NBER Macroeconomics Annual 2021

NBER Macroeconomics Annual 2021

Edited by
Martin Eichenbaum and Erik Hurst

The University of Chicago Press
Chicago and London

NBER Macroeconomics Annual 2021, Number 36

Published annually by The University of Chicago Press.
www.journals.uchicago.edu/MA/

© 2022 by the National Bureau of Economic Research.

All rights reserved. No part of this book may be reproduced in any form by any electronic or mechanical means (including photocopying, recording, or information storage and retrieval) without permission in writing from the publisher. Chapters may be copied or otherwise reused without permission only to the extent permitted by Sections 107 and 108 of the U.S. Copyright Law. Permission to copy articles for personal, internal, classroom, or library use may be obtained from the Copyright Clearance Center (www.copyright.com). For all other uses, such as copying for general distribution, for advertising or promotional purposes, for creating new collective works, or for resale, please contact Permissions Coordinator, Journals Division, University of Chicago Press, 1427 E. 60th Street, Chicago, IL 60637 USA. Fax: (773) 834-3489. E-mail: journalpermissions@press.uchicago.edu.

Subscriptions: Individual subscription rates are $95 print + electronic and $45 e-only ($23 for students). Institutional print + electronic and e-only rates are tiered according to an institution's type and research output: $153 to $321 (print + electronic), $133 to $279 (e-only). For additional information, including back-issue sales, classroom use, rates for single copies, and prices for institutional full-run access, please visit www.journals.uchicago.edu /MA/. Free or deeply discounted access is available in most developing nations through the Chicago Emerging Nations Initiative (www.journals.uchicago.edu/ceni/).

Please direct subscription inquiries to Subscription Fulfillment, 1427 E. 60th Street, Chicago, IL 60637-2902. Telephone: (773) 753-3347 or toll free in the United States and Canada (877) 705-1878. Fax: (773) 753-0811 or toll-free (877) 705-1879. E-mail: subscriptions @press.uchicago.edu.

Standing orders: To place a standing order for this book series, please address your request to The University of Chicago Press, Chicago Distribution Center, Attn. Standing Orders/Customer Service, 11030 S. Langley Avenue, Chicago, IL 60628. Telephone toll free in the U.S. and Canada: 1-800-621-2736; or 1-773-702-7000. Fax toll free in the U.S. and Canada: 1-800-621-8476; or 1-773-702-7212.

Single-copy orders: In the U.S., Canada, and the rest of the world, order from your local bookseller or direct from The University of Chicago Press, Chicago Distribution Center, 11030 S. Langley Avenue, Chicago, IL 60628. Telephone toll free in the U.S. and Canada: 1-800-621-2736; or 1-773-702-7000. Fax toll free in the U.S. and Canada: 1-800-621-8476; or 1-773-702-7212. In the U.K. and Europe, order from your local bookseller or direct from The University of Chicago Press, c/o John Wiley Ltd. Distribution Center, 1 Oldlands Way, Bognor Regis, West Sussex PO22 9SA, UK. Telephone 01243 779777 or Fax 01243 820250. E-mail: cs-books@wiley.co.uk.

The University of Chicago Press offers bulk discounts on individual titles to Corporate, Premium and Gift accounts. For information, please write to Sales Department—Special Sales, The University of Chicago Press, 1427 E. 60th Street, Chicago, IL 60637 USA or telephone 1-773-702-7723.

This book was printed and bound in the United States of America.

ISSN: 0889-3365
E-ISSN: 1537-2642
ISBN: 978-0-226-82171-9 (pb.:alk.paper)
eISBN: 978-0-226-82172-6 (e-book)

NBER Board of Directors

Officers

John Lipsky, *Chair*
Peter Blair Henry, *Vice Chair*
James M. Poterba, *President and Chief Executive Officer*
Robert Mednick, *Treasurer*
Kelly Horak, *Controller and Assistant Corporate Secretary*
Alterra Milone, *Corporate Secretary*
Denis Healy, *Assistant Corporate Secretary*

Directors at Large

Kathleen B. Cooper	Robert S. Hamada	Alicia H. Munnell
Charles H. Dallara	Peter Blair Henry	Robert T. Parry
George C. Eads	Karen N. Horn	Douglas Peterson
Jessica P. Einhorn	Lisa Jordan	James M. Poterba
Mohamed El-Erian	John Lipsky	John S. Reed
Diana Farrell	Laurence H. Meyer	Hal Varian
Helena Foulkes	Karen Mills	Mark Weinberger
Jacob A. Frenkel	Michael H. Moskow	Martin B. Zimmerman

Directors by University Appointment

Timothy Bresnahan, *Stanford*
Pierre-André Chiappori, *Columbia*
Maureen Cropper, *Maryland*
Alan V. Deardorff, *Michigan*
Graham Elliott, *California, San Diego*
Edward Foster, *Minnesota*
Benjamin Hermalin, *California, Berkeley*
Samuel Kortum, *Yale*
George Mailath, *Pennsylvania*
Joel Mokyr, *Northwestern*
Richard L. Schmalensee, *Massachusetts Institute of Technology*
Christopher Sims, *Princeton*
Richard Steckel, *Ohio State*
Lars Stole, *Chicago*
Ingo Walter, *New York*
David B. Yoffie, *Harvard*

Directors by Appointment of Other Organizations

Timothy Beatty, *Agricultural and Applied Economics Association*
Philip Hoffman, *Economic History Association*
Arthur Kennickell, *American Statistical Association*
Robert Mednick, *American Institute of Certified Public Accountants*
Maureen O'Hara, *American Finance Association*
Dana M. Peterson, *The Conference Board*
Lynn Reaser, *National Association for Business Economics*
Peter L. Rousseau, *American Economic Association*
Gregor W. Smith, *Canadian Economics Association*
William Spriggs, *American Federation of Labor and Congress of Industrial Organizations*

Directors Emeriti

George Akerlof	Don R. Conlan	Rudolph A. Oswald
Peter C. Aldrich	Ray C. Fair	Andrew Postlewaite
Elizabeth Bailey	Martin J. Gruber	John J. Siegfried
Jagdish Bhagwati	Saul H. Hymans	Craig Swan
John H. Biggs	Marjorie B. McElroy	Marina v. N. Whitman

NBER Macroeconomics Annual Advisory Board

Mark Aguiar, *Princeton University and NBER*

Fernando E. Alvarez, *University of Chicago and NBER*

Lawrence Christiano, *Northwestern University and NBER*

Jesús Fernández-Villaverde, *University of Pennsylvania and NBER*

Mark Gertler, *New York University and NBER*

Robert E. Hall, *Stanford University and NBER*

Greg Kaplan, *University of Chicago and NBER*

N. Gregory Mankiw, *Harvard University and NBER*

James M. Poterba, *Massachusetts Institute of Technology and NBER*

Valerie A. Ramey, *University of California, San Diego and NBER*

Richard Rogerson, *Princeton University and NBER*

Jón Steinsson, *Columbia University and NBER*

Laura Veldkamp, *New York University and NBER*

Annette Vissing-Jorgensen, *University of California, Berkeley and NBER*

Relation of the Directors to the Work and Publications of the NBER

1. The object of the NBER is to ascertain and present to the economics profession, and to the public more generally, important economic facts and their interpretation in a scientific manner without policy recommendations. The Board of Directors is charged with the responsibility of ensuring that the work of the NBER is carried on in strict conformity with this object.

2. The President shall establish an internal review process to ensure that book manuscripts proposed for publication DO NOT contain policy recommendations. This shall apply both to the proceedings of conferences and to manuscripts by a single author or by one or more coauthors but shall not apply to authors of comments at NBER conferences who are not NBER affiliates.

3. No book manuscript reporting research shall be published by the NBER until the President has sent to each member of the Board a notice that a manuscript is recommended for publication and that in the President's opinion it is suitable for publication in accordance with the above principles of the NBER. Such notification will include a table of contents and an abstract or summary of the manuscript's content, a list of contributors if applicable, and a response form for use by Directors who desire a copy of the manuscript for review. Each manuscript shall contain a summary drawing attention to the nature and treatment of the problem studied and the main conclusions reached.

4. No volume shall be published until forty-five days have elapsed from the above notification of intention to publish it. During this period a copy shall be sent to any Director requesting it, and if any Director objects to publication on the grounds that the manuscript contains policy recommendations, the objection will be presented to the author(s) or editor(s). In case of dispute, all members of the Board shall be notified, and the President shall appoint an ad hoc committee of the Board to decide the matter; thirty days additional shall be granted for this purpose.

5. The President shall present annually to the Board a report describing the internal manuscript review process, any objections made by Directors before publication or by anyone after publication, any disputes about such matters, and how they were handled.

6. Publications of the NBER issued for informational purposes concerning the work of the Bureau, or issued to inform the public of the activities at the Bureau, including but not limited to the NBER Digest and Reporter, shall be consistent with the object stated in paragraph 1. They shall contain a specific disclaimer noting that they have not passed through the review procedures required in this resolution. The Executive Committee of the Board is charged with the review of all such publications from time to time.

7. NBER working papers and manuscripts distributed on the Bureau's web site are not deemed to be publications for the purpose of this resolution, but they shall be consistent with the object stated in paragraph 1. Working papers shall contain a specific disclaimer noting that they have not passed through the review procedures required in this resolution. The NBER's web site shall contain a similar disclaimer. The President shall establish an internal review process to ensure that the working papers and the web site do not contain policy recommendations, and shall report annually to the Board on this process and any concerns raised in connection with it.

8. Unless otherwise determined by the Board or exempted by the terms of paragraphs 6 and 7, a copy of this resolution shall be printed in each NBER publication as described in paragraph 2 above.

Contents

Editorial

Martin Eichenbaum, *Northwestern University and NBER,* United States of America
Erik Hurst, *University of Chicago and NBER,* United States of America

The NBER's 36th Annual Conference on Macroeconomics brought together leading scholars to present, discuss, and debate five research papers on central issues in contemporary macroeconomics. In addition, we included a panel discussion on the cost associated with expanding the size of government debt. Raghu Rajan moderated the panel, which included Carmen Reinhart, Richard Reis, and Larry Summers. Given the pandemic, the conference took place via Zoom. Video recordings of the presentations of the papers and the panel discussion are accessible on the web page of the NBER Annual Conference on Macroeconomics. These videos make a useful complement to this volume and make the conference's content more widely accessible.

This conference volume contains edited versions of the five papers presented at the conference, each followed by two written discussions by leading scholars and a summary of the debates that followed each paper.

How the labor market evolves during a recession and its subsequent recovery is a key question in macroeconomics. During a recession, many workers are displaced from their employers. Over time, these workers are absorbed back into the labor force. So at the onset of a recession, the unemployment rate rises sharply, whereas the unemployment rate falls slowly during the recovery.

In their paper "Why Has the US Economy Recovered So Consistently from Every Recession in the Past 70 Years?" Robert Hall and Marianna Kudlyak explore the underpinnings of unemployment dynamics across recessions. Hall and Kudlyak start their paper by documenting a set of

NBER Macroeconomics Annual, volume 36, 2022.
© 2022 National Bureau of Economic Research. All rights reserved. Published by The University of Chicago Press for the National Bureau of Economic Research. https://doi .org/10.1086/718586

stylized facts showing that the unemployment rate falls at a relatively similar rate during the recoveries of a wide variety of postwar recessions within the United States. Hall and Kudlyak further show that the speed of decline in the unemployment rate is too slow relative to what is predicted by the standard Diamond-Mortensen-Pissarides model. Finally, the paper illustrates how a model with negative feedback from unemployment to labor market tightness provides a way to generate slow recoveries consistent with the data. In particular, Hall and Kudlyak discuss several potential forces that slow down the fall in the unemployment rate during recoveries, such as adjustment costs in vacancy creation, congestion in firm recruiting activities, and scarring effects stemming from lengthy unemployment.

Hall and Kudlyak argue that unemployment falls slowly during recoveries because of negative feedback from the unemployment rate to measures of market tightness. Both discussants caution against this interpretation. Rob Shimer notes that models with persistent fundamental shocks that caused the unemployment rate to rise in the first place or shocks that lower the value of occupation-specific human capital can generate the patterns in the data without relying on the unemployment rate being "contagious." Ayşegül Şahin mentions that it is hard to draw conclusions about the causes of the sluggish unemployment recoveries without accounting for an endogenous participation margin or allowing for employer-to-employer transitions.

One of the defining features of the pandemic recession was the large relative declines in the employment of women, particularly when compared with prior recessions. In earlier recessions, the employment rate typically falls more for men because they are more likely to work in cyclically sensitive sectors like manufacturing and construction. In their paper, "From Mancession to Shecession: Women's Employment in Regular and Pandemic Recessions," Titan Alon, Sena Coskun, Matthias Doepke, David Koll, and Michèle Tertilt explore the underpinnings of the relative decline in employment of women during the 2020 recession.

The Alon and colleagues paper begins by documenting that women's employment declined more than men's during the pandemic recession, which was a pervasive feature across most countries. In the United States, the employment declines were disproportionally concentrated among women with young children. The paper shows that both the presence of young children and differences in industries and occupation can explain a portion of why women's employment declined more than men's during the pandemic recession. In particular, women were more likely to work in sectors and occupations that shed workers during the pandemic. However, for the United States, the paper shows that childcare and industry/occupation channels each account for less than 20% of the gender gap in hours worked during the pandemic. The authors conclude that understanding the additional factors behind the gender gap in employment during the 2020 recession is an important challenge for future work.

The Alon and colleagues paper presents a comprehensive set of facts about cross-country employment declines by gender during the recent recession. The discussants—Loukas Karabarbounis and Laura Pilossoph—praise the authors for their data work. Loukas Karabarbounis develops a parsimonious model of consumption and time allocation to interpret the patterns documented in the paper. In doing so, he shows that (i) the data produced by Alon and colleagues are informative about the changing employment patterns by gender during the pandemic recession relative to prior recessions and (ii) the gender gap in employment in the United States during the pandemic is not particularly puzzling when viewed through the lens of his proposed model.

Laura Pilossoph discusses potential reasons why the gender gap in employment persists even after controlling for industry, occupation, and the presence of children in the household. Finally, Pilossoph highlights new data showing that the gender gap in employment seems to have narrowed meaningfully as the recovery has gotten underway. After the paper was presented, the discussion centered on the potential welfare implications of the patterns highlighted in the paper.

Increasing life spans have resulted in a renewed interest in the labor supply of older households. In their paper "Shocks, Institutions, and Secular Changes in Employment of Older Individuals," Richard Rogerson and Johanna Wallenius explore the time series patterns of employment rates for older households across various Organization for Economic Cooperation and Development (OECD) countries and then offer potential explanations for these patterns. Rogerson and Wallenius document that the employment rate for workers aged 55–64 has followed a U-shaped pattern over the last 40 years. In particular, the employment rates for this group of people declined sharply from the early 1970s through the mid-1990s and then increased sharply from the mid-1990s through the late 2010s. The patterns were pronounced across most OECD countries and held for both men and women. Similar U-shaped time series of employment rates were not found among younger age groups.

The paper then proceeds to explore explanations for these robust patterns across countries. Rogerson and Wallenius conclude that negative aggregate shocks in the 1970s and 1980s reduced the value of work for all workers. The negative shock during this period coincided with an expansion of institutions that incentivized older workers to retire before their normal retirement age. The endogenous response of institutions favoring retirement resulted in older workers being more responsive to the negative aggregate shocks during the 1970–1995 period. This change caused the employment rates of older individuals to fall relative to those of younger individuals during this period. Finally, the paper argues that many of these institutions were curtailed starting in the mid-1990s, resulting in an increasing employment rate for older workers.

Overall, this paper provides a set of stylized facts about the U-shaped time series patterns for employment rates of older workers during the last 40 years in OECD countries. The discussants—Mark Bils and Nir Jaimovich—both highlighted additional micro data on the employment patterns of older households. Nir Jaimovich used detailed data from the United States to show that U-shaped patterns are even more pronounced for individuals more than 65. Specifically, the increase in employment rates starting in the mid-1990s was largest for individuals ages 65–74. In addition, the increasing employment rates beginning in the mid-1990s in the United States were the largest for higher educated workers. Nir Jaimovich, in his discussion, also provided a framework to help guide future empirical work looking to quantify the role of institutions in shaping the employment rates of older households. Mark Bils used micro data from Germany to bolster the argument made by Rogerson and Wallenius that changes in pension benefits were important in explaining the employment trends for older individuals during this period.

In their paper "Climate Change Uncertainty Spillover in the Macroeconomy," Michael Barnett, William Brock, and Lars Peter Hansen explore the consequences of risk, ambiguity, and model misspecification on the design and conduct of climate policy. The authors analyze these consequences in the context of a social planner whose preferences embed ambiguity aversion. The paper notes that there is no scientific consensus on the quantitative importance of at least three determinants of climate change. These determinants are (i) carbon dynamics mapping carbon emissions into carbon in the atmosphere, (ii) temperature dynamics mapping carbon in the atmosphere into temperature changes, and (iii) economic damage functions that depict the fraction of productive capacity reduced by temperature changes.

The paper considers a social planning problem of designing the pricing of carbon emissions. The authors show how the solution to the problem depends on different sources of uncertainty. Specifically, the planning problem that they consider formally incorporates risk, model ambiguity, and misspecification.

The paper includes three computational examples designed to shed light on which sources of uncertainty have the most significant impact on policy. The first example explores what impact future information about environmental and economic damages should have on current policy. The second example assesses the relative importance of uncertainties in carbon dynamics, temperature dynamics, and damage function uncertainty. Finally, the third example investigates how uncertainty about environmental damages and the development of green technologies interact in optimal policy design.

The discussants Per Krusell and Mar Reguant focused on the extent to which the paper's results could be used to inform the current policy debate about climate change.

Per Krusell notes that the two climate-economy models are quite stylized. In his view, the models in the paper are appropriate for studying the importance of uncertainty in illustrative planning problems. But he thinks they are less well suited for analyses of achieving good climate outcomes in market economies.

Krusell emphasized that he is sympathetic to the authors' agenda of formalizing and analyzing uncertainty in the climate-economy context. At the same time, he would like to see work that combines the approach taken in this paper with a more full-fledged description and analysis of market economies and available policy instruments.

Like Krusell, the other discussant Mar Reguant agreed that a comprehensive treatment of uncertainty surrounding climate change is important and that the paper provides a good framework for doing so. She cites uncertainty regarding the ability of people to adapt to climate change and the possible presence of significant tipping points as particular important sources of uncertainty. However, she expressed concern that the analytical and quantitative assumptions built into the paper's models minimize the climate change problem. So, in her view, the paper's results about climate change per se are of limited empirical relevance.

Reguant voiced broader concerns about where the profession should place its efforts when informing the fight against climate change. She argued that economists should incorporate some of the key political economy constraints that policymakers and societies face into their climate models.

In their paper "Converging to Convergence," Michel Kremer, Jack Willis, and Yang You revisit empirical tests from the 1990s, which found little evidence that poor countries were catching up to rich countries. This finding led many people to reject the neoclassical growth model and work on alternative growth models. It also led to an important theoretical and empirical literature on conditional convergence, that is, convergence conditional on growth covariates such as government policies, institutions, and human capital.

Kremer and colleagues find substantial changes since the late 1980s in growth, in its correlates, and the fundamental determinants of total factor productivity. Their findings can be summarized as follows. First, since 2000, there has been a steady trend toward convergence, leading to absolute convergence. Second, this pattern is driven by a slowdown in the growth of countries at the frontier and a broad increase in the rate of catchup among countries away from the frontier. Finally, there has been convergence in various determinants of economic growth across countries, including the determinants of total factor productivity. Finally, they find a flattening of the relationship between growth and their covariates.

According to the authors, their results are consistent with neoclassical growth models. In their view, conditional convergence held throughout the period. Absolute convergence did not hold initially, but as policies, institutions, and human capital improved in poorer countries, differences in institutions across countries shrunk, and their explanatory power for growth and convergence declined.

The paper offers a clear challenge to many theories of growth that arose in the aftermath of early rejections of the neoclassical growth model.

The paper led to two detailed, coauthored discussions. Rohini Pande and Nils Enevoldsen agree that there has been a trend toward absolute convergence in gross domestic product (GDP) per capita and that policy convergence probably played a helpful role. They focus their discussion on the positive and normative implications of absolute convergence for individual well-being. Their analysis takes a development economics perspective, with poverty as the relevant welfare metric.

Pande and Enevoldsen's main points are as follows. First, during the period associated with absolute convergence, there was a more significant clustering of the world's poor within lower-middle-income countries and rising within-country inequality. Second, the changing nature of structural transformation has contributed to these patterns. Third, inequality combined with weak institutions for redistribution may limit progress on further reduction in poverty levels.

In their discussion, Daron Acemoglu and Carlos Molina voice skepticism about the main findings in Kremer and colleagues. Specifically, they argue that the key results in the paper are driven by the lack of country-fixed effects in the relevant regressions. These fixed effects would control for unobserved determinants of GDP per capita across countries. In their view, the failure to include country-fixed effects creates a bias in convergence coefficients toward zero. Moreover, this bias can be time-varying, even when the underlying country-level parameters are stable. Thus, in contrast to Kremer and colleagues, Acemoglu and Molina conclude that the data do not support the view that there were significant changes in patterns of convergence and, more importantly, there is no flattening of the relationship between institutional variables and economic growth.

The discussions led to numerous comments from the audience, analyzing the merits of the various points raised by the authors and the discussants. We leave it to the reader to reach their own conclusions about the critical issues raised in this session.

As in previous years, the editors posted and distributed a call for proposals in the spring and summer before the conference. Some of the papers in this volume were selected from proposals submitted in response to this call. In addition, other papers are commissioned on central and topical areas in macroeconomics. The selections are made in consultation with the advisory board, who we thank for their input and support of the conference and the published volume.

The authors and the editors would like to take this opportunity to thank Jim Poterba and the National Bureau of Economic Research for their continued support for the *NBER Macroeconomics Annual* and the associated conference. We would also like to thank the NBER conference staff, particularly Rob Shannon, for his excellent organization and support. In addition, financial assistance from the National Science Foundation is gratefully acknowledged. We also thank the rapporteurs, Laura Murphy and Marta Prato, who provided invaluable help in preparing the summaries of the discussions. Last but far from least, we are grateful to Helena Fitz-Patrick for her invaluable assistance in editing and publishing the volume.

Endnote

For acknowledgments, sources of research support, and disclosure of the authors' material financial relationships, if any, please see https://www.nber.org/books-and-chapters/nber-macroeconomics-annual-2021-volume-36/editorial-nber-macroeconomics-annual-2021-volume-36

Abstracts

1 Why Has the US Economy Recovered So Consistently from Every Recession in the Past 70 Years?
Robert E. Hall and Marianna Kudlyak

A remarkable fact about the historical US business cycle is that, after unemployment reaches its peak in a recession and a recovery begins, the annual reduction in the unemployment rate is stable at around one tenth of the current level of unemployment. We document this fact in a companion paper. Here, we consider explanations for the surprising consistency of recoveries. We show that the evolution of the labor market from recession to recovery involves more than the direct effect of persistent unemployment of job losers from the recession shock—unemployment during the recovery is above normal for people who did not lose jobs during the recession. We explore models of the labor market's self-recovery that imply gradual working off of unemployment following a recession shock. We emphasize the feedback from high unemployment to the forces driving job creation. These models also explain why the recovery of market-wide unemployment is so much slower than the rate at which individual unemployed workers find new jobs. The reasons include the fact that the path that individual job losers follow back to stable employment often includes several brief interim jobs.

NBER Macroeconomics Annual, volume 36, 2022.
© 2022 National Bureau of Economic Research. All rights reserved. Published by The University of Chicago Press for the National Bureau of Economic Research. https://doi .org/10.1086/718587

2   From Mancession to Shecession: Women's Employment in Regular and Pandemic Recessions

Titan Alon, Sena Coskun, Matthias Doepke, David Koll, and Michèle Tertilt

We examine the impact of the global recession triggered by the COVID-19 pandemic on women's versus men's employment. Whereas recent recessions in advanced economies had a disproportionate impact on men's employment, giving rise to the moniker "mancessions," we show that the pandemic recession of 2020 was a "shecession," with larger employment declines among women in most countries. We examine the causes behind this pattern using micro data from several national labor force surveys and show that both the composition of women's employment across industries and occupations and increased childcare needs during closures of schools and daycare centers made important contributions. Gender gaps in the employment impact of the pandemic arise almost entirely among workers who are unable to work from home. Among telecommuters, a different kind of gender gap arises: women working from home during the pandemic spent more work time also doing childcare and experienced greater productivity reductions than men. We identify two key challenges for future research. First, why is the pandemic gender gap pervasive, that is, why did women experience larger employment reductions than men even after accounting for industry/occupation and childcare effects? Second, how will the pandemic shape gender equality in a postpandemic labor market that will likely continue to be characterized by pervasive telecommuting?

3   Shocks, Institutions, and Secular Changes in Employment of Older Individuals

Richard Rogerson and Johanna Wallenius

Employment rates of males ages 55–64 have changed dramatically in the Organization for Economic Cooperation and Development over the last 5 decades. The average employment rate decreased by more than 15 percentage points between the mid-1970s and the mid-1990s, only to increase by roughly the same amount subsequently. One proposed explanation in the literature is that spousal nonworking times are complements and that older males are working longer as a result of secular increases in labor supply of older females. In the first part of this paper, we present evidence against this explanation. We then offer a new narrative to understand the employment rate changes for older individuals. We argue that the dramatic U-shaped pattern for older male employment rates should be understood as reflecting a mean reverting low frequency shock to labor market opportunities for all workers in combination with temporary country-specific policy responses that incentivized older individuals to withdraw from market work.

4 Climate Change Uncertainty Spillover in the Macroeconomy
Michael Barnett, William Brock, and Lars Peter Hansen

The design and conduct of climate change policy necessarily confronts uncertainty along multiple fronts. We explore the consequences of ambiguity over various sources and configurations of models that affect how economic opportunities could be damaged in the future. We appeal to decision theory under risk, model ambiguity, and misspecification concerns to provide an economically motivated approach to uncertainty quantification. We show how this approach reduces the many facets of uncertainty into a low dimensional characterization that depends on the uncertainty aversion of a decision maker or fictitious social planner. In our computations, we take inventory of three alternative channels of uncertainty and provide a novel way to assess them. These include (i) carbon dynamics that capture how carbon emissions affect atmospheric carbon in future time periods, (ii) temperature dynamics that depict how atmospheric carbon alters temperature in future time periods, and (iii) damage functions that quantify how temperature changes diminish economic opportunities. We appeal to geoscientific modeling to quantify the first two channels. We show how these uncertainty sources interact for a social planner looking to design a prudent approach to the social pricing of carbon emissions.

5 Converging to Convergence
Michael Kremer, Jack Willis, and Yang You

Empirical tests in the 1990s found little evidence of poor countries catching up with rich—unconditional convergence—since the 1960s, and divergence over longer periods. This stylized fact spurred several developments in growth theory, including AK models, poverty trap models, and the concept of convergence conditional on determinants of steady-state income. We revisit these findings, using the subsequent 25 years as an out-of-sample test, and document a trend toward unconditional convergence since 1990 and convergence since 2000, driven by both faster catch-up growth and slower growth of the frontier. During the same period, many of the correlates of growth—human capital, policies, institutions, and culture—also converged substantially and moved in the direction associated with higher income. Were these changes related? Using the omitted variable bias formula, we decompose the gap between unconditional and conditional convergence as the product of two cross-sectional slopes: (i) correlate-income slopes, which remained largely stable since 1990, and (ii) growth-correlate slopes controlling for income—the coefficients of growth regressions—which remained stable for fundamentals of the Solow model (investment rate, population growth, and human capital) but which flattened substantially for other correlates, leading unconditional convergence to converge toward conditional convergence.

1

Why Has the US Economy Recovered So Consistently from Every Recession in the Past 70 Years?

Robert E. Hall, *Stanford University and NBER,* United States of America

Marianna Kudlyak, *Federal Reserve Bank of San Francisco and Center for Economic Policy Research,* United States of America

I. Introduction

We study data from the labor market during recoveries from recessions, excluding the recovery from the pandemic recession of 2020. Our objective is to understand why the recovery phase of the US business cycle has invariably been slow but irresistible, a fact established in a companion paper, Hall and Kudlyak (2020a). The unemployment recovery process is similar in all of the past 10 recoveries: the annual reduction in the unemployment rate is stable at around 10% of the prior level.

We note that a well-documented property of the unemployment rate is that unemployment rises rapidly in response to a significant aggregate adverse shock and then gradually recovers. Like fuel prices, unemployment rises like a rocket and falls like a feather. This property was most recently confirmed by Dupraz, Nakamura, and Steinsson (2019), with many cites to the earlier literature.

Our principal claims are:

1. Recessions involve displacement of large numbers of workers, but the elevated level of unemployment along the recovery path involves far more people than the original displacement—unemployment is contagious.

2. Self-recovery occurs in the Diamond-Mortensen-Pissarides (DMP) model even without any external force. But the recovery in the model with standard parameter values is much too fast, compared with data.

3. A model with negative feedback from unemployment to labor market tightness provides an internally consistent version of the DMP model

NBER Macroeconomics Annual, volume 36, 2022.

© 2022 National Bureau of Economic Research. All rights reserved. Published by The University of Chicago Press for the National Bureau of Economic Research. https://doi .org/10.1086/718588

with reliable but slow recoveries, as in the data. No external force is involved.

4. Sources of the negative feedback include cyclical changes in the composition of the unemployed, adjustment costs in vacancy creation, congestion in recruiting, scarring effects from lengthy unemployment, and persistence of elevated separation rate.

We focus on recoveries. Our measurement starts in an economy that has just been hit by an adverse shock that triggered a recession. This paper recognizes that the shocks that propel unemployment sharply upward are heterogeneous. The major recession that began in 1981 is generally viewed as the result of a sharp monetary contraction, whereas the major recession that began at the end of 2007 got much of its strength from the financial crisis of September 2008. Historical recoveries have been much more homogeneous.

We point out the puzzle of *slow decline* of unemployment. Cole and Rogerson (1999) first called attention to the puzzle—unemployment declines much more slowly than the measured exit rates from unemployment among individuals would seem to indicate.

We then ask, What accounts for the economy's consistent, reliable record in recovering from adverse shocks? Our thesis is that the economy has a powerful tendency to self-recover from serious adverse shocks, but recovery takes time.

We consider negative feedback from high unemployment to the job-finding rate as a key mechanism behind the slow unemployment recoveries. Our discussion of unemployment is within the framework of the DMP model. The model has a well-known but counterintuitive property—it lacks feedback from unemployment to labor market tightness. When an adverse shock creates a high volume of unemployment, but the shock subsides so the determinants of tightness return to normal, the legacy of unemployment has no discouraging effect on tightness. Jobs are just as easy to find with unemployment at 10% as they are when unemployment is 4%. Much of this paper is devoted to studying modifications of the DMP model to alter this property. In the modified model, unemployment is much more persistent, because jobs are hard to find when unemployment is high.

Our view of the labor market has points in common with Pries (2004) and can be seen as responding to the challenge of Cole and Rogerson (1999) to explain why aggregate unemployment recovers much more slowly than does an individual spell of unemployment.

We proceed in the following steps: First, we study the job loss that occurs when a crisis launches a recession. A spike in job loss is visible in a variety of data sources that measure layoffs, job destruction, displacement, and unemployment insurance claims. But the spike in job loss is short-lived as compared with ensuing elevated unemployment.

Second, we ask whether the volume of job losers and their likely speed of finding long-term replacement jobs are enough to explain the long-lasting bulge of total unemployment that is only gradually worked off during even a long recovery like the one that ended in early 2020. We conclude, from data on displaced workers collected every 2 years in the Current Population Survey (CPS), that the number of workers displaced even in the severe recession starting in 2007 was not enough to explain the volume of excess unemployment present in the US economy during the period from 2009 through 2014. Something happened in the labor market during that period that caused elevated unemployment among workers who were not displaced around 2009. Unemployment proved to be infectious.

Third, we examine the puzzle of low recovery speed in the framework of the DMP model. We calculate the effective exit rate from unemployment, which is lower than the exit rate for individuals from 1 month to the next. Those individual exits are frequently temporary departures from the labor force or short-term jobs, and they are then followed by additional spells of unemployment, as described in Hall and Kudlyak (2019). Short-term jobs are an important part of the job-finding process, as studied earlier in Hall (1995). In the DMP equilibrium with our estimated low effective exit rate, the unemployment rate falls more gradually, so it accounts for some of the puzzle of low recovery speed.

We study models that explain slow but sure recoveries through feedback from the level of unemployment to the job-finding rate. We consider the feedback to various driving forces. For example, when unemployment spikes, employers' costs of recruiting rise. According to standard DMP principles, higher costs of filling vacancies discourage job creation and raise equilibrium unemployment. This model generates a generally slow decline of unemployment during a recovery. We consider mechanisms based on endogenous feedback from unemployment to vacancy-creation costs. We review the extensive literature on the feedback from unemployment to the recovery process that rebuilds employment lost in the earlier crisis. Another idea regarding slowing down the unemployment recovery in the DMP model is Fujita and Ramey's (2007) model with costs of adjustment of vacancies.

We describe a wide range of other mechanisms that participate in the gradual reduction of unemployment during a recovery. These include:

1. A gradual return to the normal mix of unemployment, away from the disproportionate role of hard-to-reemploy workers in the aftermath of a recession
2. Slow but reliable decline in labor market churn that occurs following a recession
3. Decline back to normal from strict credit standards put in place during a recession
4. Congestion effects impeding recruiting efforts when unemployment is high

We conclude that the economy includes a strong internal force toward recovery that operates apart from policy instruments and apart from productivity growth and financial developments revealed in the stock market. After a negative shock, employers gradually find it profitable to hire more aggressively. Unemployment falls as the unemployed are put back to work. Rather than a pull from expansionary policy, the growth in employment arises from a push toward lower unemployment.

We find that only a small part of the reduction in unemployment following a recession takes the form of the first jobs found by the workers who lost jobs as a direct result of the recession. Additional spells of joblessness occur within that group, and extra unemployment occurs among workers who were not immediate victims, such as people entering the labor market for the first time, after the recession. This induced unemployment gradually returns to normal in the recovery.

This paper is about recoveries from January 1948 through February 2020 and not about the recovery from the pandemic that influenced the labor market starting in late March 2020. But the principles studied in this paper apply to the recovery from the pandemic recession as well if one properly accounts for the burst in unemployment due to temporary layoffs. That pandemic created an unprecedented increase in the nonworking population—unemployed and out of the labor force. But many of these people had good prospects of recall to their earlier jobs or successful reentry to the labor force once the pandemic ended. In the previous recessions, the fraction of the unemployed on temporary layoff was small (Hall and Kudlyak 2020b). The unemployed on temporary layoff typically do not need to go through the costly and time-consuming process at the center of the mechanism studied in this paper. The principles studied in this paper apply to the rest of the unemployed.

Why has the US economy recovered so consistently from every recession in the past 70 years? Our answer: Recoveries are endogenous—there is a natural force causing job seekers to match with available jobs and to lower unemployment. The bulge of unemployment created by a crisis at the beginning of a recovery creates a negative feedback to labor market tightness, endogenously slowing the recovery.

Our results have implications for macroeconomic policy: During a recovery, unemployment seems little responsive to demand disturbances that do not throw the economy into recession. Our findings imply that welfare-maximizing macroeconomic policies should focus on preventing recessions rather than trying to ameliorate their effects, as recoveries proceed slowly but reliably.

II.   Uniform Unemployment Recovery across Recessions

In Hall and Kudlyak (2020a), we study US business cycle recoveries over the past 70 years. We focus on the unemployment rate. Our key results are (1) the recovery process takes place reliably, regardless of the nature of the shock that causes the preceding economic contraction, and (2) the recovery process is similar in all of the 10 past recoveries—unemployment falls by about 0.1 log points per year.

Figure 1 displays the log of the unemployment rate during the 10 recoveries since 1948, with the recession spells of sharply rising unemployment left blank. Throughout the paper, we exclude the recovery from the pandemic recession that started in 2020.

The key fact about recoveries is apparent in the figure: Unemployment declines smoothly but slowly throughout most recoveries most of the time, at close to the same proportional rate. In the log plot, the recoveries appear as impressively close to straight lines.

III.   Job Loss in Recessions

In this section, we examine job losses in recessions. Data on layoffs, job destruction, and long-term worker displacement show the substantial but short-lived spikes of job loss when the aggregate economy contracts. The worker-level data from the CPS and data on the initial unemployment insurance claims show the initial substantial spike and a subsequent lingering of the elevated job loss.

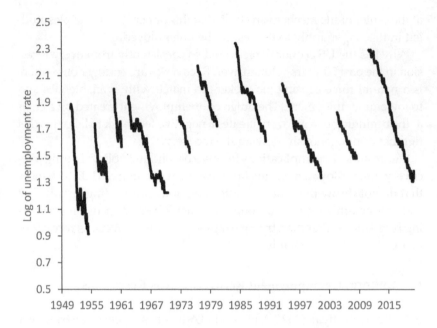

Fig. 1. The paths of log-unemployment during recoveries (Hall and Kudlyak 2020a). A color version of this figure is available online.

We consider a number of measures of job loss:

• layoffs, the flow of workers whose jobs ended at the initiative of employers

• job destruction, the amount of employment decline among establishments with shrinking employment

• worker displacement, job loss among workers with at least 3 years of tenure at the lost job

• unemployment insurance claims.

A. Layoffs

Figure 2 shows data on layoffs from the Job Openings and Labor Turnover Survey (JOLTS). A layoff occurs when an employer terminates a worker without prejudice, typically because continuing employment has become unprofitable. Most layoffs occur without any definite promise to rehire, but explicitly temporary layoffs are an important part of layoffs. On average, 20 million workers lose their jobs each year in normal

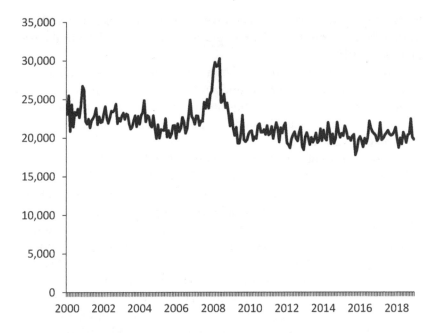

Fig. 2. Layoffs recorded in the Job Openings and Labor Turnover Survey, monthly at annual rate, in thousands of workers. A color version of this figure is available online.

times. A substantial but short-lived burst of above-normal layoffs occurred soon after the financial crisis in the fall of 2008.

B. Mass Layoffs

A mass layoff occurs when a relatively large number of a firm's employees lose their jobs. These events include high-tenured workers who tend to suffer prolonged periods of joblessness following job loss (Jacobson, LaLonde, and Sullivan 1993; Davis and von Wachter 2011).

The Mass Layoffs Statistics program of the Bureau of Labor Statistics (BLS) tracks the effects of major job cutbacks using data from state unemployment insurance databases. A *mass layoff* is defined as 50 or more initial claims for unemployment insurance benefits being filed against an employer during a 5-week period. These employers are contacted by the state agency to determine whether the separations lasted more than 30 days. Such events are termed "extended mass layoffs." The BLS obtains information on the total number of workers separated during the extended mass layoffs, including the workers who do not file for unemployment insurance, and the reasons for these separations according to the employer. These layoffs involve both people subject to recall and those who are terminated. The program operated from 1995 to the first quarter of 2013.

Figure 3 shows the number of initial claimants from extended mass layoffs. The number hovers around a million in normal times but spikes during recessions. A decline in business demand and financial difficulties are the main reasons cited behind the spikes. In 2009, extended mass layoffs spiked to 2.4 million.

Another source of data on mass layoffs is the Worker Adjustment and Retraining Notification Act (WARN), which requires employers to provide notice 60 days in advance of covered plant closings, covered mass layoffs, or sale of business that results in an employment loss. Employers are covered by WARN if they have 100 or more employees, not counting employees who have worked less than 6 months in the last 12 months and not counting employees who work an average of less than 20 hours a week. The term *employment loss* means (1) an employment termination, other than a discharge for cause, voluntary departure, or retirement; (2) a layoff exceeding 6 months; or (3) a reduction in an employee's hours of work of more than 50% in each month of any 6-month period. A plant

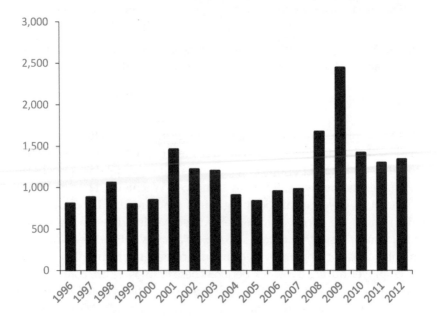

Fig. 3. Extended mass layoffs, in thousands of initial claimants per year. Data are from the Mass Layoffs Statistics program of the Bureau of Labor Statistics. The data are available from 1995 to the first quarter of 2013. A color version of this figure is available online.

closing occurs if an employment site will be shut down and the shut-down will result in an employment loss for 50 or more employees during any 30-day period. A mass layoff occurs without a plant closing if the layoff results in an employment loss at the employment site during any 30-day period for 500 or more employees, or for 50–499 employees if they make up at least 33% of the employer's active workforce. Under certain circumstances, smaller employment losses also trigger notification requirements.

The WARN data over an extended period of time are publicly available for many states. Figure 4 shows the number of layoffs for Alabama, Michigan, and Washington, as examples. The data show clear spikes in layoffs in 2009. For Alabama and Washington, the figure shows layoffs sorted by the effective date. For Michigan, we have information about the date of the WARN notice but not about the effective date of the layoff, so we sort the layoffs by the expected effective date, which is the notice date plus 2 months.

C. Job Destruction

The Business Dynamics Statistics (BDS) data report job destruction. This measure is defined as the sum of all establishment-level reductions in employment. Davis and Haltiwanger (1992) and Davis, Faberman, and Haltiwanger (2013) proposed job destruction as a measure of separations and validated the definition through study of the microdata from JOLTS. Although an employer could accomplish a reduction in employment by cutting back hiring and relying on normal attrition, in fact, almost all employment reductions take the form of separations. When an adverse shock hits the economy, separations jump and quits fall.

Figure 5 shows data from the BDS on job destruction. It shows a considerable bulge of job destruction immediately after the financial crisis.

D. Displaced Workers

Displaced workers are defined as those 20 years old and over who have worked for their employers for 3 or more years at the time of displacement, who lost or left jobs because their plants or companies closed or moved, because there was insufficient work for them to do, or because their positions or shifts were abolished. These are job losses among workers with substantial tenure, in contrast to layoffs measured in JOLTS. These are called "long-tenured displaced workers."

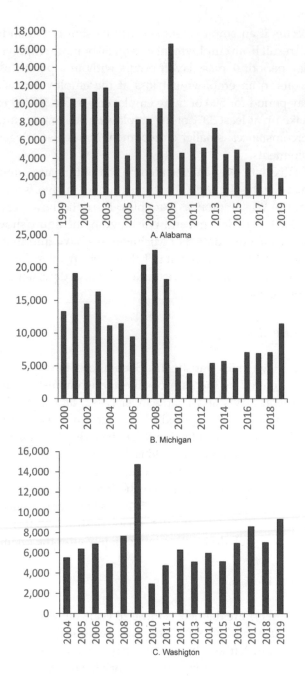

Fig. 4. Mass layoffs, by state. Data are from the layoff notices under the Worker Adjustment and Retraining Notification Act. A color version of this figure is available online.

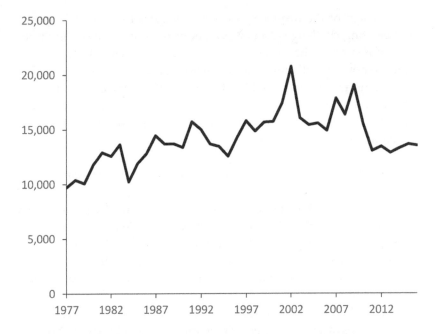

Fig. 5. Job destruction, in thousands of workers per year. Data are from the Business Dynamics Statistics. A color version of this figure is available online.

Table 1 shows the findings of the displaced workers supplement to the CPS taken in January of even-numbered years starting in 2002. The survey inquires about current unemployment and displacement in the year ended the month before, and 1 and 2 years earlier.

Table 1
Total Long-Tenured Displaced Workers and the Number of Unemployed at the Time of the Survey, in Thousands

Survey in January	Displacement Occurring in Calendar Years			Number of Displaced Workers	Unemployed at Time of Survey
2002	1999	2000	2001	3,969	841
2004	2001	2002	2003	5,329	1,076
2006	2003	2004	2005	3,815	511
2008	2005	2006	2007	3,641	655
2010	2007	2008	2009	6,938	2,505
2012	2009	2010	2011	6,121	1,634
2014	2011	2012	2013	4,292	893
2016	2013	2014	2015	3,191	507
2018	2015	2016	2017	2,981	429

Note: Data from the Worker Displacement Supplement to the Current Population Survey.

The design of the displaced workers supplement to the CPS poses an interesting challenge to inference about the time path of long-term displacements and the path of unemployment following displacement. Figure 6 shows an attempt. The annual estimates satisfy the overlapping 3-year sums and are informed by the timing of layoffs and job destruction within each 3-year span. The figure also shows a counterfactual path of displacements, which eliminates the two recession spikes present in the actual data.

E.   Comparison of Measures of the Spike of Job Loss in a Recession

Figure 7 compares the estimated long-term worker displacement counts to the tabulations of layoffs, job destruction, and extended mass layoffs. Although the normal level of displacement is far below the levels of layoffs or job destruction, the increase in displacements at the outset of the two recessions is an important fraction of the increases for layoffs and job destruction.

Figure 8 shows excess job loss associated with the 2009 recession by four measures of job loss, together with excess unemployment. We measure excess job loss as the job loss in excess of the average job loss just

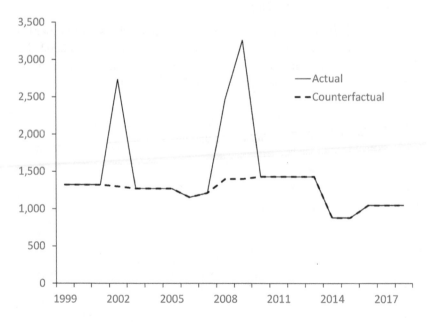

Fig. 6.   Estimated annual displacements, actual and counterfactual. A color version of this figure is available online.

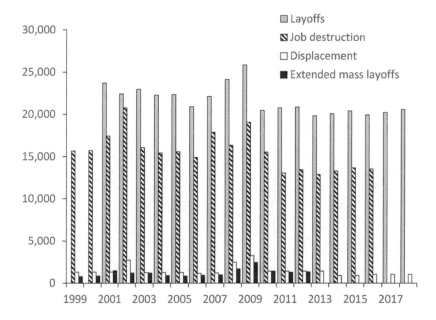

Fig. 7.   Annual levels of layoffs, job destruction, displacements, and extended mass lay-offs, in thousands. A color version of this figure is available online.

before and just after the year of the job loss spike. We measure excess unemployment as unemployment in excess of unemployment in 2007. All four job loss measures show a substantial but short-lived spike. Unemployment shows a substantial increase and slow return to its prerecession level.

F.   Initial Unemployment Insurance Claims

Figure 9 shows initial unemployment insurance claims. In contrast to layoffs (fig. 2) but similarly to unemployment, during recessions, the initial unemployment insurance claims go up like a rocket and down like a feather.

   Why is there a discrepancy between the number of layoffs and the number of initial unemployment insurance claims? One factor is that not all eligible unemployed individuals claim the benefits. Building on Blank and Card (1991), Auray, Fuller, and Lkhagvasuren (2019) find that, from 1989 through 2012, the take-up rate averaged 77%. Research shows that the number of those who are eligible but do not claim benefits increases in recession and declines in recoveries (see Fuller, Ravikumar, and Zhang 2012; Auray et al. 2019). Thus, fluctuations in take-up rates go in

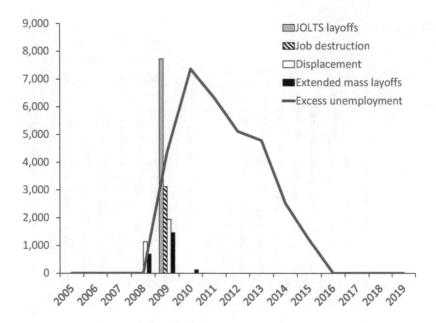

Fig. 8. Excess job loss in 2009 and excess unemployment, in thousands of workers. JOLTS = Job Openings and Labor Turnover Survey. A color version of this figure is available online.

the wrong direction as an explanation of the discrepancy between layoffs and the initial unemployment insurance claims.

G.   Flow of New Permanent Layoffs in the CPS

Figure 10 shows unemployment involving permanent job loss, by duration, from the CPS. Layoffs with duration of 5 weeks or less is the flow of new layoffs. The flow spikes at the onset of recessions and declines only slowly afterward.

IV.   The Direct Channel from Job Loss to Subsequent Lingering Unemployment

We consider the hypothesis that excess job loss directly accounts for the spike and the subsequent long slow decline of excess unemployment. We call it the *direct channel* hypothesis. According to this hypothesis, the extra individuals who become unemployed because of the recession shock follow a path similar to those found in research such as Jacobson et al. (1993) and Davis and von Wachter (2011) that tracks the

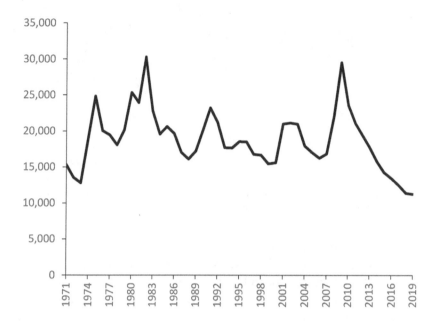

Fig. 9. Initial unemployment insurance claims, in thousands. A color version of this figure is available online.

postdisplacement paths of workers who lose their jobs from layoffs. These paths often include multiple spells of unemployment.

A. Information about the Subsequent Role in Unemployment from Job Displacement

The CPS supplement measuring job displacement contains crucial information about lingering unemployment among job losers in the years following job loss.

We fit a simple time series regression with the biennial data for unemployment in January of even-numbered years of workers suffering displacements in the previous 3 years as the left-hand variable and three lagged values of the estimated displacement counts as right-hand variables, along with a constant. The relation takes the form

$$u_t = f_1(D_{t-1}) + f_2(D_{t-2}) + f_3(D_{t-3}). \tag{1}$$

We linearize as

$$u_t \doteq \alpha + \beta_1 D_{t-1} + \beta_2 D_{t-2} + \beta_3 D_{t-3}. \tag{2}$$

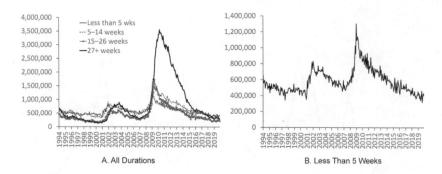

Fig. 10. Unemployment due to permanent job loss, by duration. Data are from the Current Population Survey. A color version of this figure is available online.

If market tightness were constant over time, β_1 would be the unemployment rate among workers who suffered displacement within the past year, β_2 1–2 years ago, and β_3 2–3 years ago. The design of the survey prevents learning about unemployment among people displaced more than 3 years ago. However, job-finding rates are lower in the same years that displacements are high, so $f(D)$ is a convex function of D. This property implies that the intercept α should be negative and the coefficients should be greater than the unemployment rates.

Table 2 shows the regression results. The good fit suggests that the imputation of annual timing for the displacements is reasonably successful. The fact that the third-year coefficient is somewhat larger than the second-year one is within sampling variation, but it may also reflect the fact that a worker with displacement 3 years ago also suffered an earlier displacement as well. In addition, there may be a stronger convexity effect for the third-year displacement. The negative intercept confirms the expectation of a convex relation between displacements and later unemployment.

Table 2
Regression Results for the Relation between Lagged Displacements and Current Unemployment of Workers Suffering Those Displacements

Parameter	Interpretation	Coefficient	Standard Error
A	Intercept	−991	(144)
β_1	Effect of prior year's displacements	.76	(.07)
β_2	Effect of displacement 1–2 years ago	.21	(.08)
β_3	Effect of displacement 2–3 years ago	.37	(.06)
R^2	.991		
σ	116		

Our first use of the regression is to impute unemployment of work-ers suffering displacements in the previous 3 years in January of the odd-numbered years when the supplement to the CPS was not performed. Figure 11 shows the fitted values from the regression for the years 2002 through 2018, in stripes, along with the actual unemployment counts for the even-numbered years when the supplement to the CPS occurs, in black.

Our second use of the regression results is to calculate how much lower displacement-related unemployment would have been absent the spikes of displacement in the two recessions. Figure 12 shows the results of this counterfactual and compares displacement-related unemployment from the two recessions to overall unemployment in January in the years since 2001. The rise after the recession is material relative to the overall increase in unemployment following the recession that began in 2001, but it is a small part of the large increase in unemployment following the finan-cial crisis.

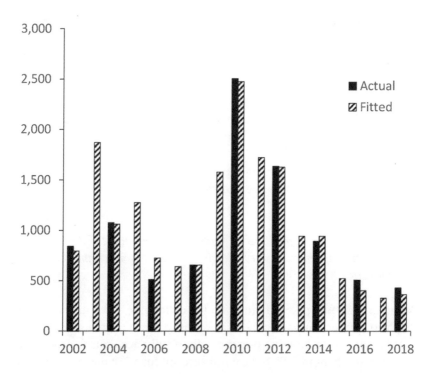

Fig. 11. Actual and fitted unemployment counts of workers suffering displacements in the previous 3 years, in thousands. A color version of this figure is available online.

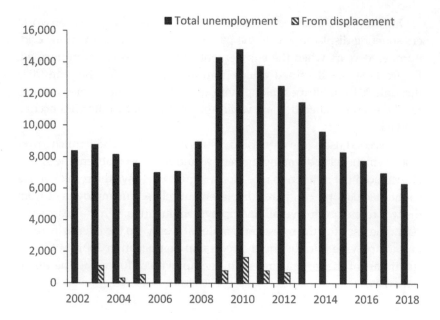

Fig. 12. Total unemployment and the component related to bursts of displacement associated with two recessions, in thousands. A color version of this figure is available online.

B. Application to Other Measures of Job Loss

We use the estimates from table 2 to calculate excess unemployment from excess job loss by the four measures shown in figure 8. Figure 13 shows the unemployment resulting from excess job loss in 2009 and total excess unemployment.

Figure 14 shows the contribution of unemployment from excess job loss in 2009 to the cumulative excess unemployment during the 2007–9 recession.

C. Conclusions about the Relation between the Magnitude of the Increase in Unemployment Following a Recession Shock and the Measures of Job Loss

An unambiguous spike in regular and mass layoffs, job destruction, and displacement accompanies the shock that marks a recession. Figure 13 shows that the spike in layoffs more than fully accounts for the spike in unemployment in 2009 but cannot account for all of the excess unemployment afterward. That is, the excess job loss accounts for the magnitude of the initial increase in unemployment, but not its persistence. The

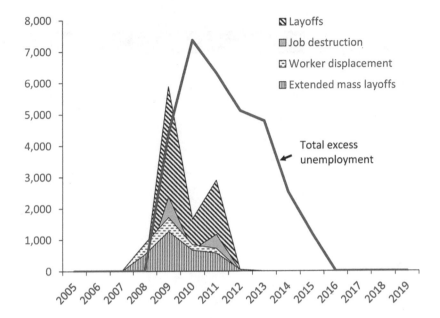

Fig. 13. Unemployment from excess job loss in 2009 and total excess unemployment, by four measures of job loss, in thousands of workers. A color version of this figure is available online.

persistence is too large to be explained as reflecting only the personal experiences of the extra job losers dating from the spike. The direct channel is only part of the story of persistent high unemployment after the crisis. This conclusion is reinforced by the rise in unemployment among new entrants to the labor force, as we show below.

The results show that the spike of job loss during recessions induces a downstream effect on unemployment. Some of subsequent unemployment comes from the unemployed who suffered the original displacement event and are circling through short employment spells, and the rest of subsequent elevated unemployment appears to come from new job loss not associated with the original job loss.

D.   Excess Unemployment of New Entrants

By definition, new entrants to the labor force are not the victims of job loss events. A bulge of unemployment of new entrants following an adverse shock indicates that unemployment is infectious or the bulge of unemployment arises from a decline in the incentives to create jobs. Figure 15 shows that new-entrant unemployment nearly doubled after the

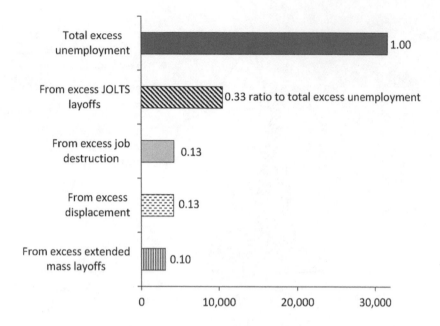

Fig. 14. Contribution of excess job loss to cumulative excess unemployment, by four measures of job loss, in thousands of worker-years. JOLTS = Job Openings and Labor Turnover Survey. A color version of this figure is available online.

financial crisis. This finding rules out the hypothesis that the sole cause of lingering unemployment following the crisis was the slow absorption of workers who suffered job loss from the crisis. The direct channel cannot be the only link between a crisis and its subsequent gradual recovery.

V. Effective Exit Rate from Unemployment

A. Defining and Measuring the Effective Exit Rate

From the data on unemployment in the displaced workers supplement, we can estimate what we call the *effective exit rate from unemployment,* denoted f_t. We know the number of people in the survey who were displaced in the prior 3 years and who are currently unemployed. We also have our estimates of the number of people displaced in each of those years. The effective exit rate is based on the assumption that the probability of being unemployed ℓ months following a displacement is the product of the monthly exit rates from the time of displacement

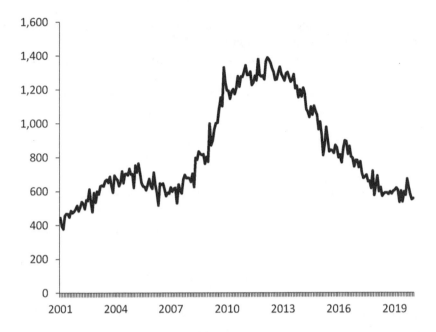

Fig. 15. Number of unemployed new entrants to the labor force, in thousands. Data are from the Current Population Survey. A color version of this figure is available online.

up to the survey. Here we adopt the perspective originated in Krueger, Cramer, and Cho (2014), and expanded in Hall and Schulhofer-Wohl (2018) and Hall and Kudlyak (2019), that the typical path from initial unemployment to current labor market activity often involves a mixture of spells of short jobs, time out of the labor force, and unemployment. As Krueger and coauthors showed, the probability of being unemployed a year later conditional on starting unemployed is much higher than would be expected from the monthly probability of unemployment ending raised to the twelfth power. Our calculation here extends the calculation by 2 additional years, as we exploit the 3-year lookback in the displaced workers supplement of the CPS.

The implied relation between the observed number of people unemployed in the January survey of month t is

$$U_t = \sum_\ell \prod_i (1 - f_{t-i}) N_\ell. \tag{3}$$

We parametrize as

$$f_\tau = a - b\, u_\tau. \tag{4}$$

The parameter b is the negative sensitivity of the effective exit rate to the standard national unemployment rate u. Not surprisingly, it turns out to be essentially 1. We estimate a and b by minimizing the sum of squared residuals of the actual values to the implied values of U_t. The estimated value is $b = 1.00$, and the monthly effective exit rates range from 0.042 in 2010 to 0.099 in 2018. By contrast, the monthly exit rate is around 0.5.

B.   Implications of Low Effective Job-Finding Rates

This subsection provides evidence that recessions are followed by long periods of high but not continuous unemployment among those who lost jobs in the recession. During the long reemployment process, the unemployed often circle among unemployment, out of the labor force, and short-term jobs.

Figure 16 shows unemployment by reason, as a share of the labor force, except for labor force new entrants. The figure shows that recessions not only involve an increase in unemployment from permanent and temporary layoffs but also are due to completion of temporary jobs and labor force reentry. This points toward an elevated number of individuals taking temporary jobs and circling between unemployment and spells out of the labor force.

When a crisis causes a spike in unemployment, there is a shift away from stable jobs and toward brief jobs in the working-age population. This shift gradually subsides during the recovery. To demonstrate this phenomenon, we study the 8-month CPS activity paths, as in Hall and Kudlyak (2019). We define short employment spells as those lasting 1 or 2 months. These are the spells that are preceded and succeeded by unemployment or out of the labor force. We define an individual to have stable employment if employed in all 8 reported months. We calculate the average number of short employment spells among CPS respondents of working age. We also calculate the average number of respondents in stable employment. We create an index of the shift toward short jobs as the difference between first and second of these calculations. Figure 17 shows the short-spell index starting in 1976 for four demographic groups. The indexes jump upward in recessions and gradually decline during the ensuing recovery for all four groups.

VI.   The DMP Model

This section describes the basic DMP model and discusses potential mechanisms and driving forces in the model that may help explain the

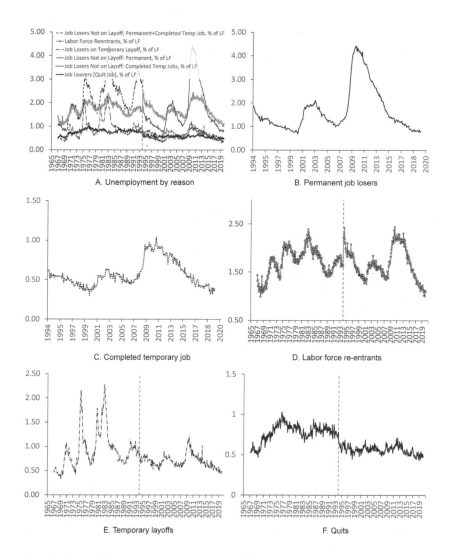

Fig. 16. Unemployment by reason, as share of labor force. Data are from the Current Population Survey. LF = labor force. A color version of this figure is available online.

slow but steady recovery of unemployment following a spike in job loss. Our goal is to explain some key features of the mechanism of the DMP model, not to create a new model at the state of the art. Put another way, we discuss the model of Chapter 1 of Pissarides (2000) and its key mechanism, which is at the heart of the models of later chapters.

The DMP class of models treats the level of unemployment as a state variable. At the outset, in our application of the model, unemployment

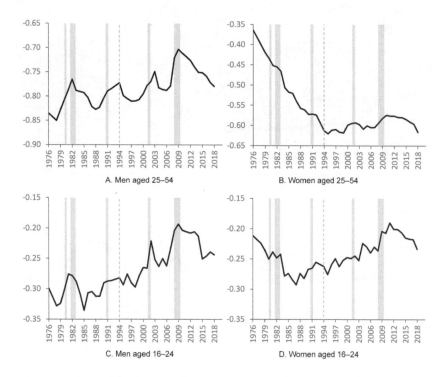

Fig. 17. Indexes of the duration of employment spells. Calculations are authors', using data from the Current Population Survey. A color version of this figure is available online.

has a high value left behind by a recession. The model traces the movements of unemployment for a decade, aiming to emulate the slow but steady decline of unemployment documented in Hall and Kudlyak (2020a). We discuss potential driving forces of the model that generate persistence. We confirm the well-known failure of the simple DMP model to account for the slow pace of recovery without invoking persistent movements of driving forces.

A. Potential Driving Forces of the DMP Model

Our discussion of the model will make the simplifying assumption that the only flow in the labor market that is sensitive to tightness is from unemployment to employment. To keep the exposition compact for now, we take the size of the labor force to be a constant. Thus we neglect variations in flows into and out of the labor market. Another important simplification is that we omit on-the-job search. A large and rich literature deals with these topics (see, e.g., Krusell et al. 2017). As we discussed in the section above, movements in and out of the labor force are an important and integral part of the job-finding process after a job loss in recessions. However, to explain the key insights of our paper, it suffices to focus on a simple textbook model with employment and unemployment. Our calibration of the model to the low effective exit rate from unemployment serves as a reduced-form representation of the churn that an unemployed worker goes through to find a long-term job.

The labor market operates on the principles of random search. The tightness of the market, denoted θ, is measured by the ratio of vacancies to job seekers. We normalize the labor force at 1 and measure vacancies as the ratio to the labor force, denoted v, and unemployment as the unemployment rate, denoted u, so

$$\theta = \frac{v}{u}. \tag{5}$$

An aggregate constant-returns matching function $m(u, v)$ gives the flow of job matches as a function of the inputs—the stock of searchers, u, and the stock of vacancies, v. We parametrize $m(u, v)$ as a Cobb-Douglas function $m(u, v) = \mu u^{1/2}v^{1/2}$. The parameter μ is matching efficiency, analogous to Hicks-neutral technical change.

The job-finding rate is the number of matches per job seeker per month,

$$f = \mu \frac{u^{1/2}v^{1/2}}{u} = \mu\, \theta^{1/2}. \tag{6}$$

Thus, tightness determines the monthly job-finding rate, an increasing function. Similarly, tightness determines the monthly job-filling rate, $q = \mu\, \theta^{-1/2}$. The latter is the number of jobs filled by holding a vacancy open for a month, so it can be greater than 1. The job-filling rate decreases with tightness.

We let P be the present value of a newly hired worker's productivity and W be the present value of their wage. The difference $P - W$ is the net benefit to the firm from hiring a new worker. For simplicity, we call W the wage, but we mean the present value the worker earns from the job, as of the time of hiring. The model operates in an environment of certainty, so expectation operators are omitted.

The flow cost of recruiting is κ. Recruiting satisfies the zero-profit condition,

$$\kappa = \mu\theta^{-1/2}(P - W). \tag{7}$$

This condition pins down tightness:

$$\theta = \left(\mu \frac{P - W}{\kappa} \right)^2. \tag{8}$$

Tightness is increasing in matching efficiency, μ, increasing in productivity, P, decreasing in the wage, W, and decreasing in the recruiting cost, κ.

The law of motion of unemployment describes the rate of change of unemployment as the net of inflows from separations and outflows from job finding:

$$\dot{u} = (1 - u)s - u\mu\theta^{1/2}. \tag{9}$$

The parameter s is the separation rate into unemployment. Its reciprocal, $1/s$, is the expected duration of a job. In addition to its visible role in the law of motion, the separation rate is one of the determinants of the present values P and W.

Separations matter in two ways. First, a shock that hits the economy just before the starting time of the model results in a pulse of separations and an elevated unemployment rate at the outset of the time span of the model. We do not model the shocks or recessions—they are simply the source of a legacy of unemployment when the model swings into action. Second, the separation rate, s, describes the flow of separations during the recovery. The separation rate controls the inflow to unemployment and the job-finding rate controls the outflow. Along a realistic recovery path, the two flows are almost equal—unemployment declines quite slowly. For now, we take the separation rate to be an exogenous constant. The job-finding rate, $\mu\theta^{1/2}$, controls the flow out of unemployment. Its reciprocal is the expected duration of a spell of unemployment. Note that matching efficiency, μ, appears in both the tightness equation and the law of motion for unemployment.

The potential driving forces of the model are

- present value of a newly hired worker's productivity, P,
- present value of their wage, W,
- flow cost of a vacancy, κ,
- matching efficiency, μ, and
- separation rate, s.

With these specified as constants, time series, or functions, the model is a first-order differential equation in the single state variable, u. Here and in the rest of the paper, we refer to driving forces, which are variables taken as exogenous to the labor market, in the sense that we do not consider that actors in the labor market can influence the variables.

We consider the path of the economy immediately after a shock has left unemployment at an elevated level. The model then evolves according to its law of motion. In the cases we consider, it converges to a stationary state because the driving forces approach constant levels.

B. Path of Unemployment Following a Recession in the Basic DMP Model

We start by describing a basic DMP model, with constant productivity, separation rate, matching efficiency, and vacancy cost. We also assume that the wage is constant even though the unemployment rate declines over time. This assumption mirrors the behavior of the canonical DMP model of Mortensen and Pissarides (1994). In that model, the wage is the endogenous result of bargaining. Under our assumptions of constant P applied to that model, the bargained wage is constant, even though unemployment follows a path that starts above its stationary value and converges over time to its stationary value. Because the wage is constant, all of the driving forces are constant and labor market tightness is constant during the recovery.

In the data, tightness rises during recoveries. Modifying the DMP model to match this key fact is one of the main topics of recent theoretical work on the model and of this paper.

We parametrize the model to resemble the economy in early 2020. Time is monthly. The stationary unemployment rate is $u^* = 0.035$, separation rate $s = 0.018$, and matching efficiency $\mu = 0.5$.

Figure 18 describes the behavior of the model in a phase diagram, with unemployment u on the horizontal axis and tightness θ on the vertical axis (see Pissarides 2000, fig. 1.3, p. 30). Equation (8) determines tightness. It describes hypothetical combinations of tightness and unemployment. It is a horizontal line in the phase diagram because in the basic model tightness is a constant, not a function of unemployment.

The downward-sloping curve in the phase diagram is the locus of stationary values of unemployment, derived from the law of motion by setting $\dot{u}$ to zero. It is

$$\theta = \left(\frac{1-u}{u}\frac{s}{\mu}\right)^2. \tag{10}$$

We call this the "$\dot{u} = 0$ curve" throughout the paper. It appears in all of our phase diagrams. It only changes when we consider different

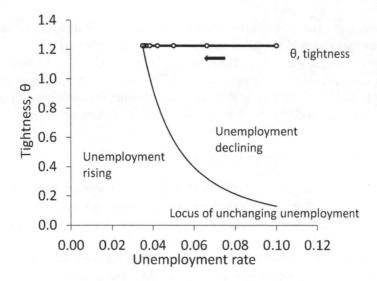

Fig. 18. Phase diagram for the basic Diamond-Mortensen-Pissarides case. A color version of this figure is available online.

values of matching efficiency μ or the separation rate s. Points above and to the right of the $\dot{u} = 0$ curve have declining unemployment, and points down and to the left have rising unemployment. At high unemployment rates, a given job-finding rate generates a higher outflow from unemployment because the rate applies to more people. With lower unemployment, constancy of unemployment along the locus requires a higher job-finding rate and thus higher tightness. Or, put another way, higher tightness means a higher rate of growth of unemployment at a given unemployment rate, and so a lower level of unemployment to achieve constancy.

All the combinations of unemployment and tightness consistent with the model will be on the horizontal line labeled θ, tightness. After a recession creates a legacy of high unemployment, the economy starts at the right end of that line. As the recovery proceeds, unemployment moves horizontally to the left according to equation (9).

Figure 19 shows the path of unemployment implied by the simple model with constant driving forces, along with the actual path starting from the peak in 2009. The dots show the progress by month. In the first month, unemployment falls substantially. As the unemployment rate falls during the recovery, the steps become smaller. The model economy closes most of the gap in just 3 or 4 months. The model's recovery is far speedier than actuality, the point made emphatically by Cole and Rogerson (1999).

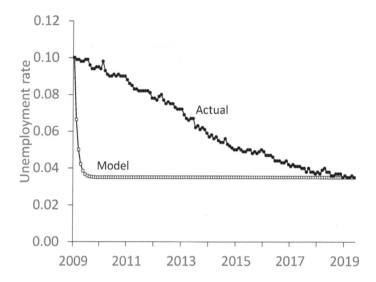

Fig. 19. Recovery path of unemployment in the standard Diamond-Mortensen-Pissarides model with constant driving forces and actual unemployment. A color version of this figure is available online.

All of our model solutions in this paper are effectively exact, that is, not based on any approximation, and using double-precision arithmetic. Petrosky-Nadeau (2014) demonstrated the importance of accurate solutions of DMP models, arising from the substantial concavity of the matching function, which impairs the accuracy of approximation by log linearization.

C.   Path of Unemployment in a Model with Low Effective Unemployment Exit Rate

We know that the 50% per month transition rate from unemployment to employment in the basic DMP model greatly overstates the actual exit rate from unemployment (see Sec. V). Figure 20 shows the phase diagram and figure 21 shows the model's unemployment path together with the actual path, with the lower effective exit rate from unemployment of 0.10 per month, in the range estimated in Section V. This alteration substantially delays the recovery but not nearly enough to match the actual path of unemployment. The phase diagram with the lower exit rate is same as the earlier one, except that the dots are closer to each other, so we do not repeat it.

We conclude that using the estimated effective unemployment exit rate of 0.10 makes an important contribution to matching the model's

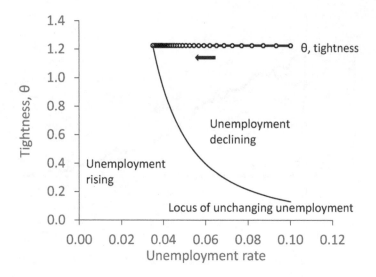

Fig. 20. Phase diagram with low effective unemployment exit rate. A color version of this figure is available online.

unemployment path but cannot be a full resolution of the high-persistence puzzle. Consequently, short-term jobs (see, e.g., Hall 1995) and movements between unemployment and out of the labor force, which are captured by the low effective exit rate, are an important ingredient of slow recoveries of unemployment but cannot fully explain it.

Pries (2004) builds a DMP model that explains the high persistence of unemployment as the result of recurrent spells of unemployment following a shock. Once a job match is made, the parties are at risk of an adverse productivity realization that reveals that the match should end and the worker should return to the labor market. In normal times, most matches will have become known to be reliable and no longer at risk of being found unproductive. At random, a cloud may form over the labor market that calls into question the earlier belief that a match is good—the parties need to receive a new signal of reliability for a fraction of the existing matches. Some of the matches end immediately, and the others are exposed to the possibility that they will be found to be unproductive from a later draw of productivity. If the aggregate shock simply knocks out some of the existing matches, the model generates little persistence—the victims of the shock regain reliable employment almost as quickly as they would without the learning-by-experience feature of the model (see Pries's fig. 3). The broader version of the shock, which induces the parties to wait to determine who are the job losers, makes the effect of the shock realistically persistent.

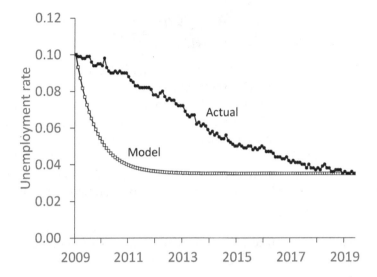

Fig. 21. Recovery path of unemployment with estimated effective exit rate from unemployment and actual unemployment, 2000–20. A color version of this figure is available online.

D. Variation of the Driving Forces over Time

So far we have discussed the model's dynamics when the driving forces are constant. The basic model generates speedy recovery of unemployment. Tightness is fixed.

In this subsection, we consider evidence of time variation in the driving forces. Where possible, we use evidence from the direct empirical counterparts of the driving forces. Otherwise, we infer variation in a combination of driving forces using the model.

Labor market tightness, θ, has five driving forces—matching efficiency, μ, productivity, P, the wage, W, the flow cost of a vacancy, κ, and the separation rate, s. We infer variation in matching efficiency from the matching function and data on hires, vacancies, and unemployment. It is the ratio of the hiring flow to weighted matching inputs:

$$\mu = \frac{H}{U^{1/2}V^{1/2}}. \tag{11}$$

The other determinants of θ—productivity, wage, and the vacancy cost—are not easily separately identified. We can identify the compound force, the job value, $J = (P - W)/\kappa$. From the zero-profit condition, this turns out to be the ratio of vacancies to hires:

$$J = \frac{\theta^{1/2}}{\mu} = \frac{\sqrt{V/U}}{H/\sqrt{VU}} = \frac{V}{H}. \tag{12}$$

Figure 22 shows the results. The labor market tightened during the long expansion starting in 2009 from a combination of rising matching efficiency, μ, and rising value of the compound job-creation incentive, J.

The remaining driving force is the separation rate into unemployment, s. Figure 23 shows the time variation in the separation rate constructed from CPS data. The separation rate increases sharply in recessions and declines slowly in recoveries. The separation rate contributes negatively to tightness, so its decline in recoveries contributes to the gradual decline in unemployment.

VII. Models That Interpret Time Variation in the Driving Forces as Exogenous to the Labor Market

Next we explore time-varying driving forces of the DMP model that are taken as exogenous to the labor market. They would be endogenous in a full general equilibrium model.

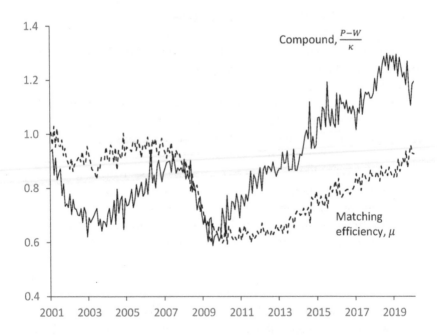

Fig. 22. Matching efficiency, μ, and the compound driving force, J, embodying productivity, wage, and vacancy cost. A color version of this figure is available online.

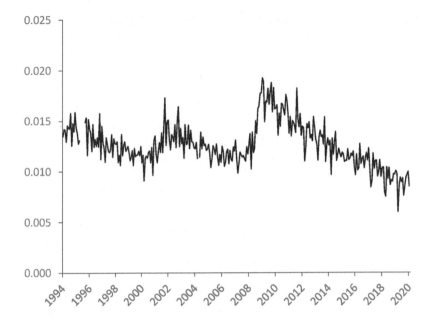

Fig. 23. Transition rate from employment to unemployment, monthly. Calculations are authors', using data from the Current Population Survey, monthly seasonally adjusted. A color version of this figure is available online.

A. Profitability of Hiring a Worker

The financial incentive to engage in job creation, $J = (P - W)/\kappa$, is at the center of the DMP class of unemployment models. If J remains at a low value after a crisis and only gradually trends upward during the recovery, tightness will gradually rise from a low value back to normal and unemployment will gradually decline. A large fraction of the DMP literature invokes this mechanism to explain movements of tightness.

This approach typically takes P as an exogenous time series process and W as an endogenous variable. Unless W changes by the same amount as P, an unlikely configuration, $P - W$ inherits some of the movements in P and so tightness will rise in a recovery. But, in fact, productivity has essentially no correlation with tightness, so this channel cannot explain the cyclical movements of tightness and unemployment, with persistent recoveries (Hall 2017).

A straightforward way to increase volatility in tightness relative to the volatility in P is through a rigid wage, W. The wage is the result of a bargaining process and is generally endogenous, although a fixed wage is an interesting special case. Wage-bargaining models different from the

Nash bargain of the canonical DMP model can deliver realistic volatility but do not generally add to persistence of recoveries. Shimer (2005) found that the movements in $P - W$, induced by movements in P and thus in unemployment, were tiny in the DMP model with Nash bargaining under plausible assumptions about parameter values. Numerous subsequent papers altered the original model to boost its response to productivity. A different and more fundamental shortcoming of the hypothesis that productivity drives unemployment is the lack of any correlation of measured productivity and unemployment.

Kudlyak (2014) studies the cyclical movements of the present value of the wage paid to newly hired workers, W. She finds that it falls in recessions and remains persistently low in later years for workers who remain in the same job during the recovery. She concludes that the job-creation equation in the basic model is missing an element that makes it unprofitable to hire in recessions, but this element is not wages because labor in recessions is cheap.

A persistent decline in the recruiting cost, κ, is another potential source of recovery in labor market tightness in recoveries, but it has been studied only in the context of endogenous sources that we will discuss shortly.

Our conclusion is that a gradual improvement in the value of the marginal revenue product of labor that results in a realistic upward trend in $P - W$ is a candidate explanation for the gradual decline in unemployment. However, the empirical support for that mechanism is weak. In particular, there is no systematic improvement in productivity above trend in recoveries.

B.   Financial Sources of Rising $P - W$ in Recoveries

Attention has turned in the DMP literature to financial factors as driving forces for unemployment (Hall 2017; Kilic and Wachter 2018; Kehoe et al. 2020). These papers observe that $P - W$ is the discounted value of the future cash flow to the employer, along with other discounted flows in more elaborate models, and thus is sensitive to fluctuations in discount rates. These fluctuations are substantial, according to financial principles set forth in Campbell and Shiller (1988) that are widely accepted in financial economics today.

Discount effects operating through $P - W$ will be present if W moves less than P, that is, if the present values of wages are somewhat sticky relative to the present value of productivity. Wage stickiness is fully consistent with DMP principles, provided it is not so severe as to dictate a wage outside the bargaining set of the worker and the employer, which would destroy a match despite its joint value to the parties (Hall 2005b).

Spikes in general financial discounts coincide with spikes in unemployment and so are logical candidates to be the source of high unemployment from recessions. But declines in discounts are not nearly persistent enough to account for the lengthy recoveries observed in unemployment.

One potential source of persistent financial effects is a crisis-induced cut in the availability of credit, which raises discount rates for credit-dependent firms and thereby cuts $P - W$. As the availability of credit gradually returns back to normal, unemployment also returns to normal. Dromel, Kolakez, and Lehmann (2010) pursue this approach to explaining the high persistence of unemployment.

We provide evidence of the persistent influence of credit conditions on unemployment in recoveries. To measure the availability of credit, we use data from the Federal Reserve Board's Survey of Senior Loan Officers. Respondents in the survey answer in terms of tightening and easing of commercial loan standards. We cumulate these answers using the statistical model in Hall (2011) to form an index of loan availability. The scale of the index is arbitrary. In figure 24, we scale it to have the

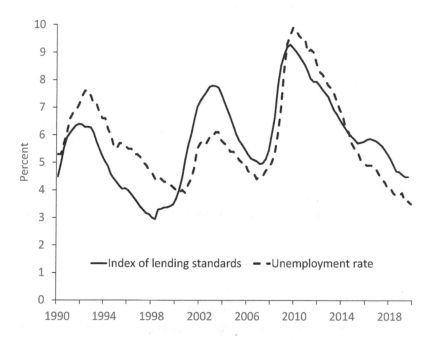

Fig. 24. Scaled index of loan availability compared with the unemployment rate. A color version of this figure is available online.

same standard deviation as the observed compound driving force, D_t, and compare the scaled index to D_t. The two variables move closely together. The slow relaxation of lending standards matches the slow decline in the driving force, D_t.

Petrosky-Nadeau (2014) introduces external financing of vacancy costs in frictional credit markets. The easing of financing constraints during an expansion as firms accumulate net worth reduces the opportunity cost for resources allocated to job creation. Agency-related credit frictions endogenously generate persistence in the dynamics of labor market tightness.

Garin (2015) studies the effects of changes in collateral requirements on the cyclical properties of unemployment and job creation. In the model, borrowing limits are linked to the firm's physical capital stock. Financial frictions arise from an imperfect enforcement contract. Financial frictions in the form of borrowing constraints create a wedge in the job-creation equation as in Petrosky-Nadeau's paper. To the extent the constraint is binding, the marginal cost of hiring an employee increases.

VIII.   Endogenous Mechanisms Implying a Slow Downward Glide in Unemployment during Recoveries

In this section, we consider self-contained mechanisms that could explain the consistent pattern of recoveries in unemployment. The high persistence of economic activity in general, and unemployment in particular, has puzzled macroeconomists for decades. Finding explanations of endogenous fluctuations in the labor market or other markets has been a goal of many generations of researchers. Our particular interest is labor market mechanisms operating to generate the observed pattern of reliable but slow recovery of the unemployment from the high levels experienced in recessions.

We study the situation immediately after a major shock has left a legacy of high unemployment. In the basic model, tightness is determined by the equation,

$$\theta = \left(\mu \frac{P - W}{\kappa} \right)^2, \tag{13}$$

which excludes any influence of unemployment except through the driving forces. Even if half the labor force is unemployed, jobs are not hard to find, as long as the driving forces are at normal levels. Instead, the volume of vacancies created by employers is at a high enough level to bring

θ, the vacancy/unemployment ratio, to a normal level. The supply of vacancies is perfectly elastic.

With instantaneous response of tightness to restored normal driving forces, unemployment returns to normal fairly quickly. Recoveries are unrealistically speedy. A number of interesting contributions to the DMP literature, mostly recent, alter the model to mimic the high persistence of unemployment.

One appealing notion in the quest for persistence is that the legacy of high unemployment from a recession creates congestion in the labor market—the high levels of vacancies hypothesized by the canonical DMP model are impractical because employers would interfere with each other, just as additional cars joining a crowded highway slow down all of the traffic. A similar mechanism derives an increase in marginal vacancy costs from convex adjustment costs—see Fujita and Ramey (2007).

A. Negative Feedback from Unemployment to Tightness

We consider a class of DMP-type models in which the unemployment rate influences labor market tightness θ. We will review an extensive literature that deals with this modification of the basic DMP model. In this class, the θ function is not a horizontal line as in figure 18 but rather slopes downward in the unemployment-tightness diagram. For clarity, we discuss a model with no exogenous movements of driving forces. The model combines the natural downward glide of unemployment intrinsic to the DMP model with an offsetting resistance from the endogenous influence of the unemployment rate.

The θ function becomes

$$\theta(u) = \left(\mu_0 \frac{P_0 - W_0}{\kappa_0} \right)^2 \gamma(u), \tag{14}$$

where $\gamma(u)$ is decreasing in u. It captures the negative effect of the current level of unemployment on labor market tightness, θ, arising from feedback effects. We normalize the variables so that $\theta(u)$ itself measures the influence of unemployment on tightness.

The observed relation between unemployment and tightness during the expansion from 2009 to 2020 is shown as the black line in figure 25. The fact that the line fits a smooth curve, except for small transitory deviations, supports the hypothesis that a functional relationship exists between u and θ.

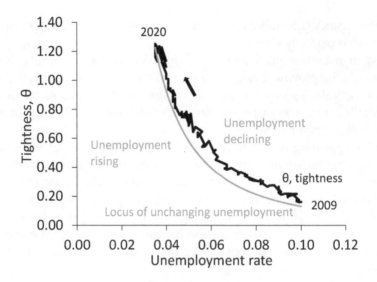

Fig. 25. Phase diagram for the Diamond-Mortensen-Pissarides model with negative dependence of tightness on unemployment. A color version of this figure is available online.

One interesting implication of this hypothesis is that the Beveridge curve should fit perfectly in recoveries. In general, the Beveridge curve has loops because vacancies constitute a jump variable controlled directly by tightness, whereas unemployment is a lagging state variable. Making tightness a function of unemployment eliminates the loops but only during recoveries.

As before, the $\dot{u}$ curve in the figure traces out the relation between unemployment and tightness such that the change in unemployment is zero. It is

$$\theta = \left(\frac{1-u}{u}\frac{s}{\mu}\right)^{2},\tag{15}$$

using the values of the parameters s and μ just discussed.

A recovery involves a gradual movement along the θ function starting at the lower right and moving toward the stationary point with unemployment u^*. Figure 25 shows that recoveries will proceed slowly, because the two curves are close to each other. In October 2009, at the beginning of the recovery, high unemployment discouraged tightness to a small fraction of its normal value. Job creation proceeded only enough to lower unemployment slowly.

Earlier, in Subsection VI.D, we calculated the values of the driving forces, matching efficiency μ and the job value J, from their definitions.

We found that both variables rose substantially in the two most recent completed recoveries. If there is no endogenous force taming the DMP model's tendency toward full employment, some other factor is needed to explain slow recoveries.

Though congestion externalities may play a role in understanding unemployment persistence, it is important to recognize that concavity of the empirical matching function captures the congestion externality to the extent it is reflected in the actual level of vacancies.

Progress in this area will either (1) revise the technology to increase the effective concavity in vacancies or (2) invoke adverse forces that counteract the incipient high level of vacancies early in recoveries. The resulting modified DMP model would have a lower elasticity of supply of vacancies and higher persistence of unemployment in comparison with the canonical DMP model.

It is clear that the story of the phase diagram only works if the effect embodied in γ is reasonably strong—enough to twist the curve clockwise from flat to downward sloping and lying close to the $\dot{u} = 0$ curve.

B.   Vacancy Costs

The cost of maintaining vacancies, κ, can be a channel of gradual decline in unemployment in recoveries. One idea is that elevated unemployment in a recession raises κ by creating congestion. In turn, as discussed earlier, higher κ slows the decline in unemployment. We consider mechanisms to describe this feedback from unemployment to tightness as we described earlier, where the θ equation involves an offset $\gamma(u)$ depending negatively on unemployment.

The effect of these models in extending unemployment persistence operates through the marginal cost of adjustment, which enters the model through the parameter κ, now reinterpreted as the derivative of a convex adjustment cost function. The analysis in the previous section considers the response to higher values of κ in the compound driving force, $D = (P - W)/\kappa$.

This alteration of the basic DMP model eliminates the disconnect of unemployment from the determination of tightness. As we noted earlier, in the basic model this property arises from the perfectly elastic supply of vacancies at cost κ, a fixed parameter of the model.

If expanding vacancies involves increasing marginal cost, making κ, the marginal cost of maintaining a vacancy, an increasing function of unemployment, the elasticity of supply of vacancies will be finite. An extensive literature on adjustment costs in vacancy creation has pursued this point.

Adding adjustment costs to the vacancy-creation technology would be a natural way to tame the behavior of vacancies at the beginning of recoveries. Fujita and Ramey (2007) is the pioneering analysis of adjustment costs in vacancy creation. Their model makes the marginal cost of creation rise in proportion to the rate that employers raise vacancy creation. The feedback generates higher persistence of unemployment. When unemployment is high and employers are creating vacancies at higher rates, κ is high, offsetting some of the incentive to hire and slowing the recovery. Creation costs induce firms to smooth the adjustment of new openings following a shock, leading the stock of vacancies to react sluggishly. Fujita and Ramey's modification of an otherwise standard DMP model eliminates the counterintuitive property of that model, that vacancies are a jump variable that increases by the full amount of the increase in unemployment in a crisis. Their model makes vacancies a state variable obeying an adjustment process. During that process, the decline in unemployment from a high initial level is slower.

Ferraro (2017) confirms the conclusion in Fujita and Ramey (2007) that the perfect elasticity of supply of vacancies assumed in the canonical DMP model is unrealistic. Within its third-moment framework, the paper argues that upward-sloping supply results in more realistic performance of the DMP model, notably in its ability to match slow recoveries. Coles and Kelishomi (2018) test and reject the assumption of the canonical DMP model that tightness is orthogonal to unemployment. They conclude that the vacancy-creation process is less than infinitely elastic.

C. Recruiting Process and Externalities

One line of modeling to support the proposition that higher unemployment raises recruiting costs is the following: Employers have a choice between costly screening of applicants or hiring without screening. In normal times, most employers do not screen because most applicants self-select to be well matched to the jobs being filled. In times of higher unemployment, self-selection breaks down and employers invest in screening prior to negotiating terms with qualified applicants. The effective cost κ of maintaining a vacancy rises and the labor market slackens rapidly. As time passes, conditions gradually reduce κ (this is the challenging part) and unemployment begins to decline. The process gains momentum as the pool of job seekers begins to increase its self-selection.

Unemployment gradually declines along the path described earlier in this paper.

This mechanism was considered in Hall (1990) and Hall (2005a). The cost of evaluation per hire depends on the fraction of applicants who are qualified for the job. Applicants may be better informed about their qualifications than are employers. If incentives induce self-selection by job seekers so that they apply mainly for jobs where they are qualified, friction and thus unemployment will be low. Self-selection is strongest in markets where unemployment is low and jobs are easy to find. Because of this positive feedback, the equilibrium in a market with self-selection is fragile—unemployment is sensitive to its determinants. Self-selection provides a mechanism for amplification of small changes in the determinants of unemployment.

Gautier (2002) focuses on an externality in the labor market that is caused by nonsequential search. The job-offer rate is increasing in the number of applications while the hiring rate is decreasing in the flow of applications per applicant. The externality arises because screening information is lost when a worker is found unsuitable for a job, and the next firm has to spend time screening the applicant again.

Villena-Roldan (2012) builds a model of search equilibrium in the labor market with endogenous recruiting effort involving the employer's choice of the number of candidates to screen for a given job opening. Although the paper does not focus on our issue, it appears that matching efficiency is lower in an equilibrium with higher unemployment.

Molavi (2018) investigates conditions that lead to an outward shift of the Beveridge curve and thus a decline in matching efficiency. To the extent that a force that shifts unemployment has this effect, his paper may contribute to an understanding of the changes that occur in the labor market during a recovery.

Engbom (2021) takes on the challenge of this paper, starting from the observation that unemployed job seekers bombard recruiting firms with vastly more applications than do on-the-job applicants. As a result, they apply for many jobs that are not actually good fits, thus imposing higher recruiting costs on employers. Higher cost results in lower labor market tightness for standard DMP reasons. He provides evidence that recruiting effort rises in times of higher unemployment.

Fishman, Parker, and Straub (2020) develop a dynamic model of credit markets in which lending standards and the quality of potential borrowers are endogenous. Lending standards set privately by the banks have negative externalities and are dynamic strategic complements—tighter screening worsens the future pool of borrowers for all banks and increases their incentives to screen in the future. Lending standards can amplify and prolong temporary downturns, affecting lending volume, credit spreads, and default rates. In the model, when markets recover, they may do so only slowly, a phenomenon the authors call "slow thawing." This line of thought may apply to labor markets.

Lockwood (1991) develops a setup where employers may administer a test. Then employers also consider unemployment duration as informative about how many times the job seeker has flunked previous tests. When unemployment is higher, this problem worsens, creating a congestion externality.

D. Composition Effects

Eeckhout and Lindenlaub (2019) observe that, in times of high unemployment, the composition of job seekers shifts toward the unemployed and away from on-the-job searchers. The latter are not included in unemployment. Thus unemployment is not a good measure of the flow of matches—calculations of matching efficiency based on the unemployment rate overstate the growth of efficiency during recoveries.

Hall and Schulhofer-Wohl (2018) study job-finding rates and match efficiency in CPS data broken down by multiple categories based on the personal circumstances of working-age individuals. These include individuals who are unemployed for various reasons, those currently employed, and those out of the labor force who are and are not interested in working. These categories are further broken down by the duration of unemployment to date in the cases of the unemployed. All categories have positive job-finding rates, ranging from high values for most of the unemployed to quite low values for those not interested in working. They calculate a measure of matching efficiency using their findings. It has a smooth trend but does not track the cycle. Our finding displayed in figure 22 of strong cyclical shifts in efficiency reflects major cyclical changes in the *composition* of unemployment. See also Sahin et al. (2014) and Hornstein and Kudlyak (2016).

Mercan, Schoefer, and Sedlacek (2020) propose a model in which newly hired workers are imperfect substitutes for seasoned workers. In their model, a greater share of the unemployed among the potential new hires in the recessions discourages job creation and helps explain the persistence of aggregate unemployment following an adverse shock.

E. Scarring Effects

Other models have incorporated the property that feedback from unemployment causes $P - W$ to decline when unemployment is high. One way for such a feedback is when P declines more than W in response to higher unemployment. Ljungqvist and Sargent (1998) propose a model in which workers accumulate skills on the job and lose skills during unemployment, although their nonemployment option remains unchanged. In turbulent economic times, the loss of skills is faster and the decline in productivity is greater.

F. The Separation Rate

The separation rate, s, is another parameter of the DMP model that could contribute to the explanation of the slow recovery of unemployment. An elevated separation rate shifts the stationary locus in the DMP phase diagram to the right. A gradual decline in the separation rate results in a gradual decline in unemployment. Our data on the separation rate support that account of unemployment persistence. Figure 23 shows that the separation rate has a general downward trend with spikes in recessions and slow recoveries back to trend. Research in the vector autoregression (VAR) framework provides evidence for the importance of job loss in understanding unemployment dynamics. See Fujita (2011), Barnichon (2012), Fujita and Ramey (2012), and Portugal and Rua (2020).

We believe that the separation rate is, apart from trend, an endogenous variable that reflects some of the same forces that keep unemployment on its slow glide path. Its own path is consistent with that hypothesis. In complete contrast to the sharp and short spike in layoffs, shown in figure 2, separations follow the same kind of glide path as unemployment. Churn set off by a recession gradually recedes, and unemployment, separations, and other measures of labor market activity calm down in parallel.

IX. Other Forces Operating during Recoveries

The DMP model provides a disciplined framework for studying the issues considered in this paper. But a great deal of business cycle thinking occurs outside the DMP framework. In this section, we examine the behavior of policy instruments and other potential driving forces without trying to determine how they might operate through the DMP model.

Next, we take a look at a variety of macro variables that may be involved in recoveries. These are policy instruments (government spending and monetary policy) and influences that might be considered exogenous determinants (productivity, labor force growth, and the stock market).

We use the NBER business cycle chronology so that our timing results are measured over the general business cycle rather than a cycle pertaining specifically to unemployment.

A. Fiscal and Monetary Policy

Government Purchases

Figure 26 displays consolidated government purchases of goods and services divided by the Congressional Budget Office's potential gross domestic product (GDP) series. The dates of peaks in the business cycle appear along the bottom—not the peaks in the purchases series itself.

Fig. 26. Real government purchases of goods and services during business cycle recoveries, as the ratio to potential gross domestic product, quarterly. A color version of this figure is available online.

Essentially all macroeconomic models agree that an increase in government purchases stimulates output. The figure shows that purchases in the first recovery, 1949 through 1953, grew rapidly because of the Korean War. The Reagan military buildup in the 1980s also accounted for rising purchases relative to potential GDP in that recovery—in all other recoveries, even the one in the 1960s containing the Vietnam War, purchases failed to keep up with potential GDP. The conclusion with respect to those, notably including the most recent recovery, is that fiscal policy taking the form of deliberate expansion of purchases—such as the American Recovery and Reinvestment Act—provided stimulus when the economy was weak. As the economy recovered, the stimulus was withdrawn.

Government Transfers

The United States has large and effective countercyclical government transfer programs and practices. Figure 27 shows the history of dollar benefits in terms of our unemployment recovery chronology. We standardize the data by dividing by nominal disposable income. Some of the countercyclical pattern arises from automatic stabilizers (programs

Fig. 27. Government transfer payments as the ratio to disposable income during business cycle recoveries, quarterly. A color version of this figure is available online.

that enroll more dependents in bad times) and some from discretionary expansion of programs and creation of new ones (such as extending unemployment insurance benefits to cover more weeks).

The figure shows that there is a good deal of heterogeneity across the recoveries. Transfers declined remarkably in the first recovery, starting in 1949. In the next four recoveries, transfers grew relative to disposable income. In four of the recent five recoveries, transfers declined.

Monetary Policy

The central instrument of monetary policy in the United States is the Federal Reserve's policy interest rate. The standard way to state its effect as an instrument is to define it as the margin of the economy's natural or equilibrium short interest rate over the policy rate. To expand, the Fed depresses the policy rate and increases the margin. And to contract, the Fed raises the policy rate above the natural rate to drive the margin negative. Laubach and Williams (2003) is a widely used estimate of the natural short rate.

Figure 28 shows the expansionary margin of interest-rate policy, according to Laubach and Williams. The Fed has chosen net expansion

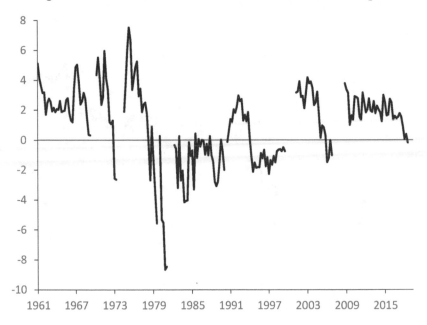

Fig. 28. The expansionary margin of interest-rate policy during business cycle recoveries, quarterly. A color version of this figure is available online.

in four expansions and net contraction in two. In the recovery from the 2007–9 recession, the Fed has chosen substantial expansion, almost as much as in the recovery of second half of the 1970s. Oddly, the late 1970s were a period of high and rising inflation, so the Fed was failing in its duty to lean against the wind.

As with the other policy instruments, we find heterogeneity in the setting of the Fed's interest-rate margin during the recoveries of the past 70 years.

B.   Other Forces during Recoveries

Financial Discounts

Forces other than macroeconomic policy may influence unemployment declines during recoveries. For example, a recent literature has described a relation between financial discounts and unemployment. See Hall (2017) in the context of the aggregate labor market and Kilic and Wachter (2018) and Kehoe et al. (2020) in general equilibrium. These papers consider DMP-type models of unemployment and events that alter economy-wide discount rates, thus changing the job value, which is the present value of the contribution of a newly hired worker net of the wage paid to the worker. Discounts sometimes jump upward almost discontinuously, as they did immediately after the Lehman bankruptcy in 2008. The job value represents the incentive to recruit. When it declines, the labor market slackens and unemployment rises. In the recovery phase, falling discounts raise the job value and unemployment falls.

According to principles of modern finance elucidated in Campbell and Shiller (1988), discount rates for risky future cash payouts are equal to the expected rates of returns associated with those payouts. In a recovery, the stock market rises, the price/dividend ratio rises, and expected rates of return decline. According to the literature linking financial events to the labor market, unemployment declines back to normal. Figure 29 shows the history of the ratio for recoveries since 1949. The ratio rose dramatically during the recovery of the 1990s. It fell substantially during the financial crisis in 2008 and 2009, but recovered during 2010, when unemployment was still rising. Its relation to the business cycle chronology in earlier years is less apparent. A rising price/dividend ratio is sometimes important for a recovery, but it does not explain the reliability of US business cycle recoveries.

Fig. 29. Price/dividend ratio of the Standard and Poor's 500 during business cycle recoveries. A color version of this figure is available online.

Productivity Growth

Another aggregate influence of unquestioned importance for GDP growth is productivity growth. If the topic of this paper were real GDP growth in recoveries, productivity would receive top billing. But the relation of productivity growth to the gradual rise of economic activity in recoveries is ambiguous and may well be small. Figure 30 shows that productivity level. The productivity growth tended to be high in recoveries through the 1980s, had a small comeback in the recovery starting in 2003, and had a spectacular shortfall in the recovery from the 2007–9 recession. Overall, productivity growth tended to be irregular in recoveries.

Variations in Labor Force Growth

The DMP model of Mortensen and Pissarides (1994) has a constant labor force. Extensions to endogenous participation may involve positive or negative comovements of participation and unemployment. Figure 31

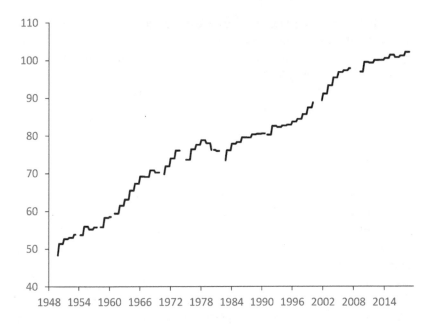

Fig. 30. Total factor productivity during business cycle recoveries, quarterly. A color version of this figure is available online.

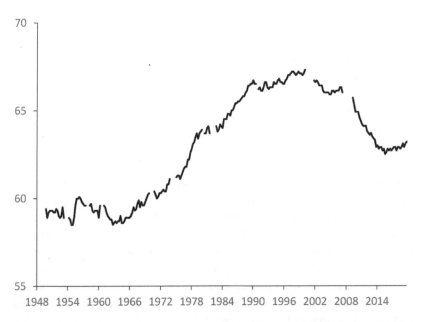

Fig. 31. Labor force participation rate during business cycle recoveries. A color version of this figure is available online.

shows that the participation rate grew during the years up to 1990 when the rising rate for women was a key factor for overall participation (to achieve a basic adjustment for demographic influences, the data refer to ages 25 through 54). In the recovery from the 2001 recession, participation was essentially unchanged. In the recovery from the 2007–9 recession, participation declined.

C.   *Discussion of Policies and Other Forces Operating
       during Recoveries*

Based on this evidence, we conclude that the economy includes a strong internal force toward recovery that operates apart from policy instruments and from financial developments or productivity growth. Policy makers understand this point and withdraw expansionary policies as the internal force does its job.

We should be clear that optimal policy that resulted in uniform growth of economic activity might be quite irregular as it fights off disturbances, so the irregularity of instruments is not conclusive evidence of the irrelevance of policy. That is, the evidence of stable outcomes and unstable policy instruments is also consistent with the view that policy makers understand the workings of the economy well and deploy the instruments to deliver stable outcomes.

Our tentative conclusion that policy has little impact on unemployment during recoveries still leaves room for effective policy to prevent or moderate recessions.

X.   Conclusions: The Sources of the Slow, Stable Downward Glide of Unemployment during Recoveries

We state our conclusions within the framework of the DMP model. That framework hypothesizes that there is a powerful economic incentive in normal times to expand employment and drive down unemployment. Early in the paper, we established the factual background for our investigation. Occasionally the US economy undergoes a crisis that results in a burst of job loss. In the ensuing years, the recovery process described in the DMP model proceeds, smoothly but slowly. We quantified job loss and the process of finding new jobs. We noted that the process has the character described in the simple DMP model but has some important complexities—even though the typical job seeker finds a job in a month or two, the net rate of job finding is much lower, because the early jobs tend to be quite short. But even taking that finding fully into account, we reach an important conclusion: the unemployment paths of the original job losers are neither as high to begin with nor as persistent as the path of elevated unemployment in the wake of the crisis.

That conclusion implies that some mechanism generates a large volume of additional unemployment beyond the initial job losers from the crisis. One possibility we consider is that the incentive to create jobs in the DMP framework is diminished for an extended period after a crisis by forces outside the labor market, possibly a continuation of the adverse force that caused the crisis. We conclude that it is difficult to pin down such a force. In the original DMP model, that force was a persistent shortfall in productivity, but we observe, along with most students in the DMP school today, that a collapse of productivity in a crisis followed by gradual restoration of productivity holds no water whatsoever. A more recent attempt to affiliate the DMP model with a financial driving force is successful in explaining the spike in unemployment in crises but not in explaining the slow rates of recoveries.

We examined some data on the availability of credit from banks that suggests a financial influence on unemployment with persistence comparable to that of unemployment. We also studied various measures of churn in the labor market, including the separation rate from jobs, which is one of the driving forces of the DMP model. Churn declines along with unemployment over the duration of a recovery.

We studied the hypothesis that unemployment is contagious—times of high unemployment in the aftermath of a crisis are times when job seekers find it hard to find jobs. It seems logical that jobs are hard to find when unemployment is high, but that is not the way that the DMP model works. With its emphasis on the incentives for job creation, the DMP model holds that the determinant of tightness in the labor market is the level of that incentive. If employers find it potentially profitable, they will exert the same effort to hire on new workers if the unemployment rate is 10% or 4%—vacancy creation is infinitely elastic. Contagion may arise from the congestion that occurs in the recruiting process when employers are flooded with applicants. Or contagion may involve changes in the equilibrium search and recruiting strategies of job seekers and employers that impede matching and lower the efficiency of the matching process. These modifications of the DMP model lower the elasticity of vacancy creation and slow down the rate of recovery of unemployment.

Invoking adjustment costs in recruiting effort is another promising alteration to the DMP model. It would tame the model's enthusiasm for hiring when unemployment is high but incentives are only normal. In the case of investment in physical capital, when the payoff to capital rises, firms do not instantly buy all the additional capital merited by the higher return. Models of adjustment costs for capital typically make the flow cost of capital installation rise with the volume of new capital installed—adjustment cost functions are often quadratic. In the presence of adjustment costs, the investment process spreads over time. The same moderating role of adjustment costs applies to investing in workers.

We noted that part of the high level of unemployment soon after a crisis reflects a change in the composition of unemployment toward individuals with naturally lower job-finding rates. This is a source of lower matching efficiency, a decline in one of the DMP model's driving forces. A related phenomenon is the lower incidence of on-the-job search when unemployment is high. Again, this is a source of lower matching efficiency.

The DMP model imposes serious restrictions on the forces that govern the speed of recovery of the labor market after a crisis creates a burst of unemployment. Most of our investigation operates within those restrictions—we take the DMP model seriously. But we do take a preliminary look at the relation between the behavior of unemployment during recoveries and other macro variables: government purchases and transfer payments, monetary policy, productivity growth, financial discounts, and labor force participation rates. We do not spot any pattern of comovement of these variables with unemployment. Our tentative conclusions do not rise to the level of firmly established causal inference. Much more remains to be done.

Endnote

Author email address: Hall (rehall@gmail.com). Hall's research was supported by the Hoover Institution. The opinions expressed are those of the authors and do not reflect those of the Federal Reserve Bank of San Francisco, the Federal Reserve System, or the National Bureau of Economic Research. For acknowledgments, sources of research support, and disclosure of the authors' material financial relationships, if any, please see https://www.nber.org/books-and-chapters/nbermacroeconomics-annual-2021-volume-36/why-has-us-economy-recovered-so-consistently-every-recession-past-70-years.

References

Auray, Stephane, David L. Fuller, and Damba Lkhagvasuren. 2019. "Unemployment Insurance Take-up Rates in an Equilibrium Search Model." *European Economic Review* 112:1–31.
Barnichon, Regis. 2012. "Vacancy Posting, Job Separation and Unemployment Fluctuations." *Journal of Economic Dynamics and Control* 36 (3): 315–30.

Blank, Rebecca M., and David Card. 1991. "Recent Trends in Insured and Uninsured Unemployment: Is There an Explanation?" *Quarterly Journal of Economics* 106 (4): 1157–89.

Campbell, John Y., and Robert J. Shiller. 1988. "The Dividend-Price Ratio and Expectations of Future Dividends and Discount Factors." *Review of Financial Studies* 1 (3): 195–228.

Cole, Harold L., and Richard Rogerson. 1999. "Can the Mortensen-Pissarides Matching Model Match the Business-Cycle Facts?" *International Economic Review* 40 (4): 933–59.

Coles, Melvyn G., and Ali Moghaddasi Kelishomi. 2018. "Do Job Destruction Shocks Matter in the Theory of Unemployment?" *American Economic Journal: Macroeconomics* 10 (3): 118–36.

Davis, Steven J., R. Jason Faberman, and John C. Haltiwanger. 2013. "The Establishment-Level Behavior of Vacancies and Hiring." *Quarterly Journal of Economics* 128 (2): 581–622.

Davis, Steven J., and John Haltiwanger. 1992. "Gross Job Creation, Gross Job Destruction, and Employment Reallocation." *Quarterly Journal of Economics* 107 (3): 819–63.

Davis, Steven J., and Till von Wachter. 2011. "Recessions and the Costs of Job Loss." *Brookings Papers on Economic Activity* 43 (2): 1–55.

Dromel, Nicolas L., Elie Kolakez, and Etienne Lehmann. 2010. "Credit Constraints and the Persistence of Unemployment." *Labour Economics* 17 (5): 823–34.

Dupraz, Stephane, Emi Nakamura, and Jon Steinsson. 2019. "A Plucking Model of Business Cycles." Working Paper no. 26351, NBER, Cambridge, MA.

Eeckhout, Jan, and Ilse Lindenlaub. 2019. "Unemployment Cycles." *American Economic Journal: Macroeconomics* 11 (4): 175–234.

Engbom, Niklas. 2021. "Contagious Unemployment." Working Paper no. 28829, NBER, Cambridge, MA.

Ferraro, Domenico. 2017. "Fast Rises, Slow Declines: Asymmetric Unemployment Dynamics with Matching Frictions." Working paper, Arizona State University.

Fishman, Michael J., Jonathan A. Parker, and Ludwig Straub. 2020. "A Dynamic Theory of Lending Standards." Working paper, Massachusetts Institute of Technology, Cambridge, MA.

Fujita, Shigeru. 2011. "Dynamics of Worker Flows and Vacancies: Evidence from the Sign Restriction Approach." *Journal of Applied Econometrics* 26:89–121.

Fujita, Shigeru, and Garey Ramey. 2007. "Job Matching and Propagation." *Journal of Economic Dynamics and Control* 31:3671–98.

———. 2012. "Exogenous versus Endogenous Separation." *American Economic Journal: Macroeconomics* 4 (4): 68–93.

Fuller, David L., B. Ravikumar, and Yuzhe Zhang. 2012. "Unemployment Insurance: Payments, Overpayments and Unclaimed Benefits." *FRB St. Louis Regional Economist*, October, 12–13.

Garin, Julio. 2015. "Borrowing Constraints, Collateral Fluctuations, and the Labor Market." *Journal of Economic Dynamics and Control* 57:112–30.

Gautier, Pieter A. 2002. "Non-Sequential Search, Screening Externalities and the Public Good Role of Recruitment Offices." *Economic Modelling* 19:179–96.

Hall, Robert E. 1990. "High and Low Unemployment Equilibria, Self-Selection, and Screening in the Labor Market." Working paper (February), NBER, Cambridge, MA.

———. 1995. "Lost Jobs." *Brookings Papers on Economic Activity* 26 (1): 221–73.

———. 2005a. *The Amplification of Unemployment Fluctuations through Self-Selection.* Stanford, CA: Stanford University.

———. 2005b. "Employment Fluctuations with Equilibrium Wage Stickiness." *American Economic Review* 95 (1): 50–65.

———. 2011. "The Long Slump." *American Economic Review* 101 (2): 431–69.

———. 2017. "High Discounts and High Unemployment." *American Economic Review* 107 (2): 305–30.

Hall, Robert E., and Marianna Kudlyak. 2019. "Job-Finding and Job-Losing: A Comprehensive Model of Heterogeneous Individual Labor-Market Dynamics." Working paper, Hoover Institution, Stanford, CA.

———. 2020a. "The Inexorable Recoveries of US Unemployment." Working Paper no. 28111, NBER, Cambridge, MA.

———. 2020b. "Unemployed with Jobs and without Jobs." Working Paper no. 27886, NBER, Cambridge, MA.

Hall, Robert E., and Sam Schulhofer-Wohl. 2018. "Measuring Job-Finding Rates and Matching Efficiency with Heterogeneous Jobseekers." *American Economic Journal: Macroeconomics* 10 (1): 1–32.

Hornstein, Andreas, and Marianna Kudlyak. 2016. "Estimating Matching Efficiency with Variable Search Effort." Working Paper no. 16–24, Federal Reserve Bank of San Francisco.

Jacobson, Louis S., Robert J. LaLonde, and Daniel G. Sullivan. 1993. "Earnings Losses of Displaced Workers." *American Economic Review* 83 (4): 685–709.

Kehoe, Patrick, Pierlauro Lopez, Virgiliu Midrigan, and Elena Pastorino. 2020. "Asset Prices and Unemployment Fluctuations." Working Paper (November), Federal Reserve Bank of Minneapolis.

Kilic, Mete, and Jessica A. Wachter. 2018. "Risk, Unemployment, and the Stock Market: A Rare-Event-Based Explanation of Labor Market Volatility." *Review of Financial Studies* 31 (12): 4762–814.

Krueger, Alan B., Judd Cramer, and David Cho. 2014. "Are the Long-Term Unemployed on the Margins of the Labor Market?" *Brookings Papers on Economic Activity* 45 (1): 229–99.

Krusell, Per, Toshihiko Mukoyama, Richard Rogerson, and Aysegul Sahin. 2017. "Gross Worker Flows over the Business Cycle." *American Economic Review* 107 (11): 3447–76.

Kudlyak, Marianna. 2014. "The Cyclicality of the User Cost of Labor." *Journal of Monetary Economics* 68:53–67.

Laubach, Thomas, and John C. Williams. 2003. "Measuring the Natural Rate of Interest." *Review of Economics and Statistics* 85 (4): 1063–70.

Ljungqvist, Lars, and Thomas J. Sargent. 1998. "The European Unemployment Dilemma." *Journal of Political Economy* 106 (3): 514–50.

Lockwood, Ben. 1991. "Information Externalities in the Labour Market and the Duration of Unemployment." *Review of Economic Studies* 58 (4): 733–53.

Mercan, Yusuf, Benjamin Schoefer, and Petr Sedlacek. 2020. "A Congestion Theory of Unemployment Fluctuations." Working Paper no. 8731, CESifo, Munich.

Molavi, Pooya. 2018. "A Theory of Dynamic Selection in the Labor Market." Technical report, Department of Economics, Massachusetts Institute of Technology, Cambridge, MA.

Mortensen, Dale T., and Christopher Pissarides. 1994. "Job Creation and Job Destruction in the Theory of Unemployment." *Review of Economic Studies* 61:397–415.

Petrosky-Nadeau, Nicolas. 2014. "Credit, Vacancies and Unemployment Fluctuations." *Review of Economic Dynamics* 17:191–205.

Pissarides, Christopher A. 2000. *Equilibrium Unemployment Theory.* Cambridge, MA: MIT Press.

Portugal, Pedro, and Antonio Rua. 2020. "How the Ins and Outs Shape Differently the U.S. Unemployment over Time and across Frequencies." *European Economic Review* 121:103348.

Pries, Michael J. 2004. "Persistence of Employment Fluctuations: A Model of Recurring Job Loss." *Review of Economic Studies* 71 (1): 193–215.

Sahin, Aysegul, Joseph Song, Giorgio Topa, and Giovanni L. Violante. 2014. "Mismatch Unemployment." *American Economic Review* 104 (11): 3529–64.

Shimer, Robert. 2005. "The Cyclical Behavior of Equilibrium Unemployment and Vacancies." *American Economic Review* 95 (1): 24–49.

Villena-Roldan, Benjamin. 2012. "Aggregate Implications of Employer Search and Recruiting Selection." Working paper, Center for Applied Economics, University of Chile.

Comment

Robert Shimer, *University of Chicago and NBER,* United States of America

In this provocative paper, Hall and Kudlyak show that during a typical recession in the United States from 1949 to 2019, a short-lived burst of job loss explains much of the rapid increase in the unemployment rate. During the subsequent expansion, unemployment declines comparatively slowly and steadily, primarily due to a sharp and persistent decline in the job finding rate, both for the initial group of job losers and for other workers who became unemployed only later in the business cycle. Hall and Kudlyak argue that the elevated jobless rate for the latter group is evidence that unemployment is "contagious" or "infectious."

For the most part, I will not take issue with their facts, although I will make the (well-known) observation that the 2020 pandemic recession and subsequent expansion featured the fastest increase in unemployment on record, followed by the fastest decrease on record. Although this recession was different in many ways from past ones, the fact that unemployment fell so quickly during the early stages of this expansion may be useful for diagnosing why unemployment declined so slowly during prior expansions.

I will focus my attention on the claim that unemployment is contagious or infectious. Hall and Kudlyak are very clear about what they mean by this: "We consider negative feedback from high unemployment to the job finding rate as a key mechanism behind the slow unemployment recoveries." The function $\gamma(u)$ in equation (14) exemplifies this logic. Section VIII of their paper sketches a number of endogenous mechanisms that can generate such feedback. I will not try to critique each—or indeed any—

NBER Macroeconomics Annual, volume 36, 2022.

© 2022 National Bureau of Economic Research. All rights reserved. Published by The University of Chicago Press for the National Bureau of Economic Research. https://doi .org/10.1086/718655

of these mechanisms, because the authors only sketch the mechanisms and a serious critique of all of them would require a book-length treatise. Indeed, I acknowledge that some of these mechanisms may be empirically relevant.

Instead, I will disagree with Hall and Kudlyak's conclusion that their analysis establishes that there must be a negative feedback loop from unemployment to the job finding rate. They reach this conclusion using the following syllogism: a short-lived initial shock dumps some workers into unemployment but does not directly affect other workers. In the subsequent years, there is elevated unemployment for workers who are initially unaffected by the shock. Therefore, it must be the case that the shock affected them indirectly, through a contagious effect of high unemployment for the initial job losers on the job finding rate for the remaining workers.

There are two problematic suppositions here. The first is that the initial shock is short lived. Although it is true that the baseline Diamond-Mortensen-Pissarides model generates almost no internal propagation, the shock itself may persist for some time after the onset of the recession. For example, credit markets did not magically revert to their prefinancial crisis state when the NBER declared the recession over in June 2009. I will not dwell here on that possibility but of course persistence of shocks is the standard assumption in virtually all models of aggregate fluctuations, including those with unemployment (Merz 1995; Andolfatto 1996; Shimer 2005, 2010).

The second problematic supposition is that the initial shock only affects workers who immediately experience unemployment. Although I recognize that this assumption is standard in certain versions of the Diamond-Mortensen-Pissarides framework, and that it is useful in some applications, it is also empirically untenable. I will argue that a different type of shock, one that lowers the value of occupation-specific human capital for many workers, is both plausible and consistent with the Hall-Kudlyak facts. Such a shock will do two things. First, it will immediately move some workers into unemployment, with a prolonged search for a new occupation. This is the initial burst of unemployment that the authors emphasize. But, second, it will also lead to subsequent elevated job loss for other now-vulnerable workers, even after the economy starts to recover. As these workers also search for a new occupation, the economy may experience a prolonged period with a (slightly) elevated job loss rate and a (significantly) depressed job finding rate. I will illustrate this possibility through a simple quantitative model, deliberately constructed to have no possibility of contagion, and argue that the key mechanism is consistent with a number of other facts that we know about how labor markets function over the business cycle.

The rest of my discussion will proceed in three steps. First, I will use some data that complement Hall and Kudlyak's to show how movements in job loss and job finding rates influence unemployment over the business cycle, emphasizing not just the countercyclicality of the job loss rate but also the fact that, once it is elevated, it stays high for many years. Second, I will describe my model, which features two distinct types of job loss, one of which is associated with a loss of occupation-specific human capital and a significant deterioration in long-run outcomes. Third, I will argue that the mechanism in my model is consistent with evidence on the concentration of secular shifts in industrial composition during recessions (Lilien 1982; Jaimovich and Siu 2020), with evidence on the long-run wage consequences of job loss during recessions (Davis and von Wachter 2011), and with the behavior of the US economy after the 2020 recession.

I. Worker Transitions over the Business Cycle

I follow a well-known methodology using matched files from the Current Population Survey to construct a measure of the flow of workers between employment (E), unemployment (U), and not in the labor force (N); see, for example, Shimer (2012). In each month, this gives me the share of workers in one state transitioning to another state; so, for example, λ_t^{EU} is the share of employed workers in month $t-1$ who are unemployed in month t. I let Λ denote the resulting 3×3 transition matrix:

$$\Lambda_t = \begin{pmatrix} 1 - \lambda_t^{EU} - \lambda_t^{EN} & \lambda_t^{EU} & \lambda_t^{EN} \\ \lambda_t^{UE} & 1 - \lambda_t^{UE} - \lambda_t^{UN} & \lambda_t^{UN} \\ \lambda_t^{NE} & \lambda_t^{NU} & 1 - \lambda_t^{NE} - \lambda_t^{NU} \end{pmatrix}. \tag{1}$$

Note that each row sums to 1. I focus here on data since 2008 to avoid overcluttering the graphs, but the basic points I make here hold in the period when I can construct these flows, since 1967.

I do two exercises with this transition matrix. First, if the economy were in steady state, with constant flows from month to month, $\Lambda_t = \Lambda$, the share of workers in each state would converge to a constant, given by the eigenvector associated with the matrix Λ's unit eigenvalue. I compare that implied steady state unemployment rate u_t^* with the actual unemployment rate u_t in each month. Figure 1 shows that the two are very similar, with u_t^* slightly larger than u_t during the two recession periods and slightly smaller during the subsequent expansions. The gaps reflect the fact that unemployment rises (falls) when the flows push it toward a higher (lower) rate. But more importantly for my purposes here, the two lines are similar because the underlying transition rates change relatively slowly over time.

Second, I construct counterfactual unemployment rates to examine the effect of each of the six transition rates in turn. More precisely, I allow just one of the six transition rates in equation (1) to vary over time and hold the other five fixed at their average value. I then look at the eigenvector associated with the unit eigenvalue of the resulting matrix to construct a counterfactual unemployment rate. The black lines in figure 2 show that the bulk of the increase in unemployment during and after the 2008–9 recession is accounted for by (the decline in) the unemployment-to-employment transition probability λ_t^{UE}, which I refer to also as the job finding rate. Interestingly, however, an early increase in the employment-to-unemployment transition probability λ_t^{EU}, which I call here the job loss rate, accounts for additional upward pressure on the unemployment rate, pushing it up to 6.3% by 2009Q1, before a slow and steady decline in job loss pulled it back

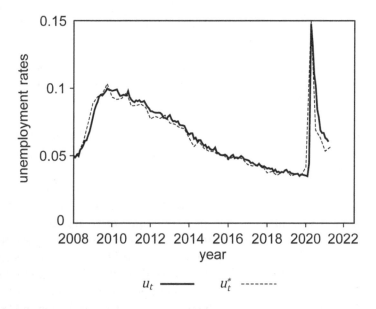

Fig. 1. The black line shows the quarterly average unemployment rate from 2008Q1 to 2021Q2 in the United States. The dotted line shows the steady state unemployment rate implied by worker flows. A color version of this figure is available online.

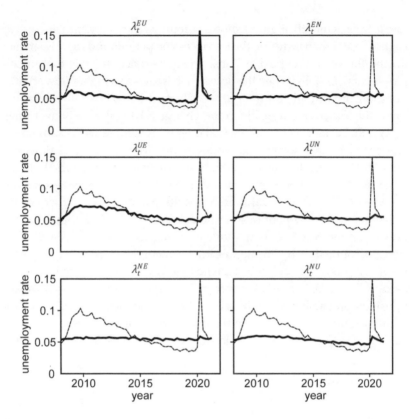

Fig. 2. Each panel shows the steady state unemployment rate implied by worker flows in dotted and the part explained by changes in one transition rate in black. US data, 2008Q1–2021Q2. A color version of this figure is available online.

down to 4.4% 10 years later. Changes in the other flows, that is, movements in and out of the labor force, had less of an impact on the steady state unemployment rate.

The story of the pandemic recession in 2020 is dramatically different but equally informative. In April 2020, the job loss rate, λ_t^{EU}, spiked, explaining virtually all of the increase in unemployment. It declined almost as rapidly, so by June 2021, elevated job loss contributed less to the unemployment rate than did the low job finding rate. Still, as I write this comment, it appears that the economy has settled into a fairly normal (and comparatively slow) recovery, with unemployment hovering near 6%.

I will argue that the difference between the pandemic recession and "normal" recessions is that during the pandemic, most workers understood that they could return to their old job, or at least their old occupation, after the worst of the pandemic had passed. In contrast, other recessions are associated with more long-term displacement as workers leave their occupation and gradually retrain for other jobs. This slow process leads to a depressed job finding rate for years after the initial shock. I conjecture that a similar phenomenon will likely arise for those workers lingering in unemployment as the United States emerges from this most recent recession.

II. Two Types of Unemployment

I now describe a mechanical model where workers can be either employed or unemployed and can have either high or low human capital. Idiosyncratic shocks move workers between the two employment statuses and between the two human capital statuses, with a positive correlation between job loss and human capital loss, as in the Ljungqvist and Sargent (1998) model of turbulence. I think of human capital as being something occupation-specific, so a high human capital worker is someone who has found an occupation that they excel at, whereas a low human capital worker is searching for such an occupation (Kambourov and Manovskii 2009; Alvarez and Shimer 2011).

I assume that unemployed workers with high (low) human capital find a job at rate f_h (f_l), whereas employed workers with high (low) human capital lose their jobs at rate s_h (s_l), all constant and exogenous. Finally, employed workers with low human capital acquire human capital at rate γ, and a fraction γ of job losses for high human capital workers are associated with a loss of human capital, the Ljungqvist and Sargent (1998) turbulence shock.

Let $u_h(t)$ and $u_l(t)$ denote the fraction of workers who are unemployed at time t with high and low human capital, respectively. Let $e_h(t)$ and $e_l(t)$ denote the corresponding employment rates. The worker flows in the previous paragraph imply these evolve according to

$$\dot{u}_l(t) = s_l e_l(t) - f_l u_l(t) + \gamma s_h e_h(t),$$

$$\dot{e}_l(t) = f_l u_l(t) - s_l e_l(t) - \gamma e_l(t),$$

$$\dot{u}_h(t) = s_h e_h(t) - f_h u_h(t) - \gamma s_h e_h(t),$$

$$\dot{e}_h(t) = f_h u_h(t) - s_h e_h(t) + \gamma e_l(t).$$

To be clear, this model is entirely and deliberately mechanical, leaving no scope for unemployment to be contagious or infectious.

I want to think quantitatively about what kinds of dynamics this model can generate, but to be clear, the numbers I use here are only suggestive. I stress that there are two critical quantitative assumptions: human capital status is much more persistent than employment status, and high human capital workers typically have shorter unemployment durations and longer employment durations than low human capital workers. I think of a time period as a month. I assume that 10% of low human capital workers switch employment status each month, $s_l = f_l = 0.1$, whereas only 2% of employed high human capital workers lose their job, $s_h = 0.02$, and 60% of unemployed high human capital workers find a job, $f_h = 0.6$. These transition rates ensure that workers with high human capital have much lower unemployment duration, much higher employment duration, and consequently much lower unemployment rates. Finally, I also assume $\gamma = 0.02$, so occupation-specific human capital is highly persistent.

In steady state, 95.9% of workers have high human capital, and the remaining 4.1% of workers have low human capital. The unemployment rate is 3.2% for the high human capital workers and 54.5% for the low human capital workers, so despite the paucity of low human capital workers, they account for almost half of the 5.3% unemployment rate. The job finding rate for the typical unemployed worker is 38.8% per month, whereas the job loss rate is 2.2% per month, both reflecting the mixture of human capital in the two pools.

Now suppose the model economy is initially in steady state but is hit by a one-time shock that adversely affects workers' human capital and throws some of them into unemployment. This might be, for example, a sharp and permanent decline in the industry demanding the worker's skills. More precisely, I assume that 10% of high human capital workers, employed and unemployed, lose their human capital. In addition, half the employed workers who lose their human capital also immediately lose their job. This combination of shocks immediately nearly doubles the unemployment rate to 10.0% and, more importantly, more than triples the share of workers with low human capital to 13.7%.

More interesting are the subsequent dynamics, which largely reflect the slow recovery of the stock of human capital. On impact, the job finding rate falls by 50 log points to 23.6%, whereas the job loss rate increases less dramatically, by 18 log points to 2.6%. Each then recovers monotonically but very slowly. As a result, we get a prolonged period of high unemployment with a very low job finding rate and a slightly elevated job loss rate. Figure 3 depicts the resulting counterfactual unemployment rates, showing persistence not unlike the response of the United States labor market to the financial crisis depicted in figure 2.

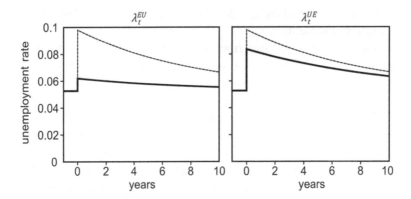

Fig. 3. Model-generated data. The dotted lines show the steady state unemployment rate implied by worker flows. The black lines show the part accounted for by one transition rate, the job loss rate λ^{EU} on the left and the job finding rate λ^{UE} on the right. A color version of this figure is available online.

Figure 4 looks at the same dynamics from a different perspective. The dotted line shows the share of the labor force that is unemployed immediately after the shock at time 0 and also unemployed at time t (possibly with one or more intervening employment spells). The black line shows the share that is employed immediately after the shock but unemployed at t. Notably, the two lines cross after 6 months, so workers who lost

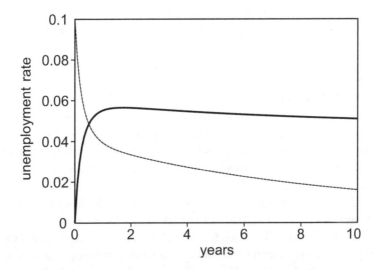

Fig. 4. Model-generated data. The dotted line shows the unemployment rate at t of workers who are unemployed at time 0. The black line shows the unemployment rate at t of workers who are employed at time 0. A color version of this figure is available online.

their job at the time of the shock subsequently account for less than half of all unemployment.

If I handed data generated from this model to Hall and Kudlyak, they would note the high unemployment rate at t of workers who remained employed through the initial shock, together with the low job finding rate for the typical unemployed worker. Putting those two facts together, I believe they would reach the same conclusion as in Subsection IV.C of their paper, "The excess job loss accounts for the magnitude of the initial increase in unemployment, but not its persistence. The persistence is too large to be explained as reflecting only the personal experiences of the extra job losers dating from the spike." Their syllogism would then lead them to conclude that unemployment is contagious.

But of course there is no contagion in this simple mechanical model. The persistent dynamics reflect the poor labor market experience of the 10% of workers who lost their human capital due to the initial shock, only some of whom immediately experienced unemployment. Unemployment persistence is a manifestation of the compositional shift in the skill distribution caused by the initial adverse shock.

III.   Relationship to Other Labor Market Facts

My simple model with two types of unemployment builds on a long tradition in macroeconomics that emphasizes that sectoral shifts are concentrated in recessions (Lilien 1982). One can think of two versions of such a model. In the first, a new sector of the economy opens up, pulling workers out of old sectors and causing a brief recession due to frictional unemployment. This version of the sectoral shifts model is empirically implausible because we do not see evidence of that growth sector during any post-World War II recession, at least in the United States (Abraham and Katz 1986). In the second version of the model, an adverse shock, say a financial crisis, leads to a recession. The pace of reallocation then accelerates during the recession, possibly due to the low opportunity cost of time (Caballero and Hammour 1994). This is the model of sectoral shifts that I have in mind.

I will offer three pieces of evidence supporting this view of recessions. First, Jaimovich and Siu (2020) show that since 1990, employment in routine tasks has looked like a step function, flat during expansions and dropping precipitously during recessions. If a worker employed in a routine task wants to find a new stable job, they typically have to retrain and look for work in a nonroutine (manual or cognitive) occupation. In a similar vein, key manufacturing industries such as steel and automobile fabrication declined sharply during the deep recessions in 1974 and 1982 with little recovery during the subsequent expansion. The road back to stable employment was arduous for those workers.

Second, Davis and von Wachter (2011) look at the subsequent earnings of men who lose a job where they had 3 or more years of tenure. There are two important conclusions in that paper. First, on average these men lose 1.4 years of discounted predisplacement earnings during the 20 years after the initial job loss. As Davis and von Wachter (2011) emphasize, this is far more than can be explained by a Diamond-Mortensen-Pissarides model where unemployed workers suffer no loss in human capital and quickly recover their employment status. It is consistent with the model I have described here, where job loss is correlated with human capital loss, because human capital and wages are positively correlated. The second conclusion is that losing a job when the unemployment rate is above 8% is twice as bad as losing a job at an average point in the business cycle. It leads to 2.8 years of lost predisplacement earnings. This is consistent with the idea that these turbulence shocks, linking job loss to skill loss, are concentrated during periods with elevated unemployment. Most job loss during expansions is not associated with human capital loss, whereas the reverse is true during recessions.

The third piece of evidence is the "dog that didn't bark," the 2020 pandemic recession. Why did unemployment recover so quickly from its peak? This recession featured a temporary stop in activity, not a period of cleansing and rapid adjustment. Many restaurant workers were laid off during the peak of the pandemic, but no one expected the restaurant industry to disappear. Indeed, many of the workers went on temporary layoff and have now returned to the same or similar establishments. Without the loss in human capital, rapid recovery was possible and has occurred. Still, even in response to this unusual shock, some jobs may be lost forever. For example, the pandemic likely accelerated a preexisting decline in brick-and-mortar retail, forcing those workers to look for new stable employment, an arduous process. My expectation is that it will take years for the employment rate to return to its prepandemic level, as in past recoveries.

I want to close by recognizing that the model I have described here probably does not account for all fluctuations in unemployment. For example, it would have a hard time explaining why the number of unemployed new entrants to the labor force gradually rises during recessions and the early stages of recoveries (Hall and Kudlyak's fig. 15). A more satisfactory model would probably have a persistent underlying shock. It would probably also have uncertainty about which growing sectors of the economy will absorb the workers leaving the declining sectors, which may propagate the shock and delay the recovery. And it may have a somewhat inelastic supply of job vacancies, which would slow expansions (even if it would not explain the observed decline in vacancies during a recession). But a proper accounting will give a large role to the importance of human capital losses during downturns and may not cede any role to contagious or infectious unemployment.

Whether unemployment is contagious matters for economic policy. According to the theories mentioned by Hall and Kudlyak, high unemployment for some workers causes high unemployment for other workers, an externality. This may create a role for programs that moderate the cyclicality of unemployment, for example, by subsidizing work sharing during recessions. In contrast, if efficient sectoral reallocation is concentrated during downturns due to the low opportunity cost of time, work-sharing programs would hinder that necessary reallocation and hence create long-run productive inefficiencies. Hall and Kudlyak have identified an interesting possibility. Future research, with better data and more serious models, will help us understand whether the possibility is correct.

Endnote

Author email address: Shimer (shimer@uchicago.edu). For acknowledgments, sources of research support, and disclosure of the author's material financial relationships, if any, please see https://www.nber.org/books-and-chapters/nbermacroeconomics-annual -2021-volume-36/comment-why-has-us-economy-recovered-soconsistently-every-recession -past-70-years-shimer.

References

Abraham, Katharine G., and Lawrence F. Katz. 1986. "Cyclical Unemployment: Sectoral Shifts or Aggregate Disturbances?" *Journal of Political Economy* 94 (3): 507–22.

Alvarez, Fernando, and Robert Shimer. 2011. "Search and Rest Unemployment." *Econometrica* 79 (1): 75–122.

Andolfatto, David. 1996. "Business Cycles and Labor-Market Search." *American Economic Review* 86 (1): 112–32.

Caballero, Ricardo J., and Mohamad L. Hammour. 1994. "The Cleansing Effect of Recessions." *American Economic Review* 84 (5): 1350–68.

Davis, Steven J., and Till von Wachter. 2011. "Recessions and the Costs of Job Loss." *Brookings Papers on Economic Activity* 43 (2): 1–72.

Jaimovich, Nir, and Henry E. Siu. 2020. "Job Polarization and Jobless Recoveries." *Review of Economics and Statistics* 102 (1): 129–47.

Kambourov, Gueorgui, and Iourii Manovskii. 2009. "Occupational Mobility and Wage Inequality." *Review of Economic Studies* 76 (2): 731–59.

Lilien, David M. 1982. "Sectoral Shifts and Cyclical Unemployment." *Journal of Political Economy* 90 (4): 777–93.

Ljungqvist, Lars, and Thomas J. Sargent. 1998. "The European Unemployment Dilemma." *Journal of Political Economy* 106 (3): 514–50.

Merz, Monika. 1995. "Search in the Labor Market and the Real Business Cycle." *Journal of Monetary Economics* 36 (2): 269–300.

Shimer, Robert. 2005. "The Cyclical Behavior of Equilibrium Unemployment and Vacancies." *American Economic Review* 95 (1): 25–49.

———. 2010. *Labor Markets and Business Cycles.* Princeton, NJ: Princeton University Press.

———. 2012. "Reassessing the Ins and Outs of Unemployment." *Review of Economic Dynamics* 15 (2): 127–48.

Comment

Ayşegül Şahin, University of Texas at Austin and NBER,
United States of America

Hall and Kudlyak start with the observation that in the typical US business cycle recovery, unemployment declines slowly but reliably from a high point at the end of a business cycle contraction. They show that the direct effect of job loss at the onset of the recession cannot account for the persistently high unemployment rate during the recovery. The recession's effects on the labor market go beyond the job losses that mark the beginning of recessions. Hall and Kudlyak then explore models where there is feedback from high unemployment to the forces driving job creation. These mechanisms include higher recruiting costs early in the recovery, congestion in recruitment, externalities from recruitment selection, lower matching efficiency, impaired profitability of new matches, and persistently higher separation rates. These models imply that the recovery of aggregate unemployment is slower than the rate at which individual unemployed workers find new jobs.

The paper tackles an interesting and eternal topic. Understanding how the labor market recovers from recessionary shocks and how firms recruit and search for workers helps us in shaping policy response to recessionary shocks. This comment reviews and interprets Hall and Kudlyak's findings and suggests new directions of research.

I. Revisiting Unemployment Recovery Patterns

Hall and Kudlyak observe that unemployment declines smoothly but slowly throughout recoveries at close to the same proportional rate. The recoveries appear as close to straight lines in the log plot, which I replicate

NBER Macroeconomics Annual, volume 36, 2022.
© 2022 National Bureau of Economic Research. All rights reserved. Published by The University of Chicago Press for the National Bureau of Economic Research. https://doi .org/10.1086/718656

in figure 1. The figure shows the log of the unemployment rate during the 10 recoveries since 1948, with the recession spells of sharply rising unemployment left blank. It is clear that, absent a new recession—which is characterized by a sharp increase in the unemployment rate—the unemployment rate goes down most of the time during recoveries. However, the uniformity in slope is hard to assess from this figure.

To facilitate the comparison of the slopes of the decline in unemployment across recoveries, I plot the log of the unemployment rate normalized at the beginning of each recovery in figure 2. This so-called spider chart is useful because it provides a direct comparison of the log of the unemployment rate starting from the peak unemployment rate, which makes it easier to detect the differences in slopes. As the figure reveals, the speed of decline varies across recoveries, especially in the earlier parts of expansions. To zoom in on the earlier periods of recoveries, figure 3 shows the evolution of unemployment in the first 4 years of each recovery. The differences are stark, with the Great Recession being particularly slow and COVID-19 recession following a steep decline in unemployment. It is also noteworthy that the difference between the 1980s recovery and the COVID-19 recovery is similar to the difference between the Great

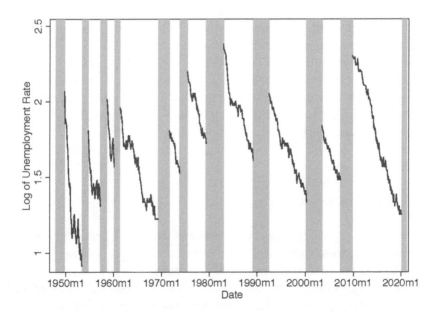

Fig. 1. The paths of log unemployment during recoveries replicated from Hall and Kudlyak. A color version of this figure is available online.

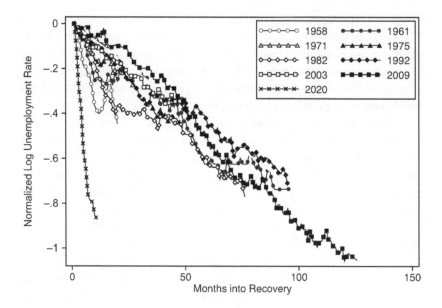

Fig. 2. The paths of log unemployment during recoveries normalized to peak unemployment rate. A color version of this figure is available online.

Recession recovery and the 1980s recovery. Moreover, whereas earlier recoveries start with steeper declines followed by a brief pause in the decline in unemployment, recent recoveries start with slower declines in the unemployment rate but do not exhibit this midcycle pause.

Examining the evidence in figures 2 and 3, I conclude that there is more heterogeneity than uniformity at the rate that the unemployment rate declines during recoveries. This finding is also consistent with the earlier studies that analyzed the causes of the slow decline in the unemployment rate following the Great Recession. See, for example, Daly et al. (2012) and references therein.

II.   The Slow Recovery Puzzle

Although the speed of recovery varies across recoveries, uniformity of the pace of recoveries is not essential for the rest of the paper, where Hall and Kudlyak move on to analyzing the reasons behind the persistence of high unemployment rate. They convincingly make two related points about unemployment dynamics. First, the number of workers laid off at the onset of recessions is not enough to explain the persistence of unemployment during the recoveries. Second, unemployment declines much more

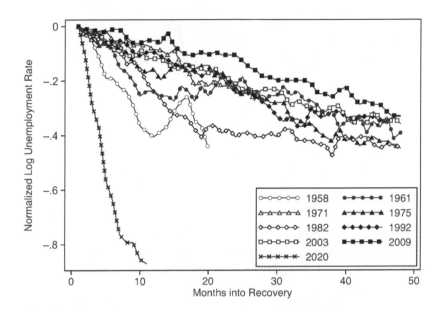

Fig. 3. The paths of log unemployment during recoveries normalized to peak unemployment rate for the first 48 months of the recoveries. A color version of this figure is available online.

slowly than implied by the measured individual exit rates from unemployment. Therefore, a stylized Diamond-Mortensen-Pissarides (DMP) framework that is calibrated to match the unemployment exit rates fails to capture the recovery dynamics as first argued by Cole and Rogerson (1999). Hall and Kudlyak refer to this observation as the "slow recovery puzzle."

It is useful to consider the flow dynamics of unemployment to illustrate the slow recovery puzzle put forth by Cole and Rogerson (1999). My point of departure is the following description of the unemployment rate, u_t,

$$\frac{du}{dt} = s_t(1 - u_t) - f_t u_t \tag{1}$$

where s_t is the inflow rate to unemployment and f_t is the outflow rate from unemployment. Shimer (2005) describes a method that uses monthly series on the number employed, the number unemployed, and the number unemployed for fewer than 5 weeks to infer the inflow and outflow rates. Figure 4 replicates the flow calculations in Crump et al. (2019) using data from the Current Population Survey and shows the evolution of

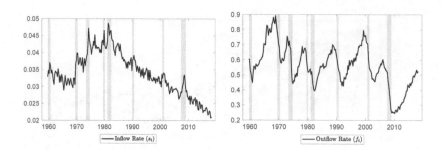

Fig. 4. Unemployment inflow (left) and outflow (right) rates

unemployment inflow and outflow rates in the last 60 years. Visual examination of inflow and outflow rates shows that the inflow rate is characterized by sharp, short-lived spikes during recessions whereas the outflow rate from unemployment is strongly procyclical with persistent
downswings during recessions.

Given the fast transitional dynamics of the unemployment rate in the
United States, the unemployment rate is closely approximated by its flow
steady-state value, u^*, given by

$$u_t^* = \frac{s_t}{s_t + f_t}. \tag{2}$$

Solving equation (1) forward implies

$$u_{t+1} = \lambda_t u_t^* + (1 - \lambda_t)u_t, \tag{3}$$

where $\lambda_t = 1 - e^{-(s_t+f_t)}$ is the speed of convergence to steady state, u^*. This
reduced form—which is implied by the DMP framework—highlights
the link between the steady-state level of the unemployment rate and
its persistence. This link has been also emphasized by Cole and Rogerson
(1999, 934), who wrote, "A key qualification, however, is that the extent
to which the model matches the business cycle facts is very dependent on
the steady state about which the model fluctuates."

To demonstrate this link, table 1 sets the inflow rate, s, to 0.018 and
computes the steady-state unemployment rate and the rate of convergence to the steady state for different values of f. It shows that there is a
tight link between the persistence of the unemployment rate and its
steady-state value. At lower values of f, the rate of convergence is slower,
but for a fixed inflow rate, a lower outflow rate implies a high steady-state
unemployment rate. Figure 5 shows the path of the unemployment rate
starting from 10% for different values of f, setting $s = 0.018$, and shows

Table 1
The Steady State Unemployment Rate and Rate of Convergence to the
Steady State for Different Values of f

f	u^* (%)	λ
.10	15.25	.11
.20	8.26	.20
.30	5.66	.27
.40	4.31	.34
.50	3.47	.40

that although the unemployment rate is more persistent for low values of
f, the steady-state unemployment rate is also higher.

Given the range of inflow and outflow rates in the United States in figure 4, convergence to steady state is very fast. Hall and Kudlyak set the
inflow rate s to 0.018 and the outflow rate to 0.50—approximately to
their 2019 levels—and compute the path of unemployment following
a recession similar to figure 2. The unemployment rate starts from 10%
and declines to its flow steady-state value of 3.5% within a few months.

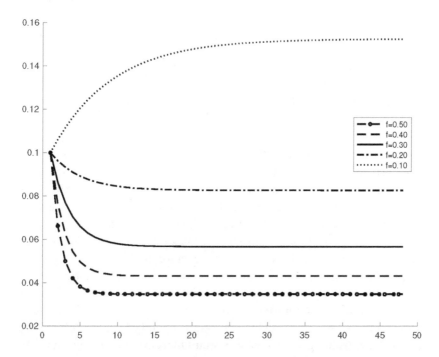

Fig. 5. The path of the unemployment rate starting from 10% for different values of f, setting $s = 0.018$.

This fast convergence stands in sharp contrast to the data where it takes several months for the unemployment rate to go back to its prerecession level.

III. Two Key Missing Margins in the Basic DMP Framework

Consistent with this tight link between the level and the persistence of unemployment that I demonstrated in table 1 and figure 5, Cole and Rogerson (1999) argued for incorporating heterogeneity in worker search intensity and allowing for quits and temporary separations—margins that are absent in the basic DMP framework. Their first point is about using data from the world in which there are three labor market states (i.e., employed, unemployed, and not in the labor force) to calibrate a model in which there are only two states. The second point is about lack of quits and temporary layoffs in the basic DMP framework. I will build on their intuition and argue that there are two key missing margins in the stylized DMP framework: the participation margin and job-to-job transitions, which are key ingredients needed to address the slow recovery puzzle.

A.   The Role of the Participation Margin for Unemployment Fluctuations

The basic model considered in Hall and Kudlyak abstracts from the participation margin and considers a two-state model with only job loss and job finding margins. However, recent research emphasized the importance of the participation margin for unemployment rate fluctuations and showed that workers' movements between participation and unemployment account for one-third of unemployment fluctuations in the data. See, for example, Elsby, Hobijn, and Şahin (2015) and Krusell et al. (2017). Moreover, entry into unemployment from nonparticipation remains persistently high even after job losses subside, contributing to a persistently high unemployment rate during recoveries.

To illustrate this point, figure 6 replicates the analysis in Elsby et al. (2015). Specifically, it shows the decomposition of the change in the unemployment rate starting from March 2007 accounted for by each of the worker flow transition rates. This episode was associated with a rise in the unemployment rate in excess of 5 percentage points, and the unemployment rate only declined by 2 percentage points 3 years after its peak in late 2009. Although the most important margin is the unemployment-to-employment transition rate, flows between nonparticipation and unemployment played an important role for the rise and the subsequent

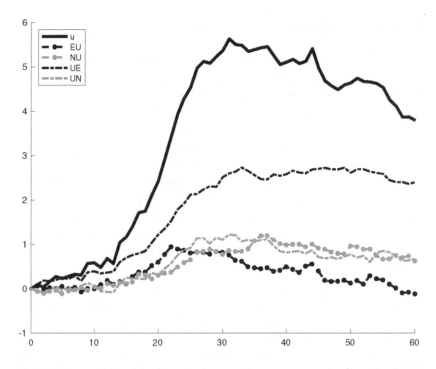

Fig. 6. Decomposition of the change in the unemployment rate starting from March 2007 accounted for by each of the worker flow transition rates following Elsby et al. (2015). A color version of this figure is available online.

decline in the unemployment rate. The role of flows between unemployment and nonparticipation was quantitatively significant and important. Notably, the inflow into unemployment from participation remained consistently high even after the employment-to-unemployment flow rate declined. This is an important observation because it shows that not all inflows into unemployment are about job loss. Workers who enter the labor market when the unemployment rate is high (such as recent college graduates) are more likely to enter through unemployment, which puts upward pressure on the unemployment rate. Incorporating this margin increases the persistence of inflows into unemployment in excess of what is implied by the job loss margin.

Hall and Kudlyak propose the gradual decline of the separation rate as a function of the unemployment rate as a potential mechanism to address the slow recovery puzzle. The participation margin provides rationale for a more gradual decline of the separation rate than implied by job losses consistent with their discussion.

B. The Role of Quits and Job-to-Job Transitions

Another key missing margin in the stylized model considered by Hall and Kudlyak is job-to-job transitions, which are an important feature of the US labor market. For example, Sedláček (2016) has documented that 30%–40% of all hires originate from employment. Faberman et al. (2020) have found that ≈60% of applications sent in 2013–17 were sent by employed workers, and employed workers accounted for around 70% of offers made during the same period in the Survey of Consumer Expectations. These findings suggest that firms' vacancy posting decisions are not only tied to unemployed searchers as suggested by the basic framework. Relatedly, once on-the-job search is taken into account, market tightness will not be captured by the vacancy to unemployed ratio but rather by the ratio of vacancies to effective searchers—which include employed workers as in Abraham, Haltiwanger, and Rendell (2020). Recent papers in the literature pursued this idea and showed that models that take into account employed searchers capture labor market dynamics better. See, for example, Moscarini and Postel-Vinay (2019), Eeckhout and Lindenlaub (2019), and Faberman et al. (2020).

To examine why job-to-job transitions are essential to address the slow recovery puzzle, figure 7 shows the quits rate along with the U-2 unemployment rate, which is a narrower unemployment rate that only includes workers who are unemployed due to job loss. Quits are strongly procyclical, and they pick up slowly even after the U-2 rate goes down. As a result, even after workers who get displaced during the recessions find jobs, employed people keep searching for better opportunities. These employed workers include the ones who delay quitting their jobs during recessions for the hope of a stronger labor market and those who were displaced during the recession and found jobs at the lower rungs of the job ladder. This reallocation over the job ladder takes longer as workers reallocate from the lower to the upper rungs of the job ladder. This idea is formalized in Eeckhout and Lindenlaub (2019) and Faberman et al. (2020), who show that traditional labor market tightness (vacancy/unemployed) and effective labor market tightness (vacancy/searchers) evolve differently over the business cycle. Employed workers' search effort declines during recessions and increases during recoveries, shifting the composition of job seekers. Firms' vacancy posting behavior responds to these shifts in the composition of searchers. As a result, even after labor demand picks up, movement of employed workers over the job ladder creates persistence in labor market conditions. Abstracting from on-the-job search

Fig. 7. U-2 and quits rate over the business cycle. A color version of this figure is available online.

ignores the compositional changes in the searcher pool, the gradual movement over the job ladder, and firms' reaction to these changes. Given the importance of employed searchers in overall search activity in the economy, on-the-job search margin should be incorporated to the DMP framework to capture labor market dynamics.

IV.   Concluding Remarks

Hall and Kudlyak revisit an important feature of the unemployment rate in the United States. Regardless of the reasons behind the rise in the unemployment rate in the preceding recession, the unemployment rate goes down at a slower pace than it rises. Put differently, unemployment fluctuations are asymmetric: it takes a long time for the unemployment to recover after a typical recession. Hall and Kudlyak offer many interesting mechanisms that would generate slow unemployment recovery dynamics that we need to better understand.

Although the mechanisms they review are interesting and likely to be important, they abstract from two key features of the labor market.

Recent research that followed up Cole and Rogerson (1999) emphasizes that labor force entrants, reentrants, and people who move from employer to employer are important in understanding firms' hiring decisions. Because their importance has been established in the last 20 years, starting from a model with these features would make the analysis more fruitful. In my view, relying on a highly stylized framework that abstracts from these two key margins and adding additional mechanisms is less conclusive than starting from a more general framework with three labor market states and on-the-job search.

To conclude, the analysis of Hall and Kudlyak is a valuable addition to the macro labor literature that focused on better understanding unemployment dynamics. The authors convincingly demonstrated that the stylized model falls short of generating realistic fluctuations in the unemployment rate. Developing models that match this feature of unemployment is key for policy analysis and design.

Endnote

Author email address: Şahin (aysegul.sahin@austin.utexas.edu). The author thanks Sadhika Bagga for excellent research assistance. For acknowledgments, sources of research support, and disclosure of the author's material financial relationships, if any, please see https://www.nber.org/books-and-chapters/nber-macroeconomics-annual-2021-volume -36/comment-why-has-us-economy-recovered-so-consistently-every-recession-past-70 -years-sahin.

References

Abraham, Katharine G., John C. Haltiwanger, and Lea E. Rendell. "How Tight Is the US Labor Market?" Brookings Papers on Economic Activity 2020, no. 1 (2020): 97–165.
Cole, Harold L., and Richard Rogerson. 1999. "Can the Mortensen-Pissarides Matching Model Match the Business-Cycle Facts?" International Economic Review 40 (4): 933–59.
Crump, Richard K., Stefano Eusepi, Marc Giannoni, and Ayşegül Şahin. "A Unified Approach to Measuring u." Brookings Papers on Economic Activity (2019): no. 1, 143–214.
Daly, Mary C., Bart Hobijn, Ayşegül Şahin, and Robert G. Valletta. 2012. "A Search and Matching Approach to Labor Markets: Did the Natural Rate of Unemployment Rise?" Journal of Economic Perspectives 26 (3): 3–26.
Eeckhout, Jan, and Ilse Lindenlaub. 2019. "Unemployment Cycles." American Economic Journal: Macroeconomics 11 (4): 175–234.
Elsby, Michael W. L., Bart Hobijn, and Ayşegül Şahin. 2015. "On the Importance of the Participation Margin for Labor Market Fluctuations." Journal of Monetary Economics 72 (2015): 64–82.

Faberman, R. Jason, Andreas I. Mueller, Ayşegül Şahin, and Giorgio Topa. 2020. "Job Search Behavior Among the Employed and Non-Employed." Forthcoming in Econometrica.

Krusell, Per, Toshihiko Mukoyama, Richard Rogerson, and Ayşegül Şahin. 2017. "Gross Worker Flows over the Business Cycle." *American Economic Review* 107 (11): 3447–76.

Moscarini, Giuseppe, and Fabien Postel-Vinay. 2019. "The Job Ladder: Inflation vs. reallocation." Mimeo. Yale University and University College London, New Haven and London.

Sedláček, Petr. 2016. "The aggregate matching function and job search from employment and out of the labor force." *Review of Economic Dynamics* 21 (2016): 16–28.

Shimer, Robert. 2005. "The Cyclical Behavior of Equilibrium Unemployment and Vacancies." *American Economic Review* 95 (1): 25–49.

Discussion

Ayşegül Şahin opened the discussion by asking how the authors' model of unemployment in recoveries differs from the existing literature and, in particular, why the mechanism is interpreted in terms of labor supply rather than labor demand. She argued that the mechanism appeared to be related to labor demand, because it is connected to the response of vacancy creation. The authors responded that in the traditional literature, unemployment declines slowly in a recovery because the exogenous forces depressing the job finding rate begin to move procyclically. In contrast, the authors' model can generate a depressed job finding rate purely through negative feedback from high unemployment back to job creation. Higher unemployment can lead to higher cost of job creation as firms need to search within a wider applicant pool. Thus, it is the high unemployment itself which creates a reduction in labor supply via the job finding rate.

The authors further responded that from a more traditional Keynesian perspective, unemployment is interpreted as a demand-determined jump variable. They regard unemployment as a fundamentally slow-moving state variable, and this carries the distinction between theirs and the traditional view. Şahin agreed with their distinction from that traditional view.

Erik Hurst then asked whether the stability of the results about the speed of the recovery across different time periods, even within the United States, implies either of the following: (i) there is not much policy variation across recessions; (ii) policy variation does not matter for the

© 2022 National Bureau of Economic Research. All rights reserved. Published by The University of Chicago Press for the National Bureau of Economic Research. https://doi .org/10.1086/718657

speed of recovery. The authors answered by stating that even in the absence of any policies, their model can generate slow self-recovery endogenously. Although policies might have contributed to stable uniform recoveries of unemployment, the model does not need policies to generate this pattern. They then discussed the model result that once unemployment rises to high levels, it is hard to bring it down quickly within a year, even when aided by policy. They highlighted that this underscores the relatively greater impact of pursuing stabilization policies during crises than during recoveries.

Giuseppe Moscarini commented that along the direction taken by discussants Robert Shimer and Ayşegül Şahin, it is time to move to a five-state model where temporary layoffs and marginally attached workers are included as separate states. Then, any residual left after taking these into account can be interpreted as aggregate demand. Although he did not take a stand on the cause of any residual, he argued that many would attribute it to monetary policy and sticky prices.

The authors concluded by responding to comments by the discussants. Robert Hall noted that although he agreed that the current state of research should push to include more states, these critiques are off point for their paper, as a simple model was purposefully included to illustrate a basic mechanism in Diamond Mortensen and Pissarides (DMP). Furthermore, he cautioned researchers on creating matching models based only on monthly transitions, as the labor transition process is of a higher order. Marianna Kudlyak agreed with discussants that temporary layoffs are important and concluded with a discussion on how their work can still apply to the current pandemic recession. She highlighted that almost 80% of the 14.7% unemployment in the COVID recession was due to temporary layoffs. The pandemic recovery looked different because the nature of unemployment due to temporary layoffs is fundamentally different from the point of view of the matching process. Unemployment from nontemporary layoffs during COVID goes down according to the principles from the previous recoveries.

2

From Mancession to Shecession: Women's Employment in Regular and Pandemic Recessions

Titan Alon, *University of California San Diego,* United States of America

Sena Coskun, *University of Mannheim, FAU Erlangen-Nuremberg, and IAB,* Germany

Matthias Doepke, *Northwestern University and NBER,* United States of America

David Koll, *European University Institute,* Italy, *and University of Mannheim,* Germany

Michèle Tertilt, *University of Mannheim,* Germany

I. Introduction

The COVID-19 pandemic has resulted in the sharpest global economic downturn since the Great Depression. Figure 1 displays deviations from long-term trends in gross domestic product (GDP) and aggregate hours worked in the United States, Canada, Germany, the Netherlands, Spain, and the United Kingdom from 2006 until the second quarter of 2020.[1] In each of these countries, the drop in output and labor supply during the pandemic recession is much larger than during any previous downturn in this period, at least twice as large even compared with the Great Recession of 2007–9. Understanding the nature and consequences of this massive economic shock is a central task for economic research.

At the onset of the crisis, Alon et al. (2020a) predicted that beyond its cause and magnitude, a key difference between the pandemic recession and others that preceded it would lie in its impact on women's employment. Recent prepandemic recessions have usually been "mancessions" in which men lost more jobs than women. The prediction by Alon et al. (2020a) that the pandemic recession would be a "shecession" with larger employment losses for women was based on two observations. First, although regular recessions heavily affect sectors such as construction and manufacturing in which many men work, it became quickly apparent that the pandemic recession would have its biggest impact on sectors

NBER Macroeconomics Annual, volume 36, 2022.
© 2022 National Bureau of Economic Research. All rights reserved. Published by The University of Chicago Press for the National Bureau of Economic Research. https://doi .org/10.1086/718660

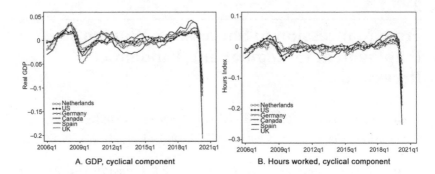

Fig. 1. The pandemic recession in six countries. See the appendix for data sources. Hours index is the index (=100 in 2006) of total hours of adult workers (20–64) in the economy. Seasonally adjusted quarterly real GDP and hours index (2006Q1–2020Q2) are Hodrick–Prescott (HP) filtered with smoothing parameter 1600 and cyclical components are reported. A color version of this figure is available online, and in our NBER Working Paper no. 28632.

such as hospitality and tourism with high female employment shares. Second, the pandemic also led to school and daycare closures that massively increased parents' childcare needs, and given that mothers provide a much larger share of childcare than fathers do, this would constrain women's ability to work more than men's.

With the benefit of hindsight, in this paper we provide a comprehensive empirical assessment of the role of women's employment in the pandemic recession of 2020. We argue that the evidence largely confirms the expectation of a larger impact on women in general and on working mothers in particular. As an illustration for the case of the United States, Figure 2 reports changes in the employment gap (the difference between the employment rate of women and men) during the pandemic recession of 2020 compared with the Great Recession of 2007–9.[2] During the Great Recession, women's employment increased compared with that of men, with gains gradually building as the recession progressed. This is the typical pattern of a mancession that puts more men than women out of employment. In the pandemic recession, in contrast, women's employment declined relative to that of men. For women without children, this decline was mild, but among women with children the drop in employment exceeded 5 percentage points 2 months into the recession compared with men with children. Employment losses declined somewhat during the summer of 2020 but expanded again in the fall.

Expanding on this evidence, we document the impact of the pandemic recession on women's versus men's employment across advanced economies; we use micro data to assess the role of childcare needs, industry

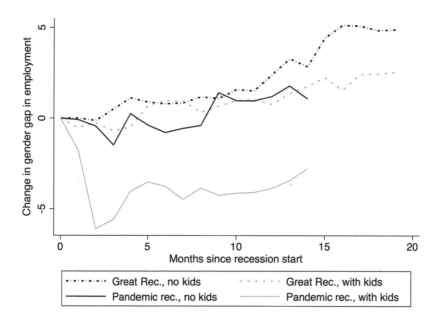

Fig. 2. Change in gender gap in employment in the United States during the Great Recession and the Pandemic Recession. The *y*-axis reports cumulative log point changes in the employment gender gap from the start of each recession (difference between women's and men's employment, negative numbers denote a decline in women's relative employment). Sample includes all civilians ages 25–55 who are either employed, unemployed, or not in the labor force. Employment series are seasonally adjusted by group from January 2000 to October 2020. The Great Recession corresponds to November 2007 to June 2009. The pandemic recession corresponds to February 2020 to April 2021. Workers "with kids" are those who have at least one own minor child (ages 0–17) residing in the same household. A color version of this figure is available online.

and occupation effects, and other factors in generating gender differences; and we assess how the gendered impact of the crisis matters for aggregate outcomes during the recession and for the evolution of gender inequality in the labor market and beyond. We find not only that the pandemic recession had an unusually large impact on working women across a large set of countries, but also that there is wide heterogeneity in the magnitude of the impact and the role of different channels underlying these impacts. The heterogeneity that we observe is informative for the role that policies and institutions play in shaping the economic impact of the recession. We also point to evidence that the pandemic recession will have long-lasting effects on the labor market. In particular, the recession is likely to result in a substantial rise in employment flexibility in the postpandemic "new normal," which has the potential to greatly benefit many working women.

To provide a baseline to compare the pandemic recession to, the first step in our analysis is to use aggregate data for 28 advanced economies to characterize the impact of regular, prepandemic business cycles on women's versus men's employment. Similar to what Doepke and Tertilt (2016) established for the United States, we find that with few exceptions regular recessions are mancessions in these countries, that is, during a typical business cycle downturn, male labor supply falls by more than female labor supply. We also show that differences in the cyclical volatility between industries with high female-versus-male employment shares play an important role in accounting for this pattern.

Turning to the pandemic recession, we find that in most countries the current recession is a shecession, that is, declines in employment and hours worked are larger among women. Moreover, in the few countries where the pandemic had a larger impact on men, the relative impact on women's labor market is usually more severe than what would be expected based on earlier recessions. Thus, a disproportionate impact on working women is a common feature of the pandemic recession that is shared among a large set of countries.

To learn more about the causes and consequences of this shecession, we turn to micro survey data from the six countries represented in figure 1: the United States, Canada, Germany, the Netherlands, Spain, and the United Kingdom. These countries represent a wide range of experiences in terms of the impact of the pandemic recession on the labor market. In the United States, Canada, and Germany, there is a substantial gender gap in the response of hours worked. In the United States, there is also a large gender gap in terms of employment changes but not so in Germany, a first indication that policy responses (such as more generous employment protection and furlough in Germany) play an important role during the crisis. In the Netherlands, Spain, and the United Kingdom, gender gaps in changes in both employment and hours worked are generally small.

Information on individual characteristics in the micro data allow us to assess the role of childcare needs, industry and occupation, and other factors in generating gender differences during the pandemic recession. Regarding childcare, we find that the impact on the gender gap is largest among parents with school-age children, pointing to the role of school closures. As figure 2 suggests, in the United States the impact of the childcare channel is large. We find large gender gaps in labor supply response among parents of school-age children, even in countries where the overall gender gap in the impact of the pandemic is small, such as

Spain. Beyond childcare, industry and occupation effects account for another sizable part of the gender gap in the impact of the crisis. Nevertheless, childcare, industry, and occupation are not the only channels at work: even when controlling for industry and occupation and considering only workers without children, we still find large gender gaps in several countries. For the United States, a decomposition analysis shows that the childcare and industry/occupation channels each account for a little less than 20% of the gender gap in terms of hours worked, with the remainder due to other factors. Understanding these additional factors behind the pervasive gender gap in the pandemic recession is an important challenge for future research.

We also analyze other dimensions of heterogeneity. A factor that matters a lot in the United States, Canada, and Spain is single parenthood: both hours and employment decline by more for single compared with married mothers. Much of the single-married divide disappears when controlling for industry and occupation, implying that the kind of jobs that single mothers hold matter. We do not find significant differences between married and single mothers in the other countries.

With regard to education, in the United States and Canada we observe larger gender gaps in the labor supply response of less-educated workers. Interestingly, the opposite finding arises in Spain and the United Kingdom (countries with a small overall gender gap in the impact of the pandemic) where we find a substantial gender gap in hours changes among parents of school-age children with college education but not among less-educated parents.

In the United States, it is well documented that the Black and Hispanic populations were particularly strongly affected by the labor market consequences of the pandemic (e.g., Hershbein and Holzer 2021). However, we generally do not find large or statistically significant differences in the gender gap in the labor supply response between different races and ethnicities or between workers with and without a migration background. The two exceptions are Germany, where the gender gap in employment losses is larger among those with a migration background, and Canada, where we observe a similar pattern in both employment and hours.

The disproportionate impact of the pandemic recession on women's employment not only matters for the distribution of the welfare cost of the pandemic recession but also has wider economic repercussions. Based on the analysis of Alon et al. (2020b), we argue that qualitative differences between shecessions and mancessions arise from the different dynamic behavior of women's and men's labor supply. Women's labor supply is generally more elastic than that of men, suggesting that in a shecession, lowered earning prospects after an unemployment spell are more likely to result in a persistent reduction in labor supply. A shecession also reduces households' ability to self-insure against income shocks, resulting in a stronger transmission from income shocks into consumption demand. In contrast, because women on average work fewer hours and earn less, shecessions can be less severe in terms of GDP losses than mancessions. Overall, whether a recession affects primarily men or women clearly matters: a shecession is not just a mancession with signs reversed.

The legacy of the pandemic recession is likely to include changes in the labor market that will long outlast the recession itself. One feature of the postpandemic new normal that is already becoming apparent now is that working from home, nearly universal among office workers during the pandemic, will have a permanent place in the future workplace (Barrero, Bloom, and Davis 2021). Alon et al. (2020b) argue that increased access to telecommuting and other forms of work flexibility have the potential to drastically reduce gender inequality in the labor market. The basis for this argument is that much of today's gender gap arises from the "motherhood penalty" (i.e., women's earnings start to lag behind those of men after having children). Work flexibility in general and telecommuting in particular are associated with a more equal division of childcare duties among mothers and fathers, thereby lowering the conflict for mothers between having a family and a career. Hence, if the future workplace indeed is more flexible, the motherhood penalty should shrink and so should overall gender inequality in the labor market.

Our empirical results reaffirm the notion that job flexibility is a particular benefit to working mothers. For the countries where we have information on telecommuting, we find that the gender gap in labor supply is concentrated among those who cannot telecommute. Among nontelecommuters, the gender gap is especially large among parents, whereas among those who can work from home, gender gaps are small regardless of whether children are present. Although several recent papers (e.g., Adams-Prassl et al. 2020b) have pointed out that the ability to telecommute protects workers from job loss in the current pandemic, our findings show that it is mothers who reap the largest gains from being able to work from home.

These findings suggest that the pandemic legacy of an expanded ability to telecommute will play an important role in advancing gender equality. Yet, there is a caveat. For the motherhood penalty to be reduced in the new normal, both mothers and fathers working from home would have to get their work done. However, evidence from the pandemic suggests that combining working from home with caring for children imposes a bigger drag on mothers' compared with fathers' productivity. In the Netherlands, we find that among parents working from home during the crisis, mothers used a larger fraction of the work time to provide childcare at the same time, particularly so if they had school-age children. Other studies document that among academic researchers (where productivity can be measured using publications and new working papers), productivity declined more among women than among men during the pandemic, with the largest productivity declines among mothers of young children (Amano-Patiño et al. 2020; Barber et al. 2021; Ribarovska et al. 2021). Hence, increased work flexibility after the pandemic opens up the potential for reduced gender inequality, but the full potential for change is unlikely to be realized without shifts in additional factors, such as social norms and workplace norms, that also determine the division of labor between mothers and fathers. Understanding the evolution and interplay of these factors shaping gender inequality in the postpandemic labor market is an important challenge for future research on the legacy of the crisis.

Our work contributes to the literature on the role of women's employment over the business cycle. Even though by now women account for the majority of the US workforce, for a long time most business cycle models have been unisex models that do not allow for gender differences. More recent studies argue that the role of women over the business cycle has substantially changed over time due to the rise in female labor force participation (Fukui, Nakamura, and Steinsson 2019; Albanesi 2020). The changed nature of business cycles also matters for policy. Bardóczy (2020) argues that the details of decision-making in the family are an important determinant of the transmission of macroeconomic shocks. Ellieroth (2019) analyzes the quantitative importance of family insurance over the business cycle using a joint-search model. Other contributions to the literature on women's employment and household decision-making within macroeconomics include Greenwood, Seshadri, and Yorukoglu (2005), Ortigueira and Siassi (2013), Doepke and Tertilt (2016), Mankart and Oikonomou (2017), Borella, De Nardi, and Yang (2018), Mennuni (2019), Olsson (2019), and Wang (2019).[3] In addition, Albanesi and Şahin (2018) and Coskun and Dalgic (2020) note the impact that the gender breakdown of employment in various industries has on the contrasting cyclicality of male and female employment. This is an important factor in the pandemic recession, because the industries hit the most by the pandemic are not those most affected by regular recessions. Finally, our work is part of the emerging literature on the impact of the COVID-19 pandemic on gender inequality in the labor market, including contributions such as Alon et al. (2020a, 2020b) and Adams-Prassl et al. (2020b). Our contribution is related in particular to Albanesi and Kim (2021), who take a similar empirical approach but focus entirely on the United States, and the studies by Dang and Nguyen (2020), Galasso and Foucault (2020), Leyva and Urrutia (2020), and Bluedorn et al. (2021), who also provide evidence across countries but without delving into detailed micro data.

In the next section, we examine the impact of the pandemic recession and earlier economic downturns on women's and men's employment in 28 countries using aggregate data. In Section III, we use micro data from national employment surveys to examine the sources of the gendered impact of the pandemic recession. In Section IV, we provide further results for the United States, where the gender gap in the impact of the pandemic recession is particularly large. In Section V, we examine heterogeneity along the dimensions of education, race, single parenthood, and the ability to telecommute. Section VI analyzes the impact of the pandemic on women's and men's productivity at work. In Section VII, we discuss the general lessons that can be learned from our analysis, and in Section VIII, we conclude.

II.   Aggregate Evidence across Countries

We start by providing an overview of the impact of earlier recessions and the pandemic recession on women's and men's employment across countries using aggregate data. We use data for 26 European countries from the European Labor Force Survey (EU-LFS), US data from the Current Population Survey (CPS), and Canadian data from the Canadian Labor Force Survey (CLFS).

A.   Regular Recessions

Doepke and Tertilt (2016) document that in the United States, women's labor supply is substantially less cyclical than that of men. In recessions, the labor supply of single men usually declines the most, whereas the drop in labor supply is smallest for married women. The same patterns can be observed in most countries in our data set. To characterize how labor supply varies over the cycle, we first compute the cyclical component of GDP as the difference between GDP and a Hodrick-Prescott trend. We then focus on the correlation between the cyclical component of GDP with the ratio of women's to men's labor supply. Figure 3 shows that in most countries in our data set, male labor supply is more cyclical than female labor supply. This is true both for the extensive and the intensive margin: panel A shows a negative correlation between the cyclical components of relative female/male employment and GDP while panel B shows a negative correlation between the cyclical components of relative hours and GDP. There are a few exceptions (Romania, Greece, and Belgium for the correlation with relative employment, and Romania and Czechia for the correlation with relative hours), but in all these cases the correlations are small.

The literature points out two primary explanations for the countercyclicality of women's relative labor supply: the distribution of women's employment by industry and occupation (Albanesi and Şahin 2018; Coskun and Dalgic 2020) and within-family insurance, that is, countercyclical adjustments of women's labor supply in response to job loss (or risk thereof) of their husbands (Doepke and Tertilt 2016). These factors give rise to substantial variation in the cyclical behavior of women's labor supply across countries, depending on factors such as the local industry composition of employment, marriage rates, and married women's labor force participation. Nevertheless, as figure 3 shows in almost all cases, the end result is a lower cyclicality of women's compared with men's labor supply.

Beyond correlations of relative labor supply and the cyclical component of GDP, we can analyze cyclical variation in women's and men's labor supply in more detail using the methodology of Doepke and Tertilt (2016). Their analysis distinguishes the total volatility of labor supply (the percentage standard deviation of the Hodrick-Prescott residual) from its cyclical volatility, which is the percentage standard deviation of the predicted value of the Hodrick-Prescott residual of labor supply on the Hodrick-Prescott residual of GDP per capita. The concept of cyclical volatility captures the part of total volatility that is related to the economic cycle, as opposed to other factors such as variation in cohort sizes.

Table 1 shows how the total and cyclical volatility of labor supply for different groups compare between the United States and five other countries: Canada, Germany, the Netherlands, Spain, and the United Kingdom. In five of the six countries, volatility is smaller for women than for men. Only the Netherlands stands out with a higher volatility for women than men.[4] When focusing on cyclical volatility, in all countries (including the Netherlands) women's hours worked vary less over the business cycle than men's. The gender gap is sizable, ranging from a modest difference in

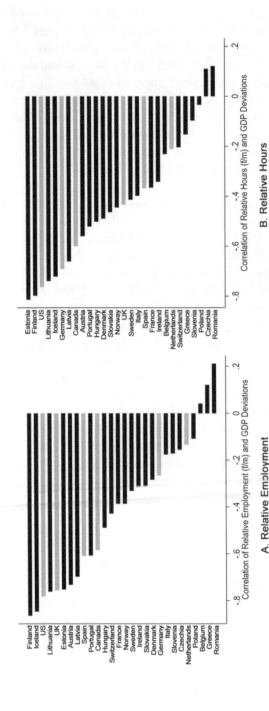

Fig. 3. In most countries, women's relative labor supply was countercyclical before 2020. The figure reports correlations between the cyclical component of relative employment/hours and the cyclical component of real GDP for each country. To compute trends, relative hours and relative employment (female/male) of individuals ages 20–64 and annual real GDP for the period 1998–2019 are HP filtered with smoothing parameter 6.25. See the appendix for data sources and details. The countries analyzed in detail in Section III are highlighted in gray. A color version of this figure is available online.

Table 1
Volatility of Hours Worked, by Gender and Marital Status, 1998–2019

	Total	All		Married		Single	
		Women	Men	Women	Men	Women	Men
			Total Volatility				
United States	1.27	.99	1.54	.80	1.23	1.29	2.12
Canada	.86	.67	1.06	.61	1.01	.93	1.31
Germany	1.02	.87	1.14	.89	.94	1.04	1.59
Netherlands	1.12	1.28	1.10	1.80	.81	1.21	1.62
Spain	1.58	1.41	1.83	1.23	1.49	1.86	2.50
United Kingdom	.74	.76	.82	.65	.60	1.07	1.27
			Cyclical Volatility				
United States	1.16	.85	1.41	.64	1.13	1.11	1.92
Canada	.71	.49	.87	.40	.73	.66	1.16
Germany	.82	.62	.93	.51	.74	.72	1.25
Netherlands	.78	.67	.83	.86	.55	.53	1.21
Spain	1.48	1.27	1.64	.90	1.22	1.76	2.26
United Kingdom	.51	.34	.62	.13	.35	.54	1.01
			Hours Share				
United States		42.96	57.04	23.57	36.15	19.39	20.89
Canada		41.97	58.03	27.53	39.83	14.44	18.20
Germany		38.27	61.73	19.86	36.76	18.41	24.97
Netherlands		35.39	64.61	17.78	37.24	17.61	27.37
Spain		38.30	61.70	20.71	38.25	17.59	23.45
United Kingdom		39.12	60.88	19.80	35.56	19.33	25.31
			Volatility Share				
United States		31.14	68.86	12.87	34.69	18.33	34.11
Canada		29.04	70.96	15.47	41.24	13.42	29.87
Germany		29.45	70.55	12.41	33.36	16.16	38.07
Netherlands		30.58	69.42	19.52	26.05	12.04	42.38
Spain		32.49	67.51	12.44	31.36	20.71	35.49
United Kingdom		26.06	73.94	5.07	24.63	20.37	49.93

Note: See appendix B for data sources. Total volatility is the percentage standard deviation of the Hodrick-Prescott residual of average labor supply per person in each group. Cyclical volatility is the percentage deviation of the predicted value of a regression of the HP-residual of hours on the HP-residual of real GDP. Hours share is the share of each component in total hours. Volatility share is share of each group in the cyclical volatility of total hours.

the Netherlands to a cyclical volatility that is almost twice as high for men relative to women in the United Kingdom.

With the exception of the Netherlands, the cyclical volatility of labor supply is lower for married women than for single women. Among singles, the cyclical volatility of women is lower than that of men in all countries. Thus, women's labor supply in general, and that of married women in particular, tends to dampen fluctuations in aggregate labor

supply over the business cycle. The overall impact of women on the behavior of aggregate labor supply not only depends on the volatility of
women's labor supply but also on their share in aggregate labor supply.
Women's share of total hours varies from 35% in the Netherlands, where
married women usually work part time, to 43% in the United States.
Women's contribution to the overall volatility of aggregate labor supply
is always lower than the hours share and varies between 26% in the United
Kingdom and 32% in Spain. Hence, in all countries women account for less
than a third of the volatility of aggregate labor supply. The volatility share
of married women differs widely across countries, ranging from only 5%
in the United Kingdom to almost 20% in the Netherlands.

Figure A1 (appendix is available online) displays the cyclical component of hours worked over time for each country. An interesting observation that has not been explored yet in the literature is that the male cycle
seems to lead the female cycle, especially for singles.

B.   The Pandemic Recession

The evidence shown so far establishes that in pre-2020 economic fluctuations, women's labor supply was less cyclical than men's across a wide
range of countries. Let us now consider what happened during the pandemic recession of 2020. Figure 4 shows how the labor supply of women
versus men changed in each country. Unlike in a regular recession,
women's labor supply fell relative to men's in 18 of 28 countries when
measured by employment, and in 19 of 28 countries when measured by
hours worked. Quantitatively, we observe larger changes in terms of hours
worked, with a drop of more than 10% in women's relative hours in Portugal.

Rather than looking at the absolute change in the ratio of women's to
men's labor supply, we can also ask how observed changes compare to
what would be expected based on the prepandemic relationship of wom-
en's and men's labor supply to the business cycle. Accordingly, figure 5
plots the actual change in labor supply in each country against the predicted
change based on prepandemic data. Here we see that most countries are
below the 45-degree line, implying that women's relative labor supply either declined or increased by less than what would have been expected
based on earlier recessions (the few exceptions are all close to the 45-degree
line). The countries that display a decline in men's relative employment
even during the COVID-19 recessions (most notably Portugal, Austria,
and the United Kingdom) are countries that have particularly pronounced
mancessions in regular times.

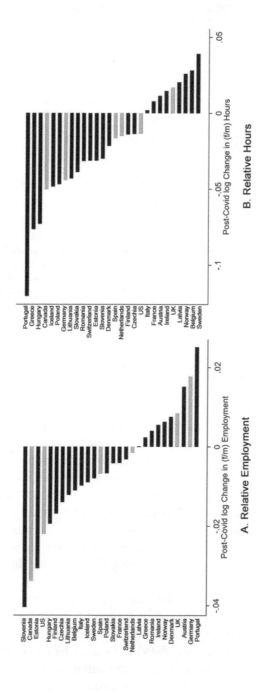

Fig. 4. Post-COVID change in relative female/male labor supply. The figure reports the log change in seasonally adjusted relative employment (female/male) and a relative hour worked index (female/male) between 2019Q4 and 2020Q2. See appendix C for further details and data sources. A color version of this figure is available online.

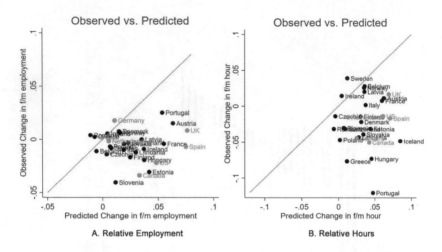

Fig. 5. Predicted versus observed changes in women's relative labor supply. Observed changes are the ones reported in figure 4. Predicted changes are calculated by multiplying the estimated coefficient from a regression of the cyclical component of relative employ-ment/hours on the cyclical component of GDP (for the years 1998–2019) and the observed GDP change between 2019Q4 and 2020Q2. A color version of this figure is available online.

C. Pattern across Industries

Why is the pandemic recession so different from usual recessions in its impact on women's versus men's employment, and what explains the substantial variation in the impact across countries? Starting with Alon et al. (2020a), the literature has focused on two explanations for the gen-dered impact of a pandemic recession. The first explanation is about the impact of the recession on different industries and occupations; be-cause the impact is related to lockdowns and social distancing measures, the parts of the economy most affected by the current downturn are not the ones that decline the most in regular recessions. Second, widespread school and daycare closures affect the ability of parents, and in particular mothers, to work.

We can use our cross-country data set to provide a first assessment of the first explanation, namely the role of the employment composition by industry. To do this, we divide industries into three groups: those with high male employment shares, those with high female employment shares, and "neutral" industries in the intermediate range. The industry classification is the same for all countries (see app. B.2 for details). We can now check how male, female, and neutral industries are affected by regular recessions and the pandemic recession in each country.

Panel *A* of figure 6 shows that, as expected, in pre-2020 data, male industries display more cyclical volatility in employment than female industries. At the same time, the figure also shows large cross-country variation; for example, in the United States the downward sloping pattern is particularly pronounced, while in Slovenia female industries are more volatile than male ones and in Germany there is little difference in the cyclical volatility between male and female industries.

Panel *B* of figure 6 shows how employment in the same set of industries in each country was affected by the pandemic recession in 2020. In a regular recession, we would expect to observe an increasing slope moving from male to female industries, that is, larger job losses during the recession in male industries. The actual pattern is the opposite: on average, female industries suffered larger employment losses than male industries. In Spain, for example, the employment decline was more than twice as large in female industries than male ones. Once again there is sizable variation across countries. For example, in the United Kingdom employment declines were slightly smaller in female industries. Differences in industry composition together with the impact of the pandemic recession on industries with relatively more female or male workers can account for some of the variation evident in figure 4. For example, women's employment was more strongly affected in Spain compared with the United Kingdom, and according to figure 6*B*, differences in the impact of the crisis across sectors (such as the large impact on and the large size of the tourism sector in Spain) can account for some of that.

Another way to see how starkly different the pandemic recession is from previous recessions is to compare it specifically to the Great Recession. In figure 7, we do this for the United States. Panel *A* shows that the most cyclical sectors, especially construction and manufacturing, also experienced the largest employment declines in the Great Recession. As panel *B* shows, in the pandemic recession the pattern is completely different: the largest employment declines were experienced by the leisure sector, which is usually not particularly cyclical. It also happens to be a sector dominated by female employees.

D.   The Childcare Channel in Cross-country Data

In addition to industry effects, increased childcare needs due to school and daycare closures are the other leading explanation for the impact of

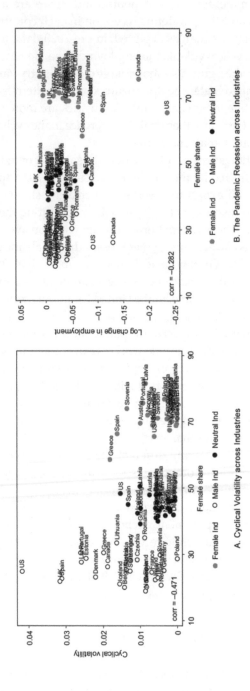

Fig. 6. Regular recessions and the pandemic recession in female versus male industries. Each dot depicts a group of industries (female, male, or neutral) in a country. See the appendix for data sources and details. Panel (b) reports log changes of seasonally adjusted aggregated industry employment between 2019Q4 and 2020Q2. Cyclical volatility is calculated for the period 2008–19 (2010–19 for Switzerland) at a quarterly frequency and is defined as the log deviation of the predicted value of a regression of the HP-residual of industry employment on the HP-residual of real GDP. The female share for each industry is the average of 2019. A color version of this figure is available online.

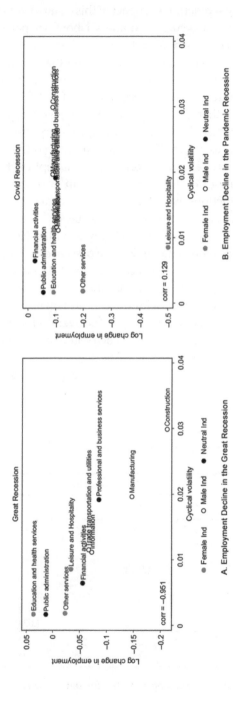

Fig. 7. Employment decline across sectors, United States. Data are from Bureau of Labor Statistics, seasonally adjusted quarterly industry employment numbers 1998–2020. Cyclical volatility has been calculated for the period 1998–2019 and is defined as the log deviation of the predicted value of a regression of the HP-residual of industry employment on the HP-residual of real GDP. Employment change in the Great Recession is the log change in industry employment from peak to trough (as defined by NBER recession dates), and for the COVID-19 recession the employment change corresponds to the period 2019Q4–2020Q2. A color version of this figure is available online.

the recession on working women. The impact of this channel varies across countries, depending on factors such as mothers' labor force participation and the length and severity of school and daycare closures. For example, in Sweden school closures were much more limited than in most other countries, and Sweden is also one of the few countries where women's relative hours increased in the pandemic recession (see fig. 4B).

Childcare (or the lack thereof) likely matters not just for the gender gap in labor supply but also for the overall employment impact of the pandemic. School closures affect all working parents, so the extent of school closures should have an impact on the overall depth of the recession. In addition, the more hours women work in normal times, the more likely it is that reductions in work hours are necessary to cope with the increased childcare needs during the pandemic.

To explore the overall impact of these channels on the labor market during the pandemic recession, in tables 2–5 we present cross-country regression results that show how various country-level characteristics are correlated with the aggregate changes in the labor market and with relative changes for women compared with men. With regard to aggregate employment, in column 1 of table 2 we regress the overall change in labor supply during the crisis (the hours index) in each country on an index that measures the severity of school closures. The regression shows that indeed, countries with more severe school closures experienced a greater

Table 2

Correlates of Change in Aggregate Hours Worked during the Pandemic Recession across Countries

	Change in Hours				
	(1)	(2)	(3)	(4)	(5)
School closure index	−.207	−.157			−.085
	(.007)	(.033)			(.241)
Prepandemic Female Hours		.011			
		(.043)			
Share of hospitality			−1.852		−1.943
			(.001)		(.00)
Teleworkable fraction				.642	.579
				(.034)	(.041)
N	28	28	28	27	27
R^2	.251	.366	.362	.168	.630

Note: p-values are in parentheses. See appendix B.2 for data sources and variable definitions.

drop in labor supply; the school closure index alone accounts for about 25% of the variation in hours changes. However, on its own the school closure index is not associated with larger employment changes or with differential impacts on women versus men (col. 1 in tables 3–5).[5]

In interpreting these results, it should be kept in mind that they represent correlations in cross-country data that are not necessarily causal and that are subject to the usual limitations of cross-country regressions. For example, differences in the severity of the pandemic across countries would be expected to generate some variation in the severity of school closures and also have a direct impact on employment (e.g., through the length of lockdowns). Hence, the results described in tables 2–5 should be interpreted as correlations that help summarize the data and can provide a first pass at assessing the importance of different channels, without being conclusive on their own.

The next variable we explore is the prepandemic level of women's labor supply. In a country where most mothers work full time, increased childcare needs during the pandemic may have a larger impact compared with a country where many mothers are either out of the labor force or working part time. Our results indicate that, when also controlling for the school closure index, countries where women's labor supply is higher experienced somewhat smaller aggregate declines in hours (col. 2 of table 2), but larger relative employment declines for women compared with men (col. 2 of table 5).

Table 3
Correlates of Change in Aggregate Employment during the Pandemic Recession across Countries

	Change in Employment				
	(1)	(2)	(3)	(4)	(5)
School closure index	−.001	−.006			.046
	(.970)	(.843)			(.080)
Prepandemic female hours		−.001			
		(.624)			
Share of hospitality			−.479		−.474
			(.016)		(.003)
Teleworkable fraction				−.026	.121
				(.764)	(.216)
N	28	28	28	27	27
R^2	0	.010	.203	.004	.357

Note: p-values are in parentheses. See appendix B.2 for data sources.

Next, we consider the role of industry composition and job characteristics. In the pandemic recession, the hospitality sector (including restaurants) has seen the largest employment decline across countries (see panel B of fig. 7 for the United States).[6] The size of the hospitality sector also varies widely across countries (in our sample, from 5.6% of total employment in Poland to 16% in Spain). Column 3 of tables 2 and 3 shows that a larger hospitality sector is indeed associated with a substantially larger overall decline in hours and employment in a country. However, there is no discernible impact on the relative changes for women versus men (col. 3 of tables 4 and 5).

In terms of job characteristics, arguably the most important one during the pandemic is whether the job can be done from home during shutdowns. Indeed, we find that countries with a larger share of telecommutable jobs experience a smaller decline in labor supply during the pandemic (col. 4 of table 2) and a smaller impact on the labor supply of women compared with men (col. 4 of table 4). When we include both measures together with the school closure index, both continue to have a substantial impact on the total hour change (col. 5 in table 2), whereas the effect of school closures turns insignificant. This regression also has the highest R^2 among specifications considered, accounting for more than 50% of the variance in overall labor supply changes across countries.

We also consider a number of other potential determinants of the labor market impact of the pandemic but find that they show little correlation with employment changes and gender differences.[7] An additional

Table 4
Correlates of Change in Relative Hours Worked (Women/Men) during the Pandemic Recession across Countries

	Change in Relative Hours (f/m)				
	(1)	(2)	(3)	(4)	(5)
School closure index	−.030	−.049			.059
	(.392)	(.182)			(.181)
Prepandemic female hours		−.004			
		(.125)			
Share of hospitality			−.110		−.250
			(.676)		(.307)
Teleworkable fraction				.313	.474
				(.016)	(.007)
N	28	28	28	27	27
R^2	.028	.117	.007	.212	.290

Note: p-values are in parentheses. See appendix B.2 for data sources.

Table 5
Correlates of Change in Relative Employment (Women/Men) during the Pandemic
Recession across Countries

	Change in Relative Employment (f/m)				
	(1)	(2)	(3)	(4)	(5)
School closure index	−.004	−.013			−.005
	(.800)	(.382)			(.806)
Prepandemic female hours		−.0026			
		(.067)			
Share of hospitality			.029		.062
			(.795)		(.587)
Teleworkable fraction				−.025	−.041
				(.648)	(.587)
N	28	28	28	27	27
R^2	.003	.130	.003	.008	.022

Note: p-values are in parentheses. See appendix B.2 for data sources.

conjecture is that the extent of employment protection may explain some of the variation in employment losses across countries. We indeed find that the Organisation for Economic Co-operation and Development (OECD) index of employment protection for temporary workers has a small correlation with overall employment changes in the expected direction, but the effect is quantitatively small and accounts for little of the observed variance across countries. Employment protection does not have a significant effect on gender differences in the impact of the pandemic.

Although the correlations documented in tables 2–5 are suggestive, only so much can be learned from cross-country correlations in aggregate data. To make progress, we now turn to household-level evidence from a smaller set of countries.

III.   Micro Data across Countries

The potential explanations for the gendered impact of the current pandemic recession generate distinct implications for which groups of women would suffer the biggest employment losses. For example, if childcare obligations during school closures were the main driving force behind women's employment losses, we would expect to observe a large impact on the employment of mothers with young children but not on women without children or women with adult children. We can use micro data from national employment surveys to examine these implications. For this analysis, we focus on a smaller set of countries for which this data is already available up to at least the second quarter of 2020, namely the United States, Canada, Germany, the Netherlands, Spain, and the United Kingdom. As table 6 shows, these countries also display a lot of variation in terms of the structure of women's labor supply, industry composition, and the policy response to the pandemic, which will provide further evidence on the additional driving forces discussed in the previous section.

A. Data and Empirical Design

The data stem from a variety of surveys and there is variation in the questionnaires, the frequency of the surveys, and sample selection.[8] We start by focusing on regressions that can be carried out in a similar way in all countries and give us a set of comparable results. The first set of regressions aims to examine the two leading explanations for the large impact of the pandemic on women's employment, namely the role of childcare and the role of industry and occupation. Our benchmark regression equation takes the form:

$$y_{it} = \beta_0 + \beta_1 F_i + \beta_2 D_t + \beta_3 F_i \times D_t + \beta_4 \mathbf{X}_{it} + \epsilon_{it}. \tag{1}$$

Here, y_{it} is the outcome variable of interest for individual i at time t, which is either a binary employment indicator or the inverse hyperbolic sine transform of hours worked last week. We apply this transformation to approximate the natural logarithm of hours worked last week while keeping the extensive margin of employment (i.e., zero hours).[9] F_i is an indicator for female, and D_t is an indicator for the COVID-19 pandemic, here corresponding to the second and third quarters of 2020 (the last two quarters in our data sets). The vector $\mathbf{X}_{it}$ consists of control variables that include gender-specific time trends in labor supply, quarterly seasonal dummies, age dummies, education categories, marital status, and race.[10] We also include a dummy for education workers in the summer months, because hours worked for this group drop strongly in the summer months. The main coefficient of interest is β_3 on the interaction of F_i and D_t. Here, $100 \times \beta_3$ captures the percentage difference in the impact of the pandemic on women versus men.[11]

We use additional regressions to characterize the extent to which the raw gender differences are due to industry, occupation, and childcare responsibilities. To get at the role of industry and occupation, we employ the following specification:

Table 6
Policies and Labor Market Structure Across Six Countries

Country	School Closure Index	Teleworkable Jobs	Average Female Hours	Share of Hospitality, Leisure, Other Services	Emp Protection Temp Worker	Emp Protection Regular Worker	Pre-COVID Cyclicality of Relative Hours
Canada	.88		23.04	.11	.28	1.68	–.60
Germany	.64	.37	22.40	.08	1.92	2.33	–.69
Netherlands	.51	.42	20.45	.09	1.48	2.88	–.21
Spain	.76	.32	20.30	.16	3.10	2.43	–.37
United Kingdom	.78	.44	23.23	.11	.54	1.90	–.43
United States	.50	.42	25.04	.15	.33	1.31	–.76

Note: See appendix B.2 for data sources.

$$y_{it} = \gamma_0 + \gamma_1 F_i + \gamma_2 D_t + \gamma_3 F_i \times D_t + \gamma_4 \text{Job}_{it} + \gamma_5 \text{Job}_{it} \times D_t + \gamma_6 X_{it} + \epsilon_{it}. \quad (2)$$

Here, Job_{it} is a vector combining occupation and industry information, with a dummy variable for each occupation-industry combination and an additional dummy variable for those not working to keep them in the sample. This job-type variable is interacted with the pandemic dummy D_t, which captures the differential impact of the recession on workers in different industries and occupations. The coefficient $100 \times \gamma_3$ captures percentage changes in the gender gap net of any industry-by-occupation-specific pandemic effects. For example, if gender differences arose entirely because more women than men work in the hospitality sector, we would expect to see a negative estimate of β_3 in regression (eq. [1]) but a zero estimate of γ_3 in regression (eq. [2]).

Our third main specification examines the role of childcare responsibilities for gender gaps in employment during the pandemic by focusing on differences between individuals with and without children. The specification has the following form:

$$y_{it} = \delta_0 \text{Kid}_{it} + \delta_1 F_i \times \text{Kid}_{it} + \delta_2 \text{Kid}_{it} \times D_t + \delta_3 F_i \times \text{Kid}_{it}$$
$$\times D_t + \delta_4 X_{it} + \epsilon_{it}. \quad (3)$$

Here, Kid_{it} is a vector of three dummy variables grouping households by age of their youngest child into three groups: pre-K (<5), school age (5–17), and a third group that combines those with no or only adult children.[12] The coefficients δ_0 to δ_3 are vectors in this regression with a separate entry corresponding to each child group. In this regression, the coefficients in δ_3 capture the gender gap in the employment impact of the pandemic conditional on the child group. If gender differences arose solely because mothers are more affected by the rise in childcare needs during the pandemic than fathers, we would expect a negative coefficient within the groups with young and school-age children but a zero coefficient in the no-child/adult-child group.

Our final specification combines equations (2) and (3) by adding the work-type controls and interactions to the child-type regressions:

$$y_{it} = \theta_0 \text{Kid}_{it} + \theta_1 F_i \times \text{Kid}_{it} + \theta_2 \text{Kid}_{it} \times D_t + \theta_3 F_i \times \text{Kid}_{it} \times D_t$$
$$+ \theta_4 \text{Job}_{it} + \theta_5 \text{Job}_{it} \times D_t + \theta_6 X_{it} + \epsilon_{it}. \quad (4)$$

Once again, adding work-type controls allows us to assess how much of the observed effects are due to industry and occupation. For example, one may conjecture that young mothers have different jobs than young fathers; the full specification allows us to measure the differential impact of the pandemic on the employment of mothers and fathers beyond what is accounted for by such industry and occupation differences.

B.   Gender Gaps across Countries in the Micro Data

Table 7 summarizes the results for these regressions with employment status (employed or not) as the left-hand side variable, and table 8 does the same for hours. For comparison, the first row displays the overall percentage employment change (table 7) and hours change (table 8) in each country during the pandemic. Employment dropped by more than 5% in the United States and Canada, by about 4% in Spain, and by less than 1% in Germany and the United Kingdom. Changes in hours are much larger and range from a decline of 36% in the United States to more than 50% in Germany.[13] The Netherlands is an outlier in both dimensions: the data actually indicate a small but insignificant rise in employment and hours during the crisis. Rather than reflecting a true increase in employment, it is more likely that this increase reflects a change in the questionnaire in the Dutch Longitudinal Internet Studies for the Social Sciences (LISS) survey that reduces comparability of reported hours before and during the pandemic.[14] We keep the Netherlands in the sample because the variation in outcomes across different groups in the crisis is still informative.

It is notable that Germany and the United Kingdom display the smallest decline in employment but among the largest drops in hours. This suggests an important role of furlough schemes in these countries that preserved employment while allowing large reductions in hours (often to zero), which should be kept in mind when interpreting the results.

The other entries in tables 7 and 8 are estimates for the gender-gap coefficients of interest β_3, γ_3, δ_3, and θ_3. Each entry in the table corresponds to an estimate from a separate regression, and p-values are displayed in parentheses. The row labeled as "basic gender gap" displays the coefficient estimate for β_3 for each outcome and for each country. In terms of employment, a sizable and statistically significant gender gap in the impact of the pandemic on employment is observed only in the United States and to a smaller extent in Spain.[15] Note that according to table 6, these two countries have the highest employment share of the hospitality sector. In terms of hours (table 8), we observe a substantially larger impact on women's compared with men's labor supply in the United States, Canada, and Germany but no statistically significant difference in the

Table 7
Pandemic-induced Change in Employment and in the Gender Gap in Employment:
Regression Coefficients from Individual Country Regressions

	USA	CAN	DEU	NLD	ESP	GBR
Overall employment decline	−6.34	−5.52	−.28	.67	−4.08	−.13
	(0.00)	(0.00)	(.55)	(.13)	(0.00)	(.59)
Basic gender gap (β_3):	−1.91	−.44	−1.34	1.51	−1.01	.15
	(0.00)	(.13)	(.13)	(.21)	(.09)	(.81)
Pre-K kids ($\delta_{3,\text{pre-K}}$)	.13	2.65		1.13	.20	1.38
	(.83)	(0.00)		(.59)	(.84)	(.16)
School-age kids ($\delta_{3,\text{school}}$)	−4.23	−1.76	−1.12	.92	−1.97	−.80
	(0.00)	(0.00)	(.43)	(.55)	(.01)	(.30)
No kids ($\delta_{3,\text{none}}$)	−1.57	−1.05	−1.04	2.06	−1.13	−.47
	(0.00)	(0.00)	(.33)	(.13)	(.12)	(.52)
w/ industry and occ controls (γ_3):	−1.09	−.46	−1.32	1.11	.04	−.34
	(0.00)	(.02)	(.16)	(.28)	(.41)	(.52)
Pre-K kids ($\theta_{3,\text{pre-K}}$)	−.81	.14		1.05	.08	.12
	(.03)	(.63)		(.56)	(.15)	(.89)
School-age kids ($\theta_{3,\text{school}}$)	−1.79	−1.63	−.99	.31	−.05	−.74
	(0.00)	(0.00)	(.50)	(.81)	(.41)	(.26)
No kids ($\theta_{3,\text{none}}$)	−.95	−.33	−1.20	1.52	.08	−.69
	(0.00)	(.15)	(.28)	(.18)	(.15)	(.25)

Note: Coefficients reported are in percentage points. Sample includes all civilians ages 25–
55 who are either employed, unemployed, or not in the labor force. The p-values are reported
in parentheses below estimates. Unless otherwise noted, all regressions include gender-
specific time trends and controls for age, education, race, and marital status, in addition
to quarterly indicators and a fixed effect for education sector workers in summer months
to control for seasonality. No controls are used in the estimation of the overall employment
decline. For Canada, Germany, the Netherlands, and Spain, we group people by migration
background instead of race. Child age brackets are assigned by the age of the youngest
child (<5 and 5–17). In Spain, the group of school-age children includes those up to the
age of 19. Due to data limitations, for Germany we can only estimate the combined effect
of having children below 16 (including pre-K), which in the table is reported in the
"school-age kids" rows. Furthermore, due to a shorter data availability, in Germany and
the Netherlands we cannot control for gender-specific time trends, quarterly indicators,
and the summer-education fixed effect. For details on the data, see appendix C.

Netherlands, Spain, and the United Kingdom.[16] One reason for these
cross-country differences is likely the different labor market structure
in these countries. The fall in relative hours was large and significant
in those countries where the pre-COVID cyclicality of relative hours
was high and where female hours worked are relatively high (see table 6).
    The following rows of tables 7 and 8 break down the gender gap be-
tween individuals with young children, school-age children, and either
no or older children. Controlling for children matters a lot, in part because
of differences within the two groups with children. In most cases, the gender gap in the "no kids" group is similar to the basic gender gap. With the

Table 8
Pandemic-induced Change in Hours and in the Gender Gap in Hours: Regression Coefficients from Individual Country Regressions

	USA	CAN	DEU	NLD	ESP	GBR
Overall hours decline	−36.17	−43.77	−52.18	6.91	−49.87	−42.20
	(0.00)	(0.00)	(0.00)	(.14)	(0.00)	(0.00)
Basic gender gap (β_3):	−7.76	−6.50	−26.39	−6.63	−2.08	4.97
	(0.00)	(0.00)	(.01)	(.46)	(.46)	(.12)
Pre-K kids ($\delta_{3,\text{pre-K}}$)	2.42	6.00		−67.85	11.02	13.80
	(.40)	(.01)		(.01)	(.03)	(.01)
School-age kids ($\delta_{3,\text{school}}$)	−17.86	−11.08	−16.23	−9.25	−4.60	−4.05
	(0.00)	(0.00)	(.29)	(.55)	(.20)	(.34)
No kids ($\delta_{3,\text{none}}$)	−6.63	−7.92	−31.25	5.89	−5.11	2.55
	(0.00)	(0.00)	(.01)	(.63)	(.13)	(.52)
w/ industry and occ controls (γ_3):	−5.20	−7.21	−22.38	−11.21	−2.16	.53
	(0.00)	(0.00)	(.03)	(.22)	(.24)	(.87)
Pre-K kids ($\theta_{3,\text{pre-K}}$)	−3.66	−5.58		−65.79	.43	7.06
	(.08)	(0.00)		(.01)	(.91)	(.16)
School-age kids ($\theta_{3,\text{school}}$)	−8.94	−11.55	−10.17	−7.66	−4.93	−6.31
	(0.00)	(0.00)	(.52)	(.61)	(.05)	(.12)
No kids ($\theta_{3,\text{none}}$)	−4.19	−4.64	−29.71	−4.05	−1.23	−1.50
	(0.00)	(0.00)	(.02)	(.72)	(.57)	(.68)

Note: Coefficients reported are log points difference of the pandemic's effect on women versus men. Hours index is calculated using inverse hyperbolic sine transformation of reported hours worked last week. Sample includes all civilians ages 25–55 who are either employed, unemployed, or not in the labor force. The p-values are reported in parentheses below estimates. Unless otherwise noted, all regressions include gender-specific time trends and controls for age, education, race, and marital status, in addition to quarterly indicators and a fixed effect for education sector workers in summer months to control for seasonality. No controls are used in the estimation of the overall hours decline. For Canada, Germany, the Netherlands, and Spain, we group people by migration background instead of race. Child age brackets are assigned by the age of the youngest child (<5 and 5–17). In Spain, the group of school-age children includes those up to the age of 19. Due to data limitations, for Germany we can only estimate the combined effect of having children below 16 (including pre-K), which in the table is reported in the "school-age kids" rows. Furthermore, due to a shorter data availability, in Germany and the Netherlands we cannot control for gender-specific time trends, quarterly indicators, and the summer-education fixed effect. For details on the data, see appendix C.

exception of the Netherlands, among individuals with pre-K kids there is either no gender gap or women experience smaller employment and hours losses than men in this group. It is among workers with school-age children where large gender gaps in the impact of the crisis arise.

In the United States, for example, there is no significant gender gap among parents of pre-K kids for both employment and hours, a gender gap of 1.6 percentage points for employment and 6.6 percentage points for hours within the no-child group but large gaps of 4.2 and 17.9 percentage points for employment and hours within the group with school-age children. The patterns in Canada, Spain, and the United Kingdom are qualitatively similar to the United States; although the magnitudes differ, in each case the gender gap is largest among parents of school-age children with the exception of the gender gap in hours in Spain where it equals the one of nonparents (in Germany, we do not have information to distinguish parents of pre-K and school-age children). The only country with a substantially larger impact on the labor supply of women in the pre-K group is the Netherlands, and even here the effect is only observed in terms of hours but not employment. Overall, these findings are consistent with a major role of school closures in explaining gender gaps during the pandemic.

C. The Role of Industry and Occupation

We next turn to the role of differential trends across industries and occupations during the pandemic. The bottom half of tables 7 and 8 shows results after adding work-type controls for all industry-occupation combinations. As shown in equation (2), these work-type controls are interacted with the pandemic dummy, so we account for the differential impact of the pandemic on workers in each industry-occupation combination. If gender differences in a given group were entirely due to a different distribution of women and men in the group across industries and occupations, we would expect to observe a zero coefficient in the regressions controlling for these trends.

The results indicate that industry and occupation effects do matter but only account for a limited fraction of gender gaps. Consider first the United States. After controlling for work type, the overall gender gap declines by 43% in terms of employment and 33% in terms of hours. Among parents of school-age kids, the gender gap declines by more than 50% in terms of employment and a little under 50% in terms of hours. Although this shows that the work-type distribution accounts for a sizable fraction of the gender gap among parents of school-age children, this group still exhibits the largest gender gaps after controlling for work type. Another notable finding is that the gender gap among parents of pre-K kids switches sign; once work type is controlled for, mothers in this group lose more employment and hours than fathers. In other words, mothers of young children are likely to hold jobs that were relatively secure during the pandemic recession. However, even after controlling work-type effects, the gender gap in this group continues to be smaller compared both to parents of older children and individuals without children.

There is a lot of variation in the role of work type across countries. In Canada, for example, gender differences among parents with pre-K children in terms of hours actually increase after controlling for work type, suggesting that fathers of young children work in jobs that were more exposed to the pandemic recession. The gender gap continues to be largest among parents of school-age children, although it shrinks for those without kids. In Germany, controlling for work type has only a small effect on the results. In Spain, controlling for work type accentuates the role of children for gender differences: a large and significant gender gap in terms of hours is only observed among parents of school-age children after including work-type controls. The pattern in the United Kingdom is similar but is just below statistical significance.

D. Interpreting the Empirical Findings

A few broader conclusions arise from the empirical analysis so far. First, in the Netherlands, Spain, and the United Kingdom, gender gaps in the impact of the pandemic are generally small and statistically insignificant for both employment and hours once work type is controlled for. Nevertheless, within this group we find a statistically significant gender gap in the hours response among parents of school-age children in Spain and parents of pre-K children in the Netherlands. In the Netherlands, this gap in hours is quantitatively large, even though there is no gender gap in employment among the same parents. Evidently, many mothers of young children in the Netherlands reduced their hours at work while holding on to their job. The ability to do so depends on the availability of flexible furlough schemes and/or additional parental leave, which is one way in which policy choices shape the gender gap in the labor market during the crisis.

The remaining countries (United States, Canada, and Germany) all display a substantial overall gender gap in the hours response to the pandemic, with or without work-type controls. In the United States and Canada, we also observe gender gaps in the employment impact of the crisis, whereas there are no statistically significant employment effects in Germany. In fact, in Germany there is no statistically significant decrease in overall employment (both men and women), even though the decline in hours is large, once again suggesting that employment protection and furlough schemes—which are extensive in Germany ("Kurzarbeit"; see table 6)—play an important role in shaping the employment effects of the recession.

Moving on to the role of childcare, in both the United States and Canada we find that the gender gap in the impact of the pandemic on employment and hours is largest among the parents of school-age children and smallest (and even reversed in sign) among the parents of pre-K children under the age of five. Although the large gender gap among parents of school-age children lines up with a notion from the existing literature that childcare responsibilities during school and daycare closures have a negative effect on mothers' employment, our findings for the parents of younger children do not support this channel and are surprising at first sight. In terms of the sign of the effect on parents of young children, it turns out that controlling for industry and occupation is crucial: without such controls mothers experience smaller employment and hours losses than fathers in this group, but mothers' losses are larger after allowing for different trends across work types. In other words, among parents of young children, mothers who are in the labor force are more likely than fathers to work in industries and occupations that were relatively protected from the effects of the pandemic.

Still, even after introducing work-type controls, the gender gap is substantially smaller among parents of young children compared with parents of school-age children. We conjecture that this observation may reflect a selection effect. The labor force participation of mothers of young children is lower than that of mothers of school-age children. Mothers who decide to work while raising a young child may have stronger labor force attachment than average women. Also, the fact that a mother of a younger child is working may reflect that she has more help with childcare, be it through a father who does a large share of the work, the presence of other family members such as grandparents who help out, or the financial means to employ a nanny. The same factors may also lead to a smaller impact of the pandemic recession on these women's employment. Mothers of young children who managed to work prior to the pandemic without using formal childcare clearly experienced less of a shock to their childcare needs compared with mothers of older children who normally attend school.

A final notable outcome is that even after allowing for the childcare and industry and occupation channels, sizable gender gaps remain. The last rows of tables 7 and 8 show that within the no-child group and after controlling for work-type effects, women suffer larger employment losses than men in the United States and larger reductions in hours of labor supply in the United States, Canada, and Germany. In fact, the gender gap within the no-child group is only slightly smaller than the overall gender gap in the United States and Canada, and larger (in terms of hours) in Germany. This shows that the gender gap in the impact of the pandemic goes well beyond the childcare and industry/occupation channels that have been emphasized by the literature so far. Understanding this pervasive nature of the gender gap in the impact of the pandemic, which constitutes a sharp difference from previous recessions, is an important challenge for future research.

E.   Relating the Findings to the Literature

Several studies have analyzed gender differences in the labor market during the pandemic, typically focusing on one country at a time. None of these studies has applied the same methodology to analyze multiple countries in a comparable way. Existing studies also analyze only a subset of the issues that we do and often only with data from the first couple of months of the pandemic. Still, to the extent that the scope of existing studies overlaps with ours, it is instructive to check how the results line up.

A number of studies have been conducted about the United States, most of them using CPS data as we do. Some of the early studies include data only until April or May 2020 and each of them looks only at a subset of the issues we do. Nevertheless, by and large the results support our findings of large gender gaps in employment and hours reductions in response to the pandemic, especially for those with children (Collins et al. 2020; Couch, Fairlie, and Xu 2020; Cowan 2020; Dias, Chance, and Buchanan 2020; Montenovo et al. 2020; Fabrizio, Gomes, and Tavares 2021). There are two papers that exploit geographic variation in school and daycare closures to isolate the effect of increased childcare needs. Heggeness (2020) studies school closures and finds that mothers living in early closure states were more likely to take temporary leave or stop working entirely. Even mothers who maintained their jobs in early closure states were 53% more likely to not be at work compared with mothers in late closure states. Russell and Sun (2020) analyze childcare center closures instead and find similar effects for mothers of younger children. Using a triple-differences approach, they find evidence that the unemployment rate of mothers of young children increased substantially.

Like we do, studies analyzing Canadian data find sizable gender gaps in labor supply declines. Qian and Fuller (2020) analyze the Canadian LFS (same data as we use) and find a large increase in the gender employment gap for parents of primary school-age (6–12) children. They find even larger gender gaps when "being employed and at work" is used as an outcome variable. Lemieux et al. (2020) document that employment and hours worked of mothers with school-age children dropped substantially early on in the pandemic. Beauregard et al. (2020) analyze data from Quebec and find a larger impact of the pandemic on mothers relative to fathers in dual-parent households. They also find larger employment declines for single parents compared with dual-parent households. They further exploit the differential timing of primary school reopenings across regions. Using a triple-difference strategy, they find a positive effect of reopenings on parental work, a more pronounced effect on single mothers, and a stronger impact when the job cannot be done from home.

For the United Kingdom, like we do, Hupkau and Petrongolo (2020) find no increase in the gender gap in paid employment using the same labor force survey that we rely on. One explanation for these findings may be a more equal division of childcare within British households. Hupkau and Petrongolo (2020) and Sevilla and Smith (2020) both document a decline in the gender childcare gap during the pandemic, especially when men can work from home or lost their jobs. Within specific subgroups, some studies do find gender gaps even in the United Kingdom. Andrew et al. (2020a) focus on two-parent families and find larger declines in employment for mothers than fathers within this group. Analyzing data from a real-time survey in April, Adams-Prassl et al. (2020b) also find gender gaps in employment losses in the United Kingdom. Adams-Prassl et al. (2020a) document a different kind of gender gap in furlough decisions: mothers were more likely than fathers to initiate furloughing (as opposed to it being the employer's decision), although no such gender gaps were found among childless workers.

For the Netherlands, Holler et al. (2021) use the same data that we employ and find little overall widening of the gender gap in employment or hours, in line with our findings. They distinguish essential from nonessential workers and find that women working in nonessential occupations reduced hours by more than men in the same occupations, but the opposite pattern is observed in essential occupations, where women reduced hours by less. Meekes, Hassink, and Kalb (2020) use administrative data for the Netherlands until June 2020. Like us, they find no significant widening of the gender employment gap in the first half of 2020. They argue that this is largely due to institutions such as a large short-time work scheme, generous paid family leave, and the availability of emergency childcare. The authors do find gender differences among subgroups: single moms of small children classified as essential workers experienced larger reductions in hours worked than other female essential workers.

González (2021) uses the Spanish labor force survey up until the third quarter and, in contrast to us, finds no evidence for a gender gap in employment losses. However, the paper uses a different definition of employment (classifying those furloughed and working zero hours as unemployed, while we define furloughed workers as employed) and does not consider hours worked, which likely explains the different result.

Previous findings for Germany are mixed. Adams-Prassl et al. (2020b) find no significant gender gap in employment losses in data from a real-time survey conducted in April 2020. Möhring, Reifenscheid, and Weiland (2021) find that women participate less in short-time work in Germany, so women's employment is more polarized between job loss and working on-site. Dullien and Kohlrausch (2021) argue that school closures played a relatively small role for aggregate employment and hours losses in Germany. Yet they also find an increase in the gender employment gap. In their survey, 20% of parents with children who need care said they reduced working time because of childcare and home-schooling requirements in April 2020, and 13% said so in June. Also more mothers than fathers perceived the situation as "extremely/strongly stressful" during the pandemic.

IV. A Closer Look at the United States

In this section, we provide a more detailed look at the case of the United States, the largest country in our study and the one with the largest gender gap in the employment impact of the pandemic.

A. Decomposition of Channels Underlying the Gender Gap

Building on the regression results in the previous section, we start by providing a decomposition analysis to assess the relative importance of the childcare and occupational channels for generating gender gaps in the impact of the pandemic. Given the results of regression equation (4), the decomposition answers the following question: how much of the pandemic-induced change in the gender gap can be explained by the presence of children, and how much is due to industry and occupational effects? We apply this decomposition to the population of workers who were employed on the eve of the pandemic.[17]

An intuitive way to understand our decomposition is as follows: for each individual, we use the regression results of equation (4) to predict their pandemic-induced change in labor supply. Given the specification, this will depend on their gender, the presence of children, and their occupation. We then calculate the pandemic-induced change in the gender gap as the difference in the average change in labor supply for women and the average change in labor supply for men (in logs). Consequently, the aggregate change will depend on the micro effects (the estimated parameters θ_2, θ_3, and θ_5) and the joint distribution of characteristics—specifically gender, children, and occupations—in the population. For example, the contribution of the childcare channel is larger when more workers have a child. For our analysis, we use the distribution of characteristics in the prepandemic data (i.e., $D_t = 0$). The decomposition then assigns aggregate changes associated with θ_5 to the labor demand channel. The childcare channel captures contributions from θ_2 and θ_3 relative to the effect on those with no kids. The residual accounts for any widening in the gender gap among workers with no kids that is not explained by occupation effects ($\theta_{3,none}$). Details on the derivation and implementation of this decomposition are provided in appendix D.

Table 9 gives the results. We find that about 14% of the gender gap in the employment decline and 18% in the hours decline can be attributed to the childcare channel. The occupational channel can account for 12% and 20%, respectively. These numbers imply that there is a large residual: two-thirds of the widening in the gender gap cannot be explained by the two channels. The size of the residual is likely related to a missing data problem: for many individuals who are temporarily not working, no information on occupation or industry is collected. This creates noise that likely reduces the measured contribution of the occupational channel. To assess the importance of this issue, we reestimate our model on the sample of employed individuals only. Conditioning on employment means we can only decompose the intensive margin, as we are losing the extensive margin by construction. We do carry out this decomposition in appendix D. The decomposition of the widening of the gender gap in hours (conditional on working) based on an estimation using employed workers only

Table 9
Decomposition of Pandemic-induced Change in the Gender Gap

Outcome	Childcare Channel (%)	Occupation/Industry Channel (%)	Residual (%)
Employment	13.7	12.4	73.9
Hours	17.7	19.8	62.5

Note: See appendix D for details.

leads to a much smaller residual: we find that 21% of the gender gap can be attributed to the childcare channel and 50.5% to the occupational channel, leaving a residual of 28.5%. Note that although the occupation channel gains in importance, the contribution of the childcare channel is similar to the decomposition based on estimates for the entire sample.

Even a residual of just under 30% suggests that in the pandemic recession, there are channels beyond childcare and occupation that have a sizable role in explaining the disparate effects of the pandemic on women and men. One possible channel is related to the gender wage gap. If families try to minimize family exposure to COVID-19, some family members may quit jobs or reduce hours to reduce the family's total infection risk. Such a behavior would make the most sense for family members with low earnings or working in high-contact occupations, such as women working as nurses, physical therapists, or grocery store clerks. A second possibility is that our estimate of the childcare channel understates the total effect because, for instance, it ignores the effects on grandmothers in multigenerational households, some of whom may also have reduced work to provide more childcare. Yet another possibility is that other care-giving responsibilities went up as women spent more time caring for elderly relatives and other family members.

B.   The Impact over Time

Because for the United States we have monthly data through October 2020, we can estimate how the gender gap changes over time. To do so, we reestimate the regression equations (2) and (4), but instead of interacting the female and job effects with a pandemic indicator, D_t, we interact them with monthly time fixed effects. To add precision, we take advantage of the longitudinal dimension of the CPS data and include individual level fixed effects in the regression.[18] Also, we simplify child groups into a binary variable by combining parents of pre-K and school-age kids into one group. This leaves us with two groups: those who have children under the age of 18 and those who do not. Results for the overall gender gap are depicted in figure 8, and figures 9 and 10 provide separate results for those with and without children. In each case, changes are reported relative to January 2020.

Figure 8 shows that the gender gap was the largest early on in the pandemic. In April and May 2020, the gender gap was 2 percentage points higher compared with January in terms of employment and 10 percentage points higher in terms of hours. The employment gender gap started

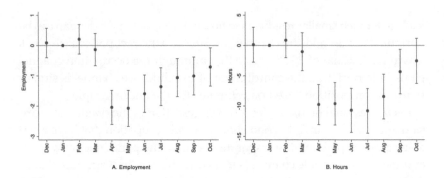

Fig. 8. Change in the gender gap over time, December 2019 to October 2020. The figure displays changes in the gender gap in the United States relative to January 2020. Error bands represent 95% confidence intervals. See appendix E for further details on the empirical specification. A color version of this figure is available online.

to narrow in June and had more than halved by October. The hours gap stayed wide for longer and started narrowing only in September. The decline over time of the gendered impact of the pandemic in the United States has also recently been pointed out by Lee, Park, and Shin (2021).

Figures 9 and 10 plot estimates over time for those with and without children. Although both groups faced a widening of the gender gap in hours and employment due to the pandemic, in April and May 2020 the gender employment gap among parents had widened by almost

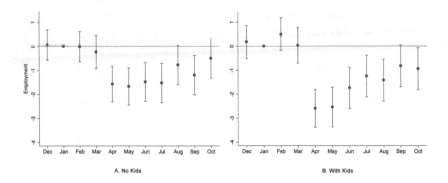

Fig. 9. Change in the employment gender gap by presence of children, December 2019 to October 2020. The figure displays changes in the gender gap in the United States relative to January 2020. Error bands represent 95% confidence intervals. See appendix E for further details on the empirical specification. A color version of this figure is available online.

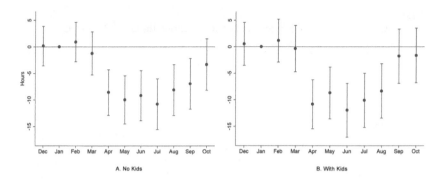

Fig. 10. Change in the hours gender gap by presence of children, December 2019 to October 2020. The figure displays changes in the gender gap in the United States relative to January 2020. Error bands represent 95% confidence intervals. See appendix E for further details on the empirical specification. A color version of this figure is available online.

3 percentage points relative to January, compared with about 2 percentage points among nonparents. For hours worked, trends across those with and without kids are similar. The gender gap in hours and employment declines over time, and by October 2020 the gender gap in employment remains statistically significant only among parents.

Generally, the impact of having children in the results displayed in figures 9 and 10 is smaller compared with the raw data displayed in figure 2 (and also fig. A4). Unlike figure 2, the regressions underlying figures 9 and 10 rely on micro data and include various controls, individual fixed effects, and differential trends across industries and occupations. Clearly, allowing for these controls and trends accounts for some of the raw gender gap displayed in figure 2.

C. Pandemic Recession versus Great Recession

In our analysis of the micro data, we have so far focused entirely on outcomes during the pandemic recession. We have already established in Section II that the aggregate impact of the pandemic recession on women versus men is drastically different from regular recessions in a large set of countries, but this still leaves open the question of whether there are gender gaps related to parenthood and childcare in other recessions too. To make one such comparison, we focus on the contrast between the pandemic recession and the Great Recession of 2007–9 in the United States.[19]

Table 10
Gender Gaps in Hours and Employment Changes during the Great Recession
in the United States, December 2007 to May 2008

	Hours		Employment	
	Benchmark	Work Controls	Benchmark	Work Controls
Basic gender gap (β_3/γ_3):	10.13	3.39	1.88	.39
	(0.00)	(0.00)	(0.00)	(.01)
Pre-K kids ($\delta_{3,pre-K}/\theta_{3,pre-K}$)	12.51	2.51	2.54	.19
	(0.00)	(.09)	(0.00)	(.44)
School-age kids ($\delta_{3,school}/\theta_{3,school}$)	8.08	3.12	1.40	.34
	(0.00)	(.01)	(0.00)	(.10)
None ($\delta_{3,none}/\theta_{3,none}$)	10.37	3.64	1.92	.44
	(0.00)	(0.00)	(0.00)	(.01)

Note: Coefficients reported are percentage points. Sample includes all civilians ages 25–55
who are either employed, unemployed, or not in the labor force (NILF). The p-values are
reported in parentheses below estimates. Unless otherwise noted, all regressions include
gender-specific time trends and controls for age, education, race, and marital status, in addition to quarterly indicators and a fixed effect for education sector workers in summer
months to control for seasonality. Child age brackets are assigned by the age of the youngest child (<5 and 5–17).

Table 10 provides results for the same specifications as in tables 7 and 8
for the Great Recession in the United States. To focus on the first 6 months
of the recession (as we do in tables 7 and 8), we set the recession indicator
D_t to one starting in December 2007 until May 2008. As expected, given
the results in Section II, the table shows that, unlike the pandemic recession, the Great Recession was a mancession with larger declines in both
hours and employment for men. Furthermore, the impacts on the gender
gap among parents and nonparents are of the same sign and of a similar
magnitude. These findings are consistent with the notion that both the
overall impact on women in the labor market and the special role of parenthood are unique to the pandemic recession of 2020.

V. Heterogeneity by Education, Race, Single Parenthood, and Ability to Work from Home

We now return to the full set of countries and explore which other dimensions of heterogeneity (beyond parenthood and industry/occupation) are
connected to gender differences in the labor market during the pandemic
recession.

A.   The Role of Education and Race

Consider, first, the role of education. Tables 11 and 12 present results analogous to tables 7 and 8 with separate results for individuals with at least college education and less-educated workers.[20] The regressions in tables 11 and 12 already include industry and occupation controls and thus capture education effects beyond those that arise because education and work type are correlated.[21]

Recall that only the United States and Canada display a large and statistically significant overall gender gap for both employment and hours after controlling for industry and occupation effects (tables 7 and 8). Tables 11 and 12 show that in the same two countries, the gender gap for both employment and hours is much larger among less-educated workers. In both countries, the gender gap for employment is more than three times larger among less-educated workers compared with workers with college education. For hours, the gender gap among less-educated workers is three times as large among the less educated in the United States and a bit more than 50% larger in Canada. The role of childcare in accounting for these differences varies across countries. In the United States, it is notable

Table 11
Pandemic-induced Changes in the Gender Gap in Employment by Education, with Occupation/Industry Controls

	USA	CAN	DEU	NLD	ESP	GBR
BA degree or higher (γ_3):	−.52	−.20	−1.92	1.71	.01	−.57
	(.03)	(.42)	(.18)	(.13)	(.78)	(.34)
Pre-K kids ($\theta_{3,\text{pre-K}}$)	−.53	.73		2.46	.10	−.28
	(.20)	(.08)		(.22)	(.23)	(.79)
School-age kids ($\theta_{3,\text{school}}$)	−1.82	−.62	−1.95	−.58	−.08	−.46
	(0.00)	(.12)	(.37)	(.67)	(.41)	(.57)
No kids ($\theta_{3,\text{none}}$)	.08	−.51	−.56	2.52	.04	−.99
	(.80)	(.09)	(.75)	(.06)	(.45)	(.19)
Less than BA degree (γ_3):	−1.59	−.66	−.83	.44	.05	−.16
	(0.00)	(0.00)	(.49)	(.73)	(.36)	(.80)
Pre-K kids ($\theta_{3,\text{pre-K}}$)	−1.24	−.32		−1.15	.08	.04
	(.03)	(.39)		(.70)	(.23)	(.98)
School-age kids ($\theta_{3,\text{school}}$)	−1.82	−2.34	.28	.77	−.04	−.84
	(0.00)	(0.00)	(.89)	(.67)	(.67)	(.31)
No kids ($\theta_{3,\text{none}}$)	−1.75	−.31	−1.55	.58	.10	−.38
	(0.00)	(.23)	(.27)	(.69)	(.20)	(.62)

Note: The notes of table 7 apply. All regressions include occupation × industry controls interacted with the pandemic indicator. For details on the data, see appendix C.

Table 12

Pandemic-induced Changes in the Gender Gap in Hours by Education,
with Occupation/Industry Controls

	USA	CAN	DEU	NLD	ESP	GBR
BA degree or higher (γ_3):	−2.24	−5.38	−22.60	−17.57	−4.06	−4.23
	(.10)	(0.00)	(.15)	(.15)	(.08)	(.27)
Pre-K kids ($\theta_{3,\text{pre-K}}$)	−4.79	−2.01		−71.19	−5.45	−.82
	(.07)	(.42)		(.01)	(.31)	(.90)
School-age kids ($\theta_{3,\text{school}}$)	−7.66	−5.32	1.56	10.05	−8.11	−12.64
	(0.00)	(.03)	(.95)	(.59)	(.03)	(.02)
No kids ($\theta_{3,\text{none}}$)	1.20	−5.46	−42.47	−15.26	−1.35	−5.15
	(.49)	(0.00)	(.01)	(.35)	(.65)	(.30)
Less than BA degree (γ_3):	−7.75	−8.75	−21.56	−4.41	−.81	4.46
	(0.00)	(0.00)	(.10)	(.73)	(.70)	(.22)
Pre-K kids ($\theta_{3,\text{pre-K}}$)	−3.22	−8.62		−50.31	5.16	14.65
	(.26)	(0.00)		(.23)	(.26)	(.03)
School-age kids ($\theta_{3,\text{school}}$)	−9.86	−15.73	−14.63	−24.28	−2.46	−2.32
	(0.00)	(0.00)	(.47)	(.27)	(.42)	(.65)
No kids ($\theta_{3,\text{none}}$)	−8.49	−5.03	−23.73	7.89	−1.59	1.91
	(0.00)	(0.00)	(.13)	(.60)	(.55)	(.67)

Note: The notes of table 8 apply. All regressions include occupation × industry controls interacted with the pandemic indicator. For details on the data, see appendix C.

that among college-educated workers, the gender gap in the impact of the crisis is entirely due to those with children—there is no significant gender gap for either employment or hours among those without kids. In contrast, among less-educated workers, women suffer larger declines in employment and hours even without children. In the United Kingdom (where the gender gap in the impact of the crisis is generally small) as well as in Spain, the only group where we observe a large and statistically significant gender gap in the decline in hours worked consists of college-educated workers with school-age children.

Another salient dimension of heterogeneity is race; in the United States for example, overall employment losses have been substantially larger among Black and Hispanic workers compared with White workers. Tables 13 and 14 examine whether the gender gap in the impact of the crisis also varies across races. The underlying regressions include industry and occupation controls and thus are not driven by differences in the distribution of workers of different races across work types.[22] Data on race are available only for the United States and the United Kingdom; for these countries, to maintain sufficiently large sample sizes, we focus on differences between white workers and all others. For Canada, Germany,

Table 13
Pandemic-induced Changes in the Gender Gap in Employment by Race or Migration
Background, with Occupation/Industry Controls

	White/Nonwhite		Migration Background			
	USA	GBR	CAN	DEU	NLD	ESP
Gender gap: whites/no migration (γ_3):	−1.14	−.32	.20	−.55	1.68	.02
	(0.00)	(.55)	(.37)	(.56)	(.11)	(.58)
Pre-K kids ($\theta_{3,\text{pre-K}}$)	−.94	.26	.39		3.50	.08
	(.02)	(.78)	(.26)		(.06)	(.23)
School-age kids ($\theta_{3,\text{school}}$)	−1.96	−.75	−.76	−.09	1.12	−.04
	(0.00)	(.26)	(.02)	(.95)	(.41)	(.49)
No kids ($\theta_{3,\text{none}}$)	−.91	−.65	.32	−.62	1.65	.05
	(0.00)	(.30)	(.19)	(.59)	(.16)	(.33)
Gender gap: nonwhites/migration (γ_3):	−.93	−.53	−1.88	−9.36	−.69	.10
	(.01)	(.61)	(0.00)	(.01)	(.67)	(.37)
Pre-K kids ($\theta_{3,\text{pre-K}}$)	−.33	−.67	−.48		−7.98	.09
	(.69)	(.74)	(.29)		(.05)	(.25)
School-age kids ($\theta_{3,\text{school}}$)	−1.26	−.68	−3.31	−8.11	−3.01	−.09
	(.04)	(.68)	(0.00)	(.10)	(.26)	(.66)
No kids ($\theta_{3,\text{none}}$)	−1.10	−.95	−1.91	−9.22	1.37	.22
	(.02)	(.53)	(0.00)	(.05)	(.49)	(.17)

Note: The notes of table 7 apply. All regressions include occupation × industry controls interacted with the pandemic indicator. For Canada, Germany, the Netherlands, and Spain, we group people by migration background instead of race. For details on the data, see appendix C.

the Netherlands, and Spain, we display analogous results focusing on differences between the native-born population and workers with a migration background (see app. C for details).

We find that in the United States, the gender gap is generally of a similar size between white and other workers. Having school-age children expands the gender gap a bit more among white workers. Likewise, in the United Kingdom there are no significant differences in patterns between white and nonwhite workers. Notice that these results reflect relative changes between women and men; even though nonwhite workers generally experienced a larger reduction in employment and hours, this does not seem to affect women more strongly than men, and in the United States it is somewhat less so if they have school-age children.

In Germany, the gender gap in the impact on employment is much larger among workers with a migration background. This difference is not driven by childcare: the gap is similar among workers with and without children. The same gap is not observed for hours. This suggests that

Table 14

Pandemic-induced Changes in the Gender Gap in Hours by Race or Migration Background, with Occupation/Industry Controls

	White/ Nonwhite		Migration Background			
	USA	GBR	CAN	DEU	NLD	ESP
Gender gap: whites/no migration (γ_3):	−5.20	−.69	−5.42	−23.06	−4.59	−1.66
	(0.00)	(.83)	(0.00)	(.03)	(.65)	(.37)
Pre-K kids ($\theta_{3,\text{pre-K}}$)	−3.23	7.32	−3.33		−50.84	2.12
	(.15)	(.17)	(.11)		(.06)	(.59)
School-age kids ($\theta_{3,\text{school}}$)	−9.73	−9.82	−8.81	−11.96	−2.54	−4.54
	(0.00)	(.02)	(0.00)	(.47)	(.88)	(.08)
No kids ($\theta_{3,\text{none}}$)	−3.89	−1.93	−3.55	−28.95	1.31	−.97
	(.01)	(.61)	(.02)	(.02)	(.92)	(.67)
Gender gap: nonwhites/migration (γ_3):	−5.16	6.67	−10.79	−15.19	−31.52	−3.51
	(.01)	(.27)	(0.00)	(.67)	(.09)	(.32)
Pre-K kids ($\theta_{3,\text{pre-K}}$)	−4.79	5.34	−10.29		−123.02	−3.95
	(.28)	(.63)	(0.00)		(.01)	(.60)
School-age kids ($\theta_{3,\text{school}}$)	−6.33	11.00	−16.79	4.13	−28.14	−6.27
	(.05)	(.26)	(0.00)	(.93)	(.44)	(.30)
No kids ($\theta_{3,\text{none}}$)	−4.95	.37	−6.66	−48.18	−16.85	−1.19
	(.05)	(.97)	(0.00)	(.32)	(.47)	(.81)

Note: The notes of table 8 apply. All regressions include occupation × industry controls interacted with the pandemic indicator. For Canada, Germany, the Netherlands, and Spain, we group people by migration background instead of race. For details on the data, see appendix C.

among workers with an immigration background, women were more likely to lose their job in the crisis, whereas immigrant men and native workers were more likely to hold on to their job but then reduce hours through the use of furlough schemes. Some of this pattern may arise because many immigrant women have "minijobs" without formal employment protection. In the Netherlands, there is a substantial gender gap for both employment and hours among parents of young children with a migration background. In Canada, the gender gap among immigrants widens substantially for both employment and hours, particularly for those with school-age children. For nonimmigrants we observe a similar effect for hours but of a smaller magnitude.

B.   The Role of Single Parenthood

Our results so far indicate that childcare obligations are one major reason why women in many countries faced a deterioration in labor market opportunities during the crisis. The role of childcare suggests that single parents, who have less flexibility in sharing responsibilities with a partner, should be particularly exposed to the effects of the crisis. To examine this possibility, we now consider differences in the impact of the crisis on single mothers versus mothers living with a partner. The regressions take the form

$$y_{it} = \kappa_0 \mathbf{Kid}_{it} + \kappa_1 S_i \times \mathbf{Kid}_{it} + \kappa_2 \mathbf{Kid}_{it} \times D_t + \kappa_3 S_i \times \mathbf{Kid}_{it}$$
$$\times D_t + \kappa_4 \mathbf{X}_{it} + \epsilon_{it}. \tag{5}$$

Here y_{it} is the outcome variable for individual i at time t, S_i is an indicator for a single mother, D_t is the indicator for the COVID-19 pandemic, and $\mathbf{Kid}_{it}$ is a vector of two dummy variables grouping households by age of their youngest child into two groups: pre-K (<5) and school age (5–17).[23] The vector $\mathbf{X}_{it}$ consists of the same control variables as in the earlier regressions. We run this regression on a sample consisting only of mothers with kids up to the age of 18 (below 20 in Spain); here we are interested in the coefficients κ_3 on the interaction of S_i, D_t, and $\mathbf{Kid}_{it}$, which captures the difference in the impact of the pandemic on single mothers versus mothers living with a partner by child age.

We also carry out a version of this regression analogous to equation (4) with work-type controls:

$$y_{it} = \lambda_0 \mathbf{Kid}_{it} + \lambda_1 S_i \times \mathbf{Kid}_{it} + \lambda_2 \mathbf{Kid}_{it} \times D_t + \lambda_3 S_i \times \mathbf{Kid}_{it} \times D_t$$
$$+ \lambda_4 \mathbf{Job}_{it} + \lambda_5 \mathbf{Job}_{it} \times D_t + \lambda_6 \mathbf{X}_{it} + \epsilon_{it}. \tag{6}$$

Table 15 shows the estimates of the parameters κ_3 and λ_3 in these regressions. In the results without work-type controls, we find that in the United States, Canada, and Spain, single mothers of school-age children experienced larger declines in employment and hours compared with mothers living with a partner. In the United States and Canada, the same is true for single mothers of younger children. In contrast, in Germany, the Netherlands, and the United Kingdom, there are no significant differences in the impact of the crisis on single versus other mothers.

The results controlling for work type indicate that a lot of the large impact on single mothers in the United States, Canada, and Spain is due to the fact that single mothers are likely to have jobs in industries and occupations that experienced larger employment declines in the crisis. In all three countries, the gap between single mothers and mothers living with a partner is substantially reduced once differential trends across job types

Table 15
Pandemic-induced Changes in Labor Supply for Single Mothers

	USA	CAN	DEU	NLD	ESP	GBR
Single mothers employment gap:						
Pre-K kids ($\kappa_{3,\text{pre-K}}$)	−5.67	−3.69		4.82	−.03	−2.64
	(0.00)	(0.00)		(.54)	(.99)	(.29)
School-age kids ($\kappa_{3,\text{school}}$)	−1.44	−2.04	6.80	−2.15	−2.82	.85
	(.03)	(0.00)	(.11)	(.42)	(.02)	(.51)
w/ ind and occ controls:						
Pre-K kids ($\lambda_{3,\text{pre-K}}$)	−.14	−.48		5.73	.10	.56
	(.82)	(.38)		(.39)	(.36)	(.80)
School-age kids ($\lambda_{3,\text{school}}$)	.28	−1.02	7.59	−4.52	−.27	.58
	(.50)	(0.00)	(.08)	(.03)	(.12)	(.57)
Single mothers hours gap:						
Pre-K kids ($\kappa_{3,\text{pre-K}}$)	−25.09	−28.10		43.64	−4.08	−15.15
	(0.00)	(0.00)		(.58)	(.73)	(.09)
School-age kids ($\kappa_{3,\text{school}}$)	−12.59	−10.99	68.71	23.20	−22.20	−2.57
	(0.00)	(0.00)	(.18)	(.43)	(0.00)	(.67)
w/ ind and occ controls:						
Pre-K kids ($\lambda_{3,\text{pre-K}}$)	−1.51	−14.40		14.41	−5.27	2.72
	(.64)	(0.00)		(.86)	(.53)	(.75)
School-age kids ($\lambda_{3,\text{school}}$)	−3.20	−5.06	84.68	7.54	−9.21	3.26
	(.13)	(.03)	(.10)	(.77)	(.01)	(.54)

Note: Hours coefficients reported are log points difference of the pandemic's effect on single mothers versus nonsingle mothers. Employment coefficients are percentage points difference. Sample includes all mothers with children (ages <5 or 5–17, by youngest child) ages 25–55 who are not in the military. In Spain, the group of school-age children includes those up to the age of 19. For Spain, Germany, and the United Kingdom, we use cohabitation-marriage status (=1 if married or cohabiting, =0 if neither cohabiting nor married). Otherwise, all notes from tables 7 and 8 apply. For further details on the data, see appendix C.

are controlled for. In the United States, in fact, all differences become statistically insignificant. In Canada, the additional impact on single mothers remains quantitatively large even after controlling for work type. For example, hours for single mothers decline by an additional 5.1 percentage points for mothers of school-age children and by 14.4 percentage points for mothers of younger children. In Spain, we observe a similarly strong decline in hours for single mothers of school-age children by an additional 9.2 percentage points when taking work type into account. In the Netherlands, the impact on the employment of single mothers with school-age kids is larger after controlling for work type.

The results not only provide support for the view that single mothers faced particularly large challenges during the crisis but also show that local conditions matter. The extent of school closures and the availability of emergency childcare varied widely across the countries considered. So does mothers' baseline labor supply. In Germany and the Netherlands, for example, relatively few mothers work full time, which may give them additional flexibility to deal with childcare needs compared with otherwise similar mothers in the United States or Canada who were working full time at the beginning of the crisis. We also note that for the Netherlands and Germany, we have only few observations of single mothers, making it more difficult to reliably identify the role of single motherhood in these countries.

C.   The Role of the Ability to Work from Home

We already saw that the impact of the pandemic on workers varied widely across industries and occupations. Among the underlying job characteristics that give rise to these differences, arguably the most important one is the ability to work from home. Job losses were highest in industries and occupations where working from home is impossible, including much of the hospitality industry. In contrast, other groups such as office workers and academics were able to continue work via telecommuting and rapidly adopted remote-working tools such as videoconferencing on Zoom and similar services in the process. The ability to work from home also interacts with childcare needs; looking after children in virtual school is easier for a parent who is working on a laptop a few feet away compared with a parent who has to commute to a workplace.

To examine how telecommuting shaped the labor market experiences of women versus men during the pandemic, we now consider how the gender gap in the impact of the crisis differs between workers who are able to work from home during the pandemic and those who are not. We focus on the United States, the United Kingdom, and the Netherlands, where information on telecommuting during the crisis is available. Moreover, we limit attention to the intensive margin of labor supply (hours worked conditional on being employed), because the place of work is only known for the employed.

For the United States, information on telecommuting during the pandemic is available from the COVID-19 supplement to the CPS.[24] The answers are available starting in May 2020, and we classify individuals as telecommuting if they worked remotely at any point from May 2020 to September 2020. We retrieve labor market outcomes predating May 2020 using the panel dimension of the CPS monthly files. In the United Kingdom, telecommuting information is available for all employed individuals, including those who report zero hours of work (i.e., workers on furlough). Note that our information is on actual telecommuting rather than just the ability to work from home, so that results could be influenced by workers' decision whether to work from home if they have the ability to do so. Nevertheless, we conjecture that during the crisis most workers who were able to work from home actually did so. In the Netherlands, the data contains information on the hours worked from home in the reference week for March, April, May, June, and September 2020. Hence, we follow the same approach as for the United States and define individuals to be able to telecommute if they have been working from home at any point between March and September 2020.

Table 16 displays how the gender gap in the impact of the crisis differs between workers who can work from home and those who cannot. For the United States, the result is straightforward to summarize: there are large gender gaps among workers who are unable to work from home but only small ones among telecommuters, which become insignificant when controlling for work types. This continues to be true when we separate results between parents and others. Among telecommuters, gender gaps are small among both parents and nonparents. In contrast, among nontelecommuters, there is a large gender gap even among workers without kids and an even larger one among parents. Unlike in our baseline results that do not control for telecommuting, this time the largest gender gap is found among parents of young (pre-K) children: in this group, mothers are estimated to reduce hours by about 17 percentage points more than fathers do. The gender gap amounts to 14 percentage points among parents of school-age children, whereas it is 9 percentage points among those without kids under the age of 18. Interestingly, the results are essentially the same regardless of whether we also introduce job-type controls or not. This suggests that the ability to work from home is the main job-type characteristic that matters during the pandemic, so that few additional effects arise when telecommuters and nontelecommuters are already separated.

The central role of the combined effect of the ability to work from home and childcare needs is also apparent from the raw data on labor supply for women and men during the pandemic. Table 17 displays average hours worked conditional on being employed in the United States broken down by gender, parental status, and telecommuting. For men, weekly work hours vary little across these groups and are close to 40 hours per week in each case. Similarly, for women who can telecommute, labor supply is roughly constant across groups, with all groups averaging between 35 and 38 hours per week. For women who cannot telecommute, however,

Table 16
Pandemic-induced Change in the Gender Gap in the Intensive Margin of Employment
by Telecommuting Status

	United States		United Kingdom		The Netherlands	
	Benchmark	Work Type	Benchmark	Work Type	Benchmark	Work Type
No telecommuting (β_3/γ_3):	−12.42	−11.87	−1.00	−2.18	6.19	7.96
	(0.00)	(0.00)	(.74)	(.49)	(.69)	(.64)
Pre-K kids ($\delta_{3,\text{pre-K}}/$ $\theta_{3,\text{pre-K}}$)	−17.18	−17.33	−3.02	−4.39	−66.07	−60.23
	(0.00)	(0.00)	(.58)	(.43)	(.21)	(.24)
School-age kids ($\delta_{3,\text{school}}/$ $\theta_{3,\text{school}}$)	−14.89	−14.09	−10.70	−9.01	−13.44	−19.01
	(0.00)	(0.00)	(.01)	(.04)	(.64)	(.51)
No kids ($\delta_{3,\text{none}}/\theta_{3,\text{none}}$)	−9.45	−8.76	2.93	−.15	18.81	22.48
	(0.00)	(0.00)	(.43)	(.97)	(.33)	(.29)
Telecommuting (β_3/γ_3):	−3.60	−2.07	9.35	12.80	−11.99	−12.32
	(.06)	(.29)	(.08)	(.02)	(.27)	(.30)
Pre-K kids ($\delta_{3,\text{pre-K}}/$ $\theta_{3,\text{pre-K}}$)	−3.52	−1.47	12.82	18.47	−41.71	−49.50
	(.34)	(.69)	(.28)	(.11)	(.13)	(.08)
School-age kids ($\delta_{3,\text{school}}/$ $\theta_{3,\text{school}}$)	−4.51	−2.90	3.50	9.95	−3.23	4.87
	(.09)	(.28)	(.67)	(.22)	(.86)	(.80)
No kids ($\delta_{3,\text{none}}/\theta_{3,\text{none}}$)	−3.51	−2.27	13.25	12.85	−7.60	−12.32
	(.11)	(.32)	(.08)	(.08)	(.61)	(.42)

Note: Coefficients reported are log percentage point differences of the pandemic's effect on women versus men. Sample includes all civilians ages 25–55 who are employed (in the United States restricted to positive hours, in the United Kingdom including those with zero hours, e.g., those on furlough). The p-values are reported in parentheses below estimates. All regressions include gender-specific time trends and controls for age, education, race, and marital status, in addition to quarterly indicators and a fixed effect for education sector workers in summer months to control for seasonality. Child age brackets are assigned by the age of the youngest child (<5 and 5–17). For details on the data, see appendix C.

motherhood makes a big difference: nontelecommuting mothers of pre-K children work more than 5 hours less per week during the pandemic compared with nontelecommuting women without children. For mothers of middle school children, there is still a gap of about 3 hours per week.

In the Netherlands, we observed in our baseline regression a large and significant gender gap in hours for parents with pre-K kids (see table 8). The coefficients in table 16 suggest that this result is to some extent driven by those parents who cannot telecommute. In this group, we observe a stark contrast between those with small children and those without children, although the results are not tightly estimated due to small sample size.

Table 17
Hours Worked during the Pandemic in the United States by Telecommuting, Gender, and Children

	Women		Men	
	Nontele	Telecommute	Nontele	Telecommute
No or adult children	35.2	37.9	39.1	39.9
Pre-K children	30.0	35.2	40.3	40.4
Middle school children	32.5	36.6	40.5	41.5
High school children	34.1	36.8	40.6	41.4

Note: Sample includes all employed individuals, ages 25–55, not in the military. Report values correspond to weighted average hours worked last week by sex, child group, and telecommuting status from May 2020 through October 2020. Child age brackets are assigned by the age of the youngest child (pre-K: <5, middle school: 5–13, high school: 14–17).

Regarding the United Kingdom, recall that unlike the other countries considered here, we did not find a substantial gender gap in the impact of the crisis. Once we separate out telecommuters, most gender-gap coefficients in table 16 continue to be small and statistically insignificant. However, we now do find a sizable gender gap among workers who cannot telecommute and who have school-age children. In this group, the negative impact on the labor supply of mothers is 9–11 percentage points larger compared with fathers. Thus, even in the United Kingdom, the combination of having to look after school-age children and being unable to work from home is associated with a large decline in mothers' labor supply.

The gender gap among parents of school-age children in the United Kingdom is related to the use of furlough schemes; there are more mothers than fathers recorded as employed but working zero hours.[25] Furloughing accounts for most of the gender gap in labor supply of nontelecommuting parents with school-age children: if we exclude those who record zero hours, the gender gap turns insignificant.[26] Hence, the data suggest that furlough schemes gave workers additional flexibility in dealing with the crisis, and that it was mothers of school-age children who used this flexibility to select into not working temporarily (i.e., asking their employer to be furloughed if telecommuting was not an option).[27]

Table 18 provides a further breakdown of the results of table 16 for the United Kingdom by allowing for separate interactions for more-educated (bachelor of arts [BA] degree or higher) and less-educated (less than BA) workers. Here we see that the option to telecommute in the presence of children matters a lot more for highly educated mothers. Among telecommuting workers with at least BA education, there is no significant

Table 18

Pandemic-induced Change in the Gender Gap in the Intensive Margin of Employment in the United Kingdom by Telecommuting Status and Education

	Benchmark		w/ Occupation × Industry	
	Less than BA	BA or Higher	Less than BA	BA or Higher
No telecommuting (β_3/γ_3):	.40	−7.97	2.83	−7.62
	(.91)	(.03)	(.47)	(.04)
Pre-K kids ($\delta_{3,\text{pre-K}}/\theta_{3,\text{pre-K}}$)	1.53	−14.54	5.72	−12.62
	(.84)	(.05)	(.46)	(.09)
School-age kids ($\delta_{3,\text{school}}/\theta_{3,\text{school}}$)	−7.96	−19.76	−3.11	−17.78
	(.14)	(0.00)	(.58)	(0.00)
No kids ($\delta_{3,\text{none}}/\theta_{3,\text{none}}$)	3.75	−3.02	3.72	−4.03
	(.43)	(.54)	(.44)	(.41)
Telecommuting (β_3/γ_3):	3.88	6.63	6.43	17.74
	(.60)	(.35)	(.38)	(.01)
Pre-K kids ($\delta_{3,\text{pre-K}}/\theta_{3,\text{pre-K}}$)	−8.76	22.34	−2.66	34.13
	(.63)	(.14)	(.88)	(.02)
School-age kids ($\delta_{3,\text{school}}/\theta_{3,\text{school}}$)	−2.83	−1.80	2.91	14.32
	(.80)	(.87)	(.79)	(.21)
No kids ($\delta_{3,\text{none}}/\theta_{3,\text{none}}$)	14.95	6.22	12.52	13.41
	(.15)	(.55)	(.22)	(.18)

Note: Coefficients reported are log points difference of the pandemic's effect on women versus men. Sample includes all civilians ages 25–55 who are employed (including those with zero and positive working hours in the last week). The p-values are reported in parentheses below estimates. All regressions include gender-specific time trends and controls for age, education, race, and marital status, in addition to quarterly indicators and a fixed effect for education sector workers in summer months to control for seasonality. Child age brackets are assigned by the age of the youngest child (<5 and 5–17). For details on the data, see appendix C.

gender gap in the impact of the crisis regardless of having children. In contrast, the gender gap among educated parents who cannot work from home is large. Depending on the age of the children and on whether we control for additional occupation and industry effects, the labor supply of nontelecommuting educated mothers falls by 13–20 percentage points more than the labor supply of fathers in this group. Among less-educated workers, these gender gaps are small or nonexistent. Thus, even though overall the gender gap in the impact of the crisis is small in the United Kingdom, even here we find that the clash of childcare needs and having to be at work during the crisis was a challenge for many mothers.

Overall, our results suggest that the ability to work from home played a central role in shaping the impact of the pandemic on working women. Being able to telecommute is a clear advantage for all workers during the pandemic, both because this reduces the probability of employment loss and because working at home reduces the risk of exposure to disease. Parents get the additional benefit of having an easier time dealing with additional childcare and supporting their children's education during school and daycare closures. Although this benefit in principle accrues to both fathers and mothers, our results show that in practice it was primarily women's employment that suffered where a conflict between children's needs and a lack of ability to telecommute arose.

VI. The Impact of the Pandemic on Workers' Productivity

So far we have focused on labor supply to document inequality in the impact of the pandemic on the labor market. Although we find a lot of evidence of gender inequality during the crisis, we also document that workplace flexibility in the form of the ability to work from home appears to protect women's labor market prospects. This could be taken as a hopeful sign for the long-run impact of the pandemic on gender inequality. The recent literature on the "motherhood penalty" shows that the combined challenge of career and family goals is at the root of much of the gender inequality in the labor market today. Our results suggest that workplace flexibility substantially reduces the conflict between work and childcare. Moreover, now that many employers have adopted working from home, liked the results, and plan to preserve work-from-home options in the future, we can expect that after the pandemic, workplace flexibility will be much more widely available than previously. Should we therefore expect a smaller motherhood penalty and lower gender gaps in the postpandemic labor market?

Although such an outcome of lower future gender equality is a possibility, our evidence on labor supply may paint an incomplete picture of the impact of the crisis on working women and men. Even though working from home allowed many parents to continue working while also supervising their children, productivity at work may still have suffered in the process. Moreover, if the division of childcare duties is unequal in the family, the productivity impact may be more severe for mothers than for fathers. The evidence indeed suggests that on average, mothers provided the larger share of the additional childcare during the pandemic. For example, Adams-Prassl et al. (2020b) show that during the pandemic, women with children who worked from home spent 1–2 hours more every day on childcare and homeschooling compared with men in the same situation, with remarkably similar patterns in the United States, Germany, and the United Kingdom.[28] This evidence suggests that combining working from home with childcare was a greater challenge for mothers compared with fathers.

Our data for the Netherlands provide direct evidence of a greater clash between work and childcare responsibilities for women compared with men. Table 19 shows that in April 2020, Dutch parents spent on average 13 hours per week working from home. A lot of this time was combined with childcare: averaging between mothers and fathers, parents report that for more than 60% of the time working at home they were simultaneously looking after their children. However, there is a large gender gap in doing double duty. In line with our other results, this gender gap is largest for those with school-age children (ages 6–14) who likely need help with homeschooling. In this group, mothers spent three quarters of their work time at home on simultaneously taking care of children, which is 30% more than the fathers in this group. As a fraction of all work hours (including those done outside the home), mothers of school-age children spent close to 40% of work time on also doing childcare, about 40% more than fathers did.

Andrew et al. (2020a) provide additional evidence of a gender gap in doing double duty of work and childcare based on a survey of parents in the United Kingdom carried out in April and May 2020. The authors find that mothers generally spent more time on childcare and house work and less time on paid work compared with fathers. To assess the extent to which other responsibilities such as childcare affect the quality of the time spent working, the authors focus on work interruptions, defined as doing

Table 19
Working from Home while Looking after Children in the Netherlands, April 2020

	Hours Worked from Home per Week	Percent of Home Work Hours also Spent on Childcare	Percent of All Work Hours also Spent on Childcare
All parents	13.0	61.1	30.8
Single parents	12.9	64.3	32.6
Mothers, kids 1–5	9.9	59.4	34.8
Fathers, kids 1–5	17.2	49.5	26.1
Mothers, kids 6–14	11.1	76.0	38.7
Fathers, kids 6–14	15.4	58.5	27.7
Mothers, kids 15–18	8.8	54.6	22.9
Fathers, kids 15–18	19.8	51.7	24.3

Note: See appendix C.4 for details.

at least one nonwork activity during an hour of paid work. Whereas prior to the pandemic, both mothers and fathers used to be interrupted proportionally to their work hours, during the crisis mothers are interrupted about 50% more often. For mothers, 90% of these interruptions are due to childcare. Overall, fathers working for pay ended up with nearly twice as many uninterrupted work hours compared with mothers working for pay.

This evidence suggests even though working from home may have cushioned the impact of school and daycare closures on employment, the quality of parents' work time and productivity are likely to have suffered in the process. This impact is much larger for mothers than for fathers. Lower productivity at work, in turn, may have implications for human capital accumulation on the job and future career prospects. Whereas in some occupations a short-run dip in productivity may be of little concern, in others mothers with high childcare obligations during the crisis may miss out on raises or promotions in the near future. In "up-or-out" occupations such as law, falling behind peers during the crisis could put up a permanent ceiling to future career prospects.

For the most part, the productivity losses of working parents during the pandemic will show up in the data only some years down the road. There is one sector characterized by "up-or-down" promotions where evidence on productivity during the crisis is already available: academia. The productivity of academic researchers can be proxied by real-time output measures such as publications and working papers. Several recent research papers document a gender gap in researchers' productivity since the beginning of the pandemic. Amano-Patiño et al. (2020) use data from the National Bureau of Economic Research (NBER) and the Centre for Economic Policy Research (CEPR) working paper series and the CEPR's *Covid Economics: Real-Time and Vetted Papers* online journal to analyze the contribution of female economists during the first wave of the pandemic. They find that while the relative number of female authors remained constant at about 20%, women constituted only 12% of all authors working on COVID-19 research. Because COVID-19 research was carried out during the pandemic, while most other working papers were likely based on research started well before the onset of the pandemic, this suggests a sizable decline in the relative research productivity of women. Similarly, Ribarovska et al. (2021) document a small reduction in female-last authors in a neurology journal, and a much larger reduction of female-first and -last authors among articles in a COVID-19 special issue. Kim and Patterson (2020) analyze Twitter posts by academic political scientists between June 2019 and June 2020 and find a larger decline in work-related tweets for women compared with men. The authors argue that this gender gap is likely driven by increased family obligations, because at the same time female researchers became relatively more likely to tweet about family-related matters. Barber et al. (2021) use a survey of members of the American Finance Association to examine determinants of research productivity during the pandemic and find that productivity fell more for women and for researchers with young children.

Many universities have announced policy changes to respond to the challenge that the crisis poses for young researchers, such as tenure-clock extensions for assistant professors. However, with few exceptions, these policies do not distinguish between women and men or make special provisions for researchers with major childcare responsibilities during the crisis. Given the emerging evidence of a relative productivity decline of women in academia, the likely result is a deterioration of many female researchers' relative prospects for tenure and career advancement. Given the broader evidence of a more severe clash between work and childcare responsibilities for mothers compared with fathers during the pandemic, it is likely that similar repercussions will occur in other industries and occupations, although it will take some time until it will be possible to verify this in the data.

VII.   What Have We Learned and Why Should We Care?

What general lessons can be learned from our analysis of data on labor market outcomes for women and men during the coronavirus pandemic? Even though there are a lot of differences across countries, a few common themes emerge. In this section, we summarize our findings and discuss what they imply for how differences in the impact on working women and men matter for economic outcomes during the crisis and beyond.

A.   Summarizing the Findings

The main conclusions arising from our empirical analysis are as follows:

1. The pandemic recession is a shecession (almost) everywhere. Figure 4 shows that in 18 out of 28 advanced economies, women's employment fell by more than men's during the pandemic, and in 19 out of 28 countries, women experienced a larger decline in hours worked. What is

more, even in countries where the impact on women and men was similar, this still presents a sharp deviation from usual recessions, which tend to be mancessions in most countries. Figure 5B shows that in all but two countries (Ireland and Sweden), the negative impact of the recession on women's hours worked relative to men's was larger than what would be expected based on earlier recessions. Overall, we conclude that the unusually large impact of the pandemic recession on working women is a common feature among a large set of economies and a key distinction between this and earlier recessions.

2. Industry/occupation effects and childcare needs are the main, but not the only, cause of gender gaps. Figure 6 demonstrates that in many countries, the pandemic recession had an unusually large impact on industries with high female employment shares, such as leisure and hospitality. Tables 7 and 8 show that in the countries with significant gender gaps in the impact of the pandemic on employment or hours, the gender gap is usually substantially reduced when controlling for different trends across industries and occupations. The same tables show larger gender gaps among parents of school-age children, indicating the importance of childcare and homeschooling obligations. Nevertheless, gender gaps go beyond industry/occupation and childcare effects. Tables 7 and 8 show that in countries where there are statistically significant overall gender gaps in the impact of the pandemic on employment or hours, a substantial and statistically significant gap is observed even among workers without children and after controlling for industry/occupation effects. The decomposition analysis for the United States in Section IV shows that the childcare and industry/occupation channels account for less than half of the total gender gap. Clearly, there are additional factors that made women's employment more vulnerable in the pandemic, and understanding these factors is an important challenge for future research on the pandemic recession.

3. Gender gaps during the pandemic recession vary widely across countries. Although qualitatively in most countries the pandemic recession is a shecession, quantitatively there is wide variation in the gaps between the impacts on women and men across countries (see fig. 4). What is more, there is only a loose correlation between the impact of the gender gap in terms of employment and hours. The United States is an example of a country with a large gender gap in the decline in employment, yet hours worked relative to men changed less than in other countries. In contrast, in countries such as Denmark and Germany, women experienced not only fewer employment losses than men but also a large reduction in

relative hours worked, implying that women's labor supply conditional on working dropped sharply.

4. Policy difference likely contributed to cross-country differences in the impact of the crisis, but evidence is inconclusive. The policy response to the pandemic varied widely across countries, for example, in terms of the severity and duration of lockdowns and the extent and duration of school closures. Given that much of the pandemic recession is due to the response of the crisis rather than a direct consequence of disease, one would expect that policy differences contribute to cross-country variation in gender gaps. Tables 2 and 3 show that the extent of school closures is indeed correlated with employment losses during the pandemic across countries. However, there is no conclusive evidence that these policy differences underlie cross-country differences in gender gaps (tables 4 and 5). Another relevant policy dimension is the use of furlough policies (such as *Kurzarbeit* in Germany) to protect employment during the crisis. Tables 7 and 8 show that in Germany there is only a small effect on overall employment and no gender gap in this dimension but a large overall impact and a large gender gap in hours. In the United States, with little use of furlough policies, the overall impact and gender gaps are much larger in terms of employment and smaller in terms of hours. These observations suggest that furlough policies in Germany protected formal employment relationships while also providing flexibility for large adjustments of labor supply on the intensive margin.

5. Work flexibility in the form of the ability to work from home greatly reduces the impact of the pandemic on gender gaps. Table 16 shows that in the United States and the United Kingdom, there is no statistically significant larger impact on women's hours worked among workers who can work from home during the crisis, regardless of industry, occupation, or childcare obligations. Table 4 shows that the fraction of jobs that allow for telecommuting is the only variable that is significantly correlated with differences in the gender gap across countries. This evidence suggests that work flexibility greatly reduces gender differences in the labor market during the pandemic. However, there is evidence that among those working from home, mothers experienced a larger decline in productivity while simultaneously engaging in work and childcare. Table 19 shows that in the Netherlands, mothers working from home spent a much larger fraction of the work time while also looking after their children than fathers did. Survey evidence for other countries and direct productivity measures for academic research also suggest a larger dip in women's work productivity during the pandemic.

B. Wider Implications for the Nature of the Pandemic Recession

Is a shecession the same as a mancession with signs reversed? For sure, the simple issue of whether the bulk of employment losses falls on women rather than men is a big part of what makes these types of recessions distinct. But there are equally important qualitative differences between shecessions and mancessions. Understanding these differences matters for policy tradeoffs during the recession and for the shape of the economic recovery that follows.

A first qualitative difference between shecessions and mancessions arises from the different dynamic behavior of women's and men's labor supply. Women's labor supply is generally more elastic at the micro level (e.g., Blundell and MaCurdy 1999). Men's labor supply elasticity is lower, and particularly so for married men. This implies that when men lose employment in a recession, they are likely to stay in the labor force and return to full-time employment in the recovery. In contrast, given their more elastic labor supply, when losing employment in a recession, women are relatively more likely to drop out of the labor force or to only seek part-time work. At the economy-wide level, these patterns suggest that in a shecession, when job losses are concentrated on women, the decline in aggregate labor supply will be more persistent and continue to be concentrated on women during the recovery (see Alon et al. 2020b for a quantitative analysis making this point).

A second difference between shecessions and mancessions relates to insurance within the household. Married couples can provide each other with insurance for income shocks. The mere presence of a second earner implies that a temporary job loss has a smaller proportional impact on earnings compared with single-earner households. Couples are also able to provide each other with active insurance, such as the "added worker effect" of a secondary earner joining the labor force in response to unemployment of the primary earner (Lundberg 1985). Blundell, Pistaferri, and Saporta-Eksten (2016) show that within-family insurance is the primary insurance channel for many households, and Bardóczy (2020) argues that this insurance channel plays a central role in the transmission of aggregate shocks.

The distinct behavior of women's and men's labor supply suggests that family insurance is less effective in the pandemic recession compared with a regular recession. The large overall impact on the employment of both women and men implies that there are many families where both husband and wife experience earnings losses, which reduces the scope for passive insurance. More importantly, active insurance relies on the ability of the spouse who did not experience unemployment or reduced earnings to increase labor supply. In a mancession, the spouse who provides insurance is usually the wife. More married women than men work either part time or are out of the labor force, which means that there is scope for increasing labor supply. Therefore, in a mancession, active insurance can play an important role in buffering income losses for households. In contrast, when married women lose employment in a shecession, their husbands are often unable to provide active insurance, because they already work full time and because married men's labor supply is generally inflexible. Overall, family insurance is much less effective in a shecession such as the current pandemic recession compared with a regular recession.

Beyond shaping labor supply responses, the lack of family insurance also matters for how aggregate consumption and savings evolve in the recession. If households have less access to insurance, economic shocks translate more directly into consumption. The strength of this transmission can be summarized by the marginal propensity to consume (MPC), which is the fraction of a one-dollar loss in income for a household that will be reflected in lower consumption in the same period (instead of in lower savings). Alon et al. (2020b) show that the loss of family insurance in a pandemic recession results in a sustained raise in MPCs relative to a regular recession. Higher economy-wide MPCs, in turn, can result in a deeper recession and in a slower recovery, because higher MPCs mean that aggregate demand will drop more sharply during the recession. To be sure, a pandemic recession has additional implications for MPCs that do not relate to the relative impact on women's versus men's employment, for example, because of reduced consumption opportunities during lockdowns and the effects of stimulus payments during the crisis. Depending on policy responses, the overall evolution of MPCs in a pandemic recession is therefore ambiguous, but the family insurance channel is a force toward higher MPCs in this type of recession.

There are also opposing channels that suggest less severe effects of shecessions compared with mancessions. First, employed women work on average fewer hours than employed men. Hence, the same employment losses in a shecession will lead to lower aggregate hours losses than a mancession of the same size (when measured by employment declines). Second, women on average earn less than men, so even the same hours losses in a shecession will lead to lower GDP declines compared with a mancession with the same aggregate hours losses. Third, one might argue that women's more elastic labor supply arises because of better alternative uses for their time, for example, home production rather than playing video games (Aguiar et al. 2020). Although this point is surely debatable, it suggests the possibility that the welfare losses of job loss differ between women and men. Relatedly, domestic violence generally goes up in recessions (van den Berg and Tertilt 2012), and one might hypothesize that this would be less true in shecessions. However, due to the pandemic-induced lockdowns, which put stress on families, studies in fact do find an increase in domestic violence (Bullinger, Carr, and Packham 2021; Leslie and Wilson 2020). But it is possible that other side effects of recessions, such as increases in the crime rate or drug abuse, are less pronounced in shecessions. Further data will be needed to evaluate such hypotheses empirically.

The impact of the pandemic recession on women's employment also matters through its interaction with policies and institutions. In many countries, unemployment insurance is the primary social insurance channel in recessions. However, women who stop working during the pandemic because of childcare needs are usually out of the labor force rather than unemployed, that is, they stop looking for work. Therefore, traditional unemployment insurance would not be accessible to women in this situation. Many countries instituted temporary changes to their insurance systems during the crisis, such as expanding furlough pay and making unemployment benefits available also to those who stop working because of family obligations. Still, some of these policy changes were temporary and implementation varied across countries and US states, so some policy-induced asymmetries remain.

C. Wider Implications for the Future Labor Market

The pandemic recession will also have repercussions for the future of the labor market that far outlast the recession and the subsequent recovery. It is well-known that losing employment during a recession is associated with persistent earnings losses for the affected workers (Stevens 1997; Davis and von Wachter 2011). The fact that more women than men were affected by employment losses will tend to increase the gender pay gap in the years after the recession. Women's higher flexibility of labor supply is also likely to result in persistent changes in labor force participation; some women (especially married women) who lost employment during the crisis will drop out of the labor force for an extended period or only return to part-time work. Hence, women's labor force participation will be lower as a result of the recession for years to come.

In addition to the direct impact on workers during the recession, the shock of the pandemic will also result in broader changes in the labor market that will shape the experience of current and future cohorts of workers alike. Arguably the most important one of these changes is increased employment flexibility, such as a much expanded ability to work from home for many workers. During the pandemic, most jobs that could be done from home in principle were switched to being done from home in practice. Office workers who spend their days primarily working with computers almost universally worked from their living rooms, kitchens, and spare bedrooms during the pandemic, rapidly adopting new remote-work tools such as videoconferencing through Zoom in the process. Much of this change is likely to persist beyond the crisis. Employers and employees have paid the fixed cost of adopting remote work; learning by doing has taken place; employers have realized that working from home does not have to result in lower productivity; and employers have started to appreciate the savings from needing much less office space (Barrero et al. 2021). Many have already announced that working from home will continue to be central to the postpandemic work environment and have started the process of canceling leases for office space.

How is this new normal in the postpandemic workplace going to change the labor market? Change is likely to occur in a number of dimensions, from commuting patterns and the commercial real estate market to new ways of fostering coherence and interaction in a workplace where face-to-face contact with coworkers is the exception rather than the norm.

For our purposes, the most interesting changes concern gender inequality in the labor market. We believe that increased work flexibility in the new normal has the potential to substantially reduce gender inequality. This expectation is based on two observations about the prepandemic labor market.

The first observation is that much gender inequality in the labor market in today's advanced economies is related to parenthood and childcare. The literature on the "motherhood penalty" establishes that gender-wage gap is small among young workers who do not have children. In contrast, after having a child, the earnings of mothers stall, whereas fathers continue climbing the career ladder (e.g., Miller 2011; Adda, Dustmann, and Stevens 2017; Gallen 2018; Kleven, Landais, and Søgaard 2019; Kleven et al. 2019). These observations suggest that the unequal division of the burden of childcare between mothers and fathers is now the primary cause of gender gaps in the labor market.

The second observation is that job flexibility can do much to reduce inequality in the division of labor between spouses in terms of childcare and other home work. The general point that workplace flexibility is a particular benefit to women's careers has been advanced by Goldin and Katz (2011) and Goldin (2014). Regarding telecommuting specifically, Alon et al. (2020a) show that in prepandemic data, the ability to telecommute is strongly predictive of mothers' and fathers' engagement in childcare. For example, fathers who are able to work from home and are married to mothers who cannot, spend about 50% more hours on childcare compared with otherwise similar fathers who cannot telecommute.

Taken together, these observations suggest that the expansion of work flexibility brought about by the pandemic recession may substantially reduce gender inequality in the labor market in the long term, by allowing a more even division of childcare responsibilities among the now much larger share of couples who can both work from home, and by reducing the motherhood penalty that is at the root of today's gender inequality in the process. Our finding above that there were hardly any gender differences in the impact of the pandemic among workers who can telecommute is an indication of how powerful this channel can be.

Although this justifies some optimism about gender equality in the future workplace, there is an important caveat. The evidence discussed in Section VI suggests that among couples with children who both worked from home during the crisis, women continued to spend substantially more time on childcare, and their productivity likely suffered as a result. Even if the effects are not immediately visible, lower productivity at work will ultimately hinder career advancement and lower mothers' future earnings prospects. Albanesi and Olivetti (2009) show that expectations of an unequal division of labor in the household, once established, can become self-fulfilling and create new barriers in the labor market. The implications of increased workplace flexibility for gender inequality are therefore closely linked to what happens to the division of labor inside the home.

Hence, the upshot is that the pandemic is likely to bring about changes in the postpandemic workplace that open up the potential for much reduced gender inequality in the labor market. But for this potential to be realized, changes in the workplace are not enough; there also needs to be a shift in social norms and expectations that lead mothers and fathers to make more equal use of the added flexibility that the new workplace offered. Without such a shift, the strain of failing to do full justice to work, family, and self-maintenance needs that were shared by many workers during the pandemic will continue to be the reality of many working mothers in the new normal. Given these countervailing forces, evaluating the actual impact of expanded workplace flexibility on gender inequality in the postpandemic labor market is an important task for future research.

VIII. Conclusions

In this paper, we have documented that in a large set of countries, the COVID-19 recession had a much larger impact on women's relative employment compared with prepandemic recessions. One cause of this disproportional impact on working women was the sectoral distribution of the recession, which fell heavily on service sectors with high female employment shares. Another cause was the increase in childcare needs during closures of schools and daycare centers, which had a bigger impact on mothers' versus fathers' labor supply. Yet even when controlling for industry and occupation and considering only workers without children, in several countries we still find large remaining gender gaps, the causes of which are not yet well understood.

The fact that the pandemic recession was a shecession matters for the shape of the economic downturn and the recovery. Moreover, the pandemic recession is also likely to result in permanent changes in the labor market, such as a wider availability of work-from-home options and other forms of employment flexibility in the postpandemic new normal. These changes are likely to result in persistent changes in women's and men's labor force participation and will shape gender inequalities in the labor market.

Beyond the employment of women and men, there are additional dimensions that make the pandemic recession of 2020 distinct from most others, and some of these dimensions are likely to interact with the issues considered here. One example is the impact of the pandemic on children's education. Early evidence suggests that virtual learning during school closures is often a poor substitute for in-person schooling and that children's skill acquisition will suffer as a result (e.g., Kuhfeld et al. 2020; Maldonado and De Witte 2020). Moreover, a growing literature suggests that school closures during the pandemic will widen educational inequality across richer and poorer families (Andrew et al. 2020b; Fuchs-Schündeln et al. 2020; Grewenig et al. 2020; Jang and Yum 2020;

Agostinelli et al. 2022). If learning losses result in a greater need for parental support in the following years, the impact on children can further amplify the persistent effect on women's employment documented here. Once again, the ability to work from home plays a central role, as parents who can work from home have an easier time supporting their children's learning (Agostinelli et al. 2022). Hence, lack of work flexibility likely had a double-negative effect on many families during the crisis, through the direct impact on employment and through the repercussions for children's education.

Another likely consequence of the pandemic is a sharp drop in fertility rates (Kearney and Levine 2020), which is already becoming evident in data on birth rates in late 2020 and early 2021. To some extent, the drop in fertility may reflect a delay in childbearing that will be compensated by higher fertility in subsequent years, leading to additional interactions with women's labor supply at that time.

Our analysis has also been limited to a set of high income countries. Many of the conditions that created a disproportionate impact on women's employment in this group are equally applicable to countries at other stages of development. For example, at the height of the COVID-19 pandemic, schools closed in most countries of the world, making increased childcare needs during the crisis a near-universal phenomenon. Researchers have addressed how the optimal response to the pandemic in terms of health policy should be modified in developing countries (e.g., Alon et al. 2020c), but there is less work to date on implications for gender inequality in the labor market. Both the short-run impact on and the long-run repercussions for working women are likely to be different in developing countries compared with the group considered here, for example, because of a bigger role of informal employment and much more limited remote-work opportunities. Addressing the impact of the global COVID-19 pandemic on the labor market for women and men in a broad set of countries is an important challenge for additional research on the crisis.

Endnotes

Authors' email addresses: Alon (talon@ucsd.edu), Coskun (sena.coskun@uni-mann heim.de), Tertilt (tertilt@uni-mannheim.de), Doepke (doepke@northwestern.edu), Koll (koll@uni-mannheim.de). We thank Suzanne Bellue, Kwok Yan Chiu, and Laura Montenbruck for excellent research assistance and the German Research Foundation (through the CRC TR 224 project A3 and the Gottfried Wilhelm Leibniz Prize) and the National Science Foundation for their financial support. We thank Laura Pilossoph and Loukas Karabarbounis for excellent discussions and Steve Davis and Claudia Goldin for helpful comments. We thank Katja Möhring and Ulrich Krieger for help and access to the German data and Hans-Martin von Gaudecker for help with the Dutch data. This paper is also based on data from Eurostat, EU-LFS, 1998–2019. The responsibility for all conclusions drawn from the data lies entirely with the authors. For acknowledgments, sources of research support, and disclosure of the authors' material financial relationships, if any, please see https://www.nber.org/books-and-chapters/nber-macroeconomics-annual-2021-volume-36/mancession-shecession-womens-employment-regular-and-pandemic-recessions.

1. The figure depicts the cyclical components of both GDP and hours worked. Fig. A2 shows the raw data.

2. An analogous figure reporting hours worked by gender is provided in the appendix (fig. A4).

3. Macroeconomic studies of the policy implications of joint household decisions include Guner, Kaygusuz, and Ventura (2012, 2020), Bick (2016), and Wu and Krueger (2019).

4. The higher volatility for women in the Netherlands is related to a large decline in hours worked of married women in 2005 (see fig. 1B). There was a break in the time series in 2005, which we attempted to correct but which may still have an impact on measured volatility.

5. The severity of school closures may also be endogenous to the labor market structure. For example, in countries where many employees have children, political pressure may have kept more schools open. Indeed, fig. A3 shows that in countries where women work more and/or a greater share of labor force is in need of childcare, schools closures were less severe.

6. In these regressions, we use a broad definition of hospitality that includes hospitality, leisure, and other services.

7. These include the existence of emergency care, the duration of short-term work allowances, a government response stringency index, and the fraction of employees with childcare obligations.

8. We use the Current Population Survey for the United States, the Canadian Labor Force Survey for Canada, the Economically Active Population Survey for Spain, the UK Labour Force Survey for the United Kingdom, the Dutch LISS Panel as described in von Gaudecker et al. (2021) for the Netherlands, and the German Internet Panel and the Mannheim Corona Study for Germany as described in Blom et al. (2015, 2020). See app. C for details on the data sources and the samples used.

9. See Bellemare and Wichman (2020) for more discussion and applications of the inverse hyperbolic sine transformation.

10. For Germany, the Netherlands, Canada, and Spain, we use migration status instead of race (see app. C for details).

11. Throughout our micro data analysis, we use this difference in the percentage point change to measure the gendered impact of the pandemic. An alternative measure would be the difference in the percent changes, which generally should lead to larger gender gaps as women's employment rates were lower than men's prior to the pandemic. Thus, we see our estimates as a lower bound of the gendered impact of the pandemic. See Bluedorn et al. (2021) for a useful comparison of the two measures in cross-country data.

12. In Spain, the group of school-age children includes children up to the age of 19, based on the available age brackets in the Spanish micro data set. Similar data limitations in Germany allow us to only form two groups of households in Germany: those with a child below 16 and those without.

13. The large impact on hours worked in Germany arises in part because the work-time measure here includes commuting time, which drops while many people work from home during the pandemic. In addition, in the German data, postpandemic hours are observed primarily in Q2/2020, potentially leading to larger effects compared with other countries that rely on hours observed all the way through September 2020. Finally, for Germany we have only one pre-COVID data point on hours dating back to 2018. See app. C.3 for details on the German data.

14. See app. C.4 for details.

15. To reconcile the results in tables 7 and 8 with fig. 4, note that the regression includes various controls such as time trends and seasonal dummies, implying that results are not directly comparable. In addition, fig. 4 displays changes between Q4/2019 and Q2/2020,

whereas the results in the current section are based on a longer time horizon. In those cases where coefficients are significant, the sign of effect does line up with fig. 4.

16. Note that our measure of hours worked for Germany includes commuting time. Because men on average spend more time commuting than women, they also likely faced larger reductions in commuting time during the pandemic. Thus, the true increase in the gender gap in hours worked (without commuting) should likely be even larger than our estimate.

17. Workers who are out of the labor force for prolonged periods lack information on industry and occupation, so that a decomposition taking occupation effects into account is more informative for initially employed workers.

18. The time trends and covariates in our benchmark model are now subsumed by the individual and time fixed effects. We continue to control for industry and occupation using nonparametric time trends by work type. More details on the specification can be found in app. E.

19. We focus on the United States here because the overall impact of the 2007–9 financial crisis on employment and the timing of the related economic downturn differed substantially across the countries we consider.

20. We include a dummy indicating college education as an additional interaction term in our regression specifications (eqs. [1]–[4]). Hence, tables 11 and 12 report the pandemic-induced gender gap interacted with the respective education level (and the presence of children).

21. Tables A3 and A4 display results without work-type controls.

22. Tables A5 and A6 display results without work-type controls.

23. In Spain, the group of school-age children includes children up to the age of 19, based on the available age brackets in the Spanish micro data set.

24. The relevant question is as follows: "At any time in the last 4 weeks, did (you/ name) telework or work at home for pay because of the coronavirus pandemic? (Enter 'No' if person worked entirely from home before the coronavirus pandemic)"

25. The percentage point difference between mothers and fathers with a school-age child reporting zero hours while being employed increases from 2.2 percentage points in Q1/2020 to 5.2 percentage points in Q2/2020 and even further to 7.8 percentage points in Q3/2020. For those with pre-K children, there is always a sizable gender gap in those employed but working zero hours (18.5 percentage points in Q1/2020), likely due to generous parental leave policies. For this group, we also observe increases, but they are less pronounced: 18.5 percentage points in Q1/2020, 19.2 percentage points in Q2/2020, and 21.7 percentage points in Q3/2020. In contrast, the difference is stable for those without kids: 2.0 percentage points in Q1/2020, 1.5 percentage points in Q2/2020, and 2.3 percentage points in Q3/2020.

26. In fact, if we exclude those who report zero hours, the impact of the pandemic on the gender gap decreases in absolute value from −10.7 to −1.0 and once we control for work type from −9.0 to −0.7.

27. Adams-Prassl et al. (2020a) indeed find that UK mothers were more likely to initiate furloughing than fathers (as opposed to the employer), while no such gender gaps were found among childless workers.

28. See also Zamarro and Prados (2021) for additional evidence for the United States.

References

Adams-Prassl, Abi, Teodora Boneva, Marta Golin, and Christopher Rauh. 2020a. "Furloughing." *Fiscal Studies* 41 (3): 591–622.

———. 2020b. "Inequality in the Impact of the Coronavirus Shock: Evidence from Real Time Surveys." *Journal of Public Economics* 189:104245.

Adda, Jérôme, Christian Dustmann, and Katrien Stevens. 2017. "The Career Costs of Children." *Journal of Political Economy* 125 (2): 293–337.

Agostinelli, Francesco, Matthias Doepke, Giuseppe Sorrenti, and Fabrizio Zilibotti. 2022. "When the Great Equalizer Shuts Down: Schools, Peers, and Parents in Pandemic Times." *Journal of Public Economics* 206:104574.

Aguiar, Mark, Mark Bils, Kerwin Kofi Charles, and Erik Hurst. 2020. "Leisure Luxuries and the Labor Supply of Young Men." *Journal of Political Economy* 129 (2): 337–82.

Albanesi, Stefania. 2020. "Changing Business Cycles: The Role of Women's Employment." Working Paper no. 25655, NBER, Cambridge, MA.

Albanesi, Stefania, and Jiyeon Kim. 2021. "The Gendered Impact of the COVID-19 Recession on the US Labor Market." Working Paper no. 28505, NBER, Cambridge, MA.

Albanesi, Stefania, and Claudia Olivetti. 2009. "Home Production, Market Production, and the Gender Wage Gap: Incentives and Expectations." *Review of Economic Dynamics* 12 (1): 80–107.

Albanesi, Stefania, and Ayşegül Şahin. 2018. "The Gender Unemployment Gap." *Review of Economic Dynamics* 30:47–67.

Alon, Titan, Matthias Doepke, Jane Olmstead-Rumsey, and Michèle Tertilt. 2020a. "The Impact of COVID-19 on Gender Equality." *Covid Economics: Vetted and Real-Time Papers* 4:62–85.

———. 2020b. "This Time It's Different: The Role of Women's Employment in a Pandemic Recession." Working Paper no. 27660, NBER, Cambridge, MA.

Alon, Titan M., Minki Kim, David Lagakos, and Mitchell VanVuren. 2020c. "How Should Policy Responses to the COVID-19 Pandemic Differ in the Developing World?" Working Paper no. 27273, NBER, Cambridge, MA.

Amano-Patiño, Noriko, Elisa Faraglia, Chryssi Giannitsarou, and Zeina Hasna. 2020. "The Unequal Effects of COVID-19 on Economists' Research Productivity." Working Paper no. 2020/22, Cambridge-INET.

Andrew, Alison, Sarah Cattan, Monica Costa Dias, Christine Farquharson, Lucy Kraftman, Sonya Krutikova, Angus Phimister, and Almudena Sevilla. 2020a. "The Gendered Division of Paid and Domestic Work under Lockdown." Discussion Paper no. 13500, IZA, Bonn.

———. 2020b. "Inequalities in Children's Experiences of Home Learning during the COVID-19 Lockdown in England." *Fiscal Studies* 41 (3): 653–83.

Barber, Brad M., Wei Jiang, Adair Morse, Manju Puri, Heather Tookes, and Ingrid M. Werner. 2021. "What Explains Differences in Finance Research Productivity during the Pandemic?" Working Paper no. 28493, NBER, Cambridge, MA.

Bardóczy, Bence. 2020. "Spousal Insurance and the Amplification of Business Cycles." Unpublished Manuscript, Northwestern University.

Barrero, Jose Maria, Nick Bloom, and Steven J. Davis. 2021. "Why Working from Home Will Stick." Unpublished Manuscript, Stanford University.

Beauregard, Pierre-Loup, Marie Connolly, Catherine Haeck, and Tímea Laura Molnár. 2020. "Primary School Reopenings and Parental Work." Working Paper no. 20-06 (August), Research Group on Human Capital, Montreal's School of Management, University of Quebec.

Bellemare, Marc F., and Casey J. Wichman. 2020. "Elasticities and the Inverse Hyperbolic Sine Transformation." *Oxford Bulletin of Economics and Statistics* 82 (1): 50–61.

Bick, Alexander. 2016. "The Quantitative Role of Child Care for Female Labor Force Participation and Fertility." *Journal of the European Economic Association* 14 (3): 639–68.

Blom, Annelies G., Carina Cornesse, Sabine Friedel, Ulrich Krieger, Marina Fikel, Tobias Rettig, Alexander Wenz, et al. 2020. "High Frequency and High Quality Survey Data Collection." *Survey Research Methods* 14 (2): 171–78.

Blom, Annelies G., Christina Gathmann, and Ulrich Krieger. 2015. "Setting Up an Online Panel Representative of the General Population: The German Internet Panel." *Field Methods* 27 (4): 391–408.

Bluedorn, John, Francesca Caselli, Niels-Jakob Hansen, Ippei Shibata, and Marina M. Tavares. 2021. "Gender and Employment in the COVID-19 Recession: Cross-Country Evidence on 'She-cessions'." *Covid Economics: Vetted and Real-Time Papers* 76:87–109.

Blundell, Richard, and Thomas MaCurdy. 1999. "Labor Supply: A Review of Alternative Approaches." In *Handbook of Labor Economics*, Vol. 3A, ed. Orley Ashenfelter and David Card. New York: Elsevier.

Blundell, Richard, Luigi Pistaferri, and Itay Saporta-Eksten. 2016. "Consumption Inequality and Family Labor Supply." *American Economic Review* 106 (2): 387–435.

Borella, Margherita, Mariacristina De Nardi, and Fang Yang. 2018. "The Aggregate Implications of Gender and Marriage." *Journal of the Economics of Ageing* 11:6–26.

Bullinger, Lindsey Rose, Jillian B. Carr, and Analisa Packham. 2021. "COVID-19 and Crime: Effects of Stay-at-Home Orders on Domestic Violence." *American Journal of Health Economics* 7 (3): 249–80.

Collins, Caitlyn, Liana C. Landivar, Leah Ruppanner, and William J. Scarborough. 2020. "COVID-19 and the Gender Gap in Work Hours." *Gender, Work, and Organization* 28 (S1): 101–12.

Coskun, Sena, and Husnu Dalgic. 2020. "The Emergence of Procyclical Fertility: The Role of Gender Differences in Employment Risk." Discussion Paper Series no. 142, CRC TR 224, University of Mannheim.

Couch, Kenneth A., Robert W. Fairlie, and Huanan Xu. 2020. "Gender and the COVID-19 Labor Market Downturn." Working Paper no. 20-037 (October), SIEPR, Stanford University, Palo Alto, CA.

Cowan, Benjamin W. 2020. "Short-run Effects of COVID-19 on U.S. Worker Transitions." Working Paper no. 27315, NBER, Cambridge, MA.

Dang, Hai-Anh H., and Cuong Viet Nguyen. 2020. "Gender Inequality during the COVID-19 Pandemic: Income, Expenditure, Savings, and Job Loss." Discussion Paper no. 13824, IZA, Bonn.

Davis, Steven J., and Till von Wachter. 2011. "Recessions and the Costs of Job Loss." *Brookings Papers on Economic Activity* 42 (2): 1–72.

Dias, Felipe A., Joseph Chance, and Arianna Buchanan. 2020. "The Motherhood Penalty and the Fatherhood Premium in Employment during Covid-19: Evidence from the United States." *Research in Social Stratification and Mobility* 69:100542.

Doepke, Matthias, and Michèle Tertilt. 2016. "Families in Macroeconomics." In *Handbook of Macroeconomics*, Vol. 2A, ed. John B. Taylor and Harald Uhlig. Amsterdam: North Holland.

Dullien, Sebastian, and Bettina Kohlrausch. 2021. "Dissecting the COVID19 Supply Shock: Which Role Did School Closures Play?" Working Paper no. 207, Hans-Böckler-Stiftung, Düsseldorf.

Ellieroth, Kathrin. 2019. "Spousal Insurance, Precautionary Labor Supply, and the Business Cycle." Unpublished Manuscript, Indiana University.

Fabrizio, Stefania, Diego B. P. Gomes, and Marina M. Tavares. 2021. "The COVID-19 She-cession: The Employment Penalty of Taking Care of Young Children." *Covid Economics: Vetted and Real-Time Papers* 72:136–66.

Fuchs-Schündeln, Nicola, Dirk Krueger, Alexander Ludwig, and Irina Popova. 2020. "The Long-Term Distributional and Welfare Effects of Covid-19 School Closures." Working Paper no. 27773, NBER, Cambridge, MA.

Fukui, Masao, Emi Nakamura, and Jón Steinsson. 2019. "Women, Wealth Effects, and Slow Recoveries." Unpublished Manuscript, University of Berkeley.

Galasso, Vincenzo, and Martial Foucault. 2020. "Working during COVID-19: Cross-country Evidence from Real-time Survey Data." Working Papers no. 246, OECD Social, Employment and Migration, Paris.

Gallen, Yana. 2018. "Motherhood and the Gender Productivity Gap." Unpublished Manuscript, University of Chicago.

Goldin, Claudia. 2014. "A Grand Gender Convergence: Its Last Chapter." *American Economic Review* 104 (4): 1091–119.

Goldin, Claudia, and Lawrence F. Katz. 2011. "The Cost of Workplace Flexibility for High-Powered Professionals." *Annals of the American Academy of Political and Social Science* 638 (1): 45–67.

González, Libertad. 2021. "The Covid-19 Crisis and the Well-being of Families in Spain." Presented at conference Policies to Cope with the COVID-19 Crisis, ZEW, Mannheim, January 2021.

Greenwood, Jeremy, Ananth Seshadri, and Mehmet Yorukoglu. 2005. "Engines of Liberation." *Review of Economic Studies* 72 (1): 109–33.

Grewenig, Elisabeth, Philipp Lergetporer, Katharina Werner, Ludger Woessmann, and Larissa Zierow. 2020. "COVID-19 and Educational Inequality: How School Closures Affect Low- and High-Achieving Students." Discussion Paper no. 13820, IZA, Bonn.

Guner, Nezih, Remzi Kaygusuz, and Gustavo Ventura. 2012. "Taxation and Household Labour Supply." *Review of Economic Studies* 79 (3): 1113–49.

———. 2020. "Child-Related Transfers, Household Labor Supply and Welfare." *Review of Economic Studies* 87 (5): 2290–321.

Heggeness, Misty L. 2020. "Why Is Mommy So Stressed? Estimating the Immediate Impact of the COVID-19 Shock on Parental Attachment to the Labor Market and the Double Bind of Mothers." Working Paper no. 33 (June), Opportunity and Inclusive Growth Institute, Federal Reserve Bank of Minneapolis, Minneapolis, MN.

Hershbein, Brad J., and Harry J. Holzer. 2021. "The COVID-19 Pandemic's Evolving Impacts on the Labor Market: Who's Been Hurt and What We Should Do." Working Paper no. 21-341, Upjohn Institute, Kalamazoo, MI.

Holler, Radost, Lena Janys, Christian Zimpelmann, Hans-Martin Gaudecker, and Bettina Siflinger. 2021. "The Early Impact of the Covid-19 Pandemic on the Gender Division of Market and Household Work." Unpublished Manuscript, University of Bonn.

Hupkau, Claudia, and Barbara Petrongolo. 2020. "Work, Care and Gender during the COVID-19 Crisis." Discussion Paper no. 15358 (October), CEPR, London.

Jang, Youngsoo, and Minchul Yum. 2020. "Aggregate and Intergenerational Implications of School Closures: A Quantitative Assessment." Discussion Paper Series no. 234 (November), CRC TR 224, Mannheim University, Germany.

Kearney, Melissa S., and Phillip B. Levine. 2020. "Half a Million Fewer Children? The Coming COVID Baby Bust." Brookings Institution Report, Washington, DC.

Kim, Eunji, and Shawn Patterson. 2020. "The Pandemic and Gender Inequality in Academia." Unpublished Manuscript, Vanderbilt University.

Kleven, Henrik, Camille Landais, Johanna Posch, Andreas Steinhauer, and Josef Zweimüller. 2019. "Child Penalties across Countries: Evidence and Explanations." *AEA Papers and Proceedings* 109:122–26.

Kleven, Henrik, Camille Landais, and Jakob Egholt Søgaard. 2019. "Children and Gender Inequality: Evidence from Denmark." *American Economic Journal: Applied Economics* 11 (4): 181–209.

Kuhfeld, Megan, James Soland, Beth Tarasawa, Angela Johnson, Erik Ruzek, and Jing Liu. 2020. "Projecting the Potential Impact of COVID-19 School Closures on Academic Achievement." *Educational Researcher* 49 (8): 549–65.

Lee, Sang Yoon (Tim), Minsung Park, and Yongseok Shin. 2021. "Hit Harder, Recover Slower? Unequal Employment Effects of the Covid-19 Shock." Working Paper no. 28354, NBER, Cambridge, MA.

Lemieux, Thomas, Kevin Milligan, Tammy Schirle, Wilfrid Laurier, and Mikal Skuterud. 2020. "Initial Impacts of the COVID-19 Pandemic on the Canadian Labour Market." *Canadian Public Policy* 46 (S1): S55–S65.

Leslie, Emily, and Riley Wilson. 2020. "Sheltering in Place and Domestic Violence: Evidence from Calls for Service during COVID-19." *Journal of Public Economics* 189:104241.

Leyva, Gustavo, and Carlos Urrutia. 2020. "Informal Labor Markets in Times of Pandemic: Evidence for Latin America and Policy Options." Unpublished Manuscript, ITAM.

Lundberg, Shelly. 1985. "The Added Worker Effect." *Journal of Labor Economics* 3 (1): 11–37.

Maldonado, Joana Elisa, and Kristof De Witte. 2020. "The Effect of School Closures on Standardised Student Test Outcomes." Discussion Paper Series no. 20.17, KU Leuven.

Mankart, Jochen, and Rigas Oikonomou. 2017. "Household Search and the Aggregate Labour Market." *Review of Economic Studies* 84 (4): 1735–88.

Meekes, Jordy, Wolter H. J. Hassink, and Guyonne Kalb. 2020. "Essential Work and Emergency Chilcare: Identifying Gender Differences in COVID-19 Effects on Labour Demand and Supply." Discussion Paper no. 13843, IZA, Bonn.

Mennuni, Alessandro. 2019. "The Aggregate Implications of Changes in the Labour Force Composition." *European Economic Review* 116:83–106.

Miller, Amalia R. 2011. "The Effects of Motherhood Timing on Career Path." *Journal of Population Economics* 24 (3): 1071–100.

Möhring, Katja, Maximiliane Reifenscheid, and Andreas Weiland. 2021. "Is the Recession a 'Shecession'? Gender Inequality in the Employment Effects of the COVID-19 Pandemic in Germany." Unpublished Manuscript, University of Mannheim.

Montenovo, Laura, Xuan Jiang, Felipe Lozano Rojas, Ian M. Schmutte, Kosali I. Simon, Bruce A. Weinberg, and Coady Wing. 2020. "Determinants of Disparities in Covid-19 Job Losses." Working Paper no. 27132, NBER, Cambridge, MA.

Olsson, Jonna. 2019. "Structural Transformation of the Labor Market and the Aggregate Economy." Unpublished Manuscript, Stockholm University.

Ortigueira, Salvador, and Nawid Siassi. 2013. "How Important is Intra-household Risk Sharing for Savings and Labor Supply?" *Journal of Monetary Economics* 60 (6): 650–66.

Qian, Yue, and Sylvia Fuller. 2020. "COVID-19 and the Gender Employment Gap among Parents of Young Children." *Canadian Public Policy* 46 (S2): S89–S101.

Ribarovska, Alana K., Mark R. Hutchinson, Quentin J. Pittman, Carmine Pariante, and Sarah J. Spencer. 2021. "Gender Inequality in Publishing during the COVID-19 Pandemic." *Brain Behavior and Immunity* 91:1–3.

Russell, Lauren, and Chuxuan Sun. 2020. "The Effect of Mandatory Child Care Center Closures on Women's Labor Market Outcomes during the COVID-19 Pandemic." *Covid Economics: Vetted and Real-Time Papers* 62:124–54.

Sevilla, Almudena, and Sarah Smith. 2020. "Baby Steps: The Gender Division of Childcare During the COVID19 Pandemic." Discussion Paper no. 14804, CEPR, London.

Stevens, Ann Huff. 1997. "Persistent Effects of Job Displacement: The Importance of Multiple Job Losses." *Journal of Labor Economics* 15 (1): 165–88.

Van den Berg, Gerard, and Michele Tertilt. 2012. "Domestic Violence over the Business Cycle." Unpublished Manuscript, University of Mannheim.

von Gaudecker, Hans-Martin, Christian Zimpelmann, Moritz Mendel, Bettina Siflinger, Lena Janys, Jürgen Maurer, Egbert Jongen, et al. 2021. "CoViD-19 Impact Lab Questionnaire Documentation." https://doi.org/10.5281/zenodo.4338730.

Wang, Haomin. 2019. "Intra-household Risk Sharing and Job Search over the Business Cycle." *Review of Economic Dynamics* 34:165–82.

Wu, Chunzan, and Dirk Krueger. 2019. "Consumption Insurance against Wage Risk: Family Labor Supply and Optimal Progressive Income Taxation." *American Economic Journal: Macroeconomics* 13 (1): 79–113.

Zamarro, Gema, and María J. Prados. 2021. "Gender Differences in Couples' Division of Childcare, Work and Mental Health during COVID-19." *Review of Economics of the Household* 19:11–40.

Comment

Laura Pilossoph, *Federal Reserve Bank of New York*, United States of America

In typical recessions, male employment falls more relative to female employment. Recessions are usually "mancessions" for several reasons. First, males are disproportionately employed in sectors and industries that are more cyclically sensitive when compared with those where women work (Albanesi and Sahin 2018). Second, women are frequently second earners in the household, and they enter the labor market during recessions if their spouse loses their job, making female employment less countercyclical (Doepke and Tertilt 2016).

These differences result in the relative employment dynamics depicted in figure 1, which plots the employment-to-population ratio of men relative to women, expressed as deviations from the beginning of a particular recessionary episode, defined using gross domestic product–based methods (Chauvet and Hamilton 2005). The dynamics of this object show that nearly all recessions in the United States since the 1970s have been mancessions, with the exception of the pandemic recession in which the gender gap in the employment-to-population ratio rose by 6 percentage points by two quarters in. The authors put together a remarkable amount of data from different countries, documenting similar patterns around the globe; the pandemic recession was thus a "shecession."

The authors next provide convincing evidence in support of a simple narrative of how the pandemic recession led to such different outcomes by gender relative to prior recessionary episodes. First, a key feature of the pandemic was a reduction in face-to-face interactions, which naturally affected some occupations more than others (Mongey, Pilossoph, and

NBER Macroeconomics Annual, volume 36, 2022.
© 2022 National Bureau of Economic Research. All rights reserved. Published by The University of Chicago Press for the National Bureau of Economic Research. https://doi.org/10.1086/718661

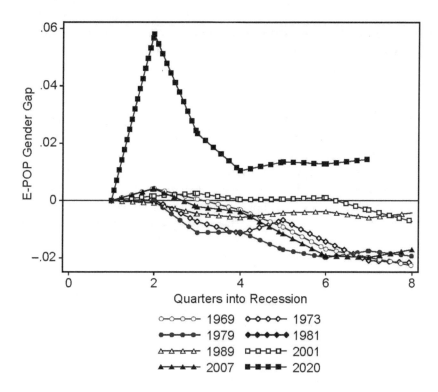

Fig. 1. The gender gap in employment-to-population (E-POP) ratios for different recessions in the United States. Calculations are author's and are based on Current Population Survey data from 1969Q2 to 2020Q4. Recession indicators are defined using gross domestic product–based methods (Chauvet and Hamilton 2005). The E-POP ratio is defined as the E-POP for men relative to the E-POP for women minus 1. The samples are limited to individuals in the civilian, noninstitutionalized population between the ages of 25 and 54 years old. Quarterly E-POPs are the average over monthly E-POPs within the quarter. A color version of this figure is available online.

Weinberg 2020). Because women were more likely to be employed in these types of occupations, their employment outcomes were worse relative to men this time around. Second, school closures and childcare needs imposed further constraints on those with children. Because women take on relatively more childcare obligations relative to men (Aguiar, Hurst, and Karabarbounis 2011), women with children were less able to work than men, and so their employment took a further relative hit.

Using monthly data from the Current Population Survey (CPS), the authors make their case as follows. First, they run regressions of the form

$$y_{it} = \beta_0 + \beta_1 F_i + \beta_2 D_t + \beta_3 F_i \times D_t + \beta_4 X_{it} + \epsilon_{it},$$

where y_{it} is either hours worked or an employment dummy in month t for individual i, F_i is a dummy taking a value of 1 if the respondent is female, D_t is a dummy taking on a value of 1 for months during the COVID recession (2020Q2–2020Q3), and X_{it} is a vector of controls including gender-specific time trends, quarterly seasonal dummies, age dummies, education dummies, marital status, and race. An estimate of $\beta_3 < 0$ implies that employment fell by $100 \times \beta_3$ percentage points more for women than for men during the pandemic, conditional on other characteristics.

If women were employed disproportionately in occupations that were harder hit by the pandemic than were men, including controls for occupations should lower the effect of being female during the pandemic on employment and hours outcomes. The authors therefore add job controls to the above regression and show that such an addition indeed lowers the estimated effect by roughly 1 percentage point (tables 7 and 8).

Similarly, if school closures are part of the story, employment losses among women with children should be even larger relative to men than women without children. To test this hypothesis, the authors add controls for children:

$$y_{it} = \theta_0 \text{Kid}_{it} + \theta_1 F_i \times \text{Kid}_{it} + \theta_2 D_t \times \text{Kid}_{it} + \theta_3 F_i \times D_t \times \text{Kid}_{it}$$
$$+ \theta_4 X_{it} + \theta_5 \text{Job}_{it} + \theta_6 \text{Job}_{it} \times D_t + \epsilon_{it},$$

where Kid_{it} is a vector of three dummy variables grouping households by the age of their youngest child (<5, 5–17, none or only adult children). Employment for women with school-age children fell by nearly 2 percentage points more than similar men, and those with children younger than five fell by 1 percentage point more (tables 7 and 8).

At first glance, one of the more puzzling results is that even women without children suffered larger employment and hours losses relative to men, even after controlling for occupation and industry. Employment fell by 1 percentage point more for women without children or with adult children relative to men, and the effect size is on the same order of magnitude as those whose youngest child is less than 5 years old. A similar pattern holds for hours as well. This begs the question: Is there something specific to the pandemic that explains the differential outcomes by gender, beyond industry and childcare?

One explanation that is consistent with a larger employment impact during the pandemic for women than for men—beyond industry and childcare—is that women tend to be more risk averse than men (Cortés et al. 2021); if so, they would be more averse to going back to work, where the virus can spread more quickly (Houstecka, Koh, and Santaeulalia-Llopis 2020).

However, examining similar regressions for other recessionary episodes sheds some light on the plausibility of this mechanism. For similar regressions run during the Great Recession, the coefficients for each category of children have a similar magnitude, consistent with the idea that childcare issues were only significant during the pandemic in driving differential outcomes by gender (table 10). However, the coefficients are all statistically significant, and they show that employment for women fell by 0.2–0.4 percentage point less than their male counterparts. Why should women fare differently than men during the Great Recession once industry and occupation have been accounted for?

A more likely explanation is that the occupation and industry controls in the above regressions do not fully capture the nature of a job, which may be better captured by the specific tasks it requires. Indeed, using data from Brazil and Costa Rica which have task-level information in addition to occupation and industry information, Gottlieb et al. (2021) find that there is substantial variation in work-from-home ability across jobs, even within occupation and industry. This partially explains the findings the authors present conditioning on teleworking outcomes during the pandemic. For those individuals who ever teleworked during the pandemic, the childcare effects disappear completely once industry and occupation have already been controlled for (table 16). Moreover, the magnitude of the coefficients is on the same order, and all three Kid_{it} categories are insignificant.

However, among those who never took up the option of working from home (or never had that option to begin with), employment still fell by a whopping 8.8 percentage points more for women without children than for men. Because a similar number cannot be constructed for the Great Recession (the telecommuting measure is unavailable because it was introduced only in the COVID Supplement to the CPS), it is possible that a version of this regression for that time period is similar, with the signs flipped. In this case, the large coefficient can be ignored. The large differential might also arise if there is a correlation between tasks that cannot be done from home and tasks that require a high degree of physical proximity, as has been documented for occupations (Mongey et al. 2020). If women are more likely employed in these types of tasks within the same occupations, their employment losses would be larger during the pandemic. Task-based information that is not aggregated to the occupation level that can be linked with employment outcomes would help clarify these issues, but no such data exist for the United States.[1]

Notwithstanding the mysterious employment effects for women without children, the paper shows convincingly the disproportionately negative role that school closures have played in female labor market outcomes during the pandemic. The question is whether these effects will be long-lasting, and whether they will outlast the typical differential employment outcomes that men experience in downturns. To conclude on a positive note, as I write this comment in June of 2021, the gender gap in the employment-to-population ratio has more than halved since three quarters into the pandemic recession. Figure 2 reproduces figure 1 using NBER recession indicators so as to include data up through 2021Q1. Although the gender gap in the employment-to-population ratio has not returned to prepandemic levels, the gap is on the same order of magnitude

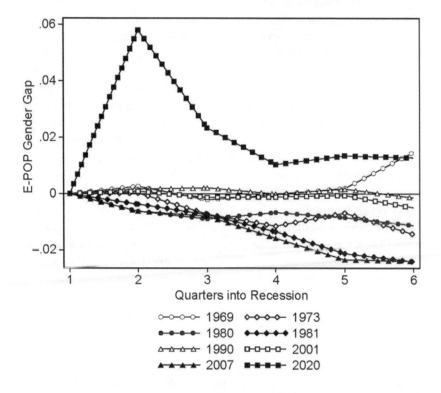

Fig. 2. The gender gap in employment-to-population (E-POP) ratios for different recessions in the United States. Calculations are author's and are based on Current Population Survey data from 1969Q2 to 2021Q1. Recession indicators are defined using the NBER recession indicators. The E-POP ratio is defined as the E-POP for men relative to the E-POP for women minus 1. The samples are limited to individuals in the civilian, noninstitutionalized population between the ages of 25 and 54 years old. Quarterly E-POPs are the average over monthly E-POPs within the quarter. A color version of this figure is available online.

as the reversed gap from the Great Recession six quarters from its onset. This makes me hopeful that the negative effects for women well documented in this paper may reverse once schools fully reopen.

Endnotes

Author email address: Pilossoph (pilossoph@gmail.com). For acknowledgments, sources of research support, and disclosure of the author's material financial relationships, if any, please see https://www.nber.org/books-and-chapters/nber-macroeconomics-annual -2021-volume-36/comment-mancession-shecession-womens-employment-regular-and-pan demic-recessions-pilossoph.

1. O*NET data have information on tasks, but only at the occupation level.

References

Aguiar, M. A., E. Hurst, and L. Karabarbounis. 2011. "Time Use During Recessions." Working Paper no. 17259, NBER, Cambridge, MA.
Albanesi, S., and A. Sahin. 2018. "The Gender Unemployment Gap." *Review of Economic Dynamics* 30:47–67.
Chauvet, M., and J. Hamilton. 2005. "Dating Business Cycle Turning Points." In *Nonlinear Time Series Analysis of Business Cycles*, vol. 276, ed. C. Milas, P. Rothman, and D. van Dijk. Bingley: Emerald Group.
Cortés, P., J. Pan, L. Pilossoph, and B. Zafar. 2021. "Gender Differences in Job Search and the Earnings Gap: Evidence from Business Majors." Working Paper no. 28820, NBER, Cambridge, MA.
Doepke, M., and M. Tertilt. 2016. "Families in Macroeconomics." In *Handbook of Macroeconomics*, vol. 2, ed. J. B. Taylor and H. Uhlig, 1789–891. Amsterdam: Elsevier.
Gottlieb, C., J. Grobovšek, M. Poschke, and F. Saltiel. 2021. "Working from Home in Developing Countries." *European Economic Review* 133:103679.
Houstecka, A., D. Koh, and R. Santaeulalia-Llopis. 2020. "Contagion at Work." Working Paper no. 1225, Barcelona Graduate School of Economics.
Mongey, S., L. Pilossoph, and A. Weinberg. 2020. "Which Workers Bear the Burden of Social Distancing?" Working Paper no. 27085, NBER, Cambridge, MA.

Comment

Loukas Karabarbounis, *University of Minnesota and NBER,* United States of America

Using a variety of microlevel data sets, Alon et al. (2021) carefully document women's and men's labor supply patterns during the pandemic recession. The pandemic recession differs from previous recessions in that, for almost all countries, women experienced a larger decline than men in their market hours. According to the analysis in the paper, two salient factors associated with this gap are the increased need for childcare and the concentration of women's employment in industries and occupations hit hardest by the pandemic.

The paper contributes a large number of observations on time allocation by gender and other demographic groups that will certainly stimulate future research on labor markets. Two questions arise when reading the paper. Are the observations informative about the causes of the decline in market hours? Filtered through standard labor supply theory, is the larger impact of the pandemic on women's labor supply puzzling or concerning?

I use a tractable model of consumption and time allocation to bridge the observations documented by Alon et al. (2021) and the lessons we draw from these observations. My first conclusion is that their observations are informative about the causes of the decline in market hours in the pandemic recession relative to previous recessions. My second conclusion is that the gender gap in decline in market hours is not particularly puzzling or concerning when filtered through the lens of the model. In reaching these conclusions, I acknowledge that I do not attempt a quantification of the model that matches every aspect of hours worked

NBER Macroeconomics Annual, volume 36, 2022.
© 2022 National Bureau of Economic Research. All rights reserved. Published by The University of Chicago Press for the National Bureau of Economic Research. https://doi .org/10.1086/718662

during the pandemic. Rather, my more modest goal is to use a quantitatively tractable framework that speaks to the most salient observations reported in the paper.

I. Model

The model considers the consumption and time allocation decisions of heterogeneous households. It has four key elements necessary to interpret the observations in the paper. First, households have heterogeneous members. Second, household members combine expenditures purchased in the market with their time to produce commodities at home. Third, female and male time inputs enter asymmetrically in home production. Finally, the model features partial insurance, with households fully insured against some shocks in the market sector and unable to insure against some others, including shocks that originate in the home sector.

A. Preferences and Technologies

Households derive utility from a market-purchased commodity c_0 and different home-produced commodities c_k for $k = 1, \ldots K$. The market commodity is produced with only market expenditures $c_0 = x_0$. Home commodities are produced with market expenditures, female time spent on home production, and male time spent on home production, $c_k(x_k, h_k^f, h_k^m)$. Households maximize the expectation of discounted sum of utility flows, where flow utility is

$$
U_t = \log \left(\omega_{0t} x_{0t}^{\frac{\phi-1}{\phi}} + \sum_k \left(\omega_{kt}^f \left(x_{kt}^{\frac{\sigma_k-1}{\sigma_k}} + \left(\theta_{kt} h_{kt}^f \right)^{\frac{\sigma_k-1}{\sigma_k}} \right)^{\frac{\sigma_k(\phi-1)}{(\sigma_k-1)\phi}} + \omega_{kt}^m (h_{kt}^m)^{\frac{\phi-1}{\phi}} \right) \right)^{\frac{\phi}{\phi-1}}. \quad (1)
$$

Consumption weights, ω_{0t}, ω_{kt}^f, and ω_{kt}^m, vary over time and across households. The variable θ_{kt} is the efficiency of female time relative to expenditures in the production of good k and also varies over time and across households.

Preferences are nested constant elasticity of substitution functions of inputs. Parameter $\phi > 0$ is the elasticity of substitution between male time h_k^m and all other commodities and parameter $\sigma_k > 0$ is the elasticity of substitution between female time h_k^f and expenditures x_k. To give a concrete example from the application below, commodity c_k can be the production of childcare. Childcare takes as input expenditures on goods and services such as childcare providers, educational programs and supplies, and other extracurricular activities. It also uses time spent with kids by household members. I will assume a key asymmetry in home technology, $\sigma_k > 1 > \phi$, which implies that female time is a closer substitute than male time with expenditures amenable to home production. This "social norm" is imposed to the analysis rather than derived from more primitive frictions or historical experiences shaping the production technology frontier of households.[1]

For every household member $g = \{f, m\}$, working in the market yields earnings:

$$y_t^g = z_t^g n_t^g = \exp(\alpha_t^g + \varepsilon_t^g)\left(T^g - \sum_k h_{kt}^g\right). \tag{2}$$

In this equation, $z_t^g = \exp(\alpha_t^g + \varepsilon_t^g)$ is the wage per unit of hour worked and $n_t^g = T^g - \sum_k h_{kt}^g$ is discretionary time devoted to working in the market. The difference between α^g and ε^g will become apparent below when I restrict attention to allocations with no insurance against changes in α^g and full insurance against changes in ε^g. Changes in α^g are, thus, capturing more permanent changes in earnings that are difficult to insure, such as differential long-run shifts in labor demand across skill or occupational groups. Changes in ε^g are capturing changes in earnings that are easier to insure through asset markets, family transfers, and government transfers. Examples are short unemployment spells, furloughs, and pay reduction programs.

B.   Sources of Heterogeneity

Households are heterogeneous in their discretionary time, consumption weights, production efficiency at home, and wages. A household is summarized by a sequence $\iota = \{T^f, T^m, \omega_{0t}, \omega_{kt}^f, \omega_{kt}^m, \theta_{kt}, \alpha_t^f, \alpha_t^m, \varepsilon_t^f, \varepsilon_t^m\}_t$. The analysis focuses on the market and home sectors. Differences in leisure across and within households are captured through differences in discretionary remaining time, T^f and T^m, allocated between market and home production. I allow discretionary time to be heterogeneous across and within households but, for simplicity, I assume it is constant over time.

C.   Planning Problems

I now introduce a sequence of island-level planning problems. An island ℓ consists of household ι's with same $\{T^f, T^m, \omega_{0t}, \omega_{kt}^f, \omega_{kt}^m, \theta_{kt}, \alpha_t^f, \alpha_t^m\}_t$. This means that all households in an island share the same sources of heterogeneity except for the $\varepsilon_t = (\varepsilon_t^f, \varepsilon_t^m)$ components of wages. In every period t, the island-ℓ planning problem is

$$\max_{\{x_{0t}, x_{kt}, h^f_{kt}, h^m_{kt}\}_\iota} \int U(x_{0t}(\iota), x_{kt}(\iota), h^f_{kt}(\iota), h^m_{kt}(\iota); \iota) d\Phi_t(\varepsilon), \qquad (3)$$

subject to the island-level resource constraint

$$\int \left(x_{0t}(\iota) + \sum_k p_{kt} x_{kt}(\iota) \right) d\Phi_t(\varepsilon) = \sum_g \int z^g_t(\iota) \left(T^g(\iota) - \sum_k h^g_{kt}(\iota) \right) d\Phi_t(\varepsilon), \qquad (4)$$

where $\Phi_t(\varepsilon)$ is the distribution function of households within an island. In the objective function (eq. [3]), U is the flow utility in equation (1). Home production is nontradable across households within an island, as evidenced by the fact that home technologies are already substituted into utility. The left-hand side of the resource constraint (eq. [4]) is total household expenditures in an island, where p_{kt} is the price of good k relative to the market good. The right-hand side is total income earned by females and males in an island.

Solving these planning problems has two advantages. First, it allows to derive equilibrium allocations in closed form. Second, the model generates partial insurance against shocks in the market sector. The ε^f_t and ε^m_t components of wages are fully insurable because planners pool resources across members of the island with different realizations of ε^f_t and ε^m_t. The α^f_t and α^m_t components of wages are uninsurable because members of a given island share the same α^f_t and α^m_t and they cannot trade securities with members of other islands. Although not essential for the results I want to emphasize, there are decentralizations that generate the same equilibrium allocations as the allocations generated by the planning problems that I study.[2]

D. Markets

Aggregate production is $Y_t = \Sigma_g \int \exp(\alpha^g_t(\iota) + \varepsilon^g_t(\iota))(T^g(\iota) - \Sigma_k h^g_{kt}(\iota)) d\Phi_t(\iota)$, where $\Phi_t(\iota)$ is the distribution function of households in the economy. Markets for labor and goods are perfectly competitive and the wage per efficiency unit of labor is 1. Production Y_t is transformed at a rate of 1 into market goods, $\int x_{0t}(\iota) d\Phi_t(\iota)$, and at a rate of A^{-1}_{kt} into home goods, $\int x_{kt}(\iota) d\Phi(\iota)$. Therefore, relative prices $p_{kt} = A^{-1}_{kt}$, and henceforth I treat p_{kt} as a primitive. The market for goods clears when $Y_t = \int (x_{0t}(\iota) + \Sigma_k p_{kt} x_{kt}(\iota)) d\Phi(\iota)$.

E. Equilibrium Allocations

An equilibrium consists of allocations $\{x_{0t}, x_{kt}, h^f_{kt}, h^m_{kt}\}_\iota$ that (i) solve the planning problem in equations (3) and (4) and (ii) clear goods and labor markets. I denote by $\lambda_t(\iota)$ the multiplier on the island-level resource constraint (eq. [4]), which equals the marginal utility of a unit of resources. By the planning problems, all households belonging to the same island have the same $\lambda_t(\iota)$. Solving the planning problems, I obtain equilibrium allocations that map primitives (i.e., sources of heterogeneity and parameters) into endogenous variables:

$$
\lambda_t(\iota) = \left(T^f(\iota) \exp(\alpha_t^f(\iota)) \int \exp(\varepsilon^f) d\Phi_t(\varepsilon^f) \right.
$$
$$
\left. + T^m(\iota) \exp(\alpha_t^m(\iota)) \int \exp(\varepsilon^m) d\Phi_t(\varepsilon) \right)^{-1},
\tag{5}
$$

$$
x_{0t}(\iota) = \frac{1}{\lambda_t(\iota) R_t(\iota)},
\tag{6}
$$

$$
x_{kt}(\iota) = \frac{\left(\frac{\omega_{kt}^f(\iota)}{\omega_{0t}(\iota)} \right)^\phi (p_{kt})^{1-\phi} \left(1 + \left(\frac{\theta_{kt}(\iota) p_{kt}}{z_t^f(\iota)} \right)^{\sigma_k - 1} \right)^{\frac{\phi - \sigma_k}{\sigma_k - 1}}}{\lambda_t(\iota) p_{kt} R_t(\iota)},
\tag{7}
$$

$$
h_{kt}^f(\iota) = \frac{\left(\frac{\theta_{kt}(\iota) p_{kt}}{z_t^f(\iota)} \right)^{\sigma_k} \left(\frac{\omega_{kt}^f(\iota)}{\omega_{0t}(\iota)} \right)^\phi (p_{kt})^{1-\phi} \left(1 + \left(\frac{\theta_{kt}(\iota) p_{kt}}{z_t^f(\iota)} \right)^{\sigma_k - 1} \right)^{\frac{\phi - \sigma_k}{\sigma_k - 1}}}{\lambda_t(\iota) p_{kt} \theta_{kt}(\iota) R_t(\iota)},
\tag{8}
$$

$$
h_{kt}^m(\iota) = \frac{\left(\frac{\omega_{kt}^m(\iota)}{\omega_{0t}(\iota)} \right)^\phi (z_t^m(\iota))^{1-\phi}}{\lambda_t(\iota) z_t^m(\iota) R_t(\iota)},
\tag{9}
$$

with $R_t(\iota) \equiv 1 + \Sigma_k((\omega_{kt}^f(\iota)/\omega_{0t}(\iota))^\phi (p_{kt})^{1-\phi}(1 + (\theta_{kt}(\iota) p_{kt}/z_t^f(\iota))^{\sigma_k-1})^{\phi-1/\sigma_k-1} + (\omega_{kt}^m(\iota)/\omega_{0t}(\iota))^\phi (z_t^m(\iota))^{1-\phi})$ in the denominators.

Marginal utility λ depends only on the realizations of the α^f and α^m components of wages. This does not imply that spending and time allocation remain constant in response to changes in other sources of heterogeneity. To see this, I use the solutions into the island-level resource constraint and rewrite λ in terms of endogenous variables:

$$
\lambda_t(\iota) = \left(x_{0t}(\iota) + \sum_k p_{kt} x_{kt}(\iota) + \sum_g z_t^g(\iota) \sum_k h_{kt}^g(\iota) \right)^{-1}.
\tag{10}
$$

With log preferences, marginal utility equals the inverse of the market value of total consumption, which consists of expenditures on market goods, $x_{0t}(\iota) + \Sigma_k p_{kt} x_{kt}(\iota)$, and the imputed market value of home production, $\Sigma_g z_t^g(\iota) \Sigma_k h_{kt}^g(\iota)$. In response to shocks other than α^f or α^m, there is intratemporal substitution between x_0, x_k, h_k^f, and h_k^m. Equation (5), however, restricts substitution patterns such that λ remains constant.[3]

Using the equilibrium allocations, we can get some insights on the economic forces that determine the allocation of time and spending. Dividing the solution for h_k^f with the solution for h_k we obtain

$$\frac{h_{kt}^f(\iota)}{x_{kt}(\iota)} = \left(\frac{p_{kt}}{z_t^f(\iota)}\right)^{\sigma_k} (\theta_{kt}(\iota))^{\sigma_k - 1}. \tag{11}$$

The first term shows that female time in home production relative to expenditures increases with the relative price of expenditures to time, p_k/z^f. The second term shows that, when female time and expenditures are substitutes, $\sigma_k > 1$, an increase in production efficiency of female time is associated with higher female time relative to expenditures.

For the allocation of time across household members we obtain

$$\frac{h_{kt}^f(\iota)}{h_{kt}^m(\iota)} = \left(\frac{\omega_{kt}^f(\iota)}{\omega_{kt}^m(\iota)}\right)^{\phi} \frac{(z_t^m(\iota))^{\phi}(\theta_{kt}(\iota))^{\sigma_k - 1}}{(z_t^f(\iota))^{\sigma_k}} \left[\left(\frac{1}{p_{kt}}\right)^{\sigma_k - 1} + \left(\frac{\theta_{kt}(\iota)}{z_t^f(\iota)}\right)^{\sigma_k - 1}\right]^{\frac{\phi - \sigma_k}{\sigma_k - 1}}. \tag{12}$$

The key comparative static is how changes in the relative price of expenditures p_k affect the allocation of time across members of the household. An increase in p_k causes households to substitute away from the female commodity bundle toward male production, which becomes relatively cheaper. This effect is parameterized by the elasticity of substitution across commodities φ. At the same time, an increase in p_k causes households to substitute away from expenditures that are more expensive toward female time. This effect is parameterized by the elasticity of substitution within commodities σ_k. When $\sigma_k > \phi$, the latter effect dominates and higher p_k is associated with higher ratio of time inputs h^f/h^m.

II. Application

I specialize the model to one aggregate home production sector, which produces commodities such as childcare, food consumption, and other household services. I proceed in four steps. First, I input to the model parameters and prepandemic consumption and time allocation data. Second, I discuss the identification of sources of heterogeneity such that the model matches perfectly the prepandemic data. Third, I perturb the model with aggregate shocks in the ε's, the α's, the ω's, and p_k and study labor supply responses. Finally, I compare the new allocations with the postpandemic observations documented in the paper.

A. Inputs to the Model

I use parameter values $\sigma_k = 3$ and $\phi = 0.8$, so that female time spent on activities such as childcare is more substitutable than male time with home expenditures. The upper panel of table 1 shows data on consumption and

Table 1
Data and Sources of Heterogeneity for Two Households

Household Data	z^f	z^m	n^f	n^m	h_k^f	h_k^m	x_0	$p_k x_k$
No kids	1	1	40	40	0	0	80	0
With kids	1	1	40	40	30	5	72	8

Sources of Heterogeneity	ω_0	ω_k^f	ω_k^m	θ_k	α^f	α^m	ε^f	ε^m
No kids	1	0	0	1	0	0	0	0
With kids	.63	.35	.02	1.94	0	0	0	0

time allocation for two hypothetical households before the pandemic. The
households belong to different islands. In the household without kids,
both spouses earn a wage of 1 per hour and both spouses work 40 hours
in the market and 0 hours at home. The household without kids spends 80
on market goods and 0 on home goods. In the household with kids, both
spouses earn a wage of 1 per hour and work 40 hours in the market. The
difference from the first household is that the female member spends
30 hours on home production whereas the male member spends only
5 hours. The household with kids spends 72 on market goods and 8 on
home goods.

B. Identification of Sources of Heterogeneity

Next, I choose sources of heterogeneity across households such that
the allocations generated by the model match perfectly with the prepandemic data.[4] In the bottom panel of table 1, the household without
kids has a weight on market goods $\omega_0 = 1$ and female production efficiency
$\theta_k = 1$. To account for differences in expenditures across households, the
household with kids has a weight on market goods $\omega_0 = 0.63$, a weight
on female commodities $\omega_k^f = 0.35$, and a weight on male commodities
$\omega_k^m = 0.02$. The model generates gender gaps in time allocations for the
household with kids when its female production efficiency at home,
$\theta_k = 1.93$, exceeds the efficiency of the household without kids. Equation (11) is useful in understanding this result. The social norm is that,
with $\sigma_k > 1$, a higher θ_k leads households with kids to allocate more resources to female time than to expenditures relative to households without kids.[5]

C. Perturbation of the Model with Aggregate Shocks

I perform comparative statics by changing the insurable component of
wages ε^f and ε^m, the uninsurable component of wages α^f and α^m, the

consumption weights ω_0, ω_k^f, ω_m^k, and the price of home-produced goods p_k. The shocks are aggregate in the sense that they affect both households equally. Owing to the planning problems, the model does not have any state variables and I consider changes across periods without specifying whether these changes are persistent or transitory and unexpected or anticipated.

Figure 1 plots comparative statics of market hours with respect to wages. Left panels display the comparative statics for the household without kids and right panels for the household with kids. In each panel, the solid line is for the female member of the household and the dashed line is for the male member of the household. Market hours are always normalized to 1 in the initial prepandemic equilibrium. Each line traces the change in market hours as we change the insurable component of female wages ε^f, the insurable component of male wages ε^m, the uninsurable component of female wages α^f, and the uninsurable component of male wages α^m.

Beginning with the four upper panels, we observe that female market hours decline in response to a decline in ε^f only for the household with kids. Though significantly smaller in magnitude, male market hours decline in response to a decline in ε^m again only for the household with kids. Because changes in the ε's are insurable and do not affect the marginal utility λ, the curves shown in the two upper panels are Frisch labor supply curves.

What explains the difference in λ-constant labor supply responses across and within households? Using the time constraint $n^g + h_k^g = T^g$, the elasticity of labor supply with respect to changes in the insurable component of wages equals

$$\frac{\partial n^g}{\partial \varepsilon^g} \frac{\varepsilon^g}{n^g} = -\frac{h^g}{n^g} \times \left(\frac{\partial h^g}{\partial \varepsilon^g} \frac{\varepsilon^g}{h^g} \right). \tag{13}$$

The Frisch elasticity of labor supply depends on the share of time devoted to home production, as shown by the first term in the right-hand side of equation (13). For the household without kids, this share is zero for both spouses and, thus, both spouses have a zero Frisch elasticity of labor supply. For the household with kids, females have a significantly larger share of home production time than males and thus experience significantly larger responses in their market hours. To get a sense of quantitative magnitudes, females with kids have a Frisch elasticity of roughly 1 for a 10% decline in wages and a Frisch elasticity of roughly 1.5 for a 20% decline in wages. For males with kids, the corresponding

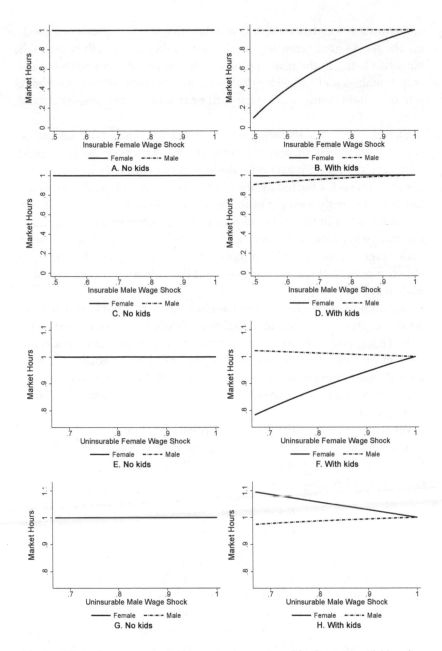

Fig. 1. Effects of wages on market hours. A color version of this figure is available online.

Frisch elasticities are 0.1 and 0.15. Frisch elasticities increase with the size of the wage shock because, in response to larger wage changes, the share of time devoted to home production increases.

In the four bottom panels, I plot changes in market hours in response to uninsurable changes in wages, α^f and α^m. With log preferences and no home production, income and substitution effects from uninsurable changes in wages cancel out. This logic explains why market hours are unresponsive to α^f and α^m for the household without kids. In models with home production, intratemporal substitution may attenuate or strengthen the substitution effect. As shown in the panels, own elasticities of labor supply are positive for both members but substantially larger for females than for males. This difference comes from the assumed elasticity values $\sigma_k = 3$ and $\phi = 0.8$. Substitution effects are substantially stronger than income effects for females because their time is substitutable with expenditures. Substitution effects are roughly of the same magnitude as income effects for males because their time is complementary to expenditures.[6]

The two upper panels of figure 2 plot comparative statics with respect to the price of home goods p_k. An increase in p_k lowers market hours for

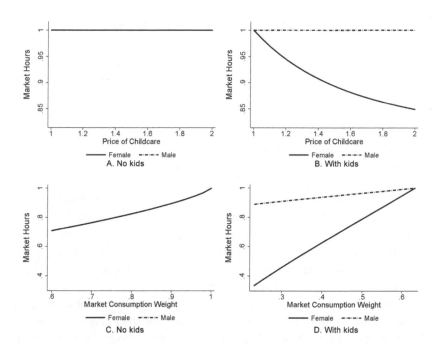

Fig. 2. Effects of relative prices and preferences on market hours. A color version of this figure is available online.

females with kids and does not affect males with kids or households without kids. The gender gap for households with kids reflects again the higher substitutability of female time with expenditures. The difference across the two households reflects differences in initial prepandemic expenditure shares. A change in relative prices does not affect significantly the allocation of expenditures and time for the household without kids because its initial expenditure share on home goods is zero.

The two lower panels of figure 2 plot comparative statics with respect to the consumption weight on market goods ω_0. For this comparative static, I allocate the remaining weight proportionally between ω_k^f and ω_k^m. Thus, as shown in equation (12), changes in ω_0 do not affect the ratio of time inputs h_k^f / h_k^m. Because time inputs are equalized for the household without kids, a decline in ω_0 leads to an equal percent decline in market hours. For the household with kids, female market hours decline by more in percent terms than male market hours. The logic is that the time constraint is additive and, therefore, the same percent change in home production time necessitates a larger percent decline in market hours for the household member who performs the larger share of home production.

D.   Comparison between US Data and Theoretical Allocations

In evaluating the implications of the model, I now use three key observations of Alon et al. (2021) for the United States. Total market hours decline by roughly $\Delta_t(\log n) = -0.36$. The gender gap in market hours for households without kids is $\Delta_t \Delta_g(\log n | \text{no kids}) = -0.06$. The gender gap in market hours for households with kids is $\Delta_t \Delta_g(\log n | \text{with kids}) = -0.18$. The last two statistics can be understood as differences-in-differences conditional on household status. The difference between the two (i.e., the "triple difference" equal to -0.12) shows that females in households with kids experienced a larger decline in their market hours than females in households without kids relative to the prepandemic state.

How do these statistics compare to the theoretical labor supply responses?[7] Insurable shocks to wages ε^f and ε^m generate a gender gap in decline in market hours for households with kids. However, if Frisch elasticities of labor supply are low, these shocks cannot account for the significant common component of the decline across all demographic groups. Uninsurable shocks to wages α^f can account for the decline in market hours of females with kids but can drive market hours of spouses in the opposite direction. The increase in the price of home-produced goods p_k generates a substantial decline in the market hours of females with kids but does not affect other demographic groups. In light of the observations of Alon et al. (2021), the most promising driver of the decline in market hours in the pandemic is the reallocation of the consumption bundle away from market goods toward home goods ω_0. The decline in ω_0 generates declines in market hours for all demographic groups. Furthermore, it generates a substantial gender gap for households with kids but not for households without kids.[8]

III. Conclusion

Alon et al. (2021) document patterns of women's and men's labor supply during the pandemic recession. I develop a model of consumption and time allocation to answer two questions. First, are the observations informative about the causes of the decline in market hours? I find that the observations are useful in discriminating between the drivers of labor supply in the pandemic recession relative to other recessions. Market hours during the pandemic recession are mainly driven by a reallocation of the consumption bundle away from market goods toward home goods such as childcare. This reallocation generates a decline in labor supply for all groups. In addition, the reallocation also accounts for the gender gap in decline in labor supply for households with kids but not for households without kids, as social norms lead women with kids to enter the pandemic with a larger share of home duties than men. Different from the pandemic recession, previous recessions are better thought of as labor demand shocks that fall disproportionately on men who work in more cyclical market sectors such as construction, manufacturing, and finance.

Second, is the larger impact of the pandemic on women's labor supply puzzling or concerning? The gender gap in decline in labor supply is not particularly puzzling or concerning when filtered through the lens of the model. Labor supply theory predicts that women's labor supply is more elastic than men's when women perform a larger share of home duties. Thus, in response to common shocks such as the reallocation of economic activity toward the home sector, we expect women's labor supply to decline by more. As argued before with the help of the solution for the marginal utility λ, this reallocation is such that λ remains constant over the pandemic for all households. In addition, there is full risk sharing within households because all household members share the same consumption bundle. Therefore, one may be tempted to conclude that the larger decline in market hours of women during the pandemic is as concerning as the larger decline in market hours of men during previous recessions.[9]

Appendix

In this appendix, I show how to identify sources of heterogeneity. The strategy is to invert equations (5), (6), (7), (8), and (9) and write the sources of heterogeneity as functions of expenditures x_0, x_k, time h_k^f, h_k^m, and wages z^f, z^m. Dropping time t and household ι subscripts for convenience, I obtain:

$$\theta_k = \left(\frac{x_k}{h_k^f}\right)^{\frac{1}{1-\sigma_k}} \left(\frac{p_k}{z^f}\right)^{\frac{\sigma_k}{1-\sigma_k}}, \tag{A1}$$

$$\frac{\omega_k^f}{\omega_0} = p_k \left(\frac{x_k}{x_0}\right)^{\frac{1}{\phi}} \left(1 + \left(\frac{\theta_k p_k}{z^f}\right)^{\sigma_k-1}\right)^{\frac{\sigma_k-\phi1}{\sigma_k-1\phi}}, \tag{A2}$$

$$\frac{\omega_k^m}{\omega_0} = z^m \left(\frac{h_k^m}{x_0}\right)^{\frac{1}{\phi}}, \tag{A3}$$

$$\omega_0 = \frac{1}{1 + \sum_k \left(p_k \left(\frac{x_k}{x_0}\right)^{\frac{1}{\phi}} \left(1 + \left(\frac{\theta_k p_k}{z^f}\right)^{\sigma_k-1}\right)^{\frac{\sigma_k-\phi1}{\sigma_k-1\phi}} + z^m \left(\frac{h_k^m}{x_0}\right)^{\frac{1}{\phi}}\right)}, \tag{A4}$$

$$\lambda(\alpha^f, \alpha^m; d\Phi(\varepsilon)) = \left(x_0 + \sum_k p_k x_k + \sum_g z^g \sum_k h_k^g\right)^{-1}, \tag{A5}$$

$$\varepsilon^f = \log z^f - \alpha^f, \tag{A6}$$

$$\varepsilon^m = \log z^m - \alpha^m. \tag{A7}$$

Equation (A5) shows that α^m and α^f are not identified because they both can account perfectly for a given market value of total consumption $x_0 + \Sigma_k p_k x_k + \Sigma_g z^g \Sigma_k h_k^g$. In the application, I have fixed α^f and used equation (A5) to infer α^m. This is without loss in generality for any of the comparative statics or conclusions.

Endnotes

Author's email address: Karabarbounis (loukas@umn.edu). For acknowledgments, sources of research support, and disclosure of the author's material financial relationships, if any, please see https://www.nber.org/books-and-chapters/nber-macroeco nomics-annual-2021-volume-36/comment-mancession-shecession-womens-employ ment-regular-and-pandemic-recessions-karabarbounis.

1. An example of such work is Alesina, Ichino, and Karabarbounis (2011), who develop a collective household model in which differences in bargaining power, perhaps due to cultural or historical reasons from a period of time when physical power mattered, generate gender gaps in career investments and labor supply elasticities. In more recent

work, Alon et al. (2020) model social norms such that a fraction of households, the traditional households, suffer a utility penalty when males work more at home than females.

2. These decentralizations require specific assumptions on the structure of asset markets and on the stochastic processes that govern the sources of heterogeneity. Heathcote, Storesletten, and Violante (2014) provide the first model with such a decentralization that generates closed-form solutions for consumption and labor supply. Their decentralization has been extended by Boerma and Karabarbounis (2020, 2021) in models with multiple home production sectors. The presentation here is closer to Boerma and Karabarbounis (2020) in that I adopt the Ghez and Becker (1975) version of the home production model instead of the Gronau (1986) version used in Boerma and Karabarbounis (2021). The model here extends these papers by adding two household members with heterogeneous substitutability, production efficiency at home, and discretionary time. The theorems that allow decentralizing of the planning problems in these papers can be extended here under further assumptions on how α^f and α^m are related and an extension of the definition of the island.

3. The constancy of λ_t in response to uninsurable shocks that originate in the home sector may be surprising. This result is special to the log specification of utility with respect to the consumption aggregator in equation (1). Log preferences generate a separability between ($\omega_{0t}, \omega_{kt}^f, \omega_{kt}^m, \theta_{kt}$) and the marginal utility.

4. The appendix shows how to invert equations (5)–(9) and identify the sources of heterogeneity. Consumption weights are normalized such that $\omega_{0t}(\iota) + \Sigma_k(\omega_{kt}^f(\iota) + \omega_{kt}^m(\iota)) = 1$. The $\alpha_t^m(\iota)$ or $\alpha_t^f(\iota)$ sources of heterogeneity are not identified because they both account perfectly for a given market value of total consumption $x_{0t}(\iota) + \Sigma_k p_{kt} x_{kt}(\iota) + \Sigma_g z_t^g(\iota) \Sigma_k h_{kt}^g(\iota)$. However, this lack of identification is inessential for the comparative statics.

5. For the household without kids I assume $h_k^f = h_k^m = x_k$ and that all these variables are very close to zero but positive. This generates a production efficiency $\theta_k = 1$.

6. Cross-elasticities of labor supply are negative and substantially larger for females, again reflecting the higher substitutability of female time.

7. Given elasticities, the statistics in the paper are informative about the shocks driving labor supply patterns. Alternatively, given observed shocks, the statistics are informative about elasticities. Without externally identified shocks, which is likely the case for the pandemic recession accompanied by school closures and lockdowns, one could use other time periods to infer elasticities and hope that elasticities did not change much during the pandemic. Here, I explore this route in the sense that I use elasticities from knowledge of prior samples.

8. The inference of shocks driving market hours in the pandemic would be sharper if it also incorporated data on expenditures. I speculate such data would attribute a more important role to p_k as it is plausible that households substituted between market goods and home goods in categories outside of childcare (e.g., food at home or home improvements). The application would need to be augmented to allow households without kids to also perform home production in these alternative activities. Similar, I interpret the increase in home production time for households without kids in response to a decline in ω_0 as a shift toward these alternative activities.

9. Intratemporal substitution between market and home production provides implicit insurance against shocks. This means that we expect total consumption, λ^{-1}, to be smoother than expenditures, $x_0 + \Sigma_k p_k x_k$, in the model. Alon et al. (2020) examine time-varying social norms in a model of consumption and time allocation with heterogeneous households. Changes in social norms toward modern family organizations with more equal division of home production weaken intratemporal substitution and strengthen the added worker effect. In the model, such a change can be conceptualized as a convergence of the elasticity σ_k toward the elasticity ϕ together with $\theta_k = 1$.

References

Alesina, A., A. Ichino, and L. Karabarbounis. 2011. "Gender-Based Taxation and the Division of Family Chores." *American Economic Journal: Economic Policy* 3 (2): 1–40.

Alon, T., S. Coskun, M. Doepke, D. Koll, and M. Tertilt. 2021. "From Mancession to Shecession: Women's Employment in Regular and Pandemic Recessions." Working Paper no. 28632, NBER, Cambridge, MA.

Alon, T., M. Doepke, J. Olmstead-Rumsey, and M. Tertilt. 2020. "This Time Is Different: The Role of Women's Employment in a Pandemic Recession." Working Paper no. 27660, NBER, Cambridge, MA.

Boerma, J., and L. Karabarbounis. 2020. "Labor Market Trends and the Changing Value of Time." *Journal of Economic Dynamics and Control* 115:103885.

————. 2021. "Inferring Inequality with Home Production." *Econometrica* 89 (5): 2517–56.

Ghez, G., and G. Becker. 1975. *The Allocation of Time and Goods Over the Life Cycle.* New York: Columbia University Press.

Gronau, R. 1986. "Home Production: A Survey." In *Handbook of Labor Economics*, ed. O. Ashenfelter and R. Layard, 274–304. Amsterdam: Elsevier.

Heathcote, J., K. Storesletten, and G. L. Violante. 2014. "Consumption and Labor Supply with Partial Insurance: An Analytical Framework." *American Economic Review* 104 (7): 2075–126.

Discussion

Steven Davis opened the discussion by questioning whether mancessions or shecessions are more socially harmful. He listed some reasons why mancessions may be more harmful, including that women are more likely to be secondary earners, women have better alternative uses of time (i.e., will spend less nonwork time pursuing sleep or leisure activities), there is a larger psychic cost of male joblessness, and male joblessness is more associated with increased crime, drug/alcohol use, and physical abuse of spouses/children. The authors responded by saying they are not making a statement on which is worse, but rather they argued that the responses of men and women to job loss are distinct, and this has macroeconomic implications. For example, differences in labor supply flexibility can have aggregate impacts. If a secondary earner (which on average is more likely to be a woman) loses their job, the primary earner (on average the man) has no margin for adjustment because they are already working full-time. In contrast, if a primary earner loses their job, the secondary earner has a margin to adjust and work more.

Martin Eichenbaum then followed up this discussion, to ask whether the difference between male and female sensitivity should be interpreted as a market failure, and whether this pattern says anything about efficiency. The authors responded that they do not think this points to any fundamental inefficiency, but the interaction of joint labor supply with policy can certainly create some. For instance, how taxation, unemployment benefits, and retirement entitlements treat secondary versus primary earners could interact with joint labor supply decisions in a way that creates inefficiency.

NBER Macroeconomics Annual, volume 36, 2022.
© 2022 National Bureau of Economic Research. All rights reserved. Published by The University of Chicago Press for the National Bureau of Economic Research. https://doi.org/10.1086/718663

Valerie Ramey expanded on comments made by the discussants and noted two reasons why women might reduce work that are not related to child care. The first is providing care to adult relatives. She mentioned anecdotal evidence that personal elder care in the San Diego area was pervasive during COVID, particularly in the Latino community. She argued that even those not increasing care may voluntarily quit a job to protect an elderly parent's health. She noted that discussant Loukas Karabarbounis's model was very helpful for thinking through these channels and could be extended to consider the whole family. The second channel is that secondary earners whose spouses increased work (e.g., because they work in an industry that expanded during the pandemic, such as construction) may reduce their hours to curtail health risk. The authors agreed with Ramey and the discussants that understanding the residual is very important. They further agreed that voluntary quits may have an impact, particularly by those wanting to minimize health exposure to the pandemic. This may be especially true for secondary earners not substantially contributing to family income, so the within-couple gender wage gap may play a role.

James Poterba noted that a common data need in calibrating Susceptible-Infected Recovered (SIR) models is contact matrices on interactions between different age groups. He suggested that to further evaluate the importance of caregiving responsibilities to elders, it may be important to unpack both the amount and nature of contact between age groups; for instance, whether contact with elders is employment-related or personal. The authors agreed.

Daron Acemoglu then commented that changes in child-care responsibilities could change the social norm going forward. This may lead to worse outcomes for gender equity in the future. The authors completely agreed that norms might be changing, but they hypothesized that it might be beneficial for gender equity. About 10% of households had the father take over more child-care responsibilities during the pandemic. This could lead to more paternal involvement down the road, either from learning by doing or role model effects. They further noted that fathers who can telecommute tend to do more child care. If telecommutability becomes more available, this could increase paternal involvement.

The authors concluded by thanking both discussants. Matthias Doepke agreed with Laura Pilossoph that the residual is a puzzle that should be fully explored. He noted that the discussion brought out some important mechanisms, and he added that the policy changes, such as the stimulus payments and increased unemployment benefits, could also have had an effect. In particular, in light of Loukas Karabarbounis's finding on the differences between labor supply flexibility, it may be that women reacted more to these policies. Michèle Tertilt added that she thought the increase in child-care costs of 100% in Loukas Karabarbounis's model, although seemingly very large, was reasonable, because the authors treated external child care as impossible (or an infinite increase in price) due to school closures. Karabarbounis agreed in the chat that 100% seemed right to him.

3

Shocks, Institutions, and Secular Changes in Employment of Older Individuals

Richard Rogerson, *Princeton University and NBER*, United States of America
Johanna Wallenius, *Stockholm School of Economics*, Sweden

I. Introduction and Background

Against a backdrop of lower fertility and increased longevity, employment levels of older individuals have become an important concern for policy makers in advanced economies. The motivation for this paper derives from figure 1, which plots the mean employment rate (i.e., employment divided by population) for males aged 55–64 for a balanced panel of 14 Organisation for Economic Co-operation and Development (OECD) economies for which there is consistent data from 1976 forward.[1]

The changes reflected in this figure are dramatic: between 1976 and 1995 the mean employment rate for this group dropped by more than 15 percentage points, only to increase by almost this same amount between 1995 and 2019. What is all the more remarkable about this figure is that the employment rate for older male workers had been declining for many decades prior to the 1970s, so that the increase since 1995 is reversing a decades-long period of declining employment rates for these workers.[2]

Understanding the factors that account for the dramatic changes in this figure is of interest in its own right in the broader context of the desire to understand the forces that shape labor supply. But it is of special importance for policy makers who want to forecast trends into the future and design appropriate policies going forward.

Although the qualitative pattern depicted in figure 1 is common to almost all of the 14 countries considered, there is considerable heterogeneity

NBER Macroeconomics Annual, volume 36, 2022.
© 2022 National Bureau of Economic Research. All rights reserved. Published by The University of Chicago Press for the National Bureau of Economic Research. https://doi .org/10.1086/718664

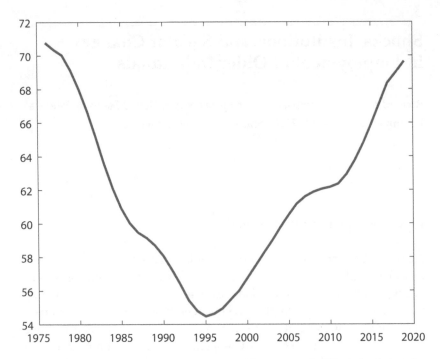

Fig. 1. Mean employment-to-population (Emp/Pop) rate, males 55–64. A color version of this figure is available online.

in the quantitative features of the U-shape across countries. Figure 2 plots 5-year moving averages for the employment-to-population ratios for males aged 55–64 for each of the 14 countries.

A complete understanding of the dynamics in figure 2 will ultimately require detailed analyses at the country level.[3] But the similarity of the qualitative pattern across countries suggests that the effort to understand the country-specific evolutions might usefully be framed within a common unifying framework. The main goal of this paper is to put forth a broad narrative that can serve to sketch this framework. Developing the main elements of our narrative reflects three features of our analysis: it contrasts outcomes across countries, it studies changes over a relatively long time period, and it seeks to understand changes in employment rates for older workers in the context of broader changes in the labor market.

Our narrative builds on the earlier literature on shocks and institutions (e.g., Bruno and Sachs 1985; Krugman 1994; Ljungqvist and Sargent 1998; Mortensen and Pissarides 1999; Blanchard and Wolfers 2000). Three facts motivated this literature. First, labor-market conditions as proxied by the unemployment rate worsened in almost all OECD economies starting in

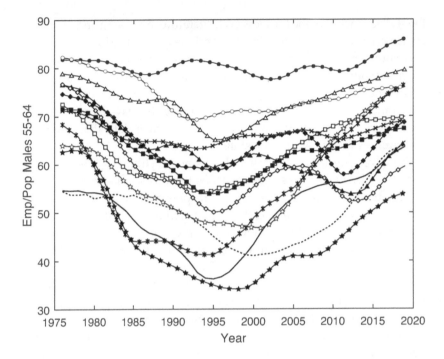

Fig. 2. Employment-to-population (Emp/Pop) rate, males 55–64 in 14 countries. A color version of this figure is available online.

the 1970s, and persisted throughout much of the 1980s. Second, the extent of deterioration varied significantly across economies. Third, there were persistent differences in labor-market institutions across countries.

This literature proposed the following broad narrative: the overall worsening of labor-market outcomes was due to a common shock (or series of shocks), and the variation in outcomes across economies arose because heterogeneous institutions differentially affected the propagation of the common shock within each economy.[4] Although some economies were plausibly more exposed to the shock, and institutions were not literally constant over time at their 1960s levels, the core message of the shocks and institutions literature was that a common shock propagated by heterogeneous institutions provided a good account for the cross-sectional heterogeneity in labor-market evolutions in the 1970s and 1980s. Notably, because this literature focused on aggregate outcomes, it did not single out the labor-market outcomes of any particular demographic group.

Similar to the earlier shocks and institutions literature, a key component of our proposed narrative is a common shock that negatively affected opportunities of all workers between 1970 and the mid-1990s. Given the stylized fact from the business cycle literature that young and old workers experience larger fluctuations than prime-aged individuals (e.g., Clark and Summers 1981; Gomme et al. 2004), it is perhaps not surprising that older individuals might also experience larger responses to low-frequency shocks. Beyond the business cycle evidence, a shock that favors new skills that complement technological change will plausibly have larger effects on older workers because they are more likely to have skills that lose value and are less able to learn new skills.

But diverging from the earlier shocks and institutions literature, our narrative also emphasizes heterogeneous responses in institutions as key to understanding the heterogeneity in responses shown in figure 2. Specifically, during the 1970s and 1980s, many countries instituted substantial expansions of what we will refer to as the "shadow social security system," thereby encouraging and accommodating the effective retirement of workers prior to reaching "normal" retirement age and entry into the formal social security system. Because many of these provisions were cut back following the mid-1990s, they constitute an additional U-shaped driving force affecting older workers in a subset of countries.

Summarizing, we argue that the dynamics in figure 1 should be understood as a combination of (at least) three processes. The first is a slow-moving trend component, reflecting the net effect of secular changes such as income, health, life expectancy, education, and the nature of work. A second process captures the effect of a low-frequency but mean-reverting negative shock to labor-market opportunities that affected all age groups, though more so in the case of older workers.[5] This process gives rise to U-shaped dynamics like those in figure 1. The third process is a temporary shock to institutional features in a subset of countries that served to significantly amplify the effect of the common shock on workers aged 55–64 in these countries. We argue that this third process is key to understanding both the magnitude of the changes in figure 1 and the heterogeneity in figure 2.[6]

By viewing the dynamics in figure 1 as largely reflecting deviations from a slow-moving trend, our narrative stands in contrast to much work studying the employment of older males. At the risk of oversimplifying, textbook discussions of this decades-long decline emphasize two key driving forces: the expansion of social security programs and secular increases in incomes.[7] To the extent that most advanced economies had instituted the key features of their social security programs by the early 1960s, explanations for the continued decline in employment rates of older males have tended to highlight ongoing increases in income.

However, it has also been recognized that the increases in income were happening alongside other secular trends that might plausibly increase employment rates for older males, including, for example, improvements in health, increases in life expectancy, and increases in educational attainment.[8] But viewed from the perspective of underlying secular trends, the widespread trend reversal following the mid-1990s is puzzling: none of the secular driving forces display trend breaks around this time, nor were there widespread changes to (formal) social security programs.[9]

For researchers wanting to connect the dynamics in figure 1 to secular trends, this has motivated a search for new trend factors that might have become important only during the 1990s. One such promising candidate was first proposed by Schirle (2008). The core mechanism in this narrative is that exogenous increases in employment rates for older females would decrease retirement incentives for older males if leisure times of couples are complements. It also holds that beginning in the 1960s, young women entered the labor market with different expectations regarding careers, leading to very significant cohort effects for female employment rates by age. Because the cohort of women that turned 20 in 1960 would turn 55 in 1995, it would be around this time that males aged 55–64 would be increasingly likely to be married to a female who was engaged in market work. In the first part of this paper, we present new evidence regarding this narrative and argue that it is unlikely to be a dominant factor in accounting for the pattern shown in figure 1. In fact, our evidence implies that rather than being a solution to the puzzle, the sharp increase in average employment rates for older females after the mid-1990s is just another piece of the puzzle that needs to be explained. Because the key elements of our narrative are gender neutral, it explains why both older males and females display large changes in employment rates in the mid-1990s.

A key question for policy makers is to forecast future employment rates of older individuals holding policy settings fixed. Our narrative has an important cautionary message for policy makers that would like to use the information in figure 1 to answer this question. Because we view much of the movement in figure 1 as reflecting responses to mean-reverting aggregate conditions and the temporary expansion and contraction of policy settings that directly affect the employment rates of older individuals, isolating the relevant trend component for predicting future changes holding policy fixed will require methods to isolate the trend components from the other factors at work.

The literature that our work relates to is too large to attempt to survey. But we single out two sources of particular interest. The first is the volume edited by Kohli et al. (1991) that summarizes the expansion of the shadow social security systems during the 1970s and 1980s in a large set of countries. The second source is the many volumes produced in the NBER series *Social Security Programs and Retirement around the World*, which has sought to provide ongoing comparable country-level studies on a variety of issues. The two most recent volumes (Coile, Milligan, and Wise 2019; Borsch-Supan and Coile 2020) are particularly relevant. Although our analysis touches on many issues that this series has addressed, we nonetheless believe our narrative offers a distinct perspective via its connection to the earlier shocks and institutions literature, its focus on mean-reverting factors, and its emphasis on analyzing the outcomes for older individuals in the context of broader labor-market developments.

Although our broad-brushstroke approach serves a useful purpose in organizing our thinking about the forces that shape the dynamics shown in figures 1 and 2, it also has some obvious limitations. First, we focus almost exclusively on highly aggregated data. Second, we do not complement our narrative with any quantitative model-based framework. As we discuss in the conclusion, important next steps in this research agenda are to document the facts at a more disaggregated level and to carry out rigorous country-level structural analyses that fully reflect the relevant context for older workers.[10]

We also offer one cautionary note to the reader. Although the United States is included in our sample of countries, we in no way focus on the particular case of the United States. We highlight this because the United States is the subject of much study and it turns out that the United States displays some but not all of the properties that hold more generally for other countries.[11] With this in mind, we caution the reader about interpreting all of our results from the perspective of a US benchmark.

An outline of the paper follows. In Section II, we discuss the key data sources and provide additional documentation regarding the key motivating fact displayed in figure 1. Section III presents evidence on the narrative emphasizing older female employment rates as the driving force behind the trend reversal found in figure 1. Section IV presents our alternative narrative and provides evidence in support of its key elements. Section V briefly overviews the evolution of the employment rate for individuals aged 65–69 and discusses how they fit with our proposed narrative. Section VI concludes and discusses directions for future research on this issue.

II.   Data

The main data for the second part of our analysis come from the OECD and relate to employment-to-population ratios by age and gender over the period 1960–2019.[12] The sample of countries that we study consists of 22 "advanced" economies: 16 from Europe, 2 from North America and 4 from Australasia. The year at which data first becomes available varies across countries, ranging from 1960 to 1994. Data availability also differs depending upon which age group we consider. In particular, there is less availability of data that considers employment-to-population ratios for each of the 55–59 and 60–64 age groups than for the 55–64 age group.[13] Although it is of interest to consider the 55–59 and 60–64 age groups separately, in the interests of space our core analysis will focus exclusively on the 55–64 group. In a later section, we will briefly examine the 65–69 age group.

For much of our analysis, we will be interested in a balanced panel and so will consider a sequence of balanced panels that differ by starting date and hence have different numbers of countries. Importantly, the key messages are robust across these different samples. Our smallest but longest panel begins in 1970 and includes Australia, Finland, Germany, Ireland, Italy, Japan, Sweden, and the United States. We will refer to this as panel 1. Panel 2 begins in 1972 and adds the Netherlands, Norway, and Spain. Panel 3 begins in 1976 and expands to include Canada, France, and Portugal. Panel 4 begins in 1984 and adds Belgium, Denmark, Greece, South Korea, and the United Kingdom. Panel 5 includes the remaining countries (Austria, New Zealand, and Switzerland) and begins in 1994.

For the first part of our analysis, we use data from the Luxembourg Income Study (LIS). This data allows us to examine employment-to-population ratios by age, gender, and marital status, which will be relevant for assessing the narrative that changes in the employment patterns of older females are a key factor in the trend reversal for males. Although this data set provides coverage for 17 of the countries in our sample, sample sizes vary and are quite small in some cases. In addition, the data are available at selected years rather than annually, and the sample period differs quite a bit across countries.

We close this section by providing a more thorough presentation of the motivating fact presented in the introduction in figure 1. Figure 3 plots the mean employment rate for males aged 55–64 for each of our five different balanced panels.

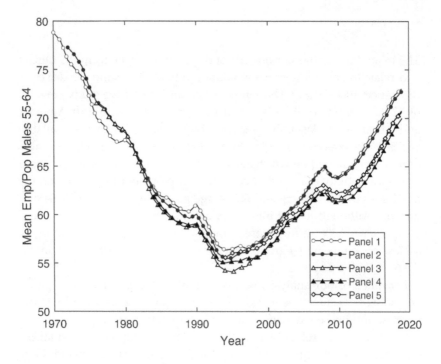

Fig. 3.   Mean employment-to-population (Emp/Pop) rate, males 55–64 by panel. A color version of this figure is available online.

Although each successive panel considers a shorter time period and a larger sample of countries, all five panels paint a consistent picture over any overlapping periods. Specifically, the key pattern that emerges is that the employment rate follows a U shaped pattern. It declines by a bit more than 20 percentage points between 1970 and the mid-1990s, at which point it reverses direction and begins a steady increase. From the mid-1990s to the end of our sample, 2019, the mean employment-to-population ratio has increased by about 15 percentage points. The effect of the Great Recession is clearly visible. As of 2019, the employment-to-population ratio is about 5 percentage points lower than it was in the early 1970s, about the same as it was in 1976, and higher than it was in 1984.

The magnitude of these changes is striking. The 20 percentage point decline between 1970 and the mid-1990s is as large as the much-studied increase in female employment rates over the period 1970–90. Although the changes are very large, a simple calculation provides useful perspective on the magnitudes. Consider a representative worker that is choosing a retirement date. If the worker retires at age 65 then the employment rate for males aged 55–64 will be 100%. Moving retirement up by 1 year will lead to a decrease of this ratio by 10 percentage points, so a 20 percentage point drop in the employment-to-population ratio for this group is equivalent to individuals choosing to retire 2 years earlier. Over a 25-year period, this would be achieved if each successive cohort retires 1 month sooner than its immediate predecessor.

If we view these changes from a lifetime perspective and consider for concreteness an individual that begins working at age 20, then a 2-year change in retirement age amounts to a less than 5% change in lifetime labor supply, so that each successive cohort is simply reducing lifetime labor supply by 0.2%. The key message here is that relatively small changes in lifetime labor supply can manifest themselves as extremely large changes in labor supply for a given age group if the change in labor supply is achieved through changes in retirement age.

III. Employment of Older Females: Driving Force or Part of the Puzzle?

In this section, we examine the narrative offered by Schirle (2008). As noted in the introduction, a key element of this narrative is that non-market work times of spouses are complements, so that holding all else constant, an exogenous increase in the employment rate for older women would decrease the value of leisure for older males, thereby creating a force for later retirement. As Schirle (2008) notes, because higher female employment also gives rise to an income effect, thereby generating an opposing force on male retirement, the complementarities between non-market times of spouses must be sufficiently strong to dominate the income effect. In the appendix, we carry out a simple exercise to explore the interaction of these two effects and the extent of complementarity that is needed to overcome the income effect. We also highlight that if the increase in female employment is accompanied by an increase in relative wages of females, it requires significantly more complementarity to overcome the income effects.

A first pass at assessing this narrative is shown in figure 4, which shows the employment rates for both males and females aged 55–64 for the same set of 14 countries as in figure 1.

The striking feature revealed by this figure is that the trend break in the employment rate series for older males occurs at virtually the same time as a trend break in the employment rate series for older females, thus lending support to the above narrative.

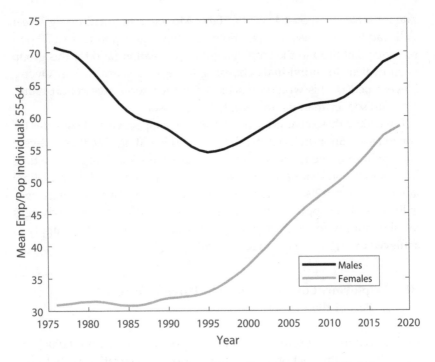

Fig. 4. Mean employment-to-population (Emp/Pop) rate for ages 55–64 by gender. A color version of this figure is available online.

Although figure 4 is consistent with the Schirle narrative, it is also consistent with an alternative narrative in which employment rates of both males and females are responding to some common factor. To address this concern, the other key element of the Schirle narrative is an argument for why the increase in employment rates for older females in the 1990s can plausibly be viewed as exogenous with regard to forces at work in the 1990s. In particular, it posits that beginning in the 1960s, young women entered the labor market with different expectations regarding careers, leading to very significant cohort effects for female employment rates by age. Because the cohort of women that turned 20 in 1960 would turn 55 in 1995, it would be around this time that males aged 55–64 would be increasingly likely to be married to a female who was engaged in market work.

In spite of the encouraging pattern reflected in figure 4, here we argue that the Schirle narrative is unlikely to be the dominant factor behind the trend reversal for males. Two facts support this position. First, examining micro data for a large set of countries, we show that the timing and magnitude of the trend reversal is effectively the same for males that live alone as it is for males that are married or living with a partner. This suggests that leisure complementarities are unlikely to be a dominant factor in explaining the trend reversal.[14]

Second, we argue that the timing of this narrative does not account for the time profile for females shown in figure 4. Using the lagged employment rate of females aged 45–54 as a way to control for cohort effects in the employment rate of females aged 55–64, we conclude that the sharp increase in employment rates for females aged 55–64 should have begun at least 10 years earlier. That is, the period prior to the mid-1990s is a period in which employment of older females is depressed relative to trend. Put somewhat differently, whereas the Schirle narrative proposes that female employment patterns are the solution to the puzzle, our analysis suggests that they are instead just another piece of a larger puzzle. Importantly, the narrative that we develop next does not emphasize gender-specific factors and so can account for why patterns are similar for both older males and older females.

A. Employment Rates and Living Arrangements

The publicly available OECD data does not allow us to break down employment-to-population ratios by age, gender, and living arrangements (i.e., living alone versus married or living with a partner). For this reason, we turn to data from the LIS, which does allow us to examine the data at this level of disaggregation. As noted earlier, two drawbacks of this data set are that the coverage is less than annual and the sample sizes are somewhat small for some countries.

In the interests of space, here we present figures showing the evolution for six countries: the three countries that Schirle (2008) originally studied (Canada, the United Kingdom, and the United States) and three countries that experienced particularly large swings in male employment (Finland, Germany, and the Netherlands). Results are shown in figure 5.

The message from all six of these plots is the same: although there are level differences between the employment rates of males aged 55–64 with different living arrangements, the timing and magnitude of trend reversals are very similar across the two groups. Although this does not imply that leisure time complementarities do not play any role, it does cast doubt on their being the dominant factor behind the trend reversal.[15]

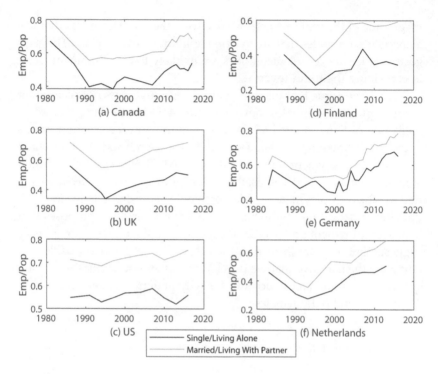

Fig. 5. Employment-to-population (Emp/Pop) rate, males 55–64 by living arrangements. A color version of this figure is available online.

B. Timing of Employment Changes for Older Females

Although the data just presented already cast doubt on the narrative that emphasizes higher female employment as the key driving force, it is instructive to consider another element of this narrative: the timing of the increase in the employment rate for older females. As previously shown in figure 4, there is a sharp increase in the trend growth of the employment rate for older females in the mid-1990s. A key element of the Schirle narrative is that this change in trend growth rates is the result of changes in female labor supply choices originating several decades previously, which in turn create ripple effects as the successive cohorts age.

This logic suggests that the growth in employment rates for females aged 45–54 between year $t-10$ and year $t-1$ should be a good proxy for the "exogenous" component of the growth in employment rates for females aged 55–64 between years t and $t+9$. In what follows we examine this relationship in both averaged across countries and each of several individual countries.

We start by presenting results based on cross-country averages. Because this exercise involves lags, we implicitly lose the first 10 years of data, making it useful to have the longest panel possible. For this reason, we carry out this exercise using panel 1, which starts in 1970 and consists of six countries. Figure 6 displays the results, where both series are normalized to zero in 1980 to focus attention on the relative trends.

The striking result is that based on this calculation, the employment rate of older females "should" have been growing steadily throughout the entire decade of the 1980s but in fact was effectively flat up until the mid-1990s. Put somewhat differently, the gap between the actual employment rate for females aged 55–64 and its predicted value based on cohort effect dynamics grew increasingly larger during the entire period from 1980 through to the mid-1990s.

Next we examine the dynamics for six individual countries: Australia, Finland, France, Italy, Sweden, and the United States. Results are displayed in figure 7. In these figures, we plot the gap between the two curves that were displayed in figure 6, with a negative value indicating

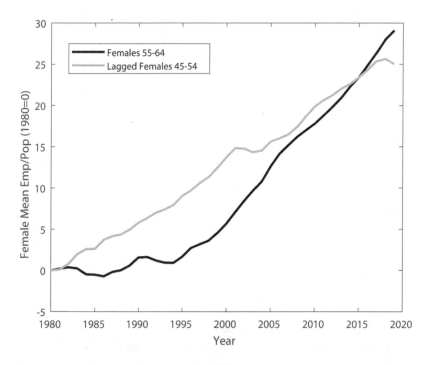

Fig. 6.   Predicted versus actual employment to population (Emp/Pop), females 55–64. A color version of this figure is available online.

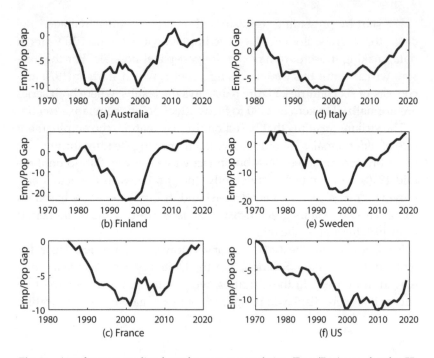

Fig. 7.   Actual versus predicted employment-to-population (Emp/Pop) gap, females 55–64. A color version of this figure is available online.

that the actual employment rate for females aged 55–64 lies below what would have been predicted based on lagged growth in the employment rate of females aged 45–54. Initial values are normalized to zero.

There are some differences across countries, but in each of these six cases we see the U-shaped dynamics that we saw in the plots for the employment rates of males aged 55–64. In several cases, the terminal value is close to zero, implying that by 2019 the overall change in the employment rate for females aged 55–64 is very close to what one would predict based on the lagged growth in the employment rate for females aged 45–54. Of course, there is no need for these to be the same, as there may well be changes in an economy that differentially affect the two groups.[16] Interestingly, the timing of the troughs for these plots is in many cases quite similar to the timing of the troughs for males.

The key message that we take away from this exercise is that once we control for cohort effects, the mid-1990s are a turning point not only for the employment behavior of males aged 55–64 but also for that of females aged 55–64. Rather than providing an answer to the puzzle regarding the trend reversal for older male employment rates, a closer examination of employment rate dynamics for older females leads us to conclude that they are actually just another piece of the same puzzle. The narrative that we describe in the next section will shed light on the common dynamics for older male and female workers.

IV.   A New Narrative: Shocks and Institutions Version 2.0

This section presents evidence to support the narrative outlined in the introduction. We proceed in three steps. In the first subsection, we document the following fact:

Fact 1.   Countries that display a larger decline in the employment rate of older males prior to the mid-1990s also display a larger increase in the period after the 1990s.

The significance of this fact is that it establishes an intimate relationship between the changes prior to the mid-1990s and those subsequent to the mid-1990s. This is important for two reasons. First, if the changes since the mid-1990s were due to the appearance of a new trend factor, it would be an unlikely coincidence that the effect of this new factor across countries would be strongly correlated with the changes associated with the distinct set of factors at play prior to the mid-1990s. Second, to the extent that changes before and after the mid-1990s are intimately related, it suggests that analyses should jointly consider changes over the two periods.

In the second subsection, we document the following two facts:

Fact 2.   The trend change for the employment rate of older males that occurs in the mid-1990s is not unique to older males. For each of the age groups 15–24, 25–34, 35–44, and 45–54, the mean employment rate across countries also displays a trend change in the mid-1990s. In particular, for each of these groups the secular pattern is a decline until the mid-1990s followed by a modest recovery that is eventually interrupted by the Great Recession.

Fact 3.   Countries with the largest decrease in the employment rate for prime-aged males (35–44) prior to the mid-1990s also have the largest decrease in the employment rate for older males.

These two facts are significant because they suggest a need to analyze employment changes for older individuals in the context of broader changes affecting all age groups. In particular, the decline in the employment rate of older males in the 1970s and 1980s should not simply be assumed to reflect the continuation of the processes that had been operating prior to the 1970s.

In the process of documenting the above facts, we will also establish that the magnitude of the low-frequency movements in the employment rate of males aged 55–64 is much greater than for prime-aged males. In particular, although the overall change between 1976 and 2019 is quite similar across age groups, the depth of the U-shape is much more pronounced for older males.

The third subsection documents the following fact:

Fact 4.   The drop in the employment rate of males aged 55–64 relative to the drop in the employment rate of males aged 45–54 between the mid-1970s and the mid-1990s varies significantly across countries.

Loosely speaking, the countries with the largest declines in the employment rate of males aged 55–64 seem to exhibit "excess" volatility in this employment rate series. This leads us to highlight the role of institutional responses as a reaction to the overall worsening of aggregate labor-market conditions. We briefly summarize the set of institutional responses for a sample of countries.

Taken together these facts highlight the important role of the three features of our analysis: contrasting outcomes across countries, focusing on a relatively long time period (at least back to the early to mid-1970s), and considering employment changes for older individuals in the context of overall employment changes.

A.   Mean Reversion

For the results presented here, we focus on the sample of countries represented by panel 3, which consists of 14 countries and starts in 1976. Table 1 reports the year in which the minimum value of the employment rate for males aged 55–64 occurs, the absolute value of the change

Table 1
Timing and Magnitude of Trend Reversals in Employment-to-Population Rate for Males 55–64

	t_{min}	$|\Delta_{1976,t_{min}}|$	$|\Delta_{2019,t_{min}}|$		t_{min}	$|\Delta_{1976,t_{min}}|$	$|\Delta_{2019,t_{min}}|$
AUS	1993	22.4	18.2	JAP	2002	5.8	10.0
CAN	1995	19.6	15.1	NET	1993	28.7	37.8
FIN	1995	21.5	29.9	NOR	1991	12.8	7.9
FRA	1998	28.7	21.6	POR	2012	26.0	14.9
GER	2000	18.3	30.7	SPA	1995	29.4	12.7
IRE	2012	20.1	15.5	SWE	1994	15.8	15.5
ITA	2001	14.3	24.2	US	1994	8.6	7.2

from 1976 to the year of the minimum, and the absolute value of the change from the year of the minimum to 2019.

The large declines in the years after 1976 are largely transitory (the mean decrease prior to the minimum is equal to 19.4 percentage points, and the mean increase following the minimum is equal to 18.7 percentage points) and the decreases prior to the minimum value being reached are highly correlated with the subsequent increases; the correlation between the decline and increase on either side of the minimum is 0.48.[17] Figure 8 presents a scatter plot of the absolute value of the decreases and increases for the 14 countries in panel 3, plus a linear regression line.

B. Negative Labor-Market Shocks in the 1970s and 1980s

An important diagnostic in the effort to understand the striking changes in the employment rate for males aged 55–64 is its behavior relative to other age groups. With this in mind, figure 9 has four panels that are analogous to figure 3 but for four other age groups: 15–24, 25–34, 35–44, and 45–54.

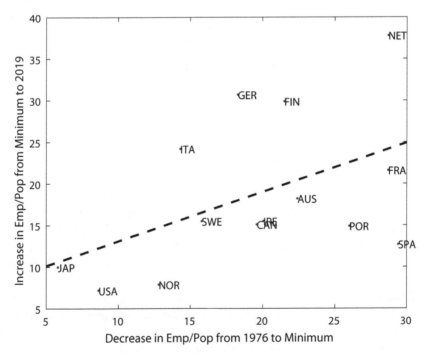

Fig. 8. Mean reversion in employment to population (Emp/Pop), males 55–64. A color version of this figure is available online.

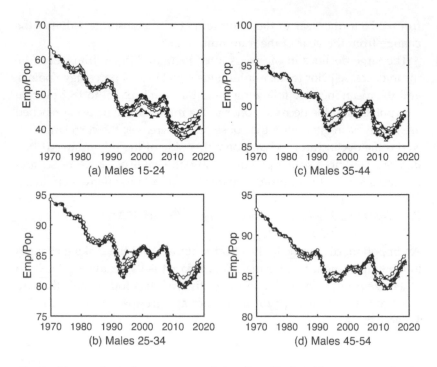

Fig. 9. Mean male employment-to-population (Emp/Pop) rate by age group. A color version of this figure is available online.

Each of the panels in figure 9 has its own scale to best illustrate the invariance of the key patterns across our samples. For purposes of comparing the results across age groups, it is useful to present results for all of the age groups in a single figure, which is done in figure 10 for the countries in panel 2.

We highlight three features of this figure. First, for all age groups, mean male employment-to-population ratios decrease significantly from 1970 to the mid-1990s. Second, subsequent to the mid-1990s, there is a modest recovery for all age groups other than 15–24, though this recovery is disrupted by the Great Recession.[18] (For those aged 15–24, the employment rate stabilizes in the mid-1990s, but there is no evidence of a subsequent recovery.) Third, both the decline and subsequent recovery for males aged 55–64 are much larger than for any of the prime-aged groups.

To highlight the connection between the changes in employment-to-population ratios across age groups, we compute the correlation coefficient between the declines in the employment rates for prime age (35–44)

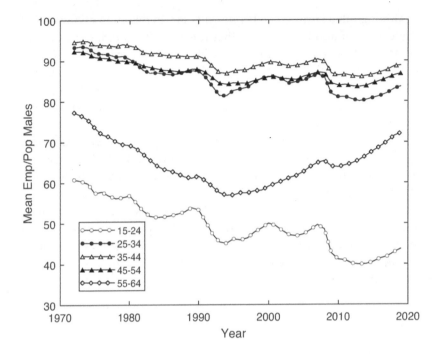

Fig. 10.   Mean employment to population (Emp/Pop) for males by age. A color version of this figure is available online.

and older (55–64) males between 1976 and 1995, using the 14 countries in panel 3. The two are highly positively correlated with a correlation coefficient of 0.69.

C.   The Role of Changing Institutions

Given the evidence presented thus far, our narrative might appear to be nothing more than a minor extension of the earlier shocks and institutions in which we explicitly note the impact on older individuals. That is, a common shock (or series of shocks) had adverse effects on overall labor-market outcomes in all economies, but the effects differed across economies, plausibly because of preexisting differences in institutions. The earlier literature did not emphasize how the effects within an economy might vary across age groups, but if one makes the additional plausible assumption that older individuals are more vulnerable to the types of shocks being experienced, then this would also account for the qualitatively different evolutions across age groups.

Although this narrative gets one quite far, in this subsection we first argue that an additional factor that directly affects older individuals differentially across countries seems likely to help account for the observed patterns. We then argue that this additional factor is plausibly related to differential institutional changes across countries that directly affect older workers by documenting specific institutional changes in a handful of countries.

We begin by contrasting the relative employment rate dynamics across age groups for two subsamples of panel 2. Subsample 1 (S1) consists of Australia, Canada, Ireland, Japan, Norway, and the United States. Subsample 2 (S2) consists of Finland, France, Germany, Italy, and Sweden.[19] For now we simply note that this partition is consistent with our reading of the literature that documents the extent of institutional changes in the period leading up to the mid-1990s. Figure 11 displays two curves for each subsample: the employment rate for males aged 45–54 and the employment rate for males aged 55–64.

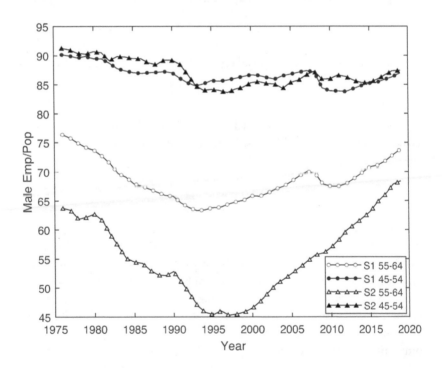

Fig. 11. Male employment-to-population (Emp/Pop) rate by age in two subsamples. A color version of this figure is available online.

Several properties of this figure are notable. First, note that for each subsample, the turning point for males aged 45–54 lines up closely with the turning point for males aged 55–64, though the turning points differ across the two subsamples by about 5 years. Second, although employment rates in 1976 are very similar for males aged 45–54 across the two subsamples, these rates are already quite different across the two subsamples for males aged 55–64. Third, although movements in the employment rate for males aged 45–54 are quantitatively quite similar across subsamples, the magnitude of movements in the employment rates for males aged 55–64 are dramatically larger in subsample 2.

It is the third property that we focus on in this subsection. An alternative way to summarize this property is to say that the elasticity of the employment rate for males aged 55–64 with respect to the employment rate for males aged 45–54 is much larger in subsample 2 than it is in subsample 1. One possibility is that this differential elasticity is explained by differences in institutions that already existed in 1970. Although there is reason to believe that this plays some role, another possibility is that the countries in subsample 2 initiated reforms in response to the shock that served to amplify its effect on males aged 55–64. Note that for this second possibility to be quantitatively important it should be the case that there were institutional changes after the mid-1990s that served to offset the effects of earlier institutional changes, a point we will document later for a sample of countries.

As another perspective on this issue, we examine the evolution of the cross-sectional dispersion of employment-to-population ratios. Figure 12 plots the time series evolution of the standard deviation of the log of employment-to-population ratios in the cross-section of countries for panel 3. To highlight the distinctive dynamics for the 55–64 age group, we also plot the same statistic for the other age groups.

The most striking feature of this figure is that the substantial variation in the extent of the decline following 1976 leads to a dramatic increase of cross-sectional dispersion in the employment-to-population ratio for older males across countries, and that the subsequent increase following the mid-1990s leads to roughly an equal decrease, so that dispersion changes relatively little between 1976 and 2019.

Although the changes in cross-sectional dispersion for the oldest age group are the single most striking feature of this figure, it is important to note that a similar hump-shaped pattern is found for each of the other three age groups prior to the Great Recession. This is consistent with the earlier shocks and institutions literature that emphasized heterogeneity

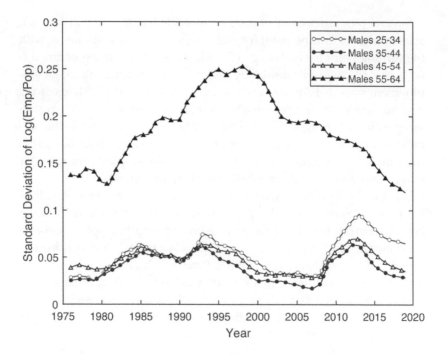

Fig. 12. Standard deviation of log male employment-to-population (Emp/Pop) rate by age. A color version of this figure is available online.

in responses at an aggregate level.[20] But importantly, the heterogeneity in responses for older individuals is much larger than the heterogeneity for other age groups.

The idea that institutional change during the 1970s and 1980s specifically targeted at older workers played a key role in the relatively large decline in their employment rate in a large set of countries is not a new one. A large literature has documented the many and varied policies enacted by various governments with the explicit goal of allowing older individuals to get by without working. (For an excellent detailed study of measures adopted in several economies, see Kohli et al. [1991].)

Importantly, whereas much previous work on the employment of older individuals has often focused on permanent features of social security rules, the relevant policy changes in this context are dominated by temporary changes to other programs that are best viewed as having created a shadow social security system. For example, some countries adopted rules that created special programs within the unemployment insurance (UI) system to allow older workers to receive benefits for a longer period of time and create a bridge to the official retirement age. As we describe below, these programs would sometimes create a pathway for an individual to receive UI for as long as 10 years starting at age 55. Other countries relaxed rules allowing older individuals to go on disability. Some adopted rules whereby older workers that were laid off would be eligible for early social security if the firm replaced the individual with a younger worker. In some cases, these changes took place via a change in the way that state agencies interpreted the policy rules about eligibility and so were not at all reflected in any statutory change in policy. One example is the issue of whether difficulty finding work for an older individual is a valid criterion for receipt of disability.

The diverse nature of the various institutional changes that were implemented makes it challenging to produce meaningful and comparable summary measures that can be used for more formal or rigorous cross-country comparisons.[21] For this reason, we will simply summarize the experiences of a few countries to illustrate some of the rather extraordinary measures that were taken. But before doing so we want to address two other issues. The first concerns motivation for the expansion of the shadow social security systems: Why did these countries adopt measures specifically targeting older individuals? The second concerns the timing of the subsequent contraction of these shadow social security programs: If the trend reversal in employment rates for males aged 55–64 is at least in part due to the gradual reduction in these measures targeted at older individuals, then why was the timing of these reforms so similar across countries?

Regarding the first issue, we highlight two points. First, older workers generally fare much worse following displacement than do younger workers. Research has shown that older workers subjected to layoffs experience both longer duration of unemployment spells and larger wage losses upon reemployment (e.g., Farber 1997). It follows that these workers will plausibly be the most affected by the type of economic restructuring that took place in response to the shocks of the 1970s and 1980s. Whether due to their concerns for overall well-being or political pressure brought by groups representing older workers, this reality might naturally lead policy makers to take special steps to shield older workers from the effects of diminished labor-market opportunities.

Second, amid the broad deterioration in overall labor-market opportunities, policy makers in several countries subscribed to the so-called "lump of labor" fallacy, which held that there were a fixed number of jobs available, so creating an employment opportunity for one individual required removing another individual from employment. In some European economies that were experiencing sharp increases in unemployment among young people, policy makers thought that encouraging older workers to leave the labor force would serve to create opportunities for younger individuals. Importantly, this rationalization implied that policy might actively encourage older workers in stable employment relationships to leave the labor force.

Why such synchronicity in the reversal of these reforms? Here we note three factors that we think are relevant. First and most important were the fiscal consequences of the accumulated reforms. The fiscal burden associated with supporting so many individuals out of work led to large budget deficits, especially in those countries with the most aggressive policy changes. These fiscal pressures would naturally be highly correlated across economies. Moreover, the planned adoption of the euro was associated with pressures for fiscal reform and so necessarily created a desire for fiscal reform that was correlated across many of the economies in our sample. Second, and related, several European economies experienced severe contractions in overall economic activity in the early to mid-1990s and policy makers came to feel that broad-based reforms were necessary. And third, policy makers came to realize the fallacy of the "lump of labor" perspective, therefore removing some of the initial rationale for the reforms that had been adopted.[22]

In the remainder of this subsection, we briefly summarize the institutional changes adopted in a few countries as a way to illustrate the types of changes that occurred. Specifically, we will highlight changes in Finland, France, Germany, and the Netherlands.

Finland

Finland is a striking example of how the UI system can be used to create a shadow social security system.[23] This system is known as the "unemployment tunnel" and consists of a few distinct programs that can be pieced together sequentially.

One piece is the unemployment pension. Beginning in the early 1970s, long-term unemployed individuals over the age of 60 became eligible for unemployment pension after collecting earnings-related unemployment benefits for 200 working days. The eligibility age was lowered to 58 in 1978 and lowered again to 55 in 1980.[24]

A second piece is extended benefits. In 1991, older individuals became entitled to earnings-related unemployment benefits until reaching the eligibility age for unemployment pension, provided they had reached the age of 55 by the time the normal unemployment benefit should have ended. Because the maximum duration for unemployment benefit collection for other age groups is roughly 2 years, this policy meant that individuals could potentially collect earnings-related unemployment benefits from age 53 until the official retirement age. This would be achieved by a combination of three separate UI programs: the regular program from age 53 to 55, the extended benefits program for older individuals from age 55 to 60, and the unemployment pension from age 60 to 65. It is this sequence of programs that is referred to as the unemployment tunnel.

One additional change was also implemented in the early 1990s. Prior to the 1990s, older individuals (i.e., individuals ages 57) could collect unemployment benefits for a maximum of 900 working days. But few individuals hit this maximum in practice, as under legislation introduced in 1987 older individuals were entitled to subsidized employment after a 1-year unemployment spell. But during the 1990s recession, the requirement to provide subsidized employment was lifted.

Starting in the mid-1990s Finland undertook a series of reforms to weaken the unemployment tunnel. In 1997, the eligibility age for the extended benefit entitlement period was increased from 53 to 55. Around the same time, the generosity of the unemployment pension benefits was reduced. A number of additional reforms to old-age retirement were implemented in 2005. These included a flexible retirement age with substantial deductions for early claiming, as well as basing the old-age retirement benefit on lifetime earnings rather than earnings from the best 10 years.

France

France is another example of how the UI system was used to initially provide income security for older workers who became displaced.[25] In 1972, the system was expanded to provide protection for older displaced workers, providing a guaranteed income to dismissed workers age 60 or older. In 1977, the system was expanded to provide access to workers aged 60 and older who quit voluntarily, making it a de facto early retirement scheme. Interestingly, these provisions for UI were actually costlier than the provisions that these workers would have received if they had instead been moved to the official social security system.

In fact, understanding the fiscal reality of the situation, in 1983 the government gave in to long-standing pressure from the unions to lower the official retirement age from 65 to 60, for the simple reason that doing so would actually reduce expenses. Not surprisingly, the lowering of the official retirement age in 1983 had no discernible effect on the employment rate of workers aged 55–64. This is because the preexisting UI reforms had already created a shadow social security system with a retirement age of 60. This episode serves as an important reminder of the importance of shadow social security programs and a cautionary tale of the danger of not accounting for the features of the shadow social security programs when evaluating the effect of changes in features of the formal social security program.

There has been a series of reforms in France in the 1990s and 2000s, starting in 1993. The number of years used to compute the retirement benefit was increased from the best 10 to the best 25 years. Required contributions were raised from 37.5 to 40 years, and later further to 41 years. The reforms in the 2000s also introduced increased benefits for delayed retirement and raised both the minimum and full retirement ages by 2 years.

Because the 1983 changes effectively codified the expansion of the shadow social security system into the formal social security system, the subsequent contractions have largely occurred within the formal social security system.

Germany

Germany provides an excellent example of the complexity of the features and circumstances that combine to define the shadow social security system. First, it illustrates the importance of both institutional features in place prior to the 1970s and changes that occurred over time in response to changing labor-market outcomes. Second, it shows that some changes were purposeful actions taken by policy makers whereas others became effective because of court decisions challenging the interpretation of statutes. Third, it illustrates the use of multiple pathways: the disability system and the UI system. In addition, the reforms in Germany since 1990 are clear evidence about policy actions taken to contract the shadow social security system, though several of these reflect changes in the formal social security system. A brief overview of these changes follows.[26]

Prior to 1970 the German social security system stipulated that 65 was the normal retirement age. However, dating back to 1957, the system had a stipulation that allowed an individual to collect a pension at age 60 if they had experienced at least 52 weeks of unemployment during the previous 1.5 years. Although this provision had little impact prior to the 1970s, it would become an important element of the early retirement pathway when labor-market prospects deteriorated. In 1973, the system was revised to allow for early retirement at age 63 with no actuarial reduction in benefits. In 1976, a court ruling stipulated that inability to find suitable employment became a criterion for receiving disability. Between 1978 and 1980 the eligibility age for old-age handicapped pensions was reduced from 62 to 60.

The late 1980s witnessed a series of expansions in the duration of UI benefits for older individuals. In 1985, the maximum duration was increased from 12 to 18 months for those aged 49 and older. In 1986, the duration was increased to 20 months for those aged 49–53 and to 24 months for those age 54 and older. In 1987, the duration was extended to 32 months for those 54 and older. Additional changes in the mid-1980s created financial incentives for firms to lay off workers aged 58 and older if they replaced them with a currently unemployed individual.

The German retirement system has subsequently been scaled back through a series of reforms, starting in 1992, reflecting changes in both the shadow social security system and the formal social security system. The 1992 reform introduced a gradual change of eligibility ages for pensions for women and unemployed individuals from age 60 to 65 and for disability pensions from age 60 to 63. Actuarial adjustments, with age 65 as the benchmark, were also implemented as part of the reform. (Prior to 1992, adjustment of benefits based on the age at retirement were only implicit via the number of years of contributions.) Another major change was the indexing of benefits to net rather than gross wages. Subsequent reforms in the 2000s have represented a shift away from a uniform system to a multipillar system with supplementary occupational and private pensions. The 2007 reform also increased the statutory retirement age from 65 to 67.

Netherlands

Generous early retirement plans were introduced in the mid-1970s with the explicit goal of replacing old workers with young ones.[27] There were two widely utilized pathways into early retirement, a pay-as-you-go early retirement program and a disability scheme. The early exit options were very generous, with replacement rates of up to 80% already at age 55.

A series of reforms in the 1990s and 2000s has curtailed disability insurance. In 1992, insurance premiums of employers with increased disability incidence were raised. In 1993, disability benefits became dependent on earnings histories, which lowered replacement rates for workers who went on disability at younger ages. Stricter medical eligibility criteria and more intensive follow-ups for disability benefit recipients were introduced in 2002. A new program was introduced in 2006 with the goal of distinguishing between fully/permanently disabled and partially/temporarily disabled individuals. The program aimed at getting disabled workers back to work.

During the same time period, the early retirement program has also been scaled back. In 1997, the program was replaced by less generous prepension arrangements with penalties for early benefit claiming. A further law change in 2006 eliminated fiscal advantages of early retirement schemes and made them more actuarially fair.

V.   Patterns for Males Aged 65–69

Our analysis has thus far focused on the dynamics in the employment rate for males aged 55–64. In doing so we found it useful to examine the dynamics for this group in the broader context of the employment rate dynamics experienced by males from younger age groups. It is similarly of interest to examine the behavior of males in an older age group, so in this section we examine the employment rate dynamics of males aged 65–69. One limiting issue is that the OECD data are more limited for this particular age group. For this reason, our analysis will focus on a somewhat smaller set of countries and a somewhat shorter time period.

We begin by presenting the dynamics for the employment rate of males aged 65–69 for the six countries that have data available prior to 1980: Australia, Canada, France, Norway, Sweden, and the United States. As before, we plot 5-year moving averages to better highlight the secular trends. Results are shown in figure 13.

Three features stand out. First, for each country this age group exhibits the same U-shaped dynamics that we observed for other age groups. Second, in most cases the bottom of the U tends to be quite flat; although the decline effectively ceases as early as the mid-1980s for several countries, the sharp increases mostly occur in the 2000s. Third, for the four countries with the earliest starting dates for data (France, Norway, Sweden, and the United States), the terminal employment rate remains below its value from the early 1970s. For Canada and Australia the terminal employment rate exceeds its initial value, but it is likely that this is an artifact of the earlier data being censored.[28]

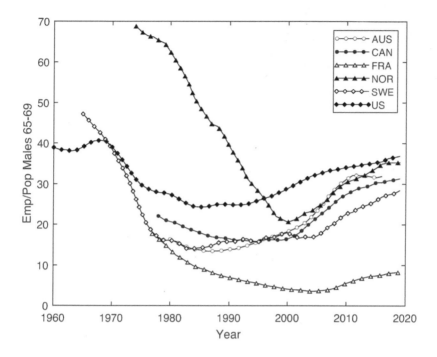

Fig. 13. Employment-to-population (Emp/Pop) rate, males 65–69. A color version of this figure is available online.

Figure 13 suggests that the 2000s are of particular interest for studying the increase in the employment rate for males aged 65–69. Because we also have a full balanced panel for this age group starting in 2002, we will focus on this time period in what follows. Figure 14 shows the behavior of the sample means for the employment rates of both the 55–64 and 65–69 age groups.

Both curves display a steady upward trend. The increase for the group aged 55–64 is about 11 percentage points, and the corresponding increase for the group aged 65–69 is about 8 percentage points. In comparing these numbers, it is useful to be mindful of the fact that the age intervals are of different length; a given percentage point increase in the employment rate for each of the two groups corresponds to an increase in person-years of employment that is twice as large for the 55–64 group.[29]

Next we focus on the cross-sectional relationship between the changes in the two employment rates. Figure 15 displays a scatter plot, where each point represents one of the countries in our sample.

Two features stand out. First, there is a positive correlation between the two changes, with the correlation coefficient being 0.33. But second,

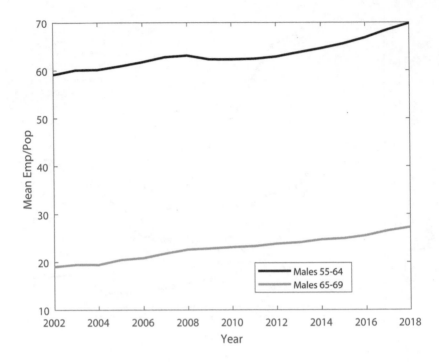

Fig. 14. Mean employment-to-population (Emp/Pop) rate for older males. A color version of this figure is available online.

the relationship seems to exhibit a sharp nonlinearity: if we focus on the countries for which the employment rate for males aged 55–64 increased by less than 15 percentage points, we see a very tight positive relationship, whereas for those countries with an increase in the employment rate for males aged 55–64 of more than 15 percentage points there appears to be no relationship.

To highlight this, figure 16 shows the scatter plot when we restrict attention to those countries that had increases of less than 15 percentage points.

Consistent with the previous discussion, this figure shows a very tight positive relationship, and the correlation coefficient is now 0.76.

The countries that are excluded from this plot are Austria, Belgium, Finland, France, Germany, Italy, and the Netherlands. Notably, this list is composed entirely of Western European countries and includes the four countries we highlighted in the previous section to exemplify countries that adopted policy changes that served to amplify the response of employment rates for individuals aged 55–64.

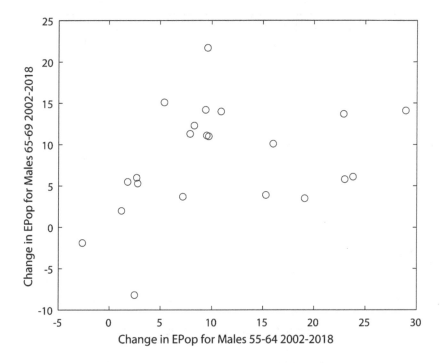

Fig. 15. Change in employment-to-population (EPop) rate for older males: full sample. A color version of this figure is available online.

To connect this evidence with our earlier narrative, recall that our narrative emphasizes two factors. First, there is a low-frequency and mean-reverting negative shock that affects labor markets over the period from the mid-1970s through to the present. Second, in some but not all countries, superimposed upon this underlying process is a process of institutional reform that first expands and later contracts the shadow social security system options available to individuals in the 55–64 age group, thereby amplifying the changes for this group. Because individuals in the 65–69 age range are affected by the true social security system rather than the shadow social security system, it is plausible to assume that they are relatively unaffected by this process of expansion and contraction of the shadow social security system.

Under this assumption, we would expect to see the sort of nonlinear relationship pictured in figure 15. For countries in which the process of institutional reform was relatively modest, the changes in employment rates for males aged 55–64 and 65–69 are largely driven by common factors and hence should be highly correlated.[30] But for those countries in

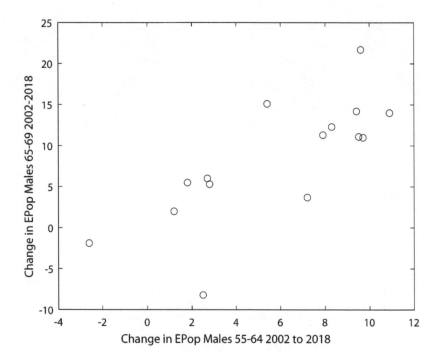

Fig. 16. Change in male employment-to-population (EPop) rate for older males: restricted sample. A color version of this figure is available online.

which the process of institutional reform had a large impact on males in the 55–64 age group, this correlation should be much less evident.

VI.   Conclusion and Directions for Future Research

The goal of this paper has been to offer a new narrative for understanding the changes in employment rates of older males as previously displayed in figure 1. Key to this narrative is that much of the decline between the mid-1970s and the mid-1990s should be understood as the result of negative shocks to aggregate labor markets as well as temporary policy measures that amplified the effects of these shocks on older males. In particular, much of the increase in the post-1995 period should be interpreted as reflecting reversion to the mean as opposed to a new "trend." We also argued that employment rates for older females experienced similar dynamics relative to trend and that our narrative can also explain why older females experienced similar dynamics.

Our analysis has focused on the broad brushstrokes associated with this narrative and so is only a first step toward a deeper understanding of the evolution of employment rates for older males. In this final section, we want to highlight what we see as four important next steps.

First, our analysis has relied almost exclusively on aggregate data. An important next step is to document the key changes over time in each country at a disaggregated level using micro data. Ideally this would be done using data that allows us to follow individuals over time to better understand the patterns of withdrawal from employment.

Second, more work needs to be done to generate comprehensive information on the family of institutional features that describe the relevant context for older workers across countries. This will be necessary for carrying out more rigorous analyses of the effects of policies on older workers. The contributions in Borsch-Supan and Coile (2020) are an important step in this direction.

Third, more effort should be directed to documenting and modeling the heterogeneous situations faced by older individuals in the labor market to better understand retirement dynamics. Whereas some individuals leave the workforce on account of having amassed sufficient resources to cover their retirement years, others are leaving despite having amassed few resources but because they have very poor prospects for paid employment. Relative to younger workers, older workers face both different shocks and different prospects following these shocks.

Fourth, and related to the previous point, the implications of the changing employment rates for older males need to be studied from a welfare perspective, and in particular need to be combined with an analysis of wage dynamics. The programs that were expanded during the 1970s and 1980s to help older workers did serve to shield these workers from the effects of adverse shocks. As these programs have contracted, many older individuals find themselves employed but much more susceptible to adverse shocks. Recent studies have begun to document these effects. See, for example, Visser et al. (2016) for the case of the Netherlands and Buchholz, Rinklake, and Blossfeld (2013) for the case of Germany.

Appendix

In this appendix, we study a simple model of family labor supply in which the nonmarket times of the two spouses are complements and report the results of some simple exercises. The household has utility from (joint) household consumption (C) and household nonmarket work time (N):

$$\log C + \frac{a}{1 - \frac{1}{\gamma}} N^{1 - \frac{1}{\gamma}}$$

where household nonmarket work time is a constant elasticity of substitution (CES) aggregate of the nonmarket work time for the male (n_m) and female (n_f) members of the household:

$$N = [a_m n_m^\rho + a_f n_f^\rho]^{1/\rho}.$$

Each individual has one unit of time and divides their time between market work, denoted by h, and nonmarket work, denoted by $n = 1 - h$. Wages are denoted by w_g for individual of gender g, and the household maximizes utility subject to the budget equation:

$$C = w_f h_f + w_m h_m.$$

We can use this simple model to think about retirement by interpreting it as a model of lifetime choices rather than choices in a particular period. That is, one can think of the variable h as measuring the length of the working life. Although somewhat abstract, the simplicity of the model allows one to focus on two key forces in a very transparent setting: income effects and complementarity of nonmarket work times.

To explore these forces quantitatively, we carry out the following exercise. First, we choose parameters so the model captures outcomes prior to the trend reversal in the mid-1990s. For our benchmark specification we consider the limiting case as γ tends to unity so that family preferences are log linear in C and N. We normalize male wages to unity and set female wages equal to 0.80. The preference parameter a cannot be determined separately from the scale of a_m and a_f so we also normalize a_m to unity. We will consider various values of ρ, but for each value of ρ we will calibrate values for a and a_f to target the length of working lives for males and females. Assuming an adult lifetime of 60 years, we target values of $h_m = 0.7$ and $h_f = 0.5$ so that men work 40% more than women.

We now carry out three exercises. In the first exercise, we simply increase h_f exogenously from 0.5 to 0.6. In subsequent exercises, we will consider changes in fundamentals, but in this exercise we do not motivate why this increase happens and instead are simply asking what the optimal response of male working time would be in response to this exogenous increase.

In the second exercise, we remove the gender gap between a_m and a_f by lowering a_f to also equal unity. This is consistent with a story in which women devote more time to the market because the value of their time in home production becomes less valuable, thereby lowering the value they place on nonmarket time. And in the third exercise, we remove both the gender gap between a_m and a_f and the gender gap in wages. In this third exercise, men and women are perfectly symmetric and so the optimal household allocation will also be symmetric.

We carry out these exercises for values of ρ in $[-10, 0]$, and the results for h_m are shown in figure A1.

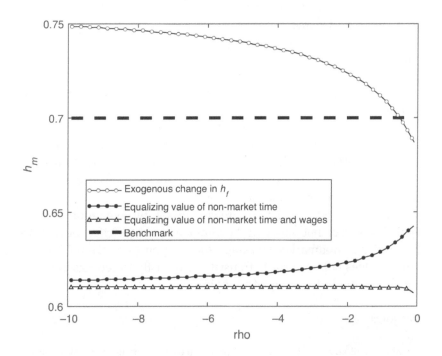

Fig. A1. Effect of female work on male work. A color version of this figure is available online.

Several patterns are worth noting. First, the top line in the figure supports the intuition that if there is enough complementarity between the nonworking times of spouses, the effect of complementarity can more than offset the income effect, so that an exogenous increase in the working time of one spouse can lead to an increase in the working time of the other spouse. In fact, as the figure shows, the level of complementarity needed is somewhat modest, as h_m increases as long as ρ is below around -0.7.

However, the figure shows that the results of this calculation do not necessarily translate into similar results when one attempts to generate the increase in the length of the working lives of females via changes in fundamentals. The "equalizing value of nonmarket time" line in the figure shows that equalizing the values of a_m and a_f leads to a decline in the working life of males for all values of ρ shown. Moreover, it is now the case that a more negative value of ρ leads to a larger decline in the working life of males. In interpreting this result, it is important to note that because each value of ρ corresponds to a different calibration of the model, equalizing the values of a_m and a_f reflects a different magnitude of change in a_f. Rather than a "bug," we want to emphasize that this feature is actually an important element of the exercise. Specifically, if one wants to argue that complementarities are large and that this is why the increased market work of women is leading to greater market work of men, one has to reconcile this with the fact that there used to be large gaps between the two, which is to say that the gap between a_m and a_f must be dependent on ρ.

The "equalizing value of nonmarket time and wages" line in the figure shows the results when we remove all asymmetries between males and females. The result is a large drop in the working lives of men and a large increase in the working lives of women, with the effect being effectively independent of the value of ρ.

To be sure, these calculations are very crude. But we report them to highlight the fact that although the intuition about the effect of complementarities in nonmarket working time of spouses is compelling, the intuition does not necessarily translate so robustly to settings in which one models the endogeneity of all choices.

Endnotes

Author email address: Rogerson (rdr@princeton.edu). We thank Mark Bils and Nir Jaimovich for comments, as well as conference participants at the NBER Annual Conference on Macroeconomics and seminar participants at the Cleveland Fed. Wallenius thanks the Knut and Alice Wallenberg Foundation for financial support. For acknowledgments, sources of research support, and disclosure of the authors' material financial relationships, if any, please see https://www.nber.org/books-and-chapters/nber-macroeconomics-annual -2021-volume-36/shocks-institutions-and-secular-changes-employment-older-individuals.

1. The countries represented in this figure are Australia, Canada, Finland, France, Germany, Ireland, Italy, Japan, Netherlands, Norway, Portugal, Spain, Sweden, and the United States.

2. We of course are not the first ones to note this pattern. A recent issue of the NBER series *Social Security Programs and Retirement around the World* (Coile et al. 2019) was entirely devoted to this issue.

3. The NBER series *Social Security Programs and Retirement around the World* promotes exactly this type of work.

4. The common shock is typically viewed as reflecting some combination of the oil shocks of the 1970s and the more persistent processes of globalization and skill-biased technical change. The key institutions were typically seen as UI, wage-setting practices, and Employment Protection Legislation.

5. We infer the presence of a mean-reverting shock by observing common low-frequency movements in employment rates for males of all age groups. The original shocks and institutions literature focused on the period prior to 2000 and so did not say anything about mean reversion. To the extent that globalization and skill-biased technical change are ongoing processes, mean reversion may seem counterintuitive. However, if one thinks of the economy as adjusting to the use of a new technology, the adjustment process can lead to dynamics that mimic those associated with a low-frequency mean-reverting shock relative to trend (e.g., Hornstein and Krusell 1996; Greenwood and Yorukoglu 1997). For our purposes, the common shock will also potentially reflect changes in overall economic policies that affect economic activity. An example would be product market regulation. This is potentially relevant for understanding some of the dynamics in Europe.

6. Several countries have also implemented reforms of their formal social security programs in the late 1990s and 2000s. Although not the focus of our analysis, these may have also contributed to the rise in employment rates in some countries and might be thought of as a fourth process, though some of these changes might best be viewed as part of the process of undoing the earlier expansion of the shadow social security system. See the various contributions in Borsch-Supan and Coile (2020) for more detail on these changes and an assessment of their effects.

7. There is good reason to believe that the effect of income becomes smaller as an economy becomes richer. First, from a theoretical perspective, subsistence constraints make income effects larger at lower levels of income. Vandenbroucke (2009) shows that this was important for understanding the changing distribution of hours worked across the wage distribution in the United States in the first half of the 1900s. But almost all wage gains in the United States since 1980 have gone to those with college education, and if anything males in this group have increased their absolute and relative level of market work.

8. As one example, Burtless (2013) argues that higher educational attainment accounts for a significant part of the increase in employment rates for older males in the United States since the mid-1990s.

9. See, e.g., the various chapters in Coile et al. (2019) for analyses that find little explanatory power in these factors for the mid-1990s reversal in older males' employment rates.

10. We note that our discussants have taken a step in this direction by analyzing patterns in the micro data for Germany and the United States. See also the various contributions in the NBER series *Social Security Programs and Retirement around the World*, including in particular the most recent volume, Borsch-Supan and Coile (2020).

11. See Costa (1998) for an extensive discussion and analysis of the history of retirement in the US context.

12. Many related studies focus on participation rates rather than employment-to-population ratios. At a broad level this distinction is not first order; figure 1 would present the basic pattern if we instead reported participation rates. We prefer to focus on employment rather than participation for the simple reason that in many countries the UI system was used as a shadow social security system for older unemployed workers, creating the possibility that the participation rate could be misleading in some countries.

13. There are a few idiosyncratic issues with the data for which we make some adjustments. The Italian data reveal a break in the early 1980s for the 45–54 and 55–64 groups. We adjust employment-to-population ratios for these two groups in the pre-1983 period so that values in 1981 are the same as in 1983. Norway does not report data for a few years in the late 1990s, and Ireland reports data at 5-year intervals in the early part of the sample. For Ireland and Norway, we fill in the missing years using linear interpolation.

14. Although we use the term leisure complementarities, the actual economic mechanism relies on complementarities between times not spent in market work, and so, e.g., does not distinguish leisure time from home-production time. Rogerson and Wallenius (2019) examine changes in time use for couples at retirement and estimate that leisure times are substitutes, not complements.

15. We emphasize that this mechanism not being the dominant force behind the trend reversal is fully consistent with the possibility that it exerts some positive effect on male employment rates, just as is true for both improving health and increasing educational attainment.

16. In fact, a prominent example of this is that several countries increased the normal retirement age for women so that it would coincide with the normal retirement age for men.

17. If we remove Portugal and Spain the correlation increases to 0.69. Because Spain and Portugal are the two poorest countries in the sample in 1976 one might expect them to experience the largest overall decline in employment of older males, and in fact this is the case. If we use panel 1 and repeat the analysis, the correlation is 0.77.

18. An interesting feature of this figure is that, in contrast to most recessions, the Great Recession seems to have had relatively smaller impacts on older individuals than prime-aged individuals. This is not something we pursue here.

19. The Netherlands is excluded because it has missing data for the younger age groups. We exclude Portugal and Spain because they are the poorest countries in our overall sample in 1976 and so are not as easily classified.

20. The significant heterogeneity of labor-market consequences during the Great Recession creates a second hump shape beginning in the late 2000s, though this is of less interest for us given our focus on secular changes. It is interesting that this effect does not show up in the series for males aged 55–64.

21. These challenges notwithstanding, see Borsch-Supan and Coile (2020) for details regarding a procedure for mapping a rich set of institutional characteristics into a single measure that summarizes the implicit tax on continuing to work at older ages.

22. The OECD Jobs Report was also released in the early 1990s, and this also represented somewhat of a turning point in terms of overall approaches to labor-market regulation and job creation.

23. See Hytti (2004) for additional details beyond the summary provided here.

24. During 1986–90, the minimum age was gradually raised back to 60, but as we note below, this was rendered irrelevant by the extension of other programs in the early 1990s.

25. See Guillemard (1991), Bozio (2008), and Charni (2016) for more extensive discussions.

26. See the discussions in Jacobs, Kohli, and Rein (1991) and Wilke (2009) for more details.

27. See de Vroom and Blomsma (1991) and Visser et al. (2016) for a more extensive summary.

28. The series for Norway is interesting in its own right. Delving into the specifics is beyond the scope of our analysis here, but we note that whereas most countries had a normal retirement age of 65 at the beginning part of our sample, Norway had a normal retirement age of 67.

29. As a different perspective on this, consider an economy with a representative agent. If the representative agent retires in the interval 55–64 and postpones retirement by 1 year, then the employment rate increases by 10 percentage points. But if the representative agent retires in the 65–69 interval and delays retirement by 1 year, the employment rate increases by 20 percentage points.

30. We note that the set of common factors includes slow-moving trends such as health and educational attainment in addition to improving labor-market prospects.

References

Blanchard, O., and J. Wolfers. 2000. "The Role of Shocks and Institutions in the Rise of European Unemployment: The Aggregate Evidence." *Economic Journal* 110:1–33.

Borsch-Supan, A., and C. Coile. 2020. *Social Security Programs and Retirement around the World: Reforms and Retirement Incentives*. Chicago: University of Chicago Press.

Bozio, A. 2008. "Impact Evaluation of the 1993 French Pension Reform on Retirement Age." *Pensions: An International Journal* 13:207–12.

Bruno, M., and J. Sachs. 1985. *Economics of Worldwide Stagflation*. Cambridge, MA: Harvard University Press.

Buchholz, S., A. Rinklake, and H. Blossfeld. 2013. "Reversing Early Retirement in Germany." *Comparative Population Studies* 38:881–906.

Burtless, G. 2013. "Can Educational Attainment Explain the Rise in Labor Force Participation at Older Ages?" Brief, Center for Retirement Research at Boston College.

Charni, K. 2016. "French Pension Reforms and their Impact on Older Unemployed Workers." Working paper, Aix-Marseille University.

Clark, K., and L. Summers. 1981. "Demographic Differences in Cyclical Employment Variation." *Journal of Human Resources* 16:61–79.

Coile, C., K. Milligan, and D. Wise. 2019. *Social Security Programs and Retirement around the World: Working Longer*. Chicago: University of Chicago Press.

Costa, D. 1998. *The Evolution of Retirement: An American History, 1880–1980*. Chicago: University of Chicago Press.

de Vroom, B., and M. Blomsma. 1991. "The Netherlands: An Extreme Case." In *Time for Retirement: Comparative Studies of Early Exit from the Labor Force*, ed. Martin Kohli, Martin Rein, Anne-Marie Guillemard, and Herman van Gunsteren. Cambridge: Cambridge University Press.

Farber, H. 1997. "The Changing Nature of Job Displacement 1881–1995." *Brookings Papers on Economic Activity: Microeconomics* 28:55–142.

Gomme, P., R. Rogerson, P. Rupert, and R. Wright. 2004. "The Life Cycle and the Business Cycle." *NBER Macroeconomics Annual* 19:415–61.

Greenwood, J., and M. Yorukoglu. 1997. "1974." *Carnegie-Rochester Conference Series on Public Policy* 46:49–95.

Guillemard, A. 1991. "Massive Exit through Unemployment Compensation." In *Time for Retirement*, ed. Martin Kohli, Martin Rein, Anne-Marie Guillemard, and Herman van Gunsteren. Cambridge: Cambridge University Press.

Hornstein, A., and P. Krusell. 1996. "Can Technology Improvements Cause Productivity Slowdowns?" *NBER Macroeconomics Annual* 11:209–76.

Hytti, H. 2004. "Early Exit from the Labour Market through the Unemployment Pathway in Finland." *European Societies* 6 (3): 265–97.

Jacobs, K., M. Kohli, and M. Rein. 1991. "Germany: The Diversity of Pathways." In *Time for Retirement*, ed. Martin Kohli, Martin Rein, Anne-Marie Guillemard, and Herman van Gunsteren. Cambridge: Cambridge University Press.

Kohli, M., M. Rein, A. Guillemard, and H. van Gunsteren, eds. 1991. *Time for Retirement*. Cambridge: Cambridge University Press.

Krugman, P. 1994. "Past and Prospective Causes of High Unemployment." *Economic Review, Federal Reserve Bank of Kansas City* 79:23–43.

Ljungqvist, L., and T. Sargent. 1998. "The European Unemployment Dilemma." *Journal of Political Economy* 106:514–50.

LIS (Luxembourg Income Study). 2019. Database. http://www.lisdatacenter
.org.
Mortensen, D., and C. Pissarides. 1999. "Unemployment Responses to Skill-Biased
Technology Shocks." *Economic Journal* 109:242–65.
Rogerson, R., and J. Wallenius. 2019. "Household Time Use among Older Couples:
Evidence and Implications for Labor Supply Parameters." *Quarterly Journal
of Economics* 134:1079–120.
Schirle, T. 2008. "Why Have Labor Force Participation Rates of Older Men In-
creased since the Mid-1990s?" *Journal of Labor Economics* 26:549–94.
Vandenbroucke, G. 2009. "Trends in the Hours: The U.S. from 1900 to 1950."
Journal of Economic Dynamics and Control 33:247–49.
Visser, M., M. Gesthuizen, G. Kraaykamp, and M. Wolbers. 2016. "Trends in
Labour Force Participation of Older Men: Examining the Influence of Policy
Reforms, Normative Change and Deindustrialization in the Netherlands, 1992–
2009." *Economic and Industrial Democracy* 37:425–47.
Wilke, Christina. 2009. *German Pension Reform: On Road towards a Sustainable
Multi-Pillar System.* Frankfurt Am Main: Peter Lang.

Comment

Nir Jaimovich, *University of Zurich and Center for Economic and Policy Research (CEPR),* United States of America

I. Introduction

In recent years, various Organisation for Economic Co-operation and Development (OECD) countries have implemented reforms targeting work incentives directed at older workers.[1] So understanding how such reforms affect the labor market is crucial. I see this interesting and important paper by Richard Rogerson and Johanna Wallenius as a first step in an exciting new research agenda. In this paper, the authors investigate the link between the labor market policy reforms targeting older workers and these workers' employment rates. The paper presents an extremely useful synthesis that brings together findings from different countries, and it suggests an important avenue for further research.

The paper contains numerous insights, and below I discuss the main argument. First, the authors document that the employment rate of men aged 55–64 has displayed a U-shaped pattern over the last 4 decades. Interestingly (and somewhat surprisingly), this pattern is common across many advanced economies, hinting that a common explanation could be responsible for it. At the same time, the reversal's magnitude varies across countries.

The explanation the authors put forth is based on three steps. First, the authors argue for the importance of "institutions" that gave rise to provisions that favored a reduction in employment rate of this older age group in many countries in the 1970s and 1980s. Second, they suggest there was a mean-reverting aggregate shock that led to a recovery in the employment

© 2022 National Bureau of Economic Research. All rights reserved. Published by The University of Chicago Press for the National Bureau of Economic Research. https://doi .org/10.1086/718665

rate. Third, they emphasize the existence of variations in reforms (institutional changes) that prompted an amplified recovery in a subset of countries.

In my discussion, I will address two issues. First, I will focus on the US experience. Doing so enables me to concentrate on key covariates that have driven the employment reversal in the United States. The hope is that the richness of the micro-level US data will deliver findings that will be useful to study in the context of the other countries the authors are interested in. Second, I will present a simple analytical framework that will enable me to identify key forces that shape the employment reversal. I will then discuss how they relate to the authors' hypothesis.

II. The US Experience

In this section, I focus on the US experience in terms of the employment rate. The goal is to identify the different covariates that matter for the employment reversal the authors emphasize. I will specifically focus on the role of age, gender, occupation, and education.[2]

A. Age

Figure 1 depicts the employment rate of five different age groups.

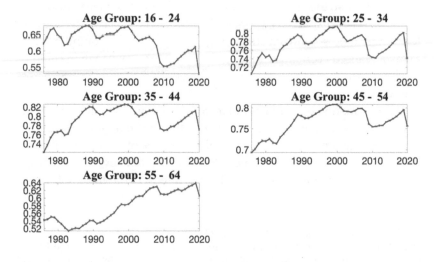

Fig. 1. Employment rate by age groups. A color version of this figure is available online.

To better understand the relative performance of these age groups, figure 2 normalizes the employment rate of each group to be equal to 1 in 1994.

Indeed, consistent with the main hypothesis of the authors and as figure 2 shows, the 55–64 age group experiences a dramatically different employment recovery vis-à-vis the other age groups.

B. Gender

Figures 1 and 2 include male and female individuals. However, since the 1960–2000 period saw a pronounced increase in female labor force participation, figure 3 concentrates on the employment rate of males, whereas figure 4 looks at the employment rate of females.

Several conclusions emerge from this analysis. First, even in the United States, the behavior of the 55–64 male group relative to the other male age groups is distinct. Second, since the turn of the twenty-first century, the female employment rate has plateaued (and has, at times, even begun to fall). However, the only female group that has shown a continued increase in employment rate is exactly the 55–64 age group. Hence, the empirical patterns relating to the 55–64 age group are not solely related to men; even in the United States, the behavior of the 55–64 female group relative to the other female age groups is distinct.

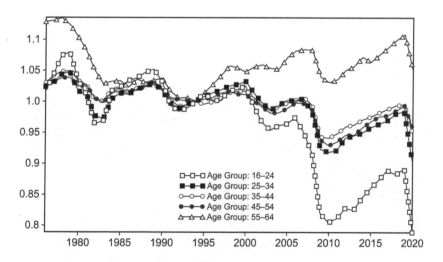

Fig. 2. Normalized employment rate by age groups. A color version of this figure is available online.

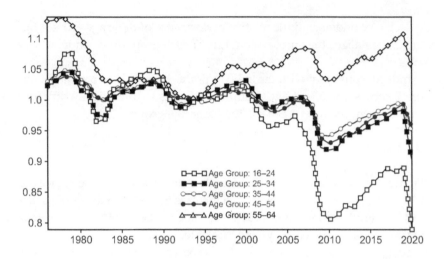

Fig. 3. Normalized employment rate by age groups: male. A color version of this figure is available online.

C. Digging into the 55+ Age Group

If the dynamics of employment are driven by an aggregate shock, then one would expect a relatively continuous response across adjacent age groups. As a result, it is useful both to further separate the 55–64 age group into 55–59 and 60–64 subgroups and to add the behavior of the

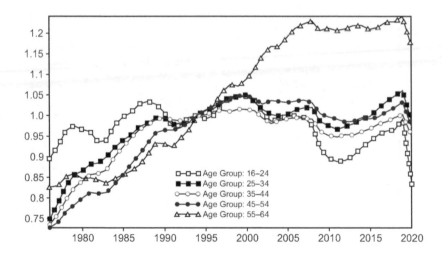

Fig. 4. Normalized employment rate by age groups: female. A color version of this figure is available online.

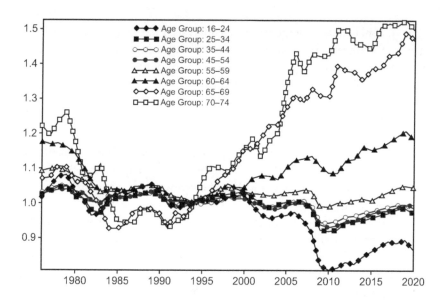

Fig. 5. Normalized employment rate by age groups: male. A color version of this figure is available online.

65–69 and 70–74 groups. In essence, at first glance, this could help to assess the importance of the "retirement institutions" hypothesis. Figures 5 and 6 show the employment rates of these different age groups for males and females, respectively.

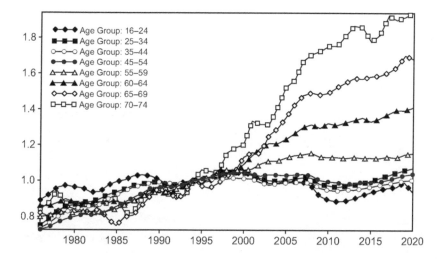

Fig. 6. Normalized employment rate by age groups: female. A color version of this figure is available online.

Two conclusions emerge from this analysis. First, within the 55–64 age group, the differential employment rate dynamics are being mainly dictated by the 60–64 age group. Second, these dynamics seem to be also affecting the 65 and above age group.

D. Occupations

To understand the covariates driving the reversal in the employment rate of the 60–64, I focus in what follows on the role of occupations. Specifically, figures 7 and 8 depict the evolution of employment and labor force participation for this age group.[3]

Figures 7 and 8 reveal that by the time the reversal in those not in the labor force (NLF) for the 60–64 age group takes place, the known decline in routine occupations (see, e.g., Autor and Dorn [2013]) has already happened. So, overwhelmingly, the increase in the labor force participation for this age group is due to a rise in employment in nonroutine cognitive occupations.[4] Thus, it seems that a key driving force in the United States is a "60+ nonroutine cognitive occupations-specific shock."

E. Education

Given the importance of nonroutine cognitive occupations, a natural question to ask is what role education plays in these dynamics. To answer this,

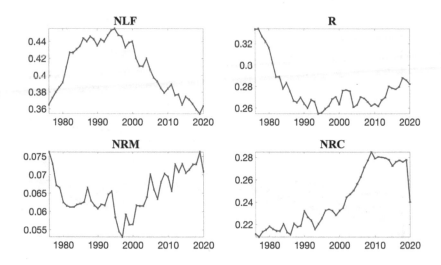

Fig. 7. Labor force participation and occupation 60–64: male. A color version of this figure is available online.

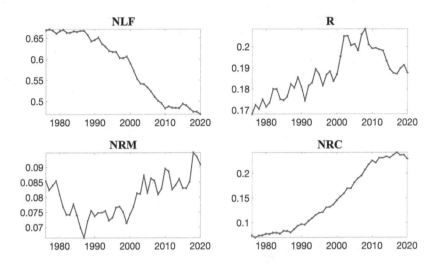

Fig. 8. Labor force participation and occupation 60–64: female. A color version of this figure is available online.

figures 9 and 10 depict the evolution of the likelihood that a given age group within a certain education level is employed.[5]

The key insight that emerges from these figures is that we only observe a rise in the employment rate for the members of the 60–64 age group who are in the high education group. This is consistent with the finding regarding the importance of the rise in nonroutine cognitive occupations discussed above.[6]

F. The Mean Reversal Shock

An additional hypothesis the authors put forth is the presence of a mean reversal aggregate shock. Is there evidence of such a shock? As a proxy for this, figure 11 depicts the normalized log wages of males. Indeed, consistent with the authors' hypothesis, all wages increased similarly across age groups within specific genders, suggesting an aggregate shock occurred. Yet, as was shown above, the reversal in employment rate did not take place in other age groups.

G. The Role of US Institutions

To summarize, the analysis of the US data suggests that even in the United States, a reversal in the employment rate of the 55–64 group is observed. The reversal was (i) present within both genders, (ii) mainly driven by the

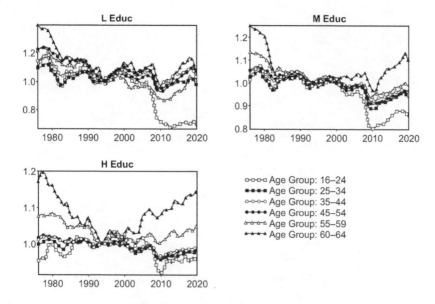

Fig. 9. Education and age group: propensity for males. A color version of this figure is available online.

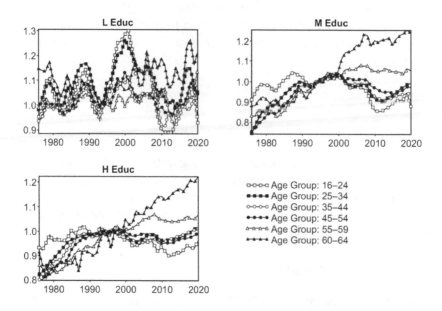

Fig. 10. Education and age group: propensity for females. A color version of this figure is available online.

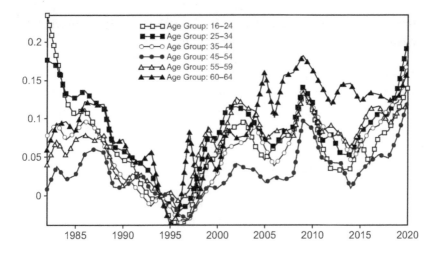

Fig. 11. Normalized log wages: male. A color version of this figure is available online.

60 and above age groups, (iii) characterized by a rise in employment in nonroutine cognitive occupations, and (iv) only held true for the high education group. These findings seem to suggest that forces affected those close to or above retirement age of very specific demographic groups, resulting in the change in their employment rate.

But what were those institutional reforms in the United States? During the period of interest, a reform in the social security system affecting cohorts reaching their 60s during the 1990s and 2000s took place. The changes induced by this reform were varied and numerous: (i) the 1983 amendments that raised the full-retirement-age (FRA) in for birth cohorts 1938 and thereafter until an FRA of 67, reducing lifetime benefits; (ii) increased incentives for delaying entitlement past the FRA (the so-called "delayed retirement credit"); and (iii) an elimination of the social security "earnings test" in 2000.[7] Indeed, a vast literature argues that these reforms can account for a significant fraction of the employment dynamics of the older age groups in the United States[8] So, consistent with the authors' view regarding the overall importance of institutional changes, the US experience seems to highlight the role of retirement institutions in shaping the employment dynamics of those near retirement.

III. A Model

In this section, I present a simple model that is useful in "identifying" the different channels and parameters that capture the mechanisms the authors are seeking. My goal with this framework is to (i) clarify what the "changes in institutions" the authors highlight mean within a structural context and (ii) emphasize that the primary elasticities that affect the employment reversal are "context" specific. Given the nature of this comment, the model makes several simplifying assumptions that enable me to get some closed-form solutions and to perform a simple quantification exercise.

A.   The Structure of the Model

Consider an individual who decides whether to retire or work for an additional period. I assume individuals differ in their ability, which is denoted by ϵ and is drawn from a distribution with a cumulative density function (CDF) $\Gamma(\epsilon)$. Individuals who work are taxed at a constant labor tax and experience a working disutility.[9] Individuals who retire receive benefits that can be indexed to their market wage, and they face a tax rate based on this benefit income. The nature of the model leads to a cutoff rule in ability that determines the employment rate. Formally, the value of working one more period is given by

$$V_E(\epsilon) = U(\underbrace{\epsilon}_{\text{Ability}} \times \underbrace{\omega}_{\text{Efficiency Wage}} \times (1 - \underbrace{\tau_\omega}_{\text{Labor Tax Rate}}) - \underbrace{G}_{\text{Working Disutility}}) + \beta V'_N, \quad (1)$$

where the value of retiring is given by

$$V_N = U(\underbrace{b(\epsilon)}_{\text{Benefits: can be indexed to the wage}} \times (1 - \underbrace{\tau_b}_{\text{Benefits Tax Rate}})) + \beta V'_N, \quad (2)$$

where V'_N denotes the continuation value.[10] This formulation leads to an implicit cutoff participation rule in ability:

$$b(\epsilon^*) \times (1 - \tau_b) = \epsilon^* \times \omega \times (1 - \tau_\omega) - G, \quad (3)$$

implying that the employment rate is given by

$$\underbrace{E}_{\text{Employment Rate}} = (1 - \underbrace{\Gamma(\epsilon^*)}_{\text{CDF}}), \quad (4)$$

which is depicted in figure 12.

Figure 12 also shows what are, within the model, the "changes in institutions" that could lead to a change in the cutoff value and, in turn, the employment rate; these could be changes in the degree of benefits or changes in either of the two tax rates.

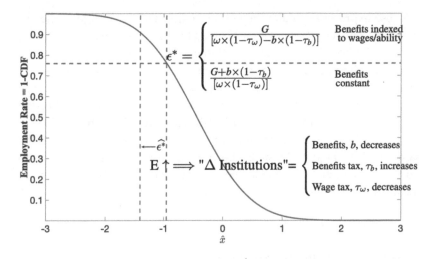

Fig. 12. Employment rate and institutions. The black line depicts the 1 − CDF values (I use the estimated values of the mean and variance of the distribution I later estimate for the United States). The specific cutoff value ϵ^* depends on whether the benefits are indexed to the wages or whether they are constant. A color version of this figure is available online.

But identical changes in the institutions do not map to the same changes in the employment rate, which is the authors' object of interest. Specifically, let a circumflex denote a variable's percentage change from its original value. Then, with a bit of tedious algebra, we can show that the percentage change in the employment rate is given by

$$\widehat{E} = \left(\frac{\Gamma'(\epsilon^*)}{E^*} \epsilon^* \right) \times \underbrace{\left(\frac{\widehat{\omega}}{\left[1 - \frac{b(1-\tau_b)}{\omega(1-\tau_\omega)}\right]} - \frac{\widehat{\tau_\omega}}{\left[\frac{(1-\tau_\omega)}{\tau_\omega} - \frac{b}{\omega}(1-\tau_b)\right]} - \frac{\widehat{b}}{\left[\frac{\omega(1-\tau_\omega)}{b(1-\tau_b)} - 1\right]} + \frac{\widehat{\tau_b}}{\left[\frac{\omega(1-\tau_\omega)}{b\tau_b} - \frac{(1-\tau_b)}{\tau_b}\right]} \right)}_{\widehat{\epsilon}^*}, \qquad (5)$$

for the case where the retirement benefits are indexed to the wage, and by

$$\widehat{E} = \left(\frac{\Gamma'(\epsilon^*)}{E^*} \epsilon^* \right) \times \underbrace{\left(\widehat{\omega} - \frac{\tau_\omega}{(1-\tau_\omega)} \widehat{\tau_\omega} + \frac{b\tau_b\widehat{\tau_b} - b(1-\tau_b)\widehat{b}}{[\omega(1-\tau_\omega)]\epsilon^*} \right)}_{\widehat{\epsilon}^*}, \qquad (6)$$

for the case where the benefits are constant.

These expressions make the simple point that the change in the employment rate (i.e., $\widehat{E}$) is not simply given by the change in the "institution variables" (the other ⌢ variables). Rather, the elasticity has two components that affect the mapping from the institutional changes to the employment rate. First, the elasticity is, in fact, institution context–dependent; the values of the two tax rates and the benefits dictate the mapping. Second, the ability distribution itself (or rather the elasticity of the ability distribution around the original employment rate) is also an object that affects that same elasticity. Figure 13 visually illustrates the basic point that, even for the same change in the cutoff value, the ability distribution's shape matters for the authors' object of interest, that is, $\widehat{E}$.

B. A Simple Quantification

Equations (5) and (6) suggest that to quantify the impact of the reforms within the context of the model, we would need to gauge the value of the different components that shape the elasticities. The obvious challenge is that, for many countries, the empirical estimates of such elasticities do not exist.

Accordingly, an alternative is to rely on the more commonly estimated (across countries) elasticities with respect to the wage. As I show below,

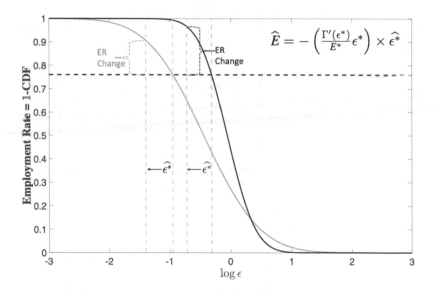

Fig. 13. Employment rate and ability. The gray and black lines depict two different distributions (i.e., two different values of 1 − CDF). A color version of this figure is available online.

such an elasticity can be used to recover the different components that determine the reform elasticities. Specifically, the elasticity of the employment rate with respect to the wage is given by

$$
\widehat{E} = \begin{cases} \left(\dfrac{\Gamma'(\epsilon^*)}{E^*} \epsilon^* \right) \times \dfrac{\widehat{\omega}}{\left[1 - \frac{b(1-\tau_b)}{\omega(1-\tau_\omega)} \right]} & \begin{array}{l} \text{Benefits indexed} \\ \text{to wages/ability} \end{array} \\[3em] \left(\dfrac{\Gamma'(\epsilon^*)}{E^*} \epsilon^* \right) \times \widehat{\omega} & \begin{array}{l} \text{Benefits} \\ \text{constant} \end{array} \end{cases} . \tag{7}
$$

If an estimate of such an elasticity exists, then we can recover all the necessary components that dictate the value of the reform elasticities. To do so, it is first useful to note that the above equation suggests there are three components that determine the elasticity of the employment rate with respect to the wage: the first term is the net pension replacement rate: $\{1 - [b(1 - \tau_b)/\omega(1 - \tau_\omega)]\}$.[11] The second one is the ability distribution $\Gamma'(\epsilon^*)$. And the third one is the employment rate E^*.

Net Pension Replacement Rate

The net pension replacement rate can be read from existing estimates.[12] As an example, figure 14 depicts the net pension rates for four countries of interest.

Ability Distribution

We need to make a parametric distribution assumption with respect to the ability distribution. Accordingly, I follow the common practice in the literature and assume that ability is distributed log-normal. To identify the mean, the variance, and the cutoff value of this distribution, I proceed with the following algorithm. I guess values for these three parameters and iteratively check whether they satisfy the following three moments. First, they need to satisfy the targeted employment rate prior to the reform, E^*. Second, in the model the after-tax wages must be proportional to ability, that is, equal to $\underbrace{\epsilon}_{\text{Ability}} \times \underbrace{\omega}_{\text{Efficiency Wage}} \times (1 - \underbrace{\tau_\omega}_{\text{Labor Tax Rate}})$, and thus it can be mapped to the observed (truncated) variance of wages for the group of interest in the data. Third, the elasticity of employment with respect to the wage is a moment that is routinely estimated in the empirical literature, so I require its value in the model, that is, $\left(\frac{\Gamma'(\log(\epsilon^*))}{E^*} \epsilon^* \right) \times \frac{1}{\{1 - b[(1 - \tau_b)/\omega(1 - \tau_\omega)]\}}$ to match the country-specific value.

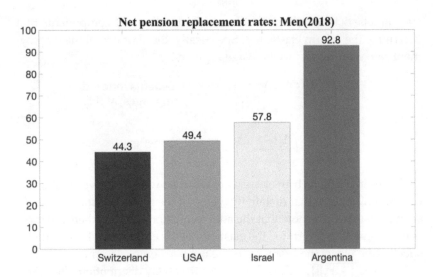

Fig. 14. Net pension replacement rates. The data are taken from the OECD "pension at a glance" project; see https://data.oecd.org/pension/net-pension-replacement-rates.htm. A color version of this figure is available online.

As an example of how I implement this approach, I consider the cases of the United States and Israel. My group of interest includes males, aged 55–64, with education above high school for the year 2012.[13] Table 1 reports the net pension replacement rate, the employment rate, and standard deviation of log wages[14] and indicates the elasticity of employment with respect to wages.[15]

Table 1
Estimates

	Israel	US
Net pension replacement rate	.578	.494
Employment rate	.83	.76
Standard deviation of logarithm wage	.61	.72
Elasticity	.43	[.13–.43]
"Identified" parameters:		
Standard ability	1.0	1.15
Mean ability	.48	.33
ϵ^*	.60	.61

Note: For the exercise reported in this comment, I took the upper bound of the elasticity in the United States because it coincided with the values reported in Israel.

Table 2
Reform Elasticity Estimates

Elasticity	US	Israel
$\eta_{\hat{E},\hat{b}}$	−.21	−.25
$\eta_{\hat{E},\hat{\tau}_a}$	−.11	−.26
$\eta_{\hat{E},\hat{\tau}_b}$	.038	.062

Armed with these values, I can implement the approach discussed above and recover the standard deviation and mean of the ability distribution. Then, given values for the tax rate,[16] I can go back to equation (5) and recover all the different reform elasticities, as now we have the implied values for all the components. Table 2 reports the estimated elasticities of the three reforms within the model.

IV. Conclusions

This important paper by Richard Rogerson and Johanna Walleniusas addresses the impact of different reforms on the labor market. As a first step, the authors chose to consider many countries to paint a general picture that points to the main insights that emerge from this study.

In the first part of my comment, my goal was to consider the US case, which enabled me to identify the key covariates shaping the employment reversal. Whether these are the same covariates that dictated the dynamics in other countries is yet to be determined, but the US experience suggests this is, at the very least, an important exercise to conduct on a country-by-country basis. Moreover, my reading of the US data is that the authors' institutional change hypothesis is, indeed, borne out in the United States.

In the second part of this comment, I presented a simple model whose goal was to highlight precisely what institutions are (at least in the eyes of the model). Moreover, the model underscored the importance of distinguishing between "institutional changes" and elasticities that jointly determine the evolution of the employment rate. Finally, I suggested a way to identify the key parameters that control the "elasticity reforms," a valuable undertaking when considering reforms for which there are no existing elasticity estimates.

I look forward to future work that quantifies the role of institutions in the employment reversal, as surely this is of first-order importance given demographic transitions.

Endnotes

Author email address: Nir Jaimovich (nir.jaimovich@uzh.ch). I am extremely grateful to Itay Saporta-Eksten and Yaniv Yedid-Levi for helpful comments and discussion while preparing this comment. I am also grateful to Gadi Barlevy for his input on the model. All remaining errors are my own. For acknowledgments, sources of research support, and disclosure of the author's material financial relationships, if any, please see https://www.nber .org/books-and-chapters/nber-macroeconomics-annual-2021-volume-36/comment -shocks-institutions-and-secular-changes-employment-older-individuals-jaimovich.

1. See, e.g., the discussion in Saporta-Eksten, Shurtz, and Weisburd (2021).

2. All data are based on a yearly aggregation of the monthly Current Population Survey files from 1976 to 2020.

3. In each of these figures, the shares of routine occupation (R), nonroutine occupation (NRM), nonroutine occupations (NRC), and not in the labor force (NLF) add to 1. In these figures, I use NLF as a proxy for the employment rate.

4. A word of caution is warranted, as there are known issues of creating time series "occupations" due to the redesign of the occupation definitions.

5. I divide the data into three education groups: Low (L), which is less than high school; Middle (M), which is high-school graduates and some college; and High (H), which is college and above.

6. In unreported results I note that there is also a composition effect that is mainly present for males. Specifically, the share within the 60+ who have higher education continued to rise during the period of interest, although in the other age groups that share plateaued. Because individuals with higher education are more likely to work, this change in the composition of education within the 60+ further contributed to the employment dynamics of this age group.

7. According to the earning test, benefits of workers aged 65–69 were reduced if earnings were above a threshold.

8. See, e.g., Friedberg (2000), Mastrobuoni (2009), Blau and Goodstein (2010), Banerjee and Blau (2013), Gelber, Isen, and Song (2016), Duggan et al. (2019), and especially Börsch-Supan and Coile (2020).

9. To derive clear predictions, I assume a no-wealth effect utility function; I include the working disutility as an argument within the utility function.

10. It is important to emphasize that in this formulation I made the simplifying assumption that the continuation value V'_N is identical whether or not the individual decides to work an additional period. That is, I assume there is no increase in assets or benefits as a result of the decision to work an additional period. This assumption enables me to derive the closed-form solution for the cutoff value ϵ^*. I am grateful to Gadi Barlevy for raising this issue.

11. I opt to show the approach for the case where the benefits are indexed to the wage because this includes an extra term of the net pension replacement rates, but naturally, the approach discussed above can easily be implemented for the second case as well.

12. See the OECD "pensions at a glance" project.

13. The choice of this specific group was guided by the availability of data for the two countries.

14. For the United States I calculate these two measures from the CPS, whereas for Israel I am grateful to Itay Saporta-Eksten for providing me with the values.

15. For the United States, the estimate is taken from Saporta-Eksten et al. (2021), whereas for Israel the estimate is taken from Chetty et al. (2013).

16. I set $\tau_\omega = 0.3$ and $\tau_b = 0.15$ for the United States and $\tau_\omega = 0.5$ and $\tau_b = 0.2$ for Israel.

References

Autor, David H., and David Dorn. 2013. "The Growth of Low-skill Service Jobs and the Polarization of the US Labor Market." *American Economic Review* 103 (5): 1553–97.

Banerjee, Sudipto, and David Blau. 2013. "Employment Trends by Age in the United States: Why Are Older Workers Different." Michigan Retirement Research Center Research Paper No. 2013-285, University of Michigan.

Blau, David, and Ryan M. Goodstein. 2010. "Can Social Security Explain Trends in Labor Force Participation of Older Men in the United States?" *Journal of Human Resources* 45 (2): 328–63.

Börsch-Supan, Axel, and Courtney Coile. 2020. *Social Security Programs and Retirement around the World: Reforms and Retirement Incentives.* Chicago: University of Chicago Press.

Chetty, Raj, Adam Guren, Dayanand S. Manoli, and Andrea Weber. 2013. "Does Indivisible Labor Explain the Difference between Micro and Macro Elasticities? A Meta-Analysis of Extensive Margin Elasticities." *NBER Macroeconomics Annual* 27 (1): 1–56.

Duggan, Mark, Irena Dushi, Sookyo Jeong, and Gina Li. 2019. "The Effect of Delayed Retirement Credit on Social Security Claiming and Employment." https://mrdrc.isr.umich.edu/publications/conference/pdf/2019RDRC%20P2%20Duggan.pdf.

Friedberg, Leora. 2000. "The Labor Supply Effects of the Social Security Earnings Test." *Review of Economics and Statistics* 82 (1): 48–63.

Gelber, Alexander M., Adam Isen, and Jae Song. 2016. "The Effect of Pension Income on Elderly Earnings: Evidence from Social Security and Full Population Data." Mimeo.

Mastrobuoni, Giovanni. 2009. "Labor Supply Effects of the Recent Social Security Benefit Cuts: Empirical Estimates Using Cohort Discontinuities." *Journal of Public Economics* 93 (11–12): 1224–33.

Saporta-Eksten, Itay, Ity Shurtz, and Sarit Weisburd. 2021. "Social Security, Labor Supply and Health of Older Workers: Quasi-Experimental Evidence from a Large Reform." *Journal of the European Economic Association* 19 (4): 2168–208.

Comment

Mark Bils, *University of Rochester and NBER,* United States of America

Rogerson and Wallenius highlight swings in employment rates for older workers for 14 Organisation for Economic Co-operation and Development (OECD) countries since the mid-1970s. The changes are really large. On average for these countries, the employment to population rate (EPOP) for men ages 55–64 falls by about 25 log points from 1976 to 1995 but then increases by roughly the same magnitude from 1995 to 2019. The shift in trends for women ages 55–64 mirror this but have to be viewed relative to a long-term rise in women's employment. Women's EPOP increases by about 5 log points from 1976 to 1995 but then by more than 55% from 1995 to 2019. These shifts are largely relative to younger workers; that is, shifts for younger workers are much more muted.[1] Shifts of this magnitude call out for an explanation, and Rogerson and Wallenius consider several. Their preferred narrative combines a combination of negative shocks and policies discouraging labor supply during the rundown in hours, then a gradual reversing of those policies during the strong rebound.

My discussion focuses on Germany, exploiting the German Socio-Economic Panel (GSOEP) described shortly. This long household panel allows me to see individual work histories. In turn, I can control for cohort effects—for example, from trends in life expectancy, schooling, or occupations—that could potentially drive the swings in employment shown by Rogerson and Wallenius from repeated cross sections. It also lets me examine trends in wage rates and household assets over time. These variables, as well as changes in taxes and transfers, should affect the labor supply of older workers.

NBER Macroeconomics Annual, volume 36, 2022.
© 2022 National Bureau of Economic Research. All rights reserved. Published by The University of Chicago Press for the National Bureau of Economic Research. https://doi .org/10.1086/718666

I find that the trend shifts for employment do not reflect cohort effects. I see the evidence for Germany supporting the Rogerson-Wallenius narrative that changing subsidies and regulations played a role in these trends, at least in the increase since the mid-1990s for men. For Germany, the data also suggest that a decline in household wealth relative to earnings played a role in employment rates rebounding for older workers. These employment swings are a striking illustration that labor supply factors are capable of generating dramatic changes in employment and total hours.

I. GSOEP Data

The GSOEP, begun in 1984, is an annual longitudinal survey of households. It surveys individuals from about 11,000 distinct households each year.[2] The GSOEP provides rich data on a working household member's earnings, employment, hours, industry, and occupation. It also provides information on the household's taxes paid and transfers received. The latter includes unemployment, old age, and disability benefits, each of which has been subject to numerous salutatory changes, especially since the mid-1990s. Starting in 2002, the GSOEP has collected data on household assets every 5 years. The GSOEP provides two channels for observing an individual's work history. One is to look back at a respondent's answers from prior years of the survey. The survey also includes retrospective histories of a respondent's employment at earlier ages.

For the purposes of this discussion, an obvious disadvantage of leaning so exclusively on Germany and the GSOEP is that it misses the other 13 OECD countries considered by Rogerson and Wallenius. Fortunately, for my purpose, the employment pattern for older workers in Germany largely mirrors that for the 14 OECD countries and, if anything, is sharper. Figure 1 displays the EPOP at ages 55–64 from the GSOEP separately for men and women. The inflection point in Germany appears closer to 1997 than 1995. For men the EPOP falls by about 25 log points just in the 13 years from 1984 to 1997; from 1997 to 2018 it then increases by nearly 50%. The comparable episodes for women are an increase of about 30 log points followed by an increase on the order of 85%.

Starting in 1984, the GSOEP misses part of the period of decline in older workers' employment shown by Rogerson and Wallenius. This is especially true of my analysis that controls for earlier work history or examines assets, only collected after 2002. But I would argue that the increase in employment rates since the mid-to-late 1990s is the most intriguing element of the German case. Longer trends are for employment and hours

Fig. 1. Employment/population (emp/pop) for ages 55–64. A color version of this figure is available online.

to decline in Germany and other countries (e.g., Boppart and Krusell 2020), making the counter-experience for older persons these past 25 years more of an outlier to explain.

II. Accounting for Cohort Effects

My figure 1, like the analysis from Rogerson and Wallenius, compares workers at ages 55–64 over time. Therefore, the variations reflect differences across cohorts. It is possible that cohorts will differ due to factors such as schooling or occupations. These may be viewed as labor supply factors. But they are not the factors that might create intertemporal movements in employment along the lines discussed by Rogerson and Wallenius.

One demographic trend has been in life expectancy. Higher life expectancy should lead to higher employment at ages 55–64, as we would not expect it to translate one-to-one to more years of retirement. But although life expectancy in Germany has trended upward, it has not accelerated since the mid-1990s.[3] If anything, the rate of increase has slowed. So I believe it is not especially important to understanding the EPOP patterns from figure 1.

Years of schooling have also trended upward. More schooling should be a powerful force for higher employment at older ages. It increases earnings, including later in the working life, while not proportionately raising permanent income given the direct and opportunity costs of schooling. It could delay retirement by engendering work that is less physically demanding and perhaps more varied. Figure 2 presents average years of schooling attainment for Germans ages 55–64 separately for men and women. Not only has years of schooling attainment increased, but it also accelerates somewhat since the late 1990s, especially for women. Figures 3 and 4 plot EPOPs for older men and women, respectively, but does so separately for individuals with more than 12 years of schooling versus those with 12 or less. The relative acceleration of EPOPs occurs across both schooling groups, regardless of gender. For men, the trough in EPOP is earlier and the subsequent rise somewhat larger for those with 12 or less years of schooling. But figures 2 and 3 suggest compositional effects by schooling do not drive much of the trends in EPOPs.

Figures 5 and 6 plot annual hours worked for ages 55–64, as well as for ages 25–34, 35–44, and 45–54. Note first that the trends in EPOP at 55–64 translate at least as strongly to annual hours. Two other points emerge. One is that the rapid increase in EPOPs since the late 1990s is

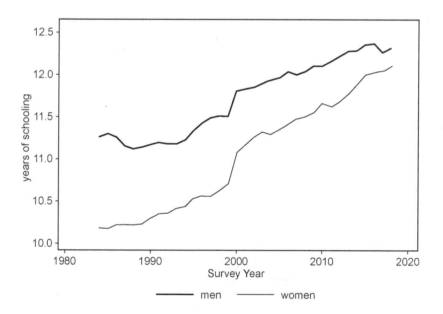

Fig. 2. Average years of schooling for ages 55–64. A color version of this figure is available online.

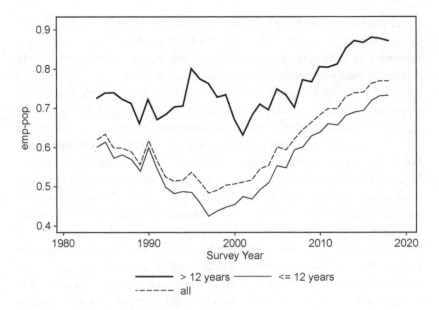

Fig. 3. Employment/population (emp/pop) by schooling for men, ages 55–64. A color version of this figure is available online.

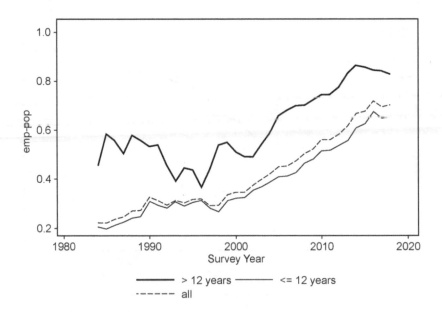

Fig. 4. Employment/population (emp/pop) by schooling for women, ages 55–64. A color version of this figure is available online.

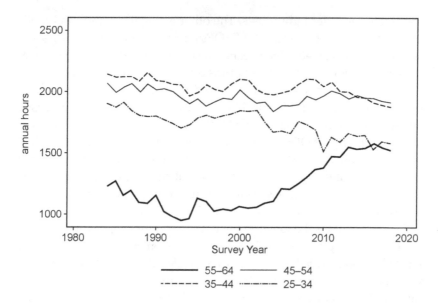

Fig. 5. Annual hours at various ages, men. A color version of this figure is available online.

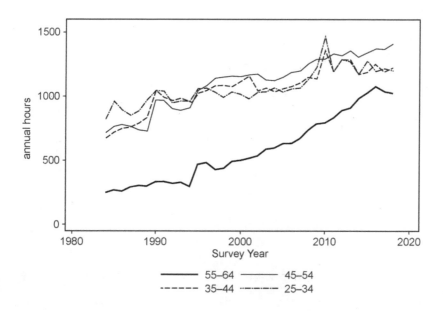

Fig. 6. Annual hours at various ages, women. A color version of this figure is available online.

specific to the older individuals. The other is that the pattern in EPOPs at ages 55–64 is not presaged by EPOPs for the same cohort 10 years earlier (looking at ages 45–54 ten years prior), 20 years earlier (ages 35–44), or 30 years earlier (ages 25–34). That runs counter to strong cohort effects.

Figures 7 and 8 make the latter point directly by plotting employment rates at ages 30, 40, and 50 for cohorts ages 55–64. These rates are based on retrospective histories in the GSOEP. The results for older men are particularly striking. EPOPs for men ages 55–64 increased from less than 50% in 1997 to more than 75% in 2018. But, from figure 7, we see that reported employment rates at earlier ages, especially at age 50, were trending down. Thus the increase in employment rates at older ages post-1997 is relative to those individuals' rates at earlier ages.

Figure 9 exploits the longitudinal data to control for older individuals' work history. It plots the EPOPs for men and women ages 55–64, but only for those who reported being employed while ages 50–54. Conditional on working at 50–54, the figure shows tremendous swings in employment rates at 55–64. For those men, the EPOP bottoms out in 2000, at about 50%, falling more than 40 log points from 1989. That rate then more than rebounds, increasing 50 plus log points by 2018. For women employed at 50–54, the EPOP shows a remarkably similar though slightly exaggerated

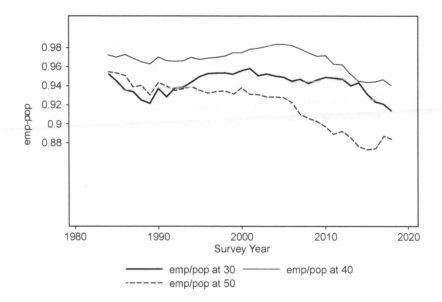

Fig. 7. Retrospective employment/population (emp/pop) for men, ages 55–64. A color version of this figure is available online.

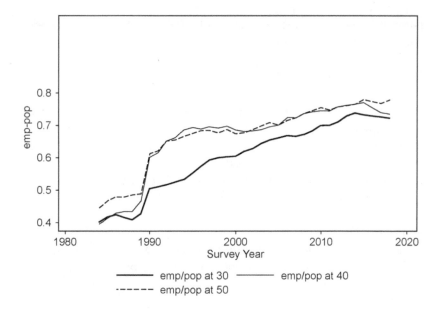

Fig. 8. Retrospective employment/population (emp/pop) for women, ages 55–64. A color version of this figure is available online.

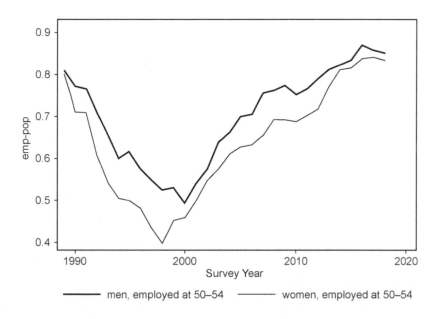

Fig. 9. Employment/population (emp/pop), 55–64, by employment status 50–54. A color version of this figure is available online.

pattern. It also starts and ends at an EPOP of about 80% but reaches a
nadir of only 40% in 1998.[4]

III. Wages versus Wealth

Figure 9 makes it crystal clear that the large trends in employment for
older persons in Germany do not reflect cohort effects. For those working in their early 50s, the EPOP halved for women, and nearly halved for
men, in a remarkably short period, then more than rebounds, again in
remarkably short order. Before turning to the type of policy changes emphasized by Rogerson and Wallenius, I first look at other variables that
should exert substitution and wealth effects on labor supply: wage rates
and assets. We should expect an individual to extend their working life if
their wage is high relative to consumption as retirement nears. Wages will
be high relative to permanent income and consumption if wage growth
has been particularly rapid or, more generally, if net wealth is low relative
to earnings.

Figure 10 presents the median real wage at ages 50–54 for the cohort
currently 55–64.[5] I present wages at ages 50–54 so that it is not too influenced by selection given the large swings in employment rates at

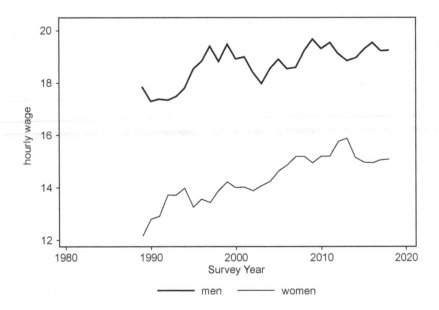

Fig. 10. Median real wage in 2018 euros at ages 50–54, for those currently 55–64. A color
version of this figure is available online.

ages 55–64. Those wages trend upward at about 0.3% per year for men and 0.8% for women. But there is no acceleration after the 1990s. In fact, the periods of highest trend growth are the mid-1990s for men and the early 1990s for women. In addition to wage levels, I examined whether individuals' wage growth increased post-2000. But the GSOEP shows no evidence that occurred.

Figure 11 plots median household assets from 2003 to 2018. The figure again presents assets at ages 50–54 for those currently 55–64 to limit the impact of employment at older ages on measured assets. Median assets decline considerably, by about 40 log points, from 2003 to 2010, then increase somewhat. That decrease is for median, not average, assets, as asset values grew more rapidly for households at higher levels. Grabka and Westermeier (2015) discuss the decline in median German assets post-2000, attributing much of it to declining real estate values.

Figure 12 presents the median of household assets relative to individual earnings, evaluated at ages 50–54 for men and for women at ages 55–64. These show more of a sustained decline post-2003, though the decline is most rapid from 2003 to 2008. Overall these ratios decline by about 45 log points for men and slightly more for women. Thus it appears quite plausible that a rise in earnings power relative to household

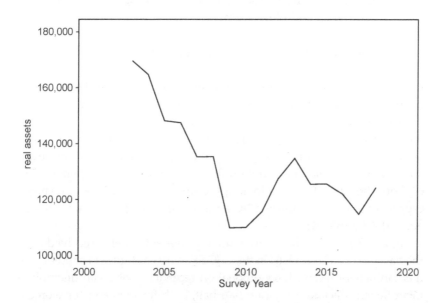

Fig. 11. Household assets at ages 50–54 in 2018 euros for those 55–64. A color version of this figure is available online.

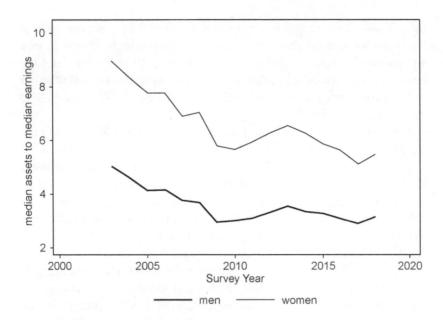

Fig. 12. Assets relative to earnings at ages 50–54, for those 55–64. A color version of this figure is available online.

wealth may have contributed somewhat to increasing employment rates both for older men and older women.

IV.   Changes in Transfers and Other Policies

Rogerson and Wallenius discuss transfer policies that arose in OECD countries in the 1970s and 1980s that would discourage employment, but were subsequently scaled back or altered. Steiner (2017) categorizes the many changes to German programs with respect to unemployment benefits and requirements to access public pensions. Here I examine the patterns in unemployment and public pension payments to persons 55–64 from the GSOEP. I then look at the timing of employment changes especially at the ages affected by some substantive policy changes (i.e., ages 60–62 or 63–64).

Figure 13 presents the mean of unemployment benefits received over the past year by those 55–64 in the GSOEP, whereas figure 14 presents the median benefit received, conditional on receiving. The mean unemployment benefit declines by more than half, both for men and for women, from the late 1990s through 2018. Of course, there is a reverse channel from employment rates, regardless of the cause, and mean unemployment

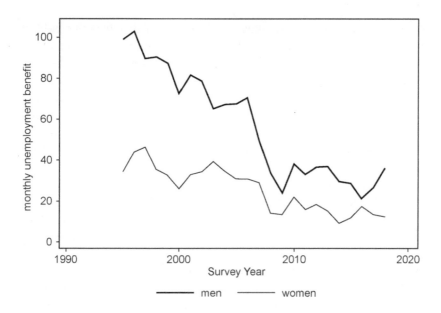

Fig. 13. Mean unemployment benefits in 2018 euros, ages 50–54 in 2018 euros, ages 55–64. A color version of this figure is available online.

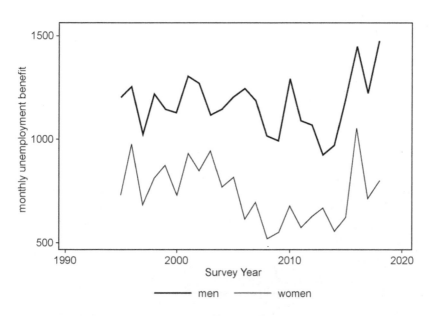

Fig. 14. Median unemployment benefits in 2018 euros conditional on receiving, ages 55–64. A color version of this figure is available online.

benefits. Figure 14 actually shows no decline in median benefit condition on receiving for men, and no sustained decline for women. Together, the figures suggest that the impact of changes to unemployment benefits, if important, must have acted through eligibility or incentives to take up unemployment, not through the generosity of the benefit. One such policy change that aligns well with the timing in figure 13 is the introduction of wage subsidies to firms hiring workers deemed difficult to place for lower wage jobs. These "Hartz" reforms were implemented in four stages from 2003 to 2005.

Many of the policy changes since the 1990s, as discussed by Rogerson and Wallenius, have been designed to scale back public pensions, those based on age or on disability. Changes drafted in Germany in the 1990s gradually reduced the generosity of benefits from 1998 to 2006 (see, for instance, Boersch-Supan and Juerges [2011]). The age required for retirement pension was raised: for men from age 63 to 65 in stages during 2000–1 and for women from 60 to 65 during 2000–4.[6] The retirement age for those classified disabled rose gradually from age 60 to 63 beginning in 2000.

Figure 15 presents the mean of public pension received by those 55–64 in the GSOEP. That mean declines substantially over time for both

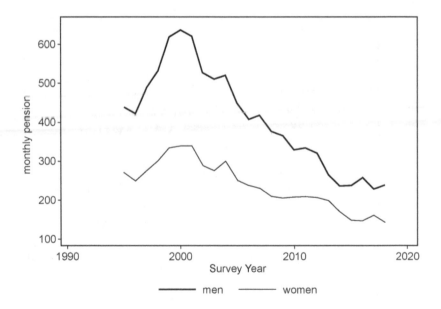

Fig. 15. Mean public pension in 2018 euros, ages 55–64. A color version of this figure is available online.

men and women, basically halving from the late 1990s to 2018. That decline is more important for men, as their average benefit received is consistently about double that for women. Figure 16 presents the median benefit, conditional on receiving. These also decline substantially, with the exception of an outlier observation for women in 2016. Figure 17 plots the differential in mean pension benefit, both old age and disability, as a function of being employed. Nonemployment is associated with higher mean benefit, but that differential declines considerably for men after the late 1990s. By contrast, no decline is perceptible for women.

I see the results in figures 13–17 as providing some support for the Rogerson-Wallenius narrative that changes in benefits were important in the employment trends for older persons. But, at least for Germany, that evidence appears stronger with respect to pension benefits and especially for men. To follow up on this, figure 18 again plots the EPOP for the older men, but separately for ages 55–59, 60–62, and 63–64. These breaks are designed to shed light on the impact of a couple of key policy changes that were phased in beginning in 2000—one making old-age pensions available at 65, rather than 63, the other increasing the age, conditional on disability, from 60 to 63. We see that the EPOP increase for men from 2000 to 2018 is driven by huge increases at ages 60–62, from

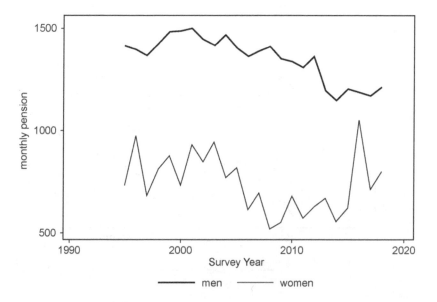

Fig. 16. Median public pension in 2018 euros, conditional on receiving, ages 55–64. A color version of this figure is available online.

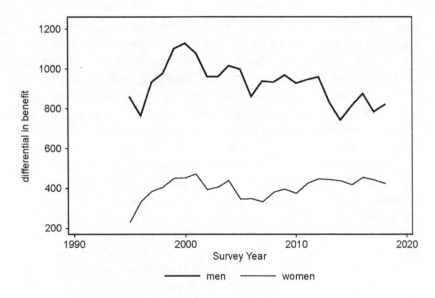

Fig. 17. Differential in mean pension in 2018 euros for not employed versus employed, ages 55–64. A color version of this figure is available online.

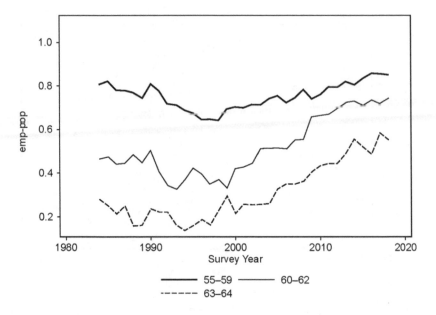

Fig. 18. Employment/population (emp/pop) rates for older men, separately by age group. A color version of this figure is available online.

about 40% to nearly 75%, and at ages 63–64, from about 20% to more than 50%. These differential trends are consistent with that expected if the changes to public pensions played an important role in employment rates for older men. One should keep in mind, however, that it may also reflect greater responsiveness of employment at ages 60–64, compared with those at 55–59, even for common forces.

V. Summary

The GSOEP sheds some light on the large swings in employment for older individuals in Germany. That swing is driven entirely by the rates of employment at ages 55–64 for those who had been employed at 50–54. From that perspective, the swings for older women are at least as striking as that for men (see fig. 9). Results from the GSOEP provide some support that policies designed to scale back transfers played a role in that trend reversal for men after 2000; but it less clearly supports that narrative for women. The GSOEP also reveals that a decline in household wealth, relative to earnings potential, probably contributed to the higher employment rates at older ages since the 1990s. Given the enormous swings in employment rates for older persons over such short periods, I believe it prudent to reserve a decent-sized role for forces as yet not identified.

Endnotes

Author email address: Bils (mark.bils@rochester.edu). Nataliya Gimpelson contributed greatly to this discussion, with suggestions as well as research assistance. For acknowledgments, sources of research support, and disclosure of the author's material financial relationships, if any, please see https://www.nber.org/books-and-chapters/nber-macroeconomics-annual-2021-volume-36/comment-shocks-institutions-and-secular-changes-employment-older-individuals-bils.

1. A number of papers have noted large long-term trends across countries, with many focused on the differential trends across countries prior to 2000. A couple of examples include Ohanian, Raffo, and Rogerson (2008) and Carbonari, Atella, and Samà (2018). The work of Carbonari et al. extends to 2007 and also breaks by ages less than 30, versus 30 and above.

2. From 1984 to 1989, the survey covered only households in West Germany. I examined figures that exclude households living in the former East Germany throughout 1984–2018. But the takeaway from those would be quite similar to that taken from the figures below.

3. See https://data.worldbank.org/indicator/SP.DYN.LE00.IN?locations=DE for World Bank indicators for Germany.

4. There have been considerable shifts in occupations over time in Germany, with an increase in those classified as white-collar. In addition, I broke the samples reflected in figure 9 between workers whose modal occupation at ages 50–54 was blue-collar versus white-collar or civil service. The patterns exhibited in figure 9 appear for individuals regardless of the occupational breaks. White-collar (and civil service) workers do tend to display about a 15 percentage points higher EPOP at 55–64 than blue-collar, for both men and

women. That differential widened to more like 25–30 percentage points, for both sexes, during the 1990s.

5. For each individual, the average wage is calculated as earnings over hours. The median represents the median of these average wages.

6. Starting in 2012, subsequent changes gradually raise that age to 67 by 2029.

References

Boersch-Supan, Axel H., and Hendrik Juerges. 2011. "Disability, Pension Reform, and Early Retirement in Germany." Working Paper no. 17079 (May), NBER, Cambridge, MA.

Boppart, Timo, and Per Krusell. 2020. "Labor Supply in the Past, Present, and Future: A Balanced-Growth Perspective." *Journal of Political Economy* 128 (1): 118–57.

Carbonari, Lorenzo, Vincenzo Atella, and Paola Samà. 2018. "Hours Worked in Selected OECD Countries: An Empirical Assessment." *International Review of Applied Economics* 32 (4): 525–45.

Grabka, Markus M., and Christian Westermeier. 2015. "Real Net Worth of Households in Germany Fell between 2003 and 2013." *DIW Economic Bulletin* 5 (34): 441–50.

Ohanian, Lee, Andrea Raffo, and R. Rogerson. 2008. "Long-term Changes in Labor Supply and Taxes: Evidence from OECD Countries, 1956–2004." *Journal of Monetary Economics* 55 (8): 1353–62.

Steiner, Viktor. 2017. "The Labor Market for Older Workers in Germany." *Journal for Labour Market Research* 50 (1): 1–14.

Discussion

Erik Hurst began the discussion by asking how much of the employment increase in older cohorts can be accounted for by increases in part-time employment. The authors noted that although certainly part-time work did increase in some countries, it does not account for all the action. Discussant Mark Bils agreed, saying that between the years 2000 and 2018, there was a 50% increase in both the employment rate and annual hours, indicating that part-time work rose in a roughly proportional way.

Daron Acemoglu then commented that although he is sympathetic to the idea that institutional differences matter greatly, he thinks that there are two other factors that should not be overlooked. The first is that shocks are not age neutral. For instance, as Nir Jaimovich discussed, occupational distributions differ across age groups, so shocks with heterogeneous employment impact will have a differential effect across age groups. The second factor is health, which may be improving differentially across age groups, and certainly has improved differently across countries. The authors agreed with these comments and pointed to a section in the paper saying that it is natural to think that certain shocks, such as automation, globalization, and changing technology, may affect older workers more, even within education groups. Daron Acemoglu responded by saying that automation affected older groups more before the year 2000, but afterward it has affected middle ages more because of their occupation distribution.

The discussion next centered on the question of whether the observed trend in employment can be explained by changes in health. Michèle Tertilt followed up on Daron Acemoglu's comment and agreed that health

© 2022 National Bureau of Economic Research. All rights reserved. Published by The University of Chicago Press for the National Bureau of Economic Research. https://doi .org/10.1086/718667

appears to be an important component, because participation in the United States has increased for ages 65-plus, and even up to 70-plus, as emerged from Nir Jaimovich's discussion. She also noted that employment increases are more extreme for the educated, who also tend to be healthier. The authors responded that it is useful to distinguish two separate phenomena. On the one hand, there are slow-moving elements, such as health and education, pushing employment in older cohorts up. On the other hand, there is a separate trend break in the employment of older cohorts in the mid-1990s that is not reflected in a change in the trend of the aforementioned slow-moving elements. Although the authors recognize the importance of health, the focus of the paper is on the changes in trend. Loukas Karabarbounis followed up on this discussion by suggesting that the authors analyze labor supply outcomes by percentiles of the age distribution, as opposed to age, to address concerns about changes to the quality of usable time.

The authors thanked the discussants, noting they agreed with much of what was said. They commented that the discussants chose countries that bracketed the effect, with the United States being moderate and Germany extreme. The US response is likely more moderate due to fewer policy changes relative to the other countries. The authors noted that the policy and institutions leading to the older cohort employment decline were a consequence of the lump of labor fallacy, that to reduce youth unemployment you needed to encourage older worker retirement.

4

Climate Change Uncertainty Spillover in the Macroeconomy

Michael Barnett, *Arizona State University,* United States of America

William Brock, *University of Wisconsin and University of Missouri,* United States of America

Lars Peter Hansen, *University of Chicago and NBER,* United States of America

I. Introduction

There are many calls for policy implementation to address climate change based on confidence in our knowledge of the adverse impact of economic activity on the climate, and conversely the negative effects of climate change on economic outcomes. Our view is that the knowledge base to support quantitative modeling in the realm of climate change and elsewhere remains incomplete. Although there is a substantial body of evidence demonstrating the adverse human imprint on the environment, uncertainty comes into play when we build quantitative models aimed at capturing the dynamic transmission of human activity on the climate and on how adaptation to climate change will play out over time. In many arenas, it has been common practice in discussions of economic policy to shunt uncertainty to the background when building and using quantitative models. To truly engage in "evidence-based policy" requires that we are clear both about the quality of the evidence and the sensitivity to the modeling inputs used to interpret the evidence. Although the importance of quantifying uncertainty has been emphasized and implemented in a variety of scientific settings, the analysis of economic policy provides some unique challenges. Specifically, our aim is to explore ways to incorporate this uncertainty for the purposes of making quantitative assessments of alternative courses of action while exploring a broader conceptualization of uncertainty than is typical in econometric analyses. We

NBER Macroeconomics Annual, volume 36, 2022.
© 2022 National Bureau of Economic Research. All rights reserved. Published by The University of Chicago Press for the National Bureau of Economic Research. https://doi .org/10.1086/718668

see this challenge as much more than putting standard errors on econometric estimates or incorporating risk (uncertainty with known probabilities) into the analysis. We turn to developments in dynamic decision theory as a guide to how we confront uncertainty in policy analysis.

In climate economics, Weitzman (2012), Wagner and Weitzman (2015), and others have emphasized uncertainty in the climate system's dynamics and how this uncertainty could create fat-tailed distributions of potential damages. Relatedly, Pindyck (2013) and Morgan et al. (2017) find existing integrated assessment models in climate economics to be of little value in the actual prudent policy. We are sympathetic to their skepticism and are not offering simple repairs to the existing integrated assessment models in this area nor quick modifications to Environmental Protection Agency (EPA) postings for the social cost of carbon (SCC). Nevertheless, we find value in the use of models to engage in a form of "quantitative storytelling" and we explore the consequences for policy when multiple models or specifications are entertained.[1] Instead of proceeding with comparing policies model by model, our ambition is to incorporate at least some of the model uncertainty into the formal analysis. That is, our aim is to explore ways to assess policies with a more explicit accounting for the limits to our understanding. In the climate-economics arena, not only is there substantial uncertainty about the economic modeling inputs, but it is also about the geoscientific inputs.

Drawing on insights from decision theory and asset valuation, Barnett, Brock, and Hansen (2020) proposed a framework for assessing uncertainty, broadly conceived, to include ambiguity over alternative models and the potential form of the misspecification of each. As is demonstrated in that paper, this broad notion of uncertainty is reflected in an endogenously determined adjustment to the probabilities used to depict meaningful economic values. This adjustment pushes well beyond the familiar discussions of social discount rates in the environmental economics literature. But the examples in Barnett et al. (2020) scratch the surface of the actual quantitative assessment of uncertainty pertinent to the economics of climate change, and they abstract from setups in which the uncertainty is at least partially resolved in the future.

In Sections III and IV, this paper takes inventory of the alternative sources of uncertainty that are pertinent to climate change policy:

- *carbon dynamics* mapping carbon emissions into carbon in the atmosphere,
- *temperature dynamics* mapping carbon in the atmosphere into temperature changes, and

- *economic damage functions* that depict the fraction of the productive capacity that is reduced by temperature changes.

We necessarily adopt some stark simplifications to make this analysis tractable. Many of the climate models are both high dimensional and nonlinear. Rather than using those models directly, we rely on outcomes of pulse
experiments applied to the models. We then take the outcomes of these
pulse experiments as inputs into our simplified specification of the climate
dynamics inside our economic model. We follow much of the environmental macroeconomic modeling literature in the use of ad hoc static damage functions, and explore the consequences of changing the curvature in
these damage functions. Even with these simplifications, our uncertainty
analysis is sufficiently rich to show how uncertainty about the alternative
channels by which emissions induce economic damages interact in important ways. Modeling extensions that confront heterogeneity in exposure to
climate change across regions will also open the door to the inclusion of
cross-sectional evidence for measuring potential environmental damages.

Decision theory provides tractable ways to explore a trade-off between
projecting the "best guess" consequences of alternative courses of action
and "worst possible" outcomes among a set of alternative models. Rather
than focusing exclusively on these extremal points, we allow our decision
maker to take intermediate positions in accordance with parameters that
govern aversions to model ambiguity and potential misspecification. We
presume a decision maker confronts many dimensions of uncertainty and
engages in a sensitivity analysis. To simplify the policy analysis, we consider a world with a "fictitious social planner." Thus, we put to the side
important questions pertaining to heterogeneity in the exposure to climate
change and to the consequent policy objectives by different decision makers. Instead, we simplify the policy implementation to that of a Pigouvian
tax that eliminates the wedge between market valuation and social valuation. We use this setup to illustrate how uncertainty can contribute to social valuation while recognizing the need for further model richness in future research. Our planner confronts risk, model ambiguity, and model
misspecification formally and deduces a socially efficient emissions trajectory. The planner's decision problem adds structure to the sensitivity
analysis and reduces a potentially high-dimensional sensitivity analysis
to a two-dimensional characterization of sensitivity parameterized by
aversion to model ambiguity and potential misspecification. We describe
formally in Section V some convenient continuous-time formulations of
decision theory designed so that recursive methods familiar in economic
dynamics can be applied with tractable modifications.

We use the SCC as a barometer for investigating the consequences of uncertainty for climate policy. In settings with uncertainty, the SCC is the economic cost to the current and future uncertain environmental and economic damages induced by an incremental increase in emissions. In effect, it is the current period cost of an adverse social cash flow. Borrowing insights from asset pricing, this cash flow should be discounted stochastically in ways that account for uncertainty. This follows in part revealing discussions in Golosov et al. (2014) and Cai, Judd, and Lontzek (2017), who explore some of the risk consequences for the SCC. We extend this by taking a broader perspective on uncertainty. The common discussion in environmental economics about what "rate" should be used to discount future social costs is ill-posed for the model ambiguity that we feature. Rather than a single rate, we borrow and extend an idea from asset pricing by representing broadly based uncertainty adjustments as a change in probability over future outcomes for the macroeconomy. As we argue formally in Section VI, when we incorporate uncertainty we are pushed away from the commonly employed modular approaches for measuring the SCC as the modular components to the SCC become much more intertwined.[2] Drawing on insights from recursive approaches to economic dynamics adds clarity to how best to rationalize and quantify the SCC in presence of decision-maker uncertainty.

Finally, this paper extends previous work by "opening the hood" of climate change uncertainty and exploring which components have the biggest impact on valuation. Rather than embrace a "one-model-fits-all-types-of-approaches" perspective, we give three computational examples designed to illustrate different points. The example presented in Section VII is by far the most ambitious and sets the stage for the other two. This first example explores what impact future information about environmental and economic damages, triggered by temperature anomaly thresholds, should have on current policy. It adds a dynamic richness missing from other treatments of model uncertainty. The second example, presented in Section VIII, implements a novel decomposition of uncertainty assessing the relative importance of uncertainties in carbon dynamics, temperature dynamics, and damage function uncertainty. The approach that is described and implemented in Section VIII is more generally applicable to other economic environments. Finally, the third example investigates the interacting implications of the uncertainties in the development of green technologies and in environmental damages for prudent policy. This example is developed in Section IX.

In the next section, we elaborate on some of the prior contributions that motivate our analysis.

II. Some Motivating Literature

Palmer and Stevens (2019) take inventory of what we know about climate change from basic principles, although they note the limits to the existing efforts at quantitative modeling. They articulate the disconnect between arguments made to advance environmental policy and the state of knowledge coming from climate science. Moreover, they argue for the systematic inclusion and quantification of stochastic components in climate models as a way to make a substantive improvement in predictive models from climate science, even though the "big picture" is quite settled. Palmer and Stevens proposed modeling improvements that are well beyond the ambition of our work, but we have a shared appreciation for explicit stochastic modeling. It is important for our uncertainty quantification methods that we incorporate explicit randomness to partially disguise the model ambiguity and misspecification from a decision maker. We aim to enrich the policy discussions by acknowledging rather than disguising uncertainty.

Our specification of damage function uncertainty can be motivated in part by "tipping points" in the climate system. Consistent with our formulation, Sharpe and Lenton (2021) and Lenton (2020), though noting that the "great majority of climate tipping points are damaging ones, and they may be closer than is often assumed," also present evidence for tipping points that open the door to a far greener and less damaged economy. Lenton, then, highlights the need to comprehensively study the uncertainty in such complicated, nonlinear settings so that we can effectively risk-manage positive and negative tipping points. Our example includes the possibility of good news with the delay in the Poisson event realization. On the other hand, although we are illustrating an important message for policy making, our example is too simplistic to connect formally to tipping-point specifications and the resulting uncertainties.[3]

Hausfather and Peters (2020) noted that policy makers and researchers have increasingly designated scenarios as "business as usual" without good justification. The formal use of decision theory allows for useful distinctions between adverse scenarios that are possible and best guesses for decision makers to trade off considerations between such projections.

In prior work, Rudik (2020) explored damage function uncertainty. He reviewed the extensive literature on damage functions and developed a

Bayesian learning framework about uncertain damage function parameters together with an analysis of the effects of robustness concerns caused by misspecification of the damage functions. Our formulation of damage function uncertainty differs substantially from his because of our Poisson event that governs damage function steepness. In our analysis, observations prior to this event are not informative about the damage function curvature beyond a threshold yet to be attained.

III.   Uncertain Climate Dynamics

In this section, we first describe some very tractable characterizations of cross-model variation in the dynamic responses of temperature to emission pulses. To support our analysis, we then build a simplified stochastic specification of the pulse responses.

A.   Simple Approximations to Climate Dynamics

Recent contributions to the climate-science literature have produced low-dimensional approximations, emulators, and pulse experiments that provide tractable alternatives to full-scale Atmospheric-Oceanic General Circulation Models (AOGCMs) used by climate scientists. These results allow for the inclusion of climate models within economic frameworks in ways that can be informative and revealing. We use the pulse experiment results of Joos et al. (2013) and Geoffroy et al. (2013) across various carbon and climate dynamics models to build the set of models we will use in our uncertainty analysis.[4]

Joos et al. (2013) report the responses of atmospheric carbon concentration to emission pulses of 100 gigatonnes of carbon for several alternative Earth System models. The emission pulse experiments follow a standardized model intercomparison analysis so that outcomes are directly comparable. We use the responses for nine such models to capture the variation and uncertainty present in models of carbon cycle dynamics.

We feed these responses for carbon concentration into log-linear approximations of temperature dynamics constructed by Geoffroy et al. (2013). In accordance with the Arrhenius (1896) equation, these dynamics relate the logarithm of carbon in the atmosphere to future temperature. The parameters that Geoffroy et al. (2013) constructed using their simplified representation differ depending on the model being approximated. We use the 16 models listed in appendix A. Thus, we take the nine different atmospheric carbon responses as inputs into the 16 temperature dynamics approximations, giving us a total of 144 different temperature responses to emissions.[5]

Figure 1 captures the resulting temperature responses across various sets of these 144 models. The top panel provides the results based on all 144 models, the middle panel provides the results based on variation in the carbon models, and the bottom panel provides the results based on variation in the temperature models. In each case, the maximal temperature response to an emission pulse occurs at about a decade and the subsequent response is very flat. These dynamics are consistent with the response patterns featured by Ricke and Caldeira (2014).

The top panel of figure 1 also reports the percentiles for each horizon computed using the 144 different temperature response functions from all the different combinations of models of carbon and temperature dynamics. Although there are similar patterns across the temperature response functions, there is considerable heterogeneity in the magnitudes of the responses. For a further characterization of this heterogeneity, we compute the exponentially weighted average of each of these response functions and use them in our computations. We report the resulting histogram in figure 2.

The eventually flat trajectories of the temperature response functions are consistent with model comparisons made using what is called the transient climate response (TCRE) to carbon dioxide emissions. The TCRE is the ratio of CO_2-induced warming realized over an interval of time to the cumulative carbon emissions over that same time interval. This linear characterization provides a simplification suggested by Matthews et al. (2009) and others by targeting the composite response of the carbon and temperature dynamics instead of the components that induce it. MacDougall, Swart, and Knutti (2017) provide a pedagogical summary of this literature and report a histogram for the TCRE computed for 150 model variants. Their histogram looks very similar to what we report in figure 2.

The middle and bottom panels of figure 1 show the contribution of uncertainty in temperature and carbon dynamics to the temperature impulse responses. In generating the middle panel of figure 1, we computed the implied temperature responses for 9 alternative models of atmospheric CO_2 dynamics averaging over the 16 models of temperature dynamics. In generating the lower panel of figure 1, we computed the 16 temperature responses for 16 temperature models while averaging over the nine models of atmospheric CO_2 dynamics. Consistent with the results reported by Ricke and Caldeira (2014), we find heterogeneity in

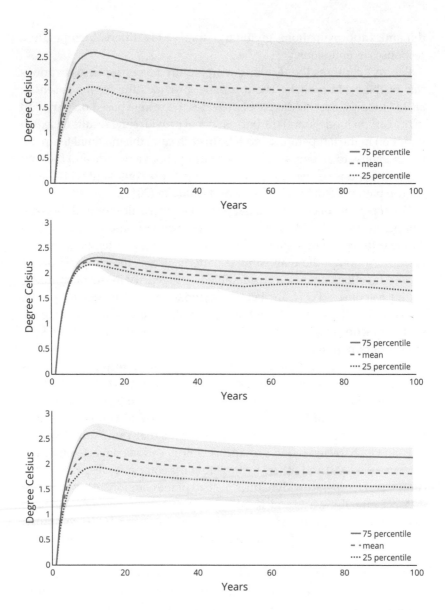

Fig. 1. Percentiles for temperature responses to emission impulses. The emission pulse was 100 gigatonnes of carbon (GtC) spread over the first year. The temperature units for the vertical axis have been multiplied by 10 to convert to degree Celsius per teratonne of carbon (TtC). The boundaries of the shaded regions are the upper and lower envelopes. Top panel: percentiles for impulse responses including both carbon and temperature dynamic uncertainty. Center panel: responses obtained for the different carbon responses for nine models each averaged more than the 16 models of temperature dynamics. Bottom panel: percentiles for the 16 temperature responses using each averaged more than the nine models of carbon concentration dynamics. A color version of this figure is available online.

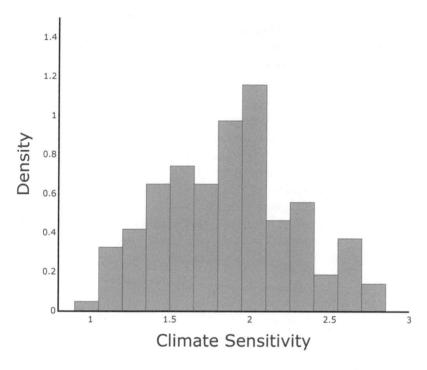

Fig. 2. Histograms for the exponentially weighted average responses of temperature to an emissions impulse from 144 different models using a rate $\delta = .01$. A color version of this figure is available online.

the temperature responses to be more prominent than that coming from the atmospheric CO_2 dynamics.[6]

B.   *Stochastic Climate Pulses*

To explore uncertainty, we introduce explicit stochasticity as a precursor to the study of uncertainty. We capture this randomness in part by an exogenous forcing process that evolves as

$$dZ_t = \mu_z(Z_t)dt + \sigma_z(Z_t)dW_t,$$

where $\{W_t : t \geq 0\}$ is a multivariate standard Brownian motion. We partition the vector Brownian motion into three subvectors as follows:

$$W_t = \begin{bmatrix} W_t^y \\ W_t^n \\ W_t^k \end{bmatrix},$$

where the first component consists of the climate change shocks, the second component contains damage shocks, and the third component captures the technology shocks. Consider an emissions "pulse" of the form

$$(\iota_y \cdot Z_t)\mathcal{E}_t(\theta dt + \varsigma \cdot dW_t^y),$$

where $\mathcal{E}_t$ is fossil-fuel emissions and $\iota_y \cdot Z = \{\iota_y \cdot Z_t : t \geq 0\}$ is a positive process that we normalize to have mean one. The $\iota_y \cdot Z$-process captures "left out" components of the climate system's reaction to an emission of $\mathcal{E}_t$ gigatonnes into the atmosphere while the $\varsigma \cdot dW_t^y$ process captures short time-scale fluctuations. We will use a positive Feller square root process for the $\iota_y \cdot Z$ process in our analysis.

Within this framework, we impose the "Matthews' approximation" by making the consequence of the pulse permanent. The temperature anomaly, $Y = \{Y_t : t \geq 0\}$, evolves stochastically as

$$dY_t = \mu_y(Z_t, \mathcal{E}_t)dt + \sigma_y(Z_t, \mathcal{E}_t)dW_t^y,$$

where

$$\mu_y(z, e) = e(\iota_y \cdot z)\theta$$
$$\sigma_y(z, e) = e(\iota_y \cdot z)\varsigma'.$$

Throughout, we will use uppercase letters to denote random vector or stochastic processes and lowercase letters to denote possible realizations. Armed with this "Matthews' approximation," we collapse the climate change uncertainty into the cross-model empirical distribution reported in figure 2. We will eventually introduce uncertainty about θ.

This specification misses the initial buildup in the temperature response and instead focuses exclusively on the flat trajectories depicted in the upper panel of figure 1. We expect that this error might be small when the prudent social planner embraces preferences that have a low rate of discounting the future, but this requires further investigation. Although others in climate sciences find linear approximations to be relevant, we recognize the need for subsequent efforts to explore systematically the potential importance of nonlinearities. Ghil and Lucarini (2020) is a thorough review of climate physics at a hierarchy of temporal and spatial scales that embraces the inherent complexity of the climate system.

Remark 3.1. For a more general starting point, let Y_t be a vector used to represent system dynamics where the temperature anomaly in this specification is the first component of Y_t. This state vector evolves according to

$$dY_t = \Lambda Y_t dt + \left(\iota_y \cdot Z_t\right)\mathcal{E}_t(\Theta dt + \Phi dW_t^y),$$

where Λ is a square matrix and Θ is a column vector. Given an initial condition Y_0, the solution for Y_t satisfies

$$Y_t = \exp(t\Lambda)Y_0 + \int_0^t \exp[(t-u)\Lambda]\left(\iota_y \cdot Z_u\right)\mathcal{E}_u(\Theta du + \Phi dW_u^y).$$

Thus under this specification, the expected future response of Y to a pulse at date zero is

$$\exp(u\Lambda)\Theta.$$

It is the first component of this function that determines the response dynamics of the temperature anomaly to an emissions pulse to the climate system. This generalization allows for multiple exponentials to approximate the pulse responses. Our introduction of a multiple exponential approximation adapts, for example, Joos et al. (2013) and Pierrehumbert (2014).[7]

As an example, we capture the initial rise in the emission responses by the following two-dimensional specification:

$$dY_t^1 = Y_t^2 dt$$
$$dY_t^2 = -\lambda Y_t^2 dt + \lambda\theta\mathcal{E}_t dt,$$

which implies the response to a pulse is

$$\theta[1 - \exp(-\lambda t)]\mathcal{E}_0.$$

A high value of λ implies more rapid convergence to the limiting response $\theta\mathcal{E}_0$. This approximation is intended as a simple representation of the dynamics where the second state variable can be thought of as an exponentially weighted average of current and past emissions.[8]

Remark 3.2. The approximation in Geoffroy et al. (2013) includes the logarithm of carbon in the atmosphere as argued for by Arrhenius (1896), which is not directly reflected in the linear approximation to the temperature dynamics that we use. The pulse experiments from Joos et al. (2013) show a more than proportional change in atmospheric carbon when the pulse size is changed. It turns out that this is enough to approximately offset the logarithmic Arrhenius adjustment so that the long-term temperature response remains approximately proportional for small pulse sizes. See also Pierrehumbert (2014), who discusses the approximate offsetting impacts of nonlinearity in temperature and climate dynamics.

IV. Uncertain Environmental and Economic Damages

Discussions of climate change policy are often simplified to specifications of temperature anomaly targets. For instance, many such discussions used a 2-degree anomaly as an upper bound on the amount of climate change that policy-makers should tolerate. More recently, this target number has been reduced to the point where numbers as low as a 1.5-degree anomaly should be entertained as a target upper bound with warnings of potentially severe consequences once warming exceeds these thresholds. There is considerable debate as to the scientific underpinnings of such thresholds. Moreover, economic analyses have often introduced so-called damage functions whereby economic opportunities are reduced by global warming depending on the curvature of the damage function. Although damage functions are ad hoc simplifications that simplify the model solution and analysis, there remains considerable uncertainty as to their steepness.

For purposes of illustration, we introduce explicitly stochastic models of damages. The specification includes an unknown threshold whereby the curvature becomes apparent. In some of our computations, this threshold occurs somewhere between 1.5 and 2 degree Celsius, but we also explore what happens when this interval is shifted to the right. Under a baseline specification, damage function curvature is realized in accordance with a Poisson event and an intensity that depends on the temperature anomaly. The event is more likely to be revealed in the near future when the temperature anomaly is larger. Although we adopt a probabilistic formulation as a baseline, we will entertain ambiguity over damage function curvature and potential misspecification of the Poisson intensity. We intend our specification of the damage function to reflect that the value of future empiricism in the near term will be limited as the climate-economic system is pushed into uncharted territory. On the other hand, we allow for the damage function steepness to be revealed in the future as the climate system moves potentially closer to an environmental tipping point.

We posit a damage process, $N_t = \{N_t : t \geq 0\}$, to capture negative externalities on society imposed by carbon emissions. The reciprocal of damages, $1/N_t$, diminishes the productive capacity of the economy because of the impact of climate change. We follow much of climate-economics literature by presuming that the process N reflects, in part, the outcome of a damage function evaluated at the temperature anomaly process. Importantly, we use a family of damage functions in place of a single function. Our construction of the alternative damage functions is similar to Barnett et al. (2020) with specifications motivated in part by prior contributions. Importantly, we modify their damage specifications in three ways:

- we entertain more damage functions, including ones that are more extreme,

- we allow for damage function steepness to emerge at an ex ante unknown temperature anomaly threshold, and

- we presume that ex post this uncertainty is resolved.

We consider a specification under which there is a temperature anomaly threshold after which the damage function could be much more curved. This curvature in the "tail" of the damage function is only revealed to decision makers when a Poisson event is triggered. As our model is highly stylized, the damages captured by the Poisson event are meant to capture more than just the economic consequences of a narrowly defined temperature movements. Temperature changes are allowed to trigger other forms of climate change that in turn can spill over into the macroeconomy.

In our computational implementation, we use a piecewise log-quadratic function for mapping how temperature changes induced by emissions alter economic opportunities. The Poisson intensity governing the jump probability is an increasing function of the temperature anomaly. We specify it so that the Poisson event is triggered prior to the anomaly hitting an upper threshold $\bar{y}$. Construct a process

$$\bar{Y}_t = \begin{cases} Y_t & t < \tau \\ Y_t - Y_\tau + \bar{y} & t \geq \tau \end{cases},$$

where τ is the date of a Poisson event. Notice that $\bar{Y}_\tau = \bar{y}$. The damages are given by

$$\log N_t = \Gamma(\bar{Y}_t) + \iota_n \cdot Z_t, \tag{1}$$

where

$$\Gamma(y) = \gamma_1 y + \frac{\gamma_2}{2} y^2 + \frac{\gamma_3^m}{2} \mathbf{1}_{y \geq \bar{y}} (y - \bar{y})^2$$

and the only component of dW pertinent for the evolution of $\iota_n \cdot Z_t$ is dW_t^n. Neither do decision makers know when the Poisson event will be triggered nor do they know ex ante what the value of γ_3^m is prior to the realization of that event. At the time of the Poisson event, one of M values of γ_3^m is realized. In our application the coefficients γ_3^m are specified so that the proportional damages are equally spaced after the threshold $\bar{y}$.

The intensity function, $\mathcal{J}$, determines the possibility of a jump over the next small increment in time. For $Y_t = y$, $\epsilon \mathcal{J}(y)$ is the approximate jump probability over small time increment ϵ. Equivalently, $\mathcal{J}$ is a local measure of probability per unit of time. In our computations, we use intensity function

$$\mathcal{J}(y) = \begin{cases} r_1 \left(\exp\left[\frac{r_2}{2} (y - \underline{y})^2 \right] - 1 \right) & y \geq \underline{y} \\ 0 & 0 \leq y < \underline{y}, \end{cases}$$

as depicted in figure 3. As $\mathcal{J}$ is increasing in y, jumps become all the more likely as Y_t approaches the upper threshold $\bar{y}$. This intensity depends on $\underline{y}$, which we refer to as the lower threshold. We set the values of (r_1, r_2) so that the probability that the Poisson event is realized prior to $Y_t = \bar{y}$ is essentially unity. Thus, the uncertainty is concentrated for state Y in the interval $[\underline{y}, \bar{y}]$. We use the intensity plotted in figure 3 in computations that follow for $\underline{y} = 1.5$ and $\bar{y} = 2$.

The probability that the process has not jumped over the time interval $[0, t)$ is

$$\exp\left[-\int_0^t \mathcal{J}(Y_\tau)d\tau\right]$$

so that a larger intensity makes the jumps more likely.

Figure 4 shows the range of damage function uncertainty that we impose in our computations. Given our intensity specification, we expect the Poisson jumps to occur between 1.5 and 2 degree Celsius. The upper panel shows the potential damage function quantiles when the jump is delayed until a 2-degree temperature anomaly. These functions are all continuous extensions of initial damage functions beyond $\bar{y}$. When a jump occurs at anomalies less than 2, the damage functions are steeper. This is illustrated in the lower panel, which shows the possible damage

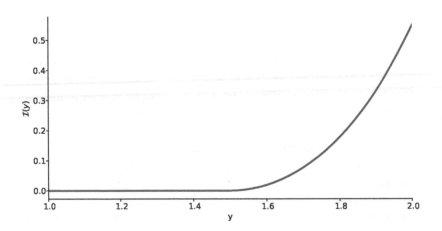

Fig. 3. Intensity function, $r_1 = 1.5$ and $r_2 = 2.5$. With this intensity function, the probability of a jump at an anomaly of 1.6 is approximately .02 per annum, increasing to about .08 per annum at an anomaly of 1.7, increasing further to approximately .18 per annum at an anomaly of 1.8 and then to about one-third per annum when the anomaly is 1.9. A color version of this figure is available online.

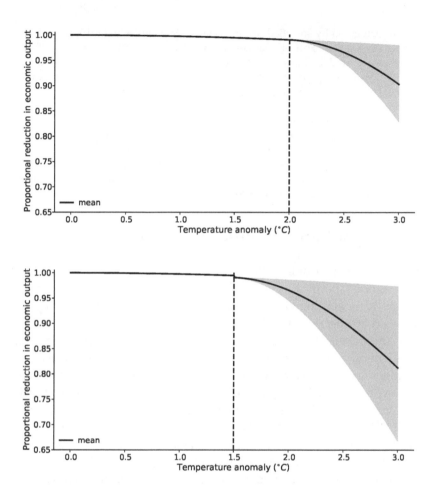

Fig. 4. Range of possible damage functions for different jump thresholds. The shaded regions in these plots give the range of possible values for exp($-n$), which measures the proportional reduction of the productive capacity of the economy. The top panel shows the damage function curvature when the jump occurs at $Y_t = 2.0$, and the bottom panel shows the damage function curvature if that jump happens at $Y_t = 1.5$. A color version of this figure is available online.

function quantiles for temperature anomalies beyond the anomaly just prior to the jump. Earlier jump dates imply steeper damage functions and are thus a form of "bad news." In contrast, delayed jumps are "good news."

Remark 4.1. Our choice of $\underline{y} = 1.5$ and $\bar{y} = 2$ degree Celsius thresholds for the temperature anomaly is motivated by discussions in the climate-science literature. Thus these damage functions are not only more than economic responses to changes in temperature but also inclusive of potentially dramatic environmental changes triggered by so-called tipping points. Drijfhout et al. (2015) provided a catalog of potential abrupt changes implied by projections from a variety of earth-science models. Motivated by such concerns about such changes, Rogelj et al. (2018) and Rogelj et al. (2019) suggested a 1.5-degree temperature anomaly as a goal for limiting human damages of the climate system. As this goal may be unachievable, they point to a 2-degree target in line with the 2015 Paris agreement, while noting the increased danger of severe damages. Although there are concerns about temperature anomalies triggering these tipping points, Ritchie et al. (2021) used recent developments in dynamical systems theory to argue that "the point of no return" for climate thresholds is highly uncertain. As an external form of sensitivity analysis, we also report results with the temperature threshold shifted to the right with $\underline{y} = 1.75$ and $\bar{y} = 2.25$.

V. Model Ambiguity and Misspecification Concerns

The model we have built so far is one in which uncertainty is captured by the stochastic specification of shocks as is typical when building dynamic stochastic models in macroeconomics. We think of this shock specification as characterizing risk. The presence of these shocks opens the door to a comprehensive assessment of uncertainty in which we entertain a broader notion of uncertainty. We include uncertainty over model specifications and parameters, which we refer to as ambiguity. In this discussion, we treat models and parameters as synonymous by thinking of each parameter as indexing an alternative model. As in our prior work, Barnett et al. (2020) and Berger and Marinacci (2020), we are led to depart from the Bayesian approach, which starts with the specification of a subjective prior over the alternative models, but does not distinguish the role of subjective probabilities over models from the probabilities given a model. Instead, we use recent formalisms from decision theory under uncertainty to explore the impact of uncertainty over the subjective inputs. Within statistics, this gave rise to robust counterparts to Bayesian inferences in the study of prior sensitivity, often outside the realm of a specific decision problem. The decision theory framework formalizes the question of "sensitivity to what?" and the formal trade-off between making best guesses versus possible bad outcomes as we look across models. Although in some settings, data richness may diminish the role of prior sensitivity, we find the economics of climate change to be a problem whereby prior sensitivity remains an important question for the decision maker. Of course, any model we write down is necessarily a simplification. We also incorporate concerns about the potential misspecification of the models under exploration using ideas from robust control theory extended to dynamic economic models.

Our use of decision theory gives rise to a form of uncertainty quantification. Uncertainty quantification in the sciences is typically done by researchers. For instance, we might ask how the SCC differs as we change the modeling ingredients. But decision makers also confront this uncertainty, including ones inside the models that we build. Thus, model ambiguity or misspecification concerns by decision makers should arguably be taken into account when determining the prudent course of action. This same uncertainty emerges as adjustments to the SCC as set by, say, a benevolent social planner. Just as risk aversion can induce caution in decision-making, the same can be said of broader notions of uncertainty aversion. Although the decision theory we use does not determine the magnitude of what this aversion should be, it reduces a potentially high-dimensional sensitivity analysis to a much lower-dimensional one captured by low-dimensional representations of uncertainty aversion.

We analyze this uncertainty using the formalism of decision theory under uncertainty. We apply two versions of such theory; one comes under the heading of variational preferences and the other under smooth ambiguity preferences. We adapt both to continuous-time specifications, which facilitates their implementation and interpretation. We use this decision theory to reduce the sensitivity analysis to a one- or two-dimensional parameterization that locates the potential misspecification that is most consequential to a decision maker. Our aim is to provide a more complete uncertainty quantification within the setting of decision problems.

A. State Dynamics

Posing our model in continuous time leads to a simplified characterization of robustness. When constructing dynamic programming solutions, it is advantageous to represent the local dynamics

$$\lim_{\epsilon \downarrow 0} \frac{1}{\epsilon} \mathbb{E}[V(X_{t+\epsilon}) - V(X_t) \mid X_t = x, a)] = \mu(x, a) \cdot \frac{\partial V}{\partial x}(x)$$
$$+ \frac{1}{2} \text{trace}\left[\frac{\partial^2 V}{\partial x \partial x'}(x)\Sigma(x, a)'\right] + \mathcal{I}(x)\int[V(\tilde{x}) - V(x)]Q(d\tilde{x} \mid x),$$

(2)

where Σ is the diffusion matrix

$$\Sigma(x, a) = \sigma(x, a)\sigma(x, a)',$$

and local exposure of X_t to a multivariate standard Brownian motion is $\sigma(X_t, a)\, dW_t$, $\mathcal{I}$ is the state-dependent jump intensity, and $Q(d\tilde{x} \mid x)$ is the jump distribution conditioned on the process jumping. Both the intensity and the jump distribution can depend on the current Markov state. The first two contributions to the drift of $V(X_t)$ are familiar from Ito's Lemma. We allow for both μ and σ to depend on a current action a. The baseline probabilities are the ones implied by this stochastic process specification.

Given our interest in recursive methods, in what follows we will describe in turn implications for misspecifying a Brownian motion, a jump process, and an ambiguity adjustment for the local mean of the dynamical system.[9] We introduce robustness by following the approach described in Anderson, Hansen, and Sargent (2003) and model ambiguity by following the approach in Hansen and Miao (2018).

B. Misspecified Brownian Increments

Following James (1992), Hansen and Sargent (2001), and others, the potential misspecification of a Brownian motion has a particularly simple form. It is known from the famed Girsanov Theorem that a change in distribution represented by a likelihood ratio replaces the standard Brownian motion by a Brownian motion with a drift. Specifically, under such a change in probability distribution, dW_t is changed from a Brownian increment to a Brownian increment with a drift or local mean that can be state (or model) dependent, which we denote $H_t d_t$. Thus, to explore the consequences of misspecification, we modify our (locally) normally distributed shocks by entertaining possible mean distortions. Allowing for arbitrary changes in the drift without a constraint or a penalty leads to an uninteresting and inflexible decision problem. Here we follow one of the preference specifications in Hansen and Sargent (2001) whereby we use an expected log-likelihood ratio measure of discrepancy called relative entropy to restrain the search over alternative possible drift specifications.[10] For Brownian motion models, the relative entropy penalty is $(\xi_r/2)|H_t|^2 dt$ where ξ_r is the penalty parameter that governs the decision maker's concern for misspecification and $(1/2)|H_t|^2 dt$ is the local contribution to relative entropy.

Given our intention to use recursive methods, we characterize the impact that the Brownian motion has for the state dynamics in terms of the local means for functions of the Markov state. We allow for the probabilities implied by a multivariate standard Brownian motion to be modified to include possible drift distortions. Equivalently, we introduce potential model misspecification by replacing μ by

$$\min{}_h \frac{\partial V}{\partial x} \cdot (\mu + \sigma h) + \frac{\xi_r}{2} h'h = \frac{\partial V}{\partial x} \cdot \mu - \frac{1}{2\xi_r} \left(\frac{\partial V}{\partial x}\right)' \Sigma \left(\frac{\partial V}{\partial x}\right), \qquad (3)$$

where the minimizing h is

$$h^* = -\frac{1}{\xi_r}\sigma'\frac{\partial V}{\partial x};$$

h is a drift distortion in the Brownian increment. This distortion is state dependent as reflected by the partial derivative of the value function. The term $(1/2)h'h$ is the local measure of relative entropy implied the local normality of Brownian motion. Large values of the penalty parameter ξ_r induce small robustness adjustments.

C. Misspecified Jump Components

To specify a Markov jump process requires both (a) a state-dependent intensity, $\mathcal{I}$, governing the probability of a jump, and (b) the distribution $Q(\cdot \mid x)$ over the postjump state given the current jump state, x. Both of these could be mistaken. We capture potential misspecification by introducing positive functions g of the postjump state:

$$\mathcal{I}(x)\int[V(\tilde{x}) - V(x)]g(\tilde{x})Q(d\tilde{x} \mid x).$$

The implied probabilities resulting from the concern about misspecification are given by

$$\frac{1}{\bar{g}(x)}g(\tilde{x})Q(d\tilde{x} \mid x)$$

and the implied intensity is given by $\bar{g}(x)\mathcal{I}(x)$, where

$$\bar{g}(x) \doteq \int g(\tilde{x})Q(d\tilde{x} \mid x).$$

Thus the choice of g determines both the jump probabilities and the jump intensities in a manner that is mathematically tractable. The local relative entropy discrepancy for a jump process is

$$\mathcal{I}(x)\int\left[1 - g(\tilde{x}) + g(\tilde{x})\log g(\tilde{x})\right]Q(d\tilde{x} \mid x).$$

This measure is nonnegative because the convex function $g \log g$ exceeds its gradient $g - 1$ evaluated at $g = 1$.

We make a robustness adjustment by solving

$$\min_{g}\mathcal{I}(x)\int[V(\tilde{x}) - V(x)]g(\tilde{x})Q(d\tilde{x} \mid x)$$
$$+ \xi_r\mathcal{I}(x)\int\left[1 - g(\tilde{x}) + g(\tilde{x})\log g(\tilde{x})\right]Q(d\tilde{x} \mid x).$$

The minimizing g is given by

$$g^*(\tilde{x}, x) = \exp\left(-\frac{1}{\xi_r}[V(\tilde{x}) - V(x)]\right)$$

with a minimized objective given by

$$\xi_r \mathcal{I}(x) \int \left[1 - \exp\left(-\frac{1}{\xi_r}[V(\tilde{x}) - V(x)]\right)\right] Q(d\tilde{x} \mid x).$$

We use this outcome in place of the jump contribution

$$\int [V(\tilde{x}) - V(x)]Q(d\tilde{x} \mid x)$$

in the local mean contribution for a continuous-time Hamilton-Jacobi-Bellman (HJB) equation.

D.   Structured Ambiguity

To assess the consequences of the heterogeneous responses from alternative climate models, we use what are called recursive smooth ambiguity preferences proposed by Klibanoff, Marinacci, and Mukerji (2009). For an important special case of these preferences, Hansen and Sargent (2007) provide a robust prior/posterior interpretation of these preferences. This alternative interpretation has advantages both in terms of calibration and representation of social valuation, which we exploit in our characterization. In deploying such preferences, we use a robust prior interpretation in conjunction with the continuous-time formulation of smooth ambiguity proposed by Hansen and Miao (2018).

To assess the consequences of the heterogeneous responses from alternative climate models, we follow Hansen and Miao (2018). Suppose that $\mu(x, a \mid \theta)$ where θ is an unknown parameter. In our applications, θ is the climate sensitivity parameter pertinent for the Matthew's approximation. Let π denote a subjective probability distribution over θ. For instance, this could be the cross-model distribution coming from the alternative pulse experiments reported in figure 1. To justify this distribution as a meaningful distribution from a decision-theoretic perspective requires that all model outputs be treated as equally plausible. In Bayesian parlance, π would be a current period posterior dependent on an initial prior and likelihood. The decision maker does not have full confidence in the posterior and engages in a robust adjustment by solving

$$\min_{f, \int f(\theta)\pi(d\theta) = 1} \frac{\partial V}{\partial x}(x) \cdot \int \mu(x, a \mid \theta) f(\theta) \pi(d\theta) + \xi_a \int f(\theta) \log f(\theta) \pi(d\theta), \quad (4)$$

where $f(\theta)$ is a density relative to a baseline probability π. The minimizing f is

$$f^*(\theta \mid x, a) \propto \exp\left[-\left(\frac{1}{\xi_a}\right) \frac{\partial V}{\partial x}(x) \cdot \mu(x, a \mid \theta)\right],$$

where the right side requires scaling to be a proper relative density.[11] The minimizing objective is

$$-\xi_a \log\left(\int \exp\left[-\left(\frac{1}{\xi_a}\right) \frac{\partial V}{\partial x}(x) \cdot \mu(x, a \mid \theta)\right] \pi(d\theta)\right),$$

which replaces

$$\frac{\partial V}{\partial x}(x) \cdot \int \mu(x, a \mid \theta) \pi(d\theta)$$

in an HJB equation.

E. A Valuation Adjustment for Uncertainty

There is much discussion in the literature on environmental economics about what discount rate to use. In our analysis so far, there is a single discount rate used to define the preferences of a fictitious social planner. But the discussions in the literature usually refer to present discounted value formulas for marginal valuation. We represented the robust adjustments in terms of altered probabilities, which we compute in conjunction with the HJB equations used for optimization. As Barnett et al. (2020) demonstrate, these same probabilities provide the uncertainty adjustments for social valuation. Thus, to account for uncertainty, broadly conceived, we are pushed beyond the question of what discount rate to use because the necessary adjustment is most conveniently depicted as an altered probability measure.

F. Other Approaches to Uncertainty Quantification across Models

We briefly discuss three prior forms of uncertainty quantification as it pertains to unknown parameters or models. We give these as illustrations, but the list is by no means exhaustive.

Olson et al. (2012) propose and implement a Bayesian method for making inferences about certain parameters of interest, including a climate sensitivity parameter coming from the UVic (University of Victoria) Earth System climate model. They document posterior sensitivity of the climate sensitivity parameter to priors and other unknown modeling inputs. In particular, they show the need to use an informative prior for climate sensitivity to obtain reasonable results, therefore demonstrating the posterior uncertainty in their informative statistical investigation. Although not the focal point of their analysis, there is additional uncertainty in the likelihood construction. These forms of uncertainty are pertinent not only to researchers presenting evidence but also to decision or policy makers in their efforts. Thus, we move the uncertainty quantification "inside the decision problem," including the sensitivity analysis. This allows us to explore the impact of model or parameter ambiguity for choosing socially prudent emissions trajectories and imputing the implied SCC.

In an alternative investigation of uncertainty within and across climate-economic models, Gillingham et al. (2018) and Nordhaus (2018) computed distributions of model outcomes given a priori distributions of parameters, specifications, and model inputs, including emissions pathways. From their analysis, they are able to produce a set of outputs associated with each parameter or model configuration to demonstrate the role of uncertainty in their setting. Their static analysis occurs "outside the decision problem," but it opens the door to exploring changes in the prior probability distribution without a systematic analysis of the sensitivity. Our framework uses recursive methods and decision-theoretic tools to determine endogenously prudent choices of emissions over time and the implied SCC trajectories when the policy maker confronts prior ambiguity. Policy outcomes include endogenous feedbacks and dynamic impacts on the SCC, and, importantly, an adjustment for uncertainty that is either unresolved or only resolved well into the future.[12]

In a third approach, Hassler, Krusell, and Olovsson (2018) conducted an analysis of uncertainty by comparing policy outcomes across two parameter intervals, one pertaining to damages and another to climate sensitivity. Instead of putting a probability distribution over parameters, they evaluate policy outcomes at the extreme points of the parameter space. Their analysis can be thought of as a simple illustration of robust decision-making allowing for arbitrary probabilities over the unknown parameters and is a revealing starting point to the policy problem they investigate. Our analysis of the policy problems is explicitly dynamic and imposes probabilistic restraints on the probabilities that could be assigned over a potentially large set of alternative model configurations. The dynamic decision theory formulation we use collapses our resulting sensitivity analysis to a low-dimensional representation in terms of ambiguity and misspecification aversion parameters.

VI. Social Cost of Carbon

The SCC is intended to be the expected discounted value of future environmental and economic damages induced by carbon emissions during the current period. In the special case in which socially efficient allocations are used, the wedge between the discounted social costs and market prices determines the Pigouvian taxes that support the efficient allocation in the presence of the environmental externality provided that the socially efficient emissions are positive.[13] More generally, the SCC is a decidedly local measure applicable to marginal changes in policy. Because the SCC can be represented as an expected discounted value, we draw on insights from asset pricing to explore the implications of uncertainty.

To place our research in a broader context of environmental economics, we draw on a recent report from the National Academies of Sciences, Engineering and Medicine (2017), which featured a four-step modular approach to measuring the SCC. We quote from the executive summary: "The committee specifies criteria for future updates to the SC – CO_2. It also recommends an integrated modular approach for SC – CO_2 estimation to better satisfy the specified criteria and to draw more readily on expertise from the wide range of scientific disciplines relevant to SC – CO_2 estimation. Under this approach, each step in SC – CO_2 estimation is developed as a module—socioeconomic, climate, damages, and discounting—that reflects the state of scientific knowledge in the current, peer-reviewed literature."[14]

The report goes on to argue, "In addition, the committee details longer-term research that could improve each module and incorporate interactions within and feedbacks across modules."

The modularization has the advantage of compartmentalizing different ingredients to the SCC estimation. Perhaps this is a valuable shortcut, but as we will argue, it misses or disguises contributions to valuation that we take to be central. This is especially true once we seek to formally integrate uncertainty into the analysis. In what follows, we will use recursive methods from control theory and economic dynamics to expose some of the considerations missed or treated inconsistently by the modular approach.

A. Impacts of Marginal Changes in Emissions

For pedagogical (and computational) simplicity, we consider a highly stylized problem to pose some important conceptual challenges. We suppose a single policy maker with a dynamic stochastic objective, but, importantly, we will not suppose that the emissions are set in a socially optimal way. We suppose that the control A_t includes emissions $\mathcal{E}_t$ as its last entry and that this control can be expressed as an invariant function of the state vector X_t. The invariance is imposed for simplicity, but the dependence on the state vector will be important in what follows. Even if we are dubious about whether the emissions will approximate a socially efficient outcome, we wish to allow for some policy responses whereby future emissions depend on, say, the magnitude of the temperature anomaly or on economic damages that emerge in the future. We allow both damages and the temperature anomaly to be components of the state vector X_t. An efficient social planner would certainly do this, but the feedback of emissions onto endogenous state variables can occur much more generally. A more complete analysis would impose a specific market structure and impose explicit constraints on the policy maker recognizing the implied market responses. The plausible assessments of exogenous scenarios arguably have such considerations in the background, but as we will see their formal presence can have an important impact on the construction of the SCC.

Consider the following recursive formulation of social valuation posed in the absence of model ambiguity or misspecification aversion:

$$0 = -\delta V(x) + U(x, a) + \mu(x, a) \cdot \frac{\partial V}{\partial x}(x) + \frac{1}{2} \text{trace} \left[\frac{\partial^2 V}{\partial x \partial x'}(x) \Sigma(x, a)' \right]$$

$$+ \mathcal{I}(x) \int [V(\tilde{x}) - V(x)] Q(d\tilde{x} \mid x), \tag{5}$$

where δ is the subjective rate of discount used by a fictitious social planner, the control is defined as $a = \psi(x)$, and U is the instantaneous contribution to the planner's continuation value function V. This relation is a version of a Feynman-Kac equation with a jump component. Intuitively, it says that the instantaneous utility contribution, U, should exactly offset the local mean of the discounted continuation value process.

B. A Discrete-Time Representation

For a measure of the net benefits (or minus net costs), we deduce the marginal impact of an additional unit of emissions into the atmosphere.

Although we will derive continuous-time formulas, we start with a discrete-time approximation with ϵ as the gap between time points. Heuristically, we aim to evaluate the ratio of

$$MV_t = \epsilon \frac{d}{d\mathcal{E}_t} \mathbb{E}\left[\sum_{j=0}^{\infty} \exp(-\delta j \epsilon) U\left(X_{t+j\epsilon}, A_{t+\epsilon j}\right) \mid \mathfrak{F}_t \right] \tag{6}$$

to the marginal utility of a numeraire consumption good at a date $t = \bar{j}\epsilon$ for some integer $\bar{j}$. We include the ϵ on the right side of (6) to view this expression as a Reimann sum approximation of an integral over time. Express

$$MV_t = \epsilon \frac{d}{d\mathcal{E}_t} \mathbb{E}\left[\sum_{j=0}^{\infty} \exp(-\delta \epsilon j) U(X_{t+j\epsilon}, A_{t+j\epsilon}) \mid \mathfrak{F}_t \right]$$

$$= \epsilon \mathbb{E}\left(\sum_{j=0}^{\infty} \exp(-\delta j \epsilon) \left[\frac{\partial U}{\partial a}(X_{t+j\epsilon}, A_{t+j\epsilon}) \frac{\partial \psi}{\partial x}(X_{t+j\epsilon}) + \frac{\partial U}{\partial x}(X_{t+j\epsilon}, A_{t+j\epsilon}) \right] R_{t+j\epsilon,t} \mid \mathfrak{F}_t \right)$$

and

$$R_{t,t+j\epsilon} = \frac{dX_{t+j\epsilon}}{d\mathcal{E}_t}$$

is the random response of the future state vector $X_{t+j\epsilon}$ to an emissions pulse $\mathcal{E}_t$ at date t. This discounted expected value is expressed in utility units and becomes the SCC once we divide by the marginal utility of the consumption numeraire. For linear dynamics, as is well known from impulse response theory, $R_{t,t+j\epsilon}, j = 0, 1, 2, \ldots$ will not be random. More generally, there are well-known methods for characterization of nonlinear impulse responses for diffusions.[15]

C.   Two Forms of Impulse Responses

As we have seen, impulse responses are inputs into the SCC computations. We consider two alternative formulations of these responses, including one that is common in scenario analysis and another that is familiar in dynamic stochastic equilibrium theory.

It is common to run "scenarios" through climate-economic models. Prominent examples in climate science are the Representative Concentration Pathway (RCP) scenarios, which are typically specified as exogenous paths of atmospheric carbon over time. See, for example, Zickfeld et al. (2013) (fig. 1), for the four main RCPs for carbon concentration. In generating these and other scenarios, the emissions or the atmospheric carbon trajectories are treated as an exogenous input and not as something that is determined endogenously by the model. Such scenarios are helpful in understanding temperature dynamics and making cross-model comparisons without attempting to complete or close the dynamical system. We call these functions "scenario response functions" (SceRFs).

In contrast, for a completely specified dynamical system, emissions and atmospheric carbon trajectories are determined endogenously. As these variables may feed back onto the state of the dynamical system, there are alternative impulse responses that take into account this endogeneity. We call these "system response functions" (SysRFs). These impulse responses are also the ones pertinent to represent the SCC when the full climate-economic model has a recursive representation of emissions as a function of the Markov state. These latter impulses are commonly used when depicting the implications of dynamic stochastic equilibrium models. In what follows, we will represent both forms of impulse responses.

For simplicity, we will abstract from the jump components, although there are direct extensions to the more general case in which they are included in the analysis.

Exogenously Specified Scenarios

Consider first a SceRF. We suppose a block recursive structure for the dynamics:

$$dX_t = \mu(X_t, A_t)dt + \sigma(X_t, A_t)dW_t$$
$$d\bar{X}_t = \bar{\mu}(\bar{X}_t)dt + \bar{\sigma}(\bar{X}_t)dW_t \tag{7}$$

and

$$A_t = \bar{\psi}(\bar{X}_t),$$

where X_t includes states used to represent climate dynamics and environmental or economic damages. We rewrite the first equation block in this system as

$$dX_t = \mu[X_t, \bar{\psi}(\bar{X}_t)]dt + \sigma[X_t, \bar{\psi}(\bar{X}_t)]dW_t$$

to represent the Markov dynamics in the composite state vector $(X_t, \bar{X}_t)$. Under this specification, the response $\bar{X}_{t+\tau}$ to an emissions pulse is zero.

In this setting, alternative scenarios are alternative specifications of $(\bar{\mu}, \bar{\sigma}, \bar{\psi})$. We construct the response functions by introducing emissions "pulses" at an initial time period.

Endogenous Emissions

Suppose that the full state dynamics are captured by

$$dX_t = \mu(X_t, A_t)dt + \sigma(X_t, A_t)dW_t,$$

where

$$A_t = \psi(X_t).$$

A special case of this is when ψ is computed as the solution to a fictitious social planner's problem. We represent the state dynamics as

$$dX_t = \mu[X_t, \psi(X_t)]dt + \sigma[X_t, \psi(X_t)]dW_t.$$

This specification allows for emissions to depend on the Markov state vector, including endogenous states that capture temperature anomalies or other forms of climate change and economic damages. A marginal change in emissions at date t induces marginal changes in emissions in future time periods because of some form of policy or market response. Suppose, for instance, that economic policies that influence carbon emissions adapt to temperature anomalies in the future. This will consequently alter the marginal impact of emissions today on future temperature anomalies in ways that are missed by treating emissions as fully exogenous. For instance, when we study a social planner's problem, emissions feed back on the temperature anomaly and mute the response of the temperature anomaly relative to the flat response featured in the Matthew's approximation.

This endogeneity illustrates the "interactions within and feedbacks across modules" mentioned in the National Academies of Sciences, Engineering and Medicine (2017) report that should be embraced in a "longer-term research" agenda.

Hybrid Approach

A third approach is a hybrid of the first two. It borrows a well-known idea from macroeconomic dynamics sometimes referred to as "big K little k." Consider a prespecified ψ giving the feedback of $a = \psi(x)$. Suppose that $\bar{X}_t = X_t$ as an equilibrium outcome. Write the dynamical system as in equation (7), where

$$\bar{\mu}(x) = \mu[x, \psi(x)]$$
$$\bar{\sigma}(x) = \sigma[x, \psi(x)] .$$

We impose the initialization $X_0 = \bar{X}_0$. A hypothetically small emissions pulse alters marginally the trajectory of $X_{t+\tau}$ but not that of $\bar{X}_{t+\tau}$. Although this approach imposes internal consistency along an equilibrium path, this consistency is not imposed in the perturbation leading to a different computation of the SCC. On the other hand, the exogenous scenario is constructed in a manner that is consistent with an endogenous policy response. As part of the equilibrium, this approach takes account of future market or policy responses when assessing plausible scenarios in a manner that is internally consistent while preserving the exogenous perspective of an emissions scenario.

D. Markov Solutions

We explore Markov solutions for the second two approaches as the first one, in an unconstrained manner, seems hard to defend from a dynamical systems perspective. For the marginal change in emissions, we are led to differentiate the right-hand side with respect to emissions e and to evaluate the derivative at $e = \psi(y)$:

$$MV(x) = \frac{\partial U}{\partial e}[x, \psi(x)] + \frac{\partial V}{\partial x}(x) \cdot \frac{\partial \mu}{\partial e}[x, \psi(x)] \tag{8}$$

$$+ \frac{1}{2}\operatorname{trace}\left[\frac{\partial^2 V}{\partial x \partial x'}(x)\frac{\partial}{\partial e}\Sigma[x, \psi(x)]\right],$$

where V solves equation (5). Recall that e is the last entry of the current period action a. Given our continuous-time specification, $MV(X_t)$ is a per-unit time measure of the marginal impact of a change in emissions. Under a social planner's solution, $MV(x) = 0$, unless the emissions solution is at a boundary.

This same logic can be modified when we proceed under the prospective of an exogenous emissions scenario. Now, the value function $\bar{V}$ depends on both x and $\bar{x}$ and satisfies a Feynman-Kac equation that is the analog to equation (5). A marginal change in e is presumed to only affect x. The formula for the net benefit in the current state is now

$$\overline{MV}(x, \bar{x}) = \frac{\partial U}{\partial e}[x, \bar{\psi}(\bar{x})] + \frac{\partial \bar{V}}{\partial x}(x, \bar{x}) \cdot \frac{\partial \mu}{\partial e}[x, \bar{\psi}(\bar{x})]$$

$$+ \frac{1}{2}\operatorname{trace}\left(\begin{bmatrix} \dfrac{\partial^2 \bar{V}}{\partial x \partial x'} & \dfrac{\partial^2 \bar{V}}{\partial x \partial \bar{x}'} \\[2ex] \dfrac{\partial^2 \bar{V}}{\partial \bar{x} \partial x'} & \dfrac{\partial^2 \overline{\bar{V}}}{\partial \bar{x} \partial \bar{x}'} \end{bmatrix}(x, \bar{x})\frac{\partial}{\partial e}\bar{\Sigma}[x, \bar{x}, \bar{\psi}(\bar{x})]\right),$$

where $a = \bar{\psi}(\bar{x})$ and

$$\bar{\Sigma}(x, \bar{x}, a) \doteq \left[\begin{array}{c} \sigma(x, a) \\ \\ \bar{\sigma}(\bar{x}) \end{array} \right] [\sigma(x, a)' \quad \bar{\sigma}(\bar{x})'],$$

although under the hybrid approach $X_t = \bar{X}_t$, it will typically be the case that

$$\overline{MV}(x, x) \neq MV(x).$$

This follows because of the differences in the implied responses to emissions pulses.

Although MV or $\overline{MV}$ are the net benefits (benefits minus costs), the separation of the two components depends on the details of the planner's problem, as we will illustrate in some example economies.

E. Uncertainty Adjustment

To accommodate ambiguity and misspecification aversion, we introduce minimization into the construction of the value function using the approaches described in Section V. The outcome of this minimization gives an uncertainty adjustment for valuation, which is conveniently represented as a probability distribution. This probabilistic adjustment emerges because of our choice to include uncertainty "inside" the decision problem. Just as external researchers confront uncertainty, so do policy makers. The discounting module in National Academies of Sciences, Engineering and Medicine (2017) misses this uncertainty adjustment. Because the outcome of the minimization depends on uncertainty in both the climate dynamics and the damage function specification, this identifies important linkages between the different modules that are missed by the simplistic discount rate sensitivity analyses often featured in the environmental economics literature. Although the choice of δ is important, so is the decision maker's aversion to ambiguity and potential model misspecification.

Remark 6.1. It is well known in the macroeconomics literature when using aggregate consumption as a numeraire for the purposes of marginal valuation that the subjective rate of discount is augmented with a growth adjustment that depends in part on the elasticity of intertemporal substitution. Relatedly, in the macroeconomic-asset pricing literature, investor risk aversion alters discounting by making it stochastic. The discounting depends on the exposure of the cash flow being discounted to aggregate risk. Cai et al. (2017) include both of these considerations in their treatment of the SCC. Our calculations extend these insights by constructing probabilistic adjustments for model ambiguity for social valuation.

Next, we show how to make the uncertainty adjustment for valuation that incorporates robustness to model ambiguity and potential misspecification. We modify the construction of MV, but the adjustment to $\overline{MV}$ is entirely analogous. To incorporate uncertainty, we modify the Feynman-Kac equation (5) by incorporating a minimization problem. Formally, the equation (5) now becomes an HJB equation pertinent for continuous-time discounted dynamic programming solutions with minimization:

$$
\begin{aligned}
0 = \min_{f, \int f(\theta)\pi(d\theta) = 1} & \min_{g(\tilde{x})} \min_{h} -\delta V(x) + U(x, a) \\
& + \frac{\partial V}{\partial x}(x) \cdot [\sigma(x, a)h] + \frac{1}{2}\text{trace}\left[\frac{\partial^2 V}{\partial x \partial x'}(x)\Sigma(x, a)\right] \\
& + \frac{\partial V}{\partial x}(x) \cdot \int \mu(x, a \mid \theta)f(\theta)\pi(d\theta) + \xi_a \int f(\theta)\log f(\theta)\pi(d\theta) \\
& + \mathcal{I}(x)\int [V(\tilde{x}) - V(x)]g(\tilde{x})Q(d\tilde{x} \mid x) \\
& + \xi_r\left[\frac{1}{2}h'h + \mathcal{I}(x)\int [1 - g(\tilde{x}) + g(\tilde{x})\log g(\tilde{x})]Q(d\tilde{x} \mid x)\right],
\end{aligned}
$$

where $a = \psi(x)$. We then use this value function solution in equation (8) to construct an uncertainty-adjusted version of MV.[16]

We next consider three example economies: the first features damage function uncertainty and its resolution, the second features a novel uncertainty decomposition that incorporates robustness to model ambiguity and misspecification, and the third investigates the impact of uncertain advances in the availability of less carbon-intensive technologies. Although our methods for making uncertainty adjustments for the SCC are more generally applicable, in all three cases we feature emission trajectories that are outcomes of social-planning problems. Even though highly stylized, each of the three examples illustrates novel impacts of uncertainty.

VII. Uncertain Damages

Our first example features how the perceived unraveling of uncertainty about economic and environmental damages influences prudent decisions.

A. Capital Evolution

We consider an AK technology for which output is proportional to capital and can be allocated between investment and consumption. Capital in this specification should be broadly conceived to include human capital or intangible capital. Suppose that there are adjustment costs to capital that are represented as the product of capital times a quadratic function of the investment-capital ratio.

As a modeling construct, we first consider "undamaged" counterparts to consumption, output, and capital. Abstracting from damages, capital evolves as

$$dK_t = K_t \left[\mu_k(Z_t)dt + \left(\frac{I_t}{K_t} \right)dt - \frac{\kappa}{2} \left(\frac{I_t}{K_t} \right)^2 dt + \sigma_k(Z_t)dW_t^k \right],$$

where K_t is the capital stock and I_t is investment. The capital evolution expressed in logarithms is

$$d \log K_t = \left[\mu_k(Z_t) + \left(\frac{I_t}{K_t} \right) - \frac{\kappa}{2} \left(\frac{I_t}{K_t} \right)^2 \right]dt - \frac{|\sigma_k(Z_t)|^2}{2}dt + \sigma_k(Z_t)dW_t^k.$$

We let consumption, C_t, and investment, I_t, sum up to output, which is proportional to capital:

$$C_t + I_t = \alpha K_t.$$

Next, we consider environmental damages. We suppose that the damage process that we depicted previously shifts proportionately consumption and capital by a multiplicative factor. For instance, the damage-adjusted consumption is $\tilde{C}_t = C_t / N_t$, and the damage-adjusted capital is $\tilde{K}_t = K_t / N_t$.

Without uncertainty aversion, preferences for the planner are time-separable with a unitary elasticity of substitution. The planner's instantaneous utility from "damaged consumption" and emissions is given by

$$(1 - \eta) \log \tilde{C}_t + \eta \log \mathcal{E}_t$$
$$= (1 - \eta)(\log C_t - \log K_t) + (1 - \eta)(\log K_t - \log N_t) + \eta \log \mathcal{E}_t,$$

where we will denote the subjective rate of discount used in preferences as δ. We can think of emissions and consumption as distinct goods, or we can think of $\tilde{C}_t$ as an intermediate good that when combined with emissions determines final consumption.

Given this formulation of the model, there are two noteworthy simplifications that we exploit in both characterizing a solution to the planner's problem and solving it numerically.

Remark 7.1. The model, as posed, has a solution that conveniently separates. We may solve two separate control problems: (i) determines "undamaged" consumption, investment, and capital; (ii) determines emissions, the temperature anomaly, and damages. It is the latter that is of particular interest. Undamaged consumption, investment, and capital are merely convenient constructs that allow us to simplify the model solution.

Remark 7.2. We obtain a further simplification by letting

$$\widetilde{\mathcal{E}}_t = \mathcal{E}_t\left(\iota_y \cdot Z_t\right).$$

We use $\widetilde{\mathcal{E}}_t$ as the control variable and then deduce the implications for $\mathcal{E}_t$.

Remark 7.3. In this illustration, the costs of emissions are given solely by the environmental and economic damages. In our previous research (Barnett et al. 2020), we followed Bornstein, Krusell, and Rebelo (2017) and Casassus, Collin-Dufresne, and Routledge (2018) by including reserves as a state variable that can be augmented by an investment in new discoveries. Although this richer specification has more substantive interest, the emissions costs implied by this technology were quite small relative to social costs induced by damages. For this example, we dropped this additional state variable to simplify further our characterization of the uncertainty implications.

Remark 7.4. As Anderson et al. (2003) note, there is a preference equivalence between a concern for model misspecification and risk aversion in the recursive utility formulation of Kreps and Porteus (1978) and Epstein and Zin (1989) when there is a unitary elasticity of substitution as we have assumed here. Our macroeconomic model, by design, can capture what is called "long-run risk" in the macrofinance literature in the absence of climate change (Bansal and Yaron 2004). The long-run risk literature explores the valuation consequence of growth-rate uncertainty using a recursive utility model of investor preferences. The preference specification presumes a full commitment to the baseline probabilities, but the rationale for this commitment appears to be weak when confronting specific forms of growth-rate uncertainty. The long-run risk literature often imposes a seemingly large risk aversion parameter that arguably can look more plausible when reinterpreted as a concern of model misspecification. In what follows, we will impose $\xi_r = 5$ as our largest value. The implied risk aversion under recursive utility is 21, which is certainly large but typically not dismissed as too large in the empirical literature on long-run risk. The Brownian drift induced by a robustness concern is quite sizable for the counterpart adjustment to the consumption/capital dynamics. Borrowing and updating a specification of growth-rate uncertainty of Hansen, Heaton, and Li (2008), Hansen and Sargent (2021) fit a simple consumption/capital model to aggregate data designed to measure macroeconomic growth-rate uncertainty. Their model is the undamaged version of the model we pose here, with two shocks. One shock is to the stochastic process for growth-rate productivity, and the other is an independent shock to only the capital productivity. These shocks imply two of the consumption shocks in Bansal and Yaron (2004).[17] The implied drift distortions for the stochastic capital evolution are

$$h = \begin{bmatrix} -.715 \\ -.170 \end{bmatrix} \quad \begin{array}{l} \text{productivity growth rate shock distortion} \\ \text{capital productivity shock distortion.} \end{array}$$

Given the relative magnitudes of the adjustments, it is the growth uncertainty channel that is of particular importance to the decision maker. Because 0.715 is large in comparison to the unit standard deviation of the shock, one might dismiss our choices of ξ_r as being too extreme.

Although we find the comparison between misspecification and risk aversion in the presence of growth-rate uncertainty to be revealing, an uncomfortable feature of the long-run risk formulation in the macro asset pricing literature is that the long-run risks are a "black box." In what follows, we will step back from the dual interpretation of risk aversion and abstract from misspecification implications for the undamaged consumption or capital evolution. The implied Brownian motion distributions for the climate dynamics will turn out to be considerably smaller than the growth-rate shock distortion reported here.

B.   HJB Equations and Robustness

We now describe our approach to solving the model and incorporating concerns about robustness and ambiguity aversion. The uncertainty that we consider has a single jump point after which the damage function uncertainty is revealed. This leads us to compute continuation value functions conditioned on each of the damage function specifications. These continuation value functions then are used to summarize postjump outcomes when we compute the initial value function. We describe the HJB equations for each of these steps in what follows. Some further details about the computations and parameter settings are provided in appendix B.

Postjump Continuation Value Functions

We first compute the value functions pertinent after the Poisson event that reveals that the damage function curvature is realized. Although the damage specification uncertainty is resolved with this event, there remains climate model uncertainty.

The state variables are the temperature anomaly and the exogenous Brownian uncertainty. Recall that after the Poisson event, the argument of the function Γ is $\bar{Y}_t = Y_t - Y_\tau + \bar{y}$, where τ is the date of the Poisson event. We abuse notation a little bit by letting y denote a potential realization of $\bar{Y}_t$. Because $-Y_\tau + \bar{y}$ is time invariant postjump, both Y_t and

$\bar{Y}_t$ share the same increment. Moreover, $\bar{Y}_\tau = \bar{y}$, which is a pertinent boundary condition for the postjump value functions.

We solve the optimization problems for the continuation value functions ϕ_m conditioned on each of the damage functions, $m = 1, 2, ..., M$. Even though the optimization problem is well posed whenever $y \geq 0$, we only care about the range in which $y \geq \bar{y}$. In our computations, we use 20 equally spaced values for γ_3^m.

In formulating the HJB equation, we include robustness considerations as described in Section V where ξ_a and ξ_r are penalty parameters. The HJB equation conditioned on a ϕ_m is given by

$$
\begin{aligned}
0 = \max_{\tilde{e}} \min_{h} \min_{\omega_j, \sum_{\ell=1}^{L} \omega_\ell = 1} \quad & -\delta\phi_m(y) + \eta \log \tilde{e} \\
& + \frac{d\phi_m(y)}{dy} \tilde{e}_\varsigma \cdot h + \frac{(\eta - 1)}{\delta}[\gamma_1 + \gamma_2 y + \gamma_3^m(y - \bar{y})]\tilde{e}_\varsigma \cdot h + \frac{\xi_r}{2} h'h \\
& + \frac{d\phi_m(y)}{dy} \sum_{\ell=1}^{L} \omega_\ell \theta_\ell \tilde{e} + \frac{1}{2}\frac{d^2\phi_m(y)}{(dy)^2}|\varsigma|^2\tilde{e}^2 \\
& + \frac{(\eta - 1)}{\delta}\left([\gamma_1 + \gamma_2 y + \gamma_3^m(y - \bar{y})]\sum_{\ell=1}^{L}\omega_\ell\theta_\ell\tilde{e} + \frac{1}{2}(\gamma_2 + \gamma_3^m)|\varsigma|^2\tilde{e}^2\right) \\
& + \xi_a\sum_{\ell=1}^{L}\omega_\ell(\log \omega_\ell - \log \pi_\ell).
\end{aligned}
\tag{9}
$$

In this calculation, the π_ℓ's are the climate model probabilities, and the ω_ℓ's are the alternative probabilities that we consider when making a robust adjustment. A jump happening in the model is equivalent to an increase in y to $\bar{y}$. After a jump, the model follows one of the m damage specifications with y reinitialized at the threshold. For computational purposes, the $\phi_m(\bar{y})'$s are a fixed set of numbers imposed in the HJB computation. For a given ω and h, the minimization over $\tilde{e}$ has a quadratic objective and can be solved quasi-analytically. For a given $\tilde{e}$, the minimization problem for h is quadratic and can also be solved analytically. Similarly, the minimizing ω_ℓ's satisfy

$$
\omega_\ell^* \propto \pi_\ell^a \exp\left(-\frac{1}{\xi_a}\left[\frac{d\phi_m(y)}{dy}\theta_\ell\tilde{e} + \frac{(\eta - 1)}{\delta}[\gamma_1 + \gamma_2 y + \gamma_3^m(y - \bar{y})]\theta_\ell\tilde{e}\right]\right).
$$

The expression on the right side requires scaling so that the resulting $\omega_\ell^{*'}$s sum to one. We exploit the resulting formulas in our recursive computations.

We solve equation (9) for the M continuation value functions that we use in our analysis.

Prejump Value Function

The prejump value function has a similar structure with two exceptions: (i) we include the intensity function discussed earlier and (ii) we introduce robustness concerns for both the intensity and distribution over the alternative γ_3^m coefficients. Given these modifications, we include

$$\mathcal{J}(y)\sum_{m=1}^{M} g_m \pi_m [\phi_m(\bar{y}) - \phi(y)] + \xi_r \mathcal{J}(y)\sum_{m=1}^{M} \pi_m (1 - g_m + g_m \log g_m)\pi_m$$

in the HJB equation and to minimize with respect to the nonnegative g_m's. The continuation value functions ϕ_m are all evaluated at $y = \bar{y}$ in this HJB equation pertinent for the prejump analysis. This occurs because immediately after a Poisson event is triggered, the damage function Γ is evaluated at the threshold point $\bar{y}$.

We now illustrate the impact of uncertainty about the magnitude and timing of damages from climate change along with uncertainty in the carbon-temperature dynamics.

Our specifications of aversion to climate model ambiguity and damage function misspecification are expressed in terms of the two penalty parameters, ξ_a and ξ_r. We use these parameters to restrain the search over alternative probabilities. The outcome of this search is an uncertainty-adjusted probability measure that is of interest for two reasons. First, it shows implied probabilities that are most problematic to the decision maker. Should these appear to be too extreme, then the penalization used in the decision problem is not severe enough. This type of inspection follows common practices for robust Bayesian methods following the proposal of Good (1952). Second, these altered probabilities provide an adjustment for social valuation implied by model ambiguity and misspecification uncertainty.

C.   *Robust Adjustments to Climate Model Uncertainty*

For the 144 carbon-climate dynamic models, we take as our baseline probabilities an equal weighting of all of the models. Although it is straightforward to explore a whole family of values for ξ_a, in the calculations that follow we set $\xi_a = .01$. To determine whether or not this is a reasonable choice of ξ_a to use in our analysis, we examine the implied distortion to the probability distribution of θ_ℓ values resulting from our choice as compared with the baseline prior probability distribution. Both the original prior probability distribution (light gray histogram) and the distorted probability distribution (medium gray histogram) of θ_ℓ values are given in figure 5. The increased concern about uncertainty over the geoscientific inputs leads to a shift to the right in the θ_ℓ probability distribution, highlighting increased concerns about worst-case climate dynamics, while still maintaining a spread in the weights on the values of θ_ℓ and not loading all the weight on the far right tail. We, therefore, view this shift in the distribution as reasonable to entertain. The implied mean distortion is about 0.26 for the unknown parameter θ. Although the concerns about geoscientific uncertainty are state dependent, the distortion in the probability distribution for θ remains roughly constant over the course of our simulations.

There is an additional mean shift in this temperature distribution that is induced by misspecification concerns. This shift is negligible for $\xi_r = 5$ and only about 0.07 for $\xi_r = 1$. Its impact is much more substantial for

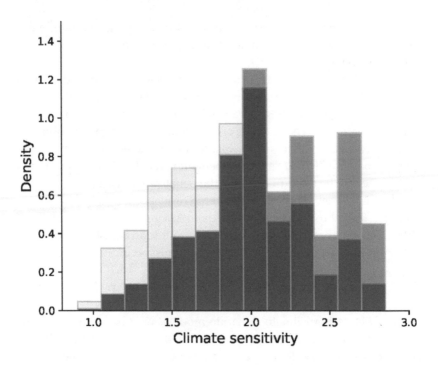

Fig. 5.   Histograms of climate sensitivity parameters. The light gray histogram is the outcome of equally weighting all 144 climate models. The medium gray histogram is the outcome of the minimization in the recursive formulations of our social planner's problem. A color version of this figure is available online.

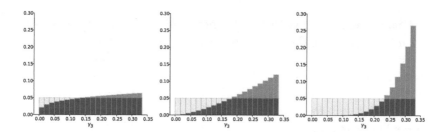

Fig. 6. Distorted probabilities of damage functions. Baseline probabilities for damage functions are 1/20 (light gray bars), and the medium gray bars are robust adjustments to the probabilities induced by model misspecification concerns (left panel: $\xi_r = 5$, center panel $\xi_r = 1$, right panel: $\xi_r = 0.3$). These histograms are the outcome of recursive minimizations. These distortions are close to being constant as the temperature anomaly increases up to the Poisson jump date. A color version of this figure is available online.

the low penalty, $\xi_r = 0.3$ with an implied mean shift of about 0.23. These distortions show very little sensitivity to the state dynamics.

D. Robust Adjustments to Damage Function Uncertainty

We next consider the penalty parameter ξ_r that governs concerns about misspecifying the Poisson jump process, including both the jump intensity and the probability distribution conditioned on a jump. Recall that we use this process to capture uncertainty of the steepness in the damage function and timing of when this steepness becomes known to the decision maker. This uncertainty is only pertinent prior to the realization of the Poisson event. We report results for three different values of this parameter $\xi_r = 5$, $\xi_r = 1$, $\xi_r = .3$ in figure 6. The distorted histogram for the lowest value, $\xi_r = .3$, is arguably extreme, although the other two choices seem considerably harder to dismiss.

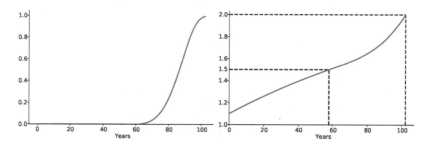

Fig. 7. The left panel shows the probabilities that a jump will occur prior to the date given on the horizontal axis. The right panel shows the simulated pathway for the temperature anomaly and the points where the anomaly reaches $\underline{y} = 1.5$ and $\bar{y} = 2.0$ (dashed lines). A color version of this figure is available online.

Finally, in figure 7, we display the probabilities that a jump will occur prior to the specified dates along the socially efficient trajectory for emissions. Again, we impose $\xi_r = 1$. The jump is pretty much assured to happen by about 100 years out, at which point the temperature anomaly is 2 degree Celsius. On so-called business-as-usual trajectories, the jump probabilities will converge to one much more quickly than what is displayed in this figure.

E.   Emission and Anomaly Trajectories

To show the effects of concerns about damage function uncertainty on policy decisions of the planner, we explore the behavior of emissions for different amounts of aversion to uncertainty. In figure 8, we report the prejump control laws for $\tilde{e}$ as a function of the temperature anomaly, and y, for three values of ξ_r in figure 8. Although the e, in contrast to $\tilde{e}$, also depends multiplicatively on the exogenous state vector, it is the dependence of the temperature anomaly that is of particular interest. For comparison, this figure also includes the control law for $\tilde{e}$ when the planner has full commitment to the baseline probabilities. We confine the domain

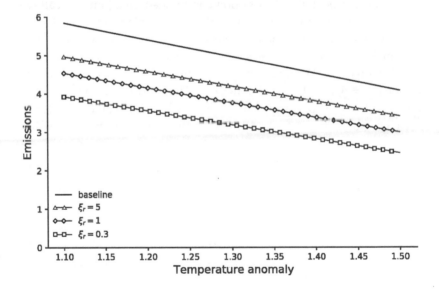

Fig. 8. Emissions as a function of the temperature anomaly for different penalty configurations. The thresholds are $\underline{y} = 1.5$ and $\bar{y} = 2.0$. We limit the domain of the function to be 1.1–1.5 because for larger temperature anomalies the Poisson event may be realized. A color version of this figure is available online.

of the control laws to temperature anomalies between 1.1 and 1.5 degree Celsius. After the temperature anomaly reaches 1.5, the probability of a jump occurring becomes nonzero.

As we see, even in advance of gaining more information about damage function curvature, the fictitious planner embraces a substantial level of precaution due to the concerns about the unknown future damage state. In light of uncertainty concerns, the control law for emissions is about 20% lower when $\xi_r = 1$ than the control law based solely on the baseline probabilities. We also see that, as the value of ξ_r is decreased, the caution is amplified and the choice of emissions is lowered even further. It follows that the emission trajectories for the lower control laws necessarily reach the $\underline{y} = 1.5$ threshold later starting from a common initial condition.

Although the 1.5- and 2-degree thresholds have dominated much of the policy discussion, there is debate as to the extent to which these are firmly backed up by evidence. For this reason, in figure 9, we report the consequences of shifting the thresholds we use in our computations to $\underline{y} = 1.75$ and $\bar{y} = 2.25$. The results for emissions are very similar, except that in comparison to figure 8, the control laws are shifted to the right as should be expected because of delay in when the more extreme damage function curvature is manifested.

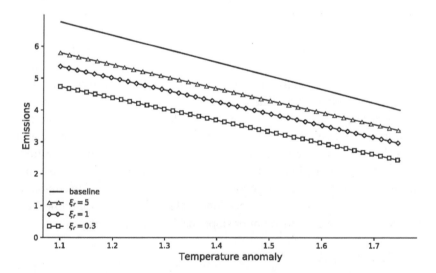

Fig. 9. Emissions as a function of the temperature anomaly for different penalty configurations. The thresholds are $\underline{y} = 1.75$ and $\bar{y} = 2.25$. We limit the domain of the function to be 1.1–1.75 because for larger temperature anomalies the Poisson event may be realized. A color version of this figure is available online.

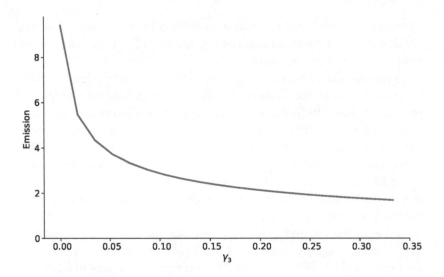

Fig. 10. Emissions choices, conditioned on a jump having occurred, for different realized damage function parameters γ_3 upon realization of the jump. A color version of this figure is available online.

Returning to our original specification, when the temperature anomaly reaches values of $y \in [\underline{y}, \bar{y}] = [1.5, 2]$, the Poisson event revealing the full damage function will at some point be realized. Once it is revealed, the emissions trajectories will jump to either a higher or a lower level depending on how much damage function curvature is realized. We report the initial emissions, postjump, in figure 10 as a function of γ_3 governing the curvature of the damage function for large temperature anomalies. Importantly, this function is highly convex. The realization of a very low damage function curvature is good news for the planner, resulting in an increase in emissions in contrast to many of the other damage function specifications that could be realized. For the damage functions with even a little more curvature, there is a large reduction in emissions as reflected in the steep slope of the function of optimal emissions choices for small values of γ_3. The emissions choices are increasingly more concentrated at similar values for higher curvature, as seen in the much flatter slope for the larger values of γ_3.

F. Temperature Anomalies

Given the probabilistic nature of the Poisson event, the emissions and resulting temperature anomalies behave probabilistically, even abstracting from Brownian motion risk. Although the planner has uncertainty about

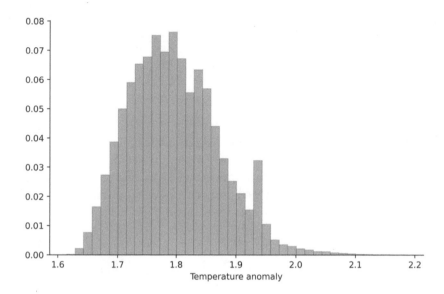

Fig. 11. Histogram of possible temperature anomaly values for the scenario, where $\xi_a = 0.01$ and $\xi_r = 1$. The temperature anomaly values are for year 100. The simulation is done under the baseline probabilities and abstracts from the Brownian motion shocks. A color version of this figure is available online.

these probabilities, we find it revealing to report the distributions under the baseline specification. We show the implied temperature anomaly distributions conditioned on the Poisson event being realized in figure 11.[18] We extend the simulation out 100 years to ensure that the no-jump probability is essentially zero. The vast majority of temperature anomaly values are less than the 2-degree threshold, though there is a small right tail going beyond that and a small right peak leading up to it. This relatively constrained distribution of temperature anomalies is driven largely by the initial caution exercised by the planner and the continued caution for most of the damage function realizations. A small fraction of realizations of the damage function curvature parameter γ_3 results in higher temperature anomalies than 2 degrees because the planner is willing to increase emissions after the Poisson event reveals "good news."

G.   Social Cost of Carbon

We use the SCC evaluated at the socially efficient trajectory as the barometer for the economic externality induced by climate change. The planner equates marginal social costs and benefits of emissions. We represent the marginal benefits in units of damaged consumption so that

$$SCC_t = \frac{\eta(\tilde{C}_t)}{(1-\eta)(\tilde{\mathcal{E}}_t)} = \frac{\eta(C_t)}{(1-\eta)(N_t)\tilde{\mathcal{E}}_t},$$

where the right-hand side variables are evaluated along the socially efficient trajectory. Taking logarithms, we get

$$\log SCC_t = \log \eta - \log(1-\eta) + \left(\log C_t - \log N_t\right) - \log \tilde{\mathcal{E}}_t.$$

As we noted previously, "undamaged consumption" evolves in a manner consistent with a long-run risk model familiar from macro asset pricing. The logarithm of consumption grows stochastically along a linear trajectory with variation increasing approximately linearly over the growth horizon. Our focus instead will be on the behavior of

$$\log \eta - \log(1-\eta) - \left(\log \tilde{N}_t\right) - \log \tilde{\mathcal{E}}_t, \tag{10}$$

where $\log \tilde{N}_t$ excludes the exogenous stochastic contribution to $\log N_t$, which is common across our specifications of the robustness parameter ξ_r. The variation of this measure over time depends entirely on the temperature anomaly trajectory prior to reaching the lower threshold $\underline{y}$. In the figures that follow, we report this dependence.

Because emissions depend on the temperature anomaly, under the planner's solution there is an important distinction between the SceRF and the SysRF discussed in Subsection IV.C. The SceRF for the temperature anomaly behaves in accordance with the Matthew's approximation whereby emissions today have a permanent impact on the future temperature anomaly. The SysRF incorporates the dependence of emissions on the temperature anomaly, and it is the SysRF that is embedded in the SCC computation for the social planner's problem. Although this dependence is a direct outcome of the planner's problem, more generally the plausibility of future emissions trajectories should be tied to the potential policy responses as we experience the impact of climate change.

To deduce the emissions contribution, we differentiate the HJB equation (9) with respect to $\tilde{e}$ and solve for $\eta/\tilde{e}$:

$$\frac{\eta}{\tilde{e}} = -\frac{d\phi(y)}{dy}\sum_{\ell=1}^{L}\omega_\ell\theta_\ell - \frac{d^2\phi(y)}{(dy)^2}|\varsigma|^2\tilde{e} + \frac{(1-\eta)}{\delta}\left[(\gamma_1 + \gamma_2 y)\sum_{\ell=1}^{L}\omega_\ell\theta_\ell + \gamma_2|\varsigma|^2\tilde{e}\right] \tag{11}$$

for $0 < \underline{y}$. For the planner's problem, because marginal benefits are equated to marginal costs, we may use either side of this equation to measure the emissions contribution to the SCC.

Figure 12 shows the log SCC for the baseline case of $\xi_r = \infty$, $\xi_a = \infty$ (line with squares), and three cases of increasing concerns about damage

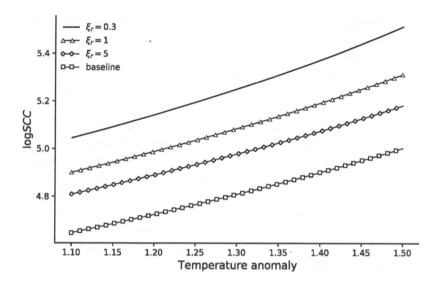

Fig. 12. Log(SCC) as functions of temperature anomaly under different penalty configurations. The SCC is state dependent, and we focus on the domain for which the anomaly is less than 1.5 degrees. The values in logarithms are translated by the initial period logarithm of consumption. A color version of this figure is available online.

function uncertainty: $\xi_r = 5$ (line with triangles), $\xi_r = 1$ (line with diamonds), and $\xi_r = 0.3$ (solid line), where $\xi_a = .01$ for all three cases. The results use the socially efficient emissions trajectories for the different values of ξ_r. The log SCC values are calculated using equations (1) and (11). In figure 12, we see substantial values of the log SCC in each case. The magnitudes are amplified as we increase concerns about damage function misspecification (by decreasing the value of ξ_r). In particular, as a function of the temperature anomaly, the SCC for $\xi_r = 1$ is between 20% and 30% higher than when we abstract from robustness concerns. Although not reported here, changing the thresholds to be $\underline{y} = 1.75$ and $\bar{y} = 2.25$ effectively shifts the curves in figure 12 degrees to the right with a corresponding smaller SCC at the initial temperature anomaly of $y = 1.1$.

H. Summary

In this example economy, the social planner adopts an emissions policy that is cautious at the outset even though considerably more information about potential damages will be available in the future. The damage function uncertainty is resolved by a single Poisson event that becomes more likely the larger the temperature anomaly. Once this event is realized, there is an asymmetric response. For a small fraction of the damage functions with the most modest curvature, emissions immediately increase. These are "good news events" and are determined endogenously within our model. For a much larger fraction of damage function specifications, the emissions responses continue to be modest, although the magnitude of these responses depends on the curvature of the damage function that is revealed. The implied SCC increases by about 20% due to the combined damage function and carbon-climate model uncertainty prior to the realization of the Poisson event. This impact can be larger or smaller depending on the social planner's aversion to ambiguity and model misspecification. Although acknowledging the simplified nature of the model used for our computations, our results demonstrate the importance of accounting not only for different uncertainty channels but also for the information dynamics when designing optimal climate policy.

VIII. Uncertainty Decomposition

An advantage to the more structured approach implemented as smooth ambiguity is that it allows us to "open the hood," so to speak, on uncertainty. We build on the work of Ricke and Caldeira (2014) by exploring the relative contributions of uncertainty in the carbon dynamics versus uncertainty in the temperature dynamics. We depart from their analysis by studying the relative contributions in the context of a decision problem, and we include robustness to model misspecification as a third source of uncertainty. This latter adjustment applies primarily to the damage function specification. We continue to use the SCC as a benchmark for assessing these contributions. We perform these computations using the model developed in the previous section, although the approach we describe is applicable more generally. For the uncertainty decomposition, we hold fixed the control law for emissions, and hence also the implied state evolution for damages, and explore the consequences of imposing constraints on minimization over the probabilities across the different models.

Recall that we use climate sensitivity parameters from combinations of 16 models of temperature dynamics and nine models of carbon dynamics. A parameter θ corresponds to climate-temperature model pair. Let Θ denote the full set of $L = 144$ pairs, and let P_j for $j = 1, 2, ... J$ be a partition of the positive integers up to L. The integer J is set to 9 or 16 depending on whether we target the temperature models or the carbon. For any given such partition, we solve a constrained version of the minimization problem (eq. [4]) by targeting the probabilities assigned to partitions while imposing the benchmark probabilities conditioned on each partition:

$$\min_{\bar{\omega}_j, j=1,2,\ldots,J} \left(\frac{\partial V}{\partial x}\right) \cdot \sum_{j=1}^{J} \bar{\omega}_j \sum_{\ell \in P_j} \left(\frac{\pi_\ell}{\sum_{\ell \in P_j} \pi_\ell}\right) \mu(x, a \mid \theta_\ell)$$

$$+ \xi_a \sum_{j=1}^{J} \bar{\omega}_j \left(\log \bar{\omega}_j - \log \bar{\pi}_j\right),$$

where $\bar{\pi}_j = \Sigma_{\ell \in P_j} \pi_\ell$ and

$$\frac{\pi_\ell}{\bar{\pi}_\ell} \ell \in P_j$$

are the baseline conditional probabilities for partition j. We only minimize the probabilities across partitions while imposing the baseline conditional probabilities within a partition.

We impose $\xi_r = \infty$ when performing this minimization and let $\xi_a = .01$ as in Section VII. We perform additional calculations where we let $\xi_r = 1$ and $\xi_a = \infty$ to target damage function uncertainty rather than temperature or climate dynamics uncertainty.[19] The two states in our problem are $x = (y, n)$, and we look for a value function of the form $V(y, n) = \phi(y) + (\eta - 1)/\delta n$ while imposing that $\tilde{e} = \epsilon(y)$. For each partition of interest, we construct the corresponding HJB equation that supports this minimization.

Because we are imposing the control law for emissions but constraining the minimization, the first-order conditions for emissions will no longer be satisfied. Recall equation (8) from Section VI with adjustments for uncertainty. In the absence of optimality, the net benefit measure $MV(x)$ is not zero with the minimization constraints imposed. Consistent with the SCC computation from the previous section, we use

$$-\frac{\partial V}{\partial x}(x) \cdot \frac{\partial \mu}{\partial e}[x, \phi(x)] - \frac{1}{2} \text{trace}\left[\frac{\partial^2 V}{\partial x \partial x'}(x) \frac{\partial}{\partial e} \Sigma[x, \phi(x)]\right]$$

for our cost contributions in the SCC decomposition.

We obtain the smallest cost measure when we preclude minimization altogether while solving for the value function and the largest one when we allow for full minimization with $\xi_r = 1$ and $\xi_a = .01$. We have three intermediate cases corresponding to temperature dynamic uncertainty, climate dynamic uncertainty, and damage function uncertainty. The smallest of these measures corresponds to a full commitment to the baseline probabilities. We form ratios with respect to the smallest measure, take

298 Barnett, Brock, and Hansen

logarithms, and multiply by 100 to convert the numbers to percentages. Importantly, we change both probabilities and value functions in this computation.

We report the results in figure 13. From this figure, we see that the uncertainty adjustments in valuation account for 20%–30% of the SCC. The contributions from temperature and carbon are essentially constant over time with the temperature uncertainty contribution being substantially larger. The damage contribution is initially below half the total uncertainty, but this changes to more than half by the time the temperature anomaly reaches the lower threshold of 1.5 degree Celsius.

Remark 8.1. The uncertainty decomposition we implement depends on the underlying emissions trajectory we impose. For the reported computations, we used the planner's solution for when all uncertainty components are considered. Because our planner cares about uncertainty, robustness considerations lead our planner to avoid excessive exposure to uncertainty when possible. In our particular setting, with uncertainty aversion, the planner will prefer to avoid being vulnerable to damage function uncertainty, which can be achieved in part by delaying when the potentially steep slope of the damage function becomes operative. Yet the exposure components of uncertainty can look very different

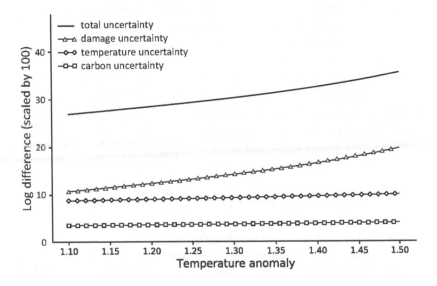

Fig. 13. Uncertainty decomposition for the logarithm of the marginal value of emissions (scaled by 100). These computations impose $\xi_a = .01$ and $\xi_r = 1$. The figures report log differences between marginal values of the different components relative to baseline probability counterparts. The uncertainty partitions account separately for temperature dynamics ambiguity, carbon dynamics ambiguity, and robustness to damage function misspecification. A color version of this figure is available online.

for, say, business-as-usual trajectories of emissions or even socially optimal trajectories of emissions that do not incorporate concerns about uncertainty. Thus, our decompositions are of potential interest for emissions trajectories other than those chosen as part of a solution to an uncertainty-averse planner's problem.

IX. Carbon Abatement Technology

Although the model posed in Section VII illustrated how the unfolding of damages should alter policy, the economic model was not designed to confront transitions to fully carbon-neutral economies. There have been several calls for such transitions with little regard for the role or impact of uncertainty. We now modify the model to allow for green technology in decades to come.

We next consider a technology that is close to the Dynamic Integrated Climate-Economy (DICE) model of Nordhaus (2017). See also Cai et al. (2017) and Cai and Lontzek (2019) for a stochastic extension (DSICE) of the DICE model.[20] For our setting, we alter the output equation from our previous specification as follows:

$$\frac{I_t}{K_t} + \frac{C_t}{K_t} + \frac{J_t}{K_t} = \alpha,$$

where

$$\frac{J_t}{K_t} = \begin{cases} \alpha \vartheta_t \left[1 - \left(\frac{\mathcal{E}_t}{\alpha \lambda_t K_t} \right) \right]^{\theta} \left(\frac{\mathcal{E}_t}{\alpha K_t} \right) & \leq \lambda_t \\ \\ 0 & \left(\frac{\mathcal{E}_t}{\alpha K_t} \right) \geq \lambda_t. \end{cases} \tag{12}$$

To motivate the term J_t, express the emissions-to-capital ratio as

$$\frac{\mathcal{E}_t}{K_t} = \alpha \lambda_t (1 - \iota_t),$$

where $0 \leq \iota_t \leq 1$ is abatement at date t. The exogenously specified process λ gives the emissions-to-output ratio in the absence of any abatement. By investing in ι_t, this ratio can be reduced, but there is a corresponding reduction in output. Specifically, the output loss is given by

$$J_t = \alpha K_t \vartheta (\iota_t)^{\theta}.$$

Equation (12) follows by solving for abatement ι_t in terms of emissions.[21] The planner's preferences are logarithmic over damaged consumption:

$$\log \tilde{C}_t = \log C_t - \log N_t = (\log C_t - \log K_t) - \log N_t + \log K_t.$$

In contrast to the previous specification, the planner's value function for this model is no longer additively separable in (y, k), although it remains additively separable in log damages, n.

For the purposes of illustration, we consider two Poisson events that reduce both (ϑ_t, λ_t), representing technological innovations that decrease the cost of abatement and improve the emissions-to-output ratio. The first jump cuts (ϑ_t, λ_t) in half, and the second jump sets $(\vartheta_t, \lambda_t) = (0, 0)$, indicating a transition to a purely carbon-neutral economy. Both events have the same constant intensity, which we set so that the expected arrival time is 20 years. The stochastic specification of damages remains the same as in the previous models. Not surprisingly, these two new Poisson events change substantially our calculations. In our discussion that follows, we highlight a few of the important differences.

The penalty parameters ξ_r and ξ_a are not necessarily transportable across the different models. Instead, it is sensible to loosen the penalty settings for more complicated economic environments to achieve probability distortions of comparable magnitudes. In our calculations, we increased $\xi_a = .02$, making the implied distorted distribution for the climate sensitivity parameter similar to the one we computed for Section VII. We again explore three settings for the robustness parameter ($\xi_r = 2.5, 5, 7.5$), and we explore which of the three Poisson events is of most concern to the social planner. Appendix C provides more detail about the parameter values we use and the approach to computation.

Figure 14 shows the baseline jump probabilities and the implied distorted probabilities for the three robustness settings. Because the second

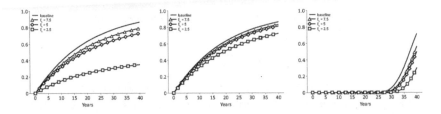

Fig. 14. Distorted probability of the Poisson events for technology changes and damages under different penalty configurations. The simulation uses the planner's optimal solution. The left panel shows the distorted jump probabilities for the first technology jump. The middle panel shows the distorted jump probabilities for the second technology jump. The right panel shows the distorted jump probabilities for the damage function curvature jump. The baseline probabilities for the right panel are computed using the state-dependent intensities when we set $\xi_a = \xi_r = \infty$. A color version of this figure is available online.

technological jump necessarily follows the first, the probabilities reported in the middle panel take as a starting point the date at which the first technology advance is realized. Comparing the probabilities across the different plots, it is clear that the probabilistic specification of the first green technology advance is of the most concern to the planner. In particular, when we set $\xi_r = 2.5$, the probability slanting is arguably extreme implying probabilities that are about 70% lower than the baseline probabilities. But even when $\xi_r = 5$, there is about a 25% reduction in the probabilities relative to the baseline. The reductions are notably smaller for the other two Poisson events. Given the prospect of advances in green technology, damage function uncertainty concerns are less concerning to the planner than the technological uncertainty. Notice that in this economy, the technological advancements make it much more plausible to avoid the more severe damages.[22]

Figure 15 reports the probability distortions for the damage function and climate sensitivity models. Here, we have imposed $\xi_a = .02$ and $\xi_r = 5.0$. Note that the damage function probability distortions are relatively modest, consistent with our previous discussion. The climate model distortions, by design, are of similar magnitude as those reported previously in figure 5.

To summarize, it is the probability of the first technological advance that is of the biggest concern to the social planner. In particular, uncertainty in the environmental and economic damages induced by climate change is now less problematic given the potential advances in green technology.

The possibilities of technological improvements appearing sometime in the future together with the extra ability to mitigate emissions by paying

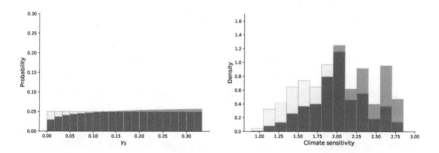

Fig. 15. Distorted probabilities of damage functions and climate models. These computations impose $\xi_a = .02$ and $\xi_r = 5.0$. Baseline probabilities are given by the light gray bars, and the medium gray bars are robust adjustments to the probabilities induced by model uncertainty concerns. The left panel shows the damage function probabilities and the right panel shows the climate model probabilities. The histograms are the outcome of recursive minimizations with the distortions calculated at year 40 of the simulation. A color version of this figure is available online.

a cost dampens the strong precautionary behavior of the fictitious planner that we found before. This finding points out the importance of adding a research and development (R&D) sector for the development of more productive green technologies and to open the door to policies that subsidize these sectors as has been explored in other studies.[23] Because R&D investments can be highly speculative, the methods in this paper would allow for an investigation of the consequent uncertainties in addition to the ones explored here.

X. Denouement

We draw our paper to end by taking inventory of what we see as the valuable messages. During the course of writing and presenting this paper, we have received a variety of comments, some of which have helped us set the stage for future research, and others that are based on a potential misunderstanding about where our research is positioned relative to other discussions of prospective emissions and the SCC.

A. Quantitative Storytelling

We have used highly stylized models to help us better understand how uncertainty should affect prudent policy making. There are two interrelated reasons for the stylized nature of our exercise: one is to preserve tractability, and the other is to ensure that mapping from model inputs to conclusions is transparent. The models we use in this paper have obvious flaws and limitations, but the resulting analyses are intended to point to where more ambitious models might contribute to the knowledge base.

Calibrating such highly stylized models is a bit like walking on a tightrope. We want the findings to have credibility, with results that are not driven by perverse or extreme parameter settings. But the models we are parameterizing deliberately omit elements of both the climate and economic dynamics. We view this research as an initial step in what we hope will be a research agenda that will become even more substantively ambitious as we explore increasingly complex dynamic models and the associated uncertainties.

B. SCC

Our choice in this paper to feature solutions to planners' problems has important ramifications for interpreting our measurement of the SCC relative to the modular approaches that we discussed previously. As we noted, others have also featured planners' approaches in part motivated by the Pigouvian approach for taxing externalities. The planner's solution pins down the contingency rule for emissions expressed in terms of the Markov states. Because the planner internalizes the impact of carbon emissions on damages, this has important ramifications for emissions trajectories and the SCC measured as a shadow price of emissions relative to a consumption numeraire. For instance, even the lower-bound temperature anomaly $\underline{y}$ where the damage function jumps begin to occur in our analysis will not be crossed for somewhere between 50 and 75 years when simulating this path going forward for our first model. This pushes the potentially extreme damage realizations far into the future relative to "business-as-usual" trajectories. The SCCs are substantial relative to other computations based on solutions to planners' problems and made larger because of the explicit adjustments for model ambiguity and robustness to potential misspecification. Recall that our approach to uncertainty quantification results in a two-parameter characterization depending on the two forms of aversion. Although we reported sensitivity to misspecification aversion in the paper, we show the impact of additional concerns about model ambiguity in our accompanying online notebook. Increasing ambiguity aversion in ways that are arguably plausible increases further the uncertainty contribution to about 35%. But these are for an illustrative model with no backup or green technology, the inclusion of which would alter substantially both the emissions trajectory and the SCC. In fact, this is what happens in the second model we consider. An interested reader can see these additional results and others in an online notebook we constructed to supplement this paper.[24] We mention such numbers to convey that the planner in our examples is responding aggressively to climate change, but such numbers are not good candidates for numerical values to post on EPA webpages because of the preliminary and stylized nature of the models including the uncertainty inputs into the computations.[25]

Although there is path uncertainty in our model because of shocks that impinge on the dynamical economic system, our approach does not include the multiple exogenous scenarios and accompanying uncertainty across the scenarios that are part of the modular approaches. The practical connection of the computation of the SCC computed from a social optimum to taxation is limited because it ignores the presence of other taxes and other constraints on policy making, including cross-country coordination. Nevertheless, in our view, the socially efficient allocation remains interesting as a benchmark to compare with existing policy outcomes. Within this context, we find the SCC to be a revealing barometer for the importance of uncertainty.

As explained in NYSERDA and RFF (2021) and elsewhere, the modular approach advocated by some for the purposes of regulation is local in nature. It is computed as a local or a small change around an existing allocation. Though perhaps suggestive, this approach does not quantify the impact of global changes in policy. As this local construct of an SCC is also forward-looking, it depends on the prospective future emissions and the damages they might induce. The actual computations depend on emissions scenarios. These are alternative emission pathways, typically imposed exogenously. The differences in the socially efficient emissions process and the array of emission scenarios can have an important impact on the SCC calculation. The treatment of uncertainty for this local approach typically (a) is static in nature; (b) presumes, at least implicitly, a priori probabilities across a small array of scenarios; and (c) is outside the decision problem. The outcome is a histogram of SCCs instead of an SCC that incorporates uncertainty. Thus, this local construct of the SCC is very different from the one used in our paper, all the more so given common implementations.[26]

The methods we describe could be applied to local measures of the SCC, provided that emissions scenarios would be specified recursively in ways amenable to the application of dynamic programming methods. Importantly, there is more to discounting than the choice of a single constant discount rate. As featured in Barnett et al. (2020), these uncertainty adjustments can be most conveniently represented as a change in the probability measure used for evaluation. These types of adjustments lead naturally to important interactions in the components of the commonly employed modular approach. SCC measurements designed to incorporate uncertainty within a decision-making or policy-design framework cannot be easily modularized.

C. Damage Functions

Our damage function specifications, like many other ones in the integrated assessment literature, should be taken with a grain of salt, so to speak. They are ad hoc primarily to support tractable illustration. As we mentioned previously, Pindyck (2013) and Morgan et al. (2017) raise valid points about the quantitative implications of integrated assessment models in part because of the ad hoc nature of the damage functions.

Most recently, Carleton and Greenstone (2021) have a valuable discussion of what is missed by this approach and the need to incorporate a broader range of empirical evidence. To incorporate such evidence in an internally consistent manner would require much more elaborate models than the ones we have used here. Such efforts would also be accompanied by a rather substantial degree of model uncertainty.

Our specification of damage possibilities included thresholds that could trigger more extreme damages. This formulation is intended to include contributions from environmental tipping points as well as reductions in economic opportunities, which adds to the challenge of how to bound uncertainties in meaningful ways. Productive discussions of our work, while still in progress, included important reminders that the announced thresholds such as a 2-degree or 1.5-degree anomaly have been set as rather arbitrary policy guides and are not firmly grounded with scientific evidence. We find our probabilistic use of such thresholds coupled with robustness concerns to be revealing, but there is little doubt that further modeling and measurement would strengthen the analysis.

Many recent policy discussions have focused on "carbon budgets," or formal limits on the cumulative amount of CO_2 emissions that should be allowed in the future based on specific temperature thresholds. Although carbon budgets allow for simplicity in communication, they are hard to defend in the presence of uncertainty as to the timing and magnitude of temperature responses to carbon emissions. A temperature threshold can be viewed as a very special type of damage function whereby losses are negligible prior to reaching the threshold and very severe (infinite) after the threshold is crossed. But again, uncertainty about the transition dynamics for future temperature changes as they respond to current emissions requires a commitment to capture carbon in the atmosphere to avoid exceeding the threshold. Though we have already noted the somewhat arbitrary nature of a single temperature threshold, we could approximate socially efficient responses to such a threshold within the framework of our models. This could be done by restricting the upper and lower temperature thresholds to be the same and embracing a steeply curved damage function. The embracing of a single steeply curved damage function could emerge formally as part of a robustness response to damage function uncertainty. Specifically, it could be viewed as the outcome of an extreme form of robustness where degenerate bounds have been placed on the probabilities over the alternative specifications for damage function curvature. Thus, a simple extension to our analysis could approximate a single temperature threshold decision criterion.

Previous commentaries have expressed valid modeling concerns about how to capture adaptation to climate change. As adaptation is inherently a dynamic process, to accommodate it in a meaningful way requires both evidence and a model to interpret the evidence while opening the door to an additional source of model uncertainty. Private-sector adaptation to climate change is an important extension of ours in other analyses, but we should also expect policies to adapt to observed changes in the environment that partially resolve the damage function uncertainty. A modular approach that treats uncertainty in emissions trajectories to be independent of damage function uncertainty seems ill-conceived once we take a more dynamic interactive perspective. Such considerations suggest that sensitivity analyses in the specification of baseline probabilities of the type that we propose would be a revealing way to addressing this potential dependence.

Our model of damage function "learning" is purposefully simplified to illustrate some important points. The stark way in which information is revealed is no doubt extreme, but one needs only to read the recent Intergovernmental Panel on Climate Change (IPCC) Sixth Assessment Report to see claims that observed damages to climate are speeding up our ability to learn about climate change. In our example economy, in spite of the one-shot nature of the learning, the social planner adopts caution in advance of becoming more fully informed about damage functions. It is too costly to delay action until after the uncertainty is resolved. Also, there is an asymmetric response to the revelation of the damage function curvature. As with any form of rational learning, there is a potential for good news. In this case, the good news is that there might be less damage function curvature than was feared. In our computations, this news response is only really notable for a small portion of the good news realizations. Our purpose in this example is to illustrate the potential importance of going beyond what some in environmental economics, such as Nordhaus (2018), call "learn, then act," and instead to incorporate informational dynamics into the analysis.

D. Technology

One concern from our model is the use of a Cobb-Douglas specification and the energy input share of fossil fuels that we use with that specification. As in Barnett et al. (2020), we use empirical estimates of the energy input share from Finn (1995), adjusted by the approximate proportion of fossil-fuel energy consumption, for our value of the energy input share of fossil fuels. This parameter value allows us to match the optimal emissions choice for the solution to the model without climate impacts to the annual emissions of 10 gigatonnes of carbon per year (GtC/yr) measured by Figueres et al. (2018). In addition, the value is similar to the mean value for the fossil-fuel income share found recently by Hassler, Krusell, and Olovsson (2021). Importantly, even with this energy share value, uncertainty is still of first-order importance. Larger energy input share values would serve to amplify the importance of uncertainty for the SCC.

Although the Cobb-Douglas specification allows us to simplify the computations and exploit numerically value function separability, a flaw in this specification is that it allows for the planner to reduce energy usages freely without incurring any abatement costs. Our second model follows the DICE literature by explicitly introducing abatement into the production technology whereby output is reduced when deviating from a fixed proportions technology. This allows us to further evaluate the impacts of uncertainty when adjusting carbon emissions is somewhat costly. This model opens the door to more interesting discussions of technological change and exploring the impact of greener technologies that might arrive in the future. Because there is uncertainty about the arrival of cleaner technologies, this model includes an additional channel whereby uncertainty has an important impact on the analysis.[27]

Each of the models we presented was designed to tell an interesting quantitative story. Although we explored the uncertainty within each setup, we could have had our decision maker entertain both models simultaneously as possibilities. Instead, we find it more productive to push further the computational boundaries in studying a more ambitious model of technology with interesting special cases.

XI. Conclusion

In many dynamic settings, our understanding of the true underlying model relevant for economic decision-making is limited because existing evidence is weak along some important dimensions. As a result, the design and conduct of policy occurs in settings in which policy outcomes are uncertain. We offer the economics of climate change as an example, but there are many others. We turned to decision theory under uncertainty to serve as a guide for how we conduct uncertainty quantification as it contributes to the design of policy. Furthermore, we showed how different forms of uncertainty affect our quantification, how information about environmental and economic damages revealed in the future influence current policies, and how different sources of uncertainty contribute to the SCC in the presence of model and ambiguity and misspecification concerns.

Our analysis in this paper is made simpler here by posing the resource allocation problem as one faced by a single policy maker or social planner. To push closer to a realistic policy setting, multiple decision makers come into play, including alternative policy makers as well as private-sector consumers and investors. Because these different agents confront uncertainty from different perspectives, their uncertainty concerns are expressed in different ways. Moreover, in more realistic policy settings, political constraints prevent first-best solutions. Although we fully appreciate the need to extend our analysis of uncertainty to address these modeling challenges, we have little reason to doubt that the uncertainty considerations should remain as first-order concerns and not be shunted to the background as they often are in policy discussions.

Appendix A

Carbon and Temperature Model Sets

As mentioned previously, we use 16 models of temperature dynamics from Geoffroy et al. (2013) and nine models of carbon dynamics models from Joos et al. (2013). We briefly describe the model experiments used in these papers, list the models we include in our analysis, and provide details for the reader to find additional information about these models and model experiments.

Geoffroy et al. (2013) approximate the temperature dynamics of 16 different models using a two-layer energy-balance model (EBM) to study properties of AOGCMs. Table A1 lists the model name for each of the 16 models used in their and our analysis and direct the reader to Geoffroy et al. (2013) and Seshadri (2017) for additional details about each of the models.

The Geoffroy et al. (2013) EBM model uses the following specification:

$$c_s \frac{dT^s}{dt} = F - \gamma T^s - \epsilon \chi (T^s - T^o)$$

$$c_o \frac{dT^o}{dt} = -\chi (T^o - T^s)$$

$$F = 5.35 (\log CO_2 - \log \underline{CO_2}),$$

where T^s is the surface temperature, T^o is the ocean temperature, CO_2 is atmospheric carbon dioxide, and $\underline{CO_2}$ is the preindustrial benchmark.

The construction of F comes from the "Arrhenius" equation (Arrhenius 1896). The EBM model is solved for explicit solutions, calibrated to fit the responses of 16 AOGCMs that participated in the Coupled Model Intercomparison Project Phase 5 (CMIP5), and then validated by using the AOGCM responses to the linear forcing experiments of 1% of CO_2 per year. The parameters they estimate in this simplified representation differ depending on the model used in the calibration of the approximation, providing a measure of the heterogeneity and uncertainty present in models of temperature dynamics. We use this specification along with Geoffroy et al.'s estimates of the 16 temperature dynamics models in our simulations to capture the carbon-to-temperature component of climate model uncertainty.

Joos et al. (2013) use a carbon cycle-climate model intercomparison analysis to study the impulse response timescales of Earth System models. From their analysis, we use the impulse response functions of nine models based on a 100GtC emission pulse added to a constant CO_2 concentration of 389 parts per million.[28] All of the models we use are Earth System Models of Intermediate Complexity, except for the reduced form model Bern-SAR. We list the model name for each of the models used in our analysis in table A2. We direct the reader to appendix A in Joos et al. (2013) for detailed descriptions of these and other models used in their intercomparison analysis.

Table A1
List of Temperature Dynamics Models from Geoffroy et al. (2013) and Seshadri (2017) Used in our Analysis

Temperature Dynamics Models
BCC-CSM1–1
BNU-ESM
CanESM2
CCSM
CNRM-CM5
CSIRO-Mk3.6.0
FGOALS-s2
GFDL-ESM2M
GISS-E2-R
HadGEM2-ES
INM-CM4
IPSL-CM5A-LR
MIROC
MPI-ESM-LR
MRI-CGCM3
NorESM1-M

Table A2
List of Carbon Dynamics Models from Joos et al. (2013)
Used in our Analysis

Carbon Dynamics Models
Bern3D-LPJ (reference)
Bern2.5D-LPJ
CLIMBER2-LPJ
DCESS
GENIE (ensemble median)
LOVECLIM
MESMO
UVic2.9
Bern-SAR

Appendix B

Value Function Components for Section VII Model

In Section VII, we discussed a climate-economics HJB equation in the state variable y. This HJB equation uses a quasianalytical simplification for the damages state n of the form $\phi(y) - 1 - \eta/\delta n$, which derive using the "guess and verify" method. This is part of a larger system that can be solved with two additional subsystems of equations. The three subsystem solutions, when combined, give a solution to the composite HJB equation of the planner.

B.1. Climate-Economics System Parameters

Table B1
Climate-Economics System Parameters

Parameter	Value
ς'	$[2.23 \quad 0 \quad 0]$
γ_1	.000177
γ_2	.0044
γ_3^m	$\frac{.333(m-1)}{19}$, $m = 1, 2, \ldots, 20$
η	.032
δ	.01

Note: To understand better the implications of the ς specification, note that for a constant emissions path, the implied standard deviation associated with the coefficient of the Matthew's approximation is 0.446 at 25 years, 0.315 for 50 years, and 0.223 for 100 years.

B.2. Consumption-Capital Dynamics

The undamaged version of the consumption-capital model, by design, has a straightforward solution. We use the "guess and verify" method to derive a solution for this subsystem, guessing a value function of $v_k \log k + \varsigma(z)$. The HJB equation for this component is

$$0 = \max_{i} \min_{h} -\delta\left[v_k \log k + \varsigma(z)\right] + (1 - \eta)\left[\log(\alpha - i) + \log k\right] + \frac{\xi_r}{2}|h|^2$$

$$+ v_k\left[\mu_k(z) + i - \frac{\kappa}{2}(i)^2 + \sigma_k(z)'h - \frac{|\sigma_k(z)|^2}{2}\right]$$

$$+ \frac{\partial \varsigma}{\partial z}(z)[\mu_z(z) + \sigma(z)'h] + \frac{1}{2}\text{trace}\left[\sigma(z)'\frac{\partial^2 \varsigma}{\partial z \partial z'}(z)\sigma(z)\right].$$

From this equation, we derive the constant scaling the capital component of the value function v_k and can see that it must be

$$v_k = \frac{1 - \eta}{\delta}.$$

Solving for the first-order conditions, we see that the first-order condition for h is

$$\xi_r h + \sigma_k v_k + \sigma_z \frac{\partial \varsigma}{\partial z} = 0,$$

and the first-order conditions for the investment-capital ratio is

$$-(1 - \eta)\left(\frac{1}{\alpha - i}\right) + v_k(1 - \kappa i) = 0.$$

Notice that the equation for the optimal h is therefore

$$h = -\frac{1}{\xi_r}\left[\sigma_k v_k + \sigma_z \frac{\partial \varsigma}{\partial z}\right]$$

and that the investment-capital ratio is constant. Although there are two solutions for the first-order conditions for i, only one is positive. In our illustration, we set $\alpha = .115$ and $\kappa = 6.667$.

The solution for h will be state dependent if we allow for σ_k or σ_z to depend on z or if there is nonlinearity in the drift specifications. Such dependence is common in the macro-finance literature as a form of stochastic volatility. In the computations that follow, we will abstract from this dependence and impose linear dynamics for z. We impose that

$$\mu_k(z) = -.043 + .04(\iota_k \cdot z)$$

and

$$\sigma_k = .01[.87 \ .38]dW_t^k,$$

where dW^k is a two-dimensional subvector of the Brownian increment vector dW. The evolution for the process $\iota_k \cdot Z$ is given by a continuous-time autoregression:

$$d(\iota_k \cdot Z_t) = -.056(\iota_k \cdot Z_t)dt + [\ 0 \ \ .055\ ]dW_t^k.$$

In this case, $\varsigma(z) = \varsigma_0 + \varsigma_1\iota_k \cdot z$, where ς_1 satisfies

$$-\delta\varsigma_1 + \upsilon_k(.04) + \varsigma_1(-.056) = 0.$$

The implied solution for h is constant and equal to

$$h^* = -\frac{1}{\xi_r}\begin{bmatrix} .85 \\ 3.58 \end{bmatrix}.$$

The implied consumption dynamics in this setting are consistent with the ones given in Hansen and Sargent (2021):[29]

$$d \log C_t = .0194 + .04Z_t dt + .01[.87 \ .38] \cdot dW_t^k.$$

B.3.   Contribution of $\iota_y \cdot z$

There is one remaining contribution to the planner's HJB equation for each of our models. Note that although $\log \iota_y \cdot z$ is included in the objective of the planner, this term has not been accounted for in our solution so far. Thus there is a third contribution, $\tilde{\varsigma}$, to the value function that solves

$$\min_h -\delta\tilde{\varsigma}(z) - \eta \log(\iota_y \cdot z) + \left[\frac{\partial\tilde{\varsigma}}{\partial z}(z)\right] \cdot [\mu_z(z) + \sigma_z(z)h] + \frac{\xi_r}{2}h'h$$

$$\tag{13}$$

$$+\frac{1}{2}\text{trace}\left[\sigma_z(z)'\frac{\partial^2\tilde{\varsigma}}{\partial z\partial z'}(z)\sigma_z(z)\right] = 0.$$

To support this value function separation, we impose that $\iota_y \cdot Z$ and $\iota_k \cdot Z$ are independent processes with $\iota_y \cdot Z$ constructed as a function of the dW^y increments and $\iota_k \cdot Z$ constructed in terms of the dW^k increments. Moreover, we assume that

$$\varsigma' \sigma_z(z)' \left[\frac{\partial \tilde{\varsigma}}{\partial z}(z) \right] = 0, \tag{14}$$

where $\tilde{\varsigma}$ is the solution to HJB equation $[\partial \tilde{\varsigma}/\partial z(z)]$.

As a special case, suppose that $\iota_y \cdot Z_t$ evolves as Feller square root process with mean one:

$$d(\iota_y \cdot Z_t) = -\chi(\iota_y \cdot Z_t - 1)dt + \sqrt{\iota_y \cdot Z_t} \tilde{\varsigma} \cdot dW_t^y,$$

where $\tilde{\varsigma} \cdot \varsigma = 0$. Then the solution of interest to equation (13) can be expressed as a functional equation in the scalar argument $\iota_y \cdot z$. Given the separability, this value function contribution is used for the figures that we produce.

As part of a "guess and verify" solution method, we add the three value function components and the three components for the minimizing h together along with the proposed solutions for the investment-capital ratio i and for scaled emissions $\tilde{e}$. In fact there may be good reasons to relax assumption (eq. [14]) and combine the climate-economics HJB contribution and that coming from (eq. [13]) into a single HJB equation to be solved instead of two lower-dimensional functional equations.

Appendix C

Value Function Components for Section IX Model

The HJB equation for the model in Section IX depends on the state variables y and k. As with the previous model, this HJB equation uses a quasianalytical simplification for the damages state n, as well as a separable subsystem for the exogenous forcing state z. The value function that solves the HJB equation is of the form $\varphi(y, k) - (1/\delta)n + \varsigma(z)$, which is derived using the "guess and verify" method. The two subsystem solutions, one for $\varphi(y, k) - (1/\delta)n$ and one for $\varsigma(z)$, when combined, give a solution to the composite HJB equation of the planner.

C.1.   HJB Equations Details

As was the case for the model in Section VII, this model has pre- and postjump values functions. These HJB equations are similar in structure to those shown in the previous model. However, in this case there are additional layers for two reasons: (i) the potential for two different technology jumps related to the abatement technology and (ii) the lack of separability between y and k due to the functional form of abatement technology. As a result, we must compute numerous continuation value functions based on postjump outcomes across multiple dimensions, as well as a prejump value function. We denote the predamage jump value functions as $\varphi_i(y, k)$ and the postdamage jump value functions as $\varphi_{i,m}(y, k)$, where i denotes the number of technology jumps that have already occurred, and thus the values for (λ_t, ϑ_t), so that $i \in \{0, 1, 2\}$. We denote the intensity rate for each technology jump as $\mathcal{H}$, given that it is constant and equal for each jump scenario.

C.2. Additional Parameters Values and Initial Conditions

We provide a table of the consumption-capital parameters and the abatement technology parameters (table C1). Except for the parameters pertaining to abatement, which were not included in the previous model, the parameters for this model match those given in appendix B.

Table C1
Abatement Parameters

Parameter	Value
Θ	3.0
(ϑ_0, λ_0)	(.0453, .1206)
$\mathcal{H}$	.05

Note: The initial values for the abatement technology (ϑ_0, λ_0) are based on the implied values for 2020 from Cai and Lontzek (2019). We set the initial value of capital so that our initial gross domestic product (GDP) matches the 2020 World GDP value of $85 trillion in the World Bank National Accounts data. Therefore, $K_0 = 739.13$. We set the initial value of atmospheric temperature anomaly to match recent estimates provided by the IPCC. Therefore, $Y_0 = 1.1$ degree Celsius.

Endnotes

    Author email address: Hansen (lhansen@uchicago.edu). An online notebook, which includes supplemental results and the code used to derive our model solutions, is available at https://climateuncertaintyspillover.readthedocs.io/en/latest. We thank Shirui Chen, Han Xu, and Jiaming Wang for the computational support on this research. Zhenhuan Xie, Samuel Zhao, and especially Diana Petrova provided valuable help in preparing this manuscript. We benefited from valuable feedback from Fernando Alvarez, Marty Eichenbaum, Michael Greenstone, Kevin Murphy, Tom Sargent, and Chris Sims during helpful conversations while preparing this manuscript. Finally, Per Krusell, Ishan Nath, and Mar Reguant provided thoughtful discussions of earlier versions of the research that helped us in subsequent revisions of this manuscript. Financial support for this project was provided by the Alfred P. Sloan Foundation (grant G-2018-11113). For acknowledgments, sources of research support, and disclosure of the authors' material financial relationships, if any, please see https://www.nber.org/books-and-chapters/nber-macroeconomics-annual-2021 -volume-36/climate-change-uncertainty-spillover-macroeconomy.

1. The term "model" is used differentially in statistical discussions of uncertainty. For us, a model conditions on any unknown parameters. Thus, we differentiate a model from a parameterized family of models.

2. See, e.g., National Academies of Sciences, Engineering and Medicine (2017) for a discussion and a defense for the modular approach.

3. See Lemoine and Traeger (2016) and Cai, Lenton, and Lontzek (2016) for an example of an economic analysis with tipping point uncertainty.

4. See Seshadri (2017), Eby et al. (2009), Matthews et al. (2009), and MacDougall et al. (2017) for additional examples of work in this area.

5. Appendix A provides additional details on the emission pulse responses from Joos et al. (2013) and the approximating model of Geoffroy et al. (2013), and lists the specific models we use from these two studies.

6. Ricke and Caldeira (2014) also consider separately two sources of temperature dynamics.

7. See eq. (5) of Joos et al. (2013) and eqs. (1)–(3) of Pierrehumbert (2014). Pierrehumbert puts the change in radiative forcing equal to a constant times the logarithm of the ratio of atmospheric CO_2 at date t to atmospheric CO_2 at baseline date zero. His figs. 1 and 2 illustrate how an approximation of the Earth System dynamics by three exponentials plus a constant tracks a radiative forcing induced by a pulse into the atmosphere at a baseline date from the atmosphere works quite well with half-lives of approximately 6, 65, and 450 years.

8. In independent work, Dietz and Venmans (2019) and Barnett et al. (2020) have used such simplified approximations within an explicit economic optimization framework. The former contribution includes the initial rapid upswing in the impulse response functions. The latter contribution abstracts from this. Barnett et al. instead explore ways to confront uncertainty, broadly conceived, while using the Matthews approximation.

9. See Hansen and Sargent (2022) and Cerreia-Vioglio et al. (2021) for decision-theoretic discussions of the distinct roles for model ambiguity and misspecification concerns.

10. This approach is a continuous-time version of the dynamic variational preferences of Maccheroni, Marinacci, and Rustichini (2006).

11. In particular, the right-hand side needs to integrate to one over θ.

12. See Lemoine and Rudik (2017) who provided a related commentary, arguing why recursive methods from economic dynamic can open the door to important extensions in climate economics including parameter learning. Nordhaus (2018) noted the inability of his framework to address such endogenous feedbacks and unresolved uncertainty, and also pointed out the potential value to using the type of recursive methods we employ in our analysis as a way to address such issues.

13. As Cai and Lontzek (2019) noted and encountered in some of their simulations, when emissions hit a zero constraint, the SCC may reflect a desire for negative emissions while Pigouvian taxes are needed only to reach the zero emissions outcome.

14. We use units of carbon as opposed to CO_2 in our computation, which is in effect a different choice of units.

15. See, e.g., Borovička, Hansen, and Scheinkman (2014) for a pedagogical treatment of nonlinear impulse response functions for diffusions and related computations pertinent for valuation. The calculations relate closely to two well-known mathematical tools, the method of characteristics and Malliavin differentiation.

16. Including parameter learning requires additional state variables that serve as sufficient statistics for the unknown parameter vector θ under the base probability specification.

17. These shocks imply two of the consumption shocks in Bansal and Yaron (2004). Bansal and Yaron also include a shock to stochastic volatility that we abstract from here and consider implications for changing the intertemporal elasticity of substitution.

18. The number of outcomes in the histograms is determined by the number of values of γ_3^m, which is 20, and the time discretization used in the simulation.

19. Although the robustness adjustment also applies to the climate dynamics, as we saw in the previous section, this adjustment was small relative to the ambiguity adjustment.

20. Among other stochastic components, the DSICE incorporates tipping elements and characterizes the SCC as a stochastic process. From a decision theory perspective, DSICE

focuses on risk aversion and intertemporal substitution under an assumption of rational expectations.

21. The link to the specification used in Cai and Lontzek (2019) is then:

$$\sigma_t = \lambda_t$$

$$\vartheta_t = \theta_{1,t}$$

$$\theta = \theta_2$$

$$\mu_t = \iota_t$$

22. To provide further confirmation of this interpretation, the initial emissions are a little higher for this model than the ones from Section VII that are depicted in figure 9. They now range between 6.9 and 8.1, depending on the value of ξ_r.

23. See, e.g., Acemoglu et al. (2016).

24. Our online notebook, which includes these supplemental results and the code used to derive our model solutions, is available at https://climateuncertaintyspillover.read thedocs.io/en/latest.

25. As readers of Koonin (2021) and of the challenges by climate scientists to some of its claims such those noted in Bellanger (2021), we expect rather heterogeneous views about plausible uncertainty bounds to use in quantitative investigations like ours.

26. The National Academies of Sciences, Engineering and Medicine (2017) report suggests investigating sensitivity to discount rates. With discount rates as low as 2%, some of the scenario paths must be projected far out into the future to compute present discounted values. It is well known that present-value calculations can be highly sensitive to assumptions about the distant future. Of course, recursive methods do not escape this challenge but address it by positing dynamic evolutions rather than paths.

27. In contrast to our earlier work, Barnett et al. (2020), and some other contributions to the climate-economics literature, we also abstracted from production or resource extraction costs for fossil fuels. This was done for pedagogical simplicity because these costs are typically internalized in the productive process.

28. We thank Fortunat Joos for graciously providing the data for these and other response experiments on his website: https://climatehomes.unibe.ch/~joos/IRF_Intercom parison/results.html.

29. Hansen and Sargent (2021) represent the dynamics in terms of a time unit of 1 quarter instead of 1 year, and they report a different but observationally equivalent orthogonalization of the Brownian increments.

References

Acemoglu, Daron, Funk Akcigit, Douglas Hanley, and William Kerr. 2016. "Transition to Clean Technology." *Journal of Political Economy* 124 (1): 52–104.

Anderson, Evan W., Lars Peter Hansen, and Thomas J. Sargent. 2003. "A Quartet of Semigroups for Model Specification, Robustness, Prices of Risk, and Model Detection." *Journal of the European Economic Association* 1 (1): 68–123.

Arrhenius, Svante. 1896. "On the Influence of Carbonic Acid in the Air upon Temperature of the Ground." *Philosophical Magazine and Journal of Science* Series 5 (41): 237–76.

Bansal, Ravi, and Amir Yaron. 2004. "Risks for the Long Run: A Potential Resolution of Asset Pricing Puzzles." *Journal of Finance* 59 (4): 1481–509.

Barnett, Michael, William A. Brock, and Lars Peter Hansen. 2020. "Pricing Uncertainty Induced by Climate Change." *Review of Financial Studies* 33 (3): 1024–66.

Bellanger, Boris, ed. 2021. *"Wall Street Journal* Article Repeats Multiple Incorrect and Misleading Claims Made in Steven Koonin's New Book *Unsettled."* Review on ClimateFeedback.org, May 3.

Berger, Loïc, and Massimo Marinacci. 2020. "Model Uncertainty in Climate Change Economics: A Review and Proposed Framework for Future Research." *Environmental and Resource Economics* 77:475–501.

Bornstein, Gideon, Per Krusell, and Sergio Rebelo. 2017. "Lags, Costs, and Shocks: An Equilibrium Model of the Oil Industry." Working Paper no. 23423, NBER, Cambridge, MA.

Borovička, Jaroslav, Lars Peter Hansen, and Jose A. Scheinkman. 2014. "Shock Elasticities and Impulse Responses." *Mathematics and Financial Economics* 8 (4): 333–54.

Cai, Yongyang, Kenneth L. Judd, and Thomas S. Lontzek. 2017. "The Social Cost of Carbon with Climate Risk." Technical report, Hoover Institution, Stanford, CA.

Cai, Yongyang, Timothy M. Lenton, and Thomas S. Lontzek. 2016. "Risk of Multiple Interacting Tipping Points Should Encourage Rapid CO_2 Emission Reduction." *Nature Climate Change* 6 (5): 520–25.

Cai, Yongyang, and Thomas S. Lontzek. 2019. "The Social Cost of Carbon with Economic and Climate Risks." *Journal of Political Economy* 127 (6): 2684–734.

Carleton, Tamma, and Michael Greenstone. 2021. "Updating the United States Government's Social Cost of Carbon." SSRN Working Paper no. 2021-04, University of Chicago, Becker Friedman Institute for Economics.

Casassus, Jaime, Pierre Collin-Dufresne, and Bryan R. Routledge. 2018. "Equilibrium Commodity Prices with Irreversible Investment and Non-Linear Technologies." *Journal of Banking and Finance* 95:128–47.

Cerreia-Vioglio, Simone, Lars Peter Hansen, Fabio Maccheroni, and Massimo Marinacci. 2021. "Making Decisions under Model Misspecification." Becker Friedman Institute for Economics Working Paper no. 2020-103, University of Chicago.

Dietz, Simon, and Frank Venmans. 2019. "Cumulative Carbon Emissions and Economic Policy: In Search of General Principles." *Journal of Environmental Economics and Management* 96:108–29.

Drijfhout, Sybren, Sebastian Bathiany, Claudie Beaulieu, Victor Brovkin, Martin Claussen, Chris Huntingford, Marten Scheffer, Giovanni Sgubin, and Didier Swingedouw. 2015. "Catalogue of Abrupt Shifts in Intergovernmental Panel on Climate Change Climate Models." *Proceedings of the National Academy of Sciences* 112 (43): E5777–E5786.

Eby, M., K. Zickfeld, A. Montenegro, D. Archer, K. J. Meissner, and A. J. Weaver. 2009. "Lifetime of Anthropogenic Climate Change: Millennial Time Scales of Potential CO_2 and Surface Temperature Perturbations." *Journal of Climate* 22 (10): 2501–11.

Epstein, Larry G., and Stanley E. Zin. 1989. "Substitution, Risk Aversion and the Temporal Behavior of Consumption and Asset Returns: A Theoretical Framework." *Econometrica* 57 (4): 937–69.

Figueres, Christiana, Corinne Le Quéré, Anand Mahindra, Oliver Bäte, Gail Whiteman, Glen Peters, and Dabo Guan. 2018. "Emissions Are Still Rising: Ramp Up the Cuts." *Nature* 564:27–30.

Finn, Mary G. 1995. "Variance Properties of Solow's Productivity Residual and Their Cyclical Implications." *Journal of Economic Dynamics and Control* 19 (5–7): 1249–81.

Geoffroy, O., D. Saint-Martin, D. J. L. Olivié, A. Voldoire, G. Bellon, and S. Tytéca. 2013. "Transient Climate Response in a Two-Layer Energy-Balance

Model. Part I: Analytical Solution and Parameter Calibration Using CMIP5 AOGCM Experiments." *Journal of Climate* 26 (6): 1841–57.

Ghil, Michael, and Valerio Lucarini. 2020. "The Physics of Climate Variability and Climate Change." *Reviews of Modern Physics* 92 (3): 035002.

Gillingham, Kenneth, William Nordhaus, David Anthoff, Geoffrey Blanford, Valentina Bosetti, Peter Christensen, Haewon McJeon, and John Reilly. 2018. "Modeling Uncertainty in Integrated Assessment of Climate Change: A Multimodel Comparison." *Journal of the Association of Environmental and Resource Economists* 5 (4): 791–826.

Golosov, Mikhail, John Hassler, Per Krusell, and Aleh Tsyvinski. 2014. "Optimal Taxes on Fossil Fuel in General Equilibrium." *Econometrica* 82 (1): 41–88.

Good, Irving J. 1952. "Rational Decisions." *Journal of the Royal Statistical Society Series B (Methodological)* 14 (1): 107–14.

Hansen, Lars Peter, John C. Heaton, and Nan Li. 2008. "Consumption Strikes Back? Measuring Long-Run Risk." *Journal of Political Economy* 116 (2): 260–302.

Hansen, Lars Peter, and Jianjun Miao. 2018. "Aversion to Ambiguity and Model Misspecification in Dynamic Stochastic Environments." *Proceedings of the National Academy of Sciences* 115 (37): 9163–68.

Hansen, Lars Peter, and Thomas J. Sargent. 2001. "Robust Control and Model Uncertainty." *American Economic Review* 91 (2): 60–66.

———. 2007. "Recursive Robust Estimation and Control without Commitment." *Journal of Economic Theory* 136 (1): 1–27.

———. 2021. "Macroeconomic Uncertainty Prices When Beliefs Are Tenuous." *Journal of Econometrics* 223 (1): 222–50.

———. 2022. "Structured Ambiguity and Model Misspecification." *Journal of Economic Theory* 199:105165.

Hassler, John, Per Krusell, and Conny Olovsson. 2018. "The Consequences of Uncertainty: Climate Sensitivity and Economic Sensitivity to the Climate." *Annual Review of Economics* 10:189–205.

———. 2021. "Directed Technical Change as a Response to Natural Resource Scarcity." *Journal of Political Economy* 129 (11): 3039–72.

Hausfather, Z., and G. P. Peters. 2020. "Emissions—The 'Business as Usual' Story Is Misleading." *Nature* 577 (7792): 618–20.

James, Matthew R. 1992. "Asymptotic Analysis of Nonlinear Stochastic Risk-Sensitive Control and Differential Games." *Mathematics of Control, Signals and Systems* 5 (4): 401–17.

Joos, F., R. Roth, J. S. Fuglestvedt, G. P. Peters, I. G. Enting, W. Von Bloh, V. Brovkin, et al. 2013. "Carbon Dioxide and Climate Impulse Response Functions for the Computation of Greenhouse Gas Metrics: A Multi-Model Analysis." *Atmospheric Chemistry and Physics* 13 (5): 2793–825.

Klibanoff, P., M. Marinacci, and S. Mukerji. 2009. "Recursive Smooth Ambiguity Preferences." *Journal of Economic Theory* 144:930–76.

Koonin, Steven E. 2021. *Unsettled: What Climate Science Tells Us, What It Doesn't, and Why It Matters.* Dallas, TX: BenBella.

Kreps, David M., and Evan L. Porteus. 1978. "Temporal Resolution of Uncertainty and Dynamic Choice." *Econometrica* 46 (1): 185–200.

Lemoine, Derek, and Ivan Rudik. 2017. "Managing Climate Change under Uncertainty: Recursive Integrated Assessment at an Inflection Point." *Annual Review of Resource Economics* 9:117–42.

Lemoine, Derek, and Christian P. Traeger. 2016. "Ambiguous Tipping Points." *Journal of Economic Behavior and Organization* 132:5–18.

Lenton, Timothy M. 2020. "Tipping Positive Change." *Philosophical Transactions of the Royal Society* B 375 (1794): 20190123.

Maccheroni, Fabio, Massimo Marinacci, and Aldo Rustichini. 2006. "Dynamic Variational Preferences." *Journal of Economic Theory* 128 (1): 4–44.

MacDougall, Andrew H., Neil C. Swart, and Reto Knutti. 2017. "The Uncertainty in the Transient Climate Response to Cumulative CO_2 Emissions Arising from the Uncertainty in Physical Climate Parameters." *Journal of Climate* 30 (2): 813–27.

Matthews, H. Damon, Nathan P. Gillett, Peter A. Stott, and Kirsten Zickfeld. 2009. "The Proportionality of Global Warming to Cumulative Carbon Emissions. *Nature* 459 (7248): 829–32.

Morgan, M. Granger, Parth Vaishnav, Hadi Dowlatabadi, and Ines L. Azevedo. 2017. "Rethinking the Social Cost of Carbon Dioxide." *Issues in Science and Technology* 33 (4): 43–50.

National Academies of Sciences, Engineering and Medicine. 2017. *Valuing Climate Damages: Updating Estimation of the Social Cost of Carbon Dioxide.* Washington, DC: National Academies Press.

Nordhaus, William D. 2017. "Revisiting the Social Cost of Carbon." *Proceedings of the National Academy of Sciences* 114 (7): 1518–23.

———. 2018. "Projections and Uncertainties about Climate Change in an Era of Minimal Climate Policies." *American Economic Journal: Economic Policy* 10 (3): 333–60.

NYSERDA and RFF (New York State Energy and Resource Development Authority and Resources for the Future). 2021. "Estimating the Value of Carbon: Two Approaches." Technical report (April), NYSERDA and RFF, Albany, NY.

Olson, Roman, Ryan Sriver, Marlos Goes, Nathan M. Urban, H. Damon Matthews, Murali Haran, and Klaus Keller. 2012. "A Climate Sensitivity Estimate Using Bayesian Fusion of Instrumental Observations and an Earth System Model." *Journal of Geophysical Research Atmospheres* 117 (D04103): 1–11.

Palmer, Tim, and Bjorn Stevens. 2019. "The Scientific Challenge of Understanding and Estimating Climate Change." *Proceedings of the National Academy of Sciences* 116 (49): 24390–95.

Pierrehumbert, Ramond T. 2014. "Short-Lived Climate Pollution." *Annual Review of Earth and Planetary Science* 42:341–79.

Pindyck, Robert S. 2013. "Climate Change Policy: What Do the Models Tell Us?" *Journal of Economic Literature* 51 (3): 860–72.

Ricke, Katharine L., and Ken Caldeira. 2014. "Maximum Warming Occurs about One Decade After a Carbon Dioxide Emission." *Environmental Research Letters* 9 (12): 1–8.

Ritchie, Paul D. L., Joseph J. Clarke, Peter M. Cox, and Chris Huntingford. 2021. "Overshooting Tipping Point Thresholds in a Changing Climate." *Nature* 592 (7855): 517–23.

Rogelj, Joeri, Daniel Huppmann, Volker Krey, Keywan Riahi, Leon Clarke, Matthew Gidden, Zebedee Nicholls, and Malte Meinshausen. 2019. "A New Scenario Logic for the Paris Agreement Long-Term Temperature Goal." *Nature* 573 (7774): 357–63.

Rogelj, Joeri, Alexander Popp, Katherine V. Calvin, Gunnar Luderer, Johannes Emmerling, David Gernaat, Shinichiro Fujimori, et al. 2018. "Scenarios Towards Limiting Global Mean Temperature Increase below 1.5 C." *Nature Climate Change* 8 (4): 325–32.

Rudik, Ivan. 2020. "Optimal Climate Policy When Damages Are Unknown." *American Economic Journal: Economic Policy* 12 (2): 340–73.

Seshadri, Ashwin K. 2017. "Fast-Slow Climate Dynamics and Peak Global Warming." *Climate Dynamics* 48 (7–8): 2235–53.

Sharpe, Simon, and Timothy M. Lenton. 2021. "Upward-Scaling Tipping Cas-
cades to Meet Climate Goals: Plausible Grounds for Hope." *Climate Policy*
21 (4): 421–33.

Wagner, Gernot, and Martin Weitzman. 2015. *Climate Shock*. Princeton, NJ:
Princeton University Press.

Weitzman, Martin L. 2012. "GHG Targets as Insurance against Catastrophic Climate Damages." *Journal of Public Economic Theory* 14 (2): 221–44.

Zickfeld, Kirsten, Michael Eby, Andrew J. Weaver, Kaitlin Alexander, Elisabeth
Crespin, Neil R. Edwards, Alexey V. Eliseev, et al. 2013. "Long-Term Climate
Change Commitment and Reversibility: An EMIC Intercomparison." *Journal
of Climate* 26 (16): 5782–809.

Comment

Mar Reguant, Northwestern University and NBER, United States of America

Barnett, Brock, and Hansen build a theoretical and quantitative framework to incorporate concepts of uncertainty and ambiguity aversion to
climate policy modeling. Their primary focus is on building a tractable
dynamic model that includes uncertainty about carbon dynamics, temperature dynamics, and damage functions in a parsimonious way. Their
model features state-of-the-art tools in asset pricing with a continuous-
time model, emphasizing specific processes of uncertainty, such as regime
changes (jump processes) and misspecified Brownian increments. This
model extends the authors' previous work (Barnett, Brock, and Hansen
2020). Climate carbon and temperature dynamics follow scientific inputs
that combine various climate models (Joos et al. 2013). The static economic
game is simple, focused on investment and consumption choices over
time. There are no explicit prices. The use of emissions in production,
which are costly from a climate-change perspective, largely determines
the shadow price of consumption.

The paper presented by Barnett et al. is a serious attempt at modeling
uncertainty from a mathematical point of view. A comprehensive treatment of uncertainty surrounding climate change, such as the one proposed in this paper, seems warranted. I agree that there are significant
uncertainties to be studied, particularly regarding the ability of humanity to adapt and mitigate the change (policy and economic uncertainty)
as well as surrounding the possibility of major tipping points (Cai et al.
2015; Lemoine and Traeger 2016). Indeed, the authors find that uncertainty

© 2022 National Bureau of Economic Research. All rights reserved. Published by The
University of Chicago Press for the National Bureau of Economic Research. https://doi
.org/10.1086/718669

about climate-change damages is the most significant uncertainty influencing optimal policy.

My primary concern is that the analytical and quantitative assumptions built into the exercise minimize the climate-change problem and are of limited empirical relevance. Therefore, it is unclear what the broader takeaway from the quantification should be for climate-change policy.

I. Assumptions Matter

The model in Barnett et al. has a novel treatment of uncertainty, but it is otherwise highly stylized. A key question emerges: Can such a stylized model inform the discussion surrounding uncertainty and optimal climate-change policy?

A. Economic Assumptions

In Barnett et al., utility is a function of effective consumption and energy following a Cobb-Douglas specification:

$$U(C_t, E_t) = \tilde{C}_t^{1-\eta} E_t^{\eta},$$

where $\tilde{C}_t = C_t/N_t$ and N_t depends on the accumulations of E_t via increasing temperatures, Y_t. In their empirical specification, $\eta = 0.032$. As in Barnett et al., the model has no equilibrium prices. This parameterization implies that cutting emissions by half only reduces utility by 2.2%. More importantly, it implies that cutting emissions by 99% only reduces utility by 13.7%. This assumption has crucial implications for the role of uncertainty. Sharply cutting emissions can avoid adverse outcomes in the model, but the welfare costs from such cuts in emissions are, by construction, limited. The model studies relatively extreme outcomes via the economic damage function but assumes that avoiding such events can be done at a relatively lower cost via the utility function.

One can make a similar comment about the lack of dynamics in energy use. The social planner can cut emissions instantly as a function of the information set and the temperature levels. However, in practice, the existing capital assets in the fossil fuel industry make the transition extremely difficult and much more costly. In the model, not only can the social planner cut emissions very rapidly today, but it can also quickly update the policy if conditions change. This assumption is unrealistic and very relevant for shaping optimal policy under uncertainty.

B.   Damage Assumptions

The economic assumptions regarding the production function understate the welfare impacts from climate change, as it enables the social planner to avoid adverse outcomes at a low cost. This assumption is even more concerning considering that, in the model, climate damages only start to significantly matter after temperature increases 1.5°C. According to the model, this event does not endogenously occur for several decades. Therefore, the authors assume not only that it is cheap to control emissions via the economic assumptions but also that it is feasible to cut those emissions sharply and avoid any relevant climate damages altogether via the delay in the climate damage function.[1]

C.   Uncertainty Assumptions

As I just explained, significant damages in the model only occur very far out in time. In addition, once damages start happening, the social planner already knows the extent of the gravity, and uncertainty about economic climate damages is resolved. The authors interpret early news as "bad news," given that, in expectation, damages are more significant the sooner they start occurring. However, early news also resolves all uncertainty surrounding climate damages, and such resolution is treated in a symmetric way regarding low versus high damage scenarios. This assumption minimizes to a great extent the uncertainty problem with climate change. Once uncertainty is resolved, it can lead to an increase in emissions after learning that the climate-change problem is minor, or at least not extreme. I am not aware of any scientific or economic evidence that suggests that we will achieve such certainty, given all the potential nonlinearities in damages and the high degree of uncertainty regarding how humanity will fare in front of such a complex problem (Burke, Hsiang, and Miguel 2015). Therefore, I find the previous treatment of uncertainty by the authors in Barnett et al. (2020) more compelling, even if it is simpler.

II.   Reexamining the Discussion with a Very Simple Cake-Eating Problem

I present a stylized model to highlight some of the tensions expressed above. The model serves as an illustration, and it is not intended to offer a comprehensive assessment. The very simple cake-eating problem is inspired by the model in Barnett et al. but in an extremely parsimonious form. There is no growth or investment, available capital is constant, and the only decision that the social planner needs to make is the speed at which emissions are released into the atmosphere. Damages permanently accumulate, as in Barnett et al.

Three equations govern the variables in the model:

[Utility] $$U(C_t, E_t) = (\bar{C}/N_t)^{1-\eta}E_t^{\eta},$$

[Temperature] $$Y_{t+1} = Y_t + \zeta_t E_t,$$ and

[Damages] $$\log(N_t) = \gamma_1 Y_t + \gamma_2 Y_t^2/2.0 + \gamma_{3,t}(Y_t - Y_0)^2,$$

in which E_t represents emissions at time t, Y_t temperature, and N_t damages to consumption. The social planner maximizes the net present value of utility U, discounted at rate β. As fossil fuels are being used, temperature increases and so do economic damages. All variables are determined in equilibrium by the chosen emissions path and the uncertainty draws. The variable ζ_t is a shock to the temperature process described by scientific models. There is also uncertainty regarding $\gamma_{3,t}$, as in Barnett et al., which affects the convexity of damages as temperature increases.

I implement this simple model using a discrete-time finite-horizon formulation that allows for limited uncertainty in the form of a tree. Each period represents 10 years. I simulate the model for 200 years. Temperature increases and damages evolve as a function of emissions, with some stochasticity. Uncertainty about ζ_t is modeled as a random draw from the scientific distribution of temperature used in Barnett et al. Uncertainty about $\gamma_{3,t}$ is modeled with probabilities surrounding alternative scenarios. To mimic the assumptions in Barnett et al. coarsely, I also consider simulations in which there is growing certainty about the relevant damage scenario along a particular branch of the tree.

For the baseline simulation, the tree structure is only focused on the temperature increases ζ_t. The uncertainty about climate damages is not revealed along the tree. There are equal probabilities of a benign, medium, and extreme scenario, whose damages are shown in figure 1a. These damages are in the spirit of what is covered by Barnett et al., but I simplify the mathematical formula and remove the unknown structural break.[2] As in Barnett et al., this treatment of climate damages leads to substantial abatement when compared with a business-as-usual scenario in which there is limited action to reduce emissions (case 1), as shown in figure 1b. The figure also highlights that the recommended optimal paths are aggressive, reducing emissions by about two-thirds already in 2020.

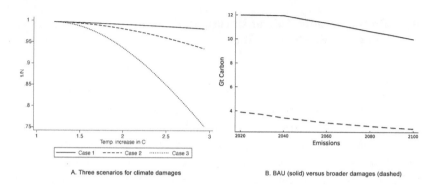

A. Three scenarios for climate damages   B. BAU (solid) versus broader damages (dashed)

Fig. 1. Three uncertain scenarios leading to substantial abatement. Gt = gigatonne, BAU = business as usual.

Given that climate damages are most important, I consider two situations to highlight that the uncertainty treatment in Barnett et al. does not necessarily make the planner conservative. First, I consider one mimicking ambiguity aversion in which the planner effectively puts more weight on the most extreme scenarios. Naturally, as shown in figure 2a, this makes the planner more conservative. Second, I consider a case in which climate damages become known after a specific date. This assumption has the opposite effect on the social planner, who becomes less conservative, as shown in figure 2b. Once the uncertainty is resolved, emissions can even increase on average. This issue highlights that the assumptions behind the treatment of uncertainty can affect the robustness of the policy recommendations if uncertainty is not truly resolved.

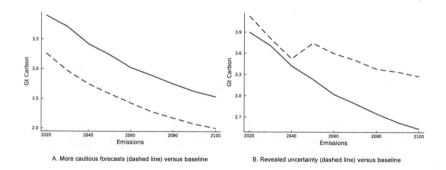

A. More cautious forecasts (dashed line) versus baseline   B. Revealed uncertainty (dashed line) versus baseline

Fig. 2. Uncertainty modeling choices. Gt = gigatonne.

III.   On the Broader Role of Uncertainty
and Climate-Change Policy

Taking a step back, I have some concerns about where the profession should place its efforts when informing the fight against climate change. Annual world emissions show no signs of decline despite the drastic reductions most integrated assessment models (IAMs) recommend. Therefore, it seems worthwhile to investigate climate policy under much more inefficient second-best environments. In particular, the feasible constrained policy is very likely to fall short of any of the optimal policies derived in these simulations.[3] We should aim at incorporating some of the political economy constraints that policy makers and societies face, as also recently emphasized by several IAM experts (Peng et al. 2021).

Uncertainty about our future is high, but it seems unlikely that, under the current political economy constraints, there is a risk of fighting "too hard" against climate change. To support such a statement, I introduce two constraints to the simple model above. First, the emissions can only decrease by 40% each decade. Second, I introduce a leak of about 4 gigatonnes (Gt) of carbon that cannot be prevented by the social planner, for example because some nations do not comply or because technological barriers hinder further decarbonization. Figure 3 shows the optimal policies under the medium and extreme scenarios. Under such very different uncertainty scenarios, the constraints are binding, and the optimal paths are the same. The optimal policy from the modeling exercise, in line with what the scientific community and Intergovernmental Panel on Climate Change reports are demanding, is to reduce emissions swiftly in the next 2 decades (fig. 3a), and go to zero emissions if there are remaining leaks (fig. 3b).[4] Because the political economy constraints are binding,

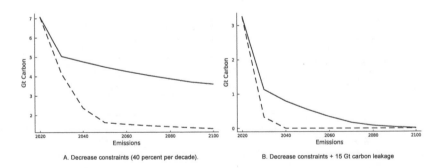

A. Decrease constraints (40 percent per decade).   B. Decrease constraints + 15 Gt carbon leakage

Fig. 3.   Likely constraints in policy limit the impact of uncertainty. Gt = gigatonne.

similar recommendations arise under expectations about future damages that are dramatically different (case 2 and case 3 in fig. 1*a*).

One could conclude, a bit provocatively, that we are so late to act against climate change that uncertainty modeling does not matter. Instead, expanding the feasible set of climate action is crucial. That said, the quantification of uncertainty could still be essential precisely on this front. Correctly modeling extreme events and their economic and uneven consequences can help shift global preferences toward coordinated action. Current events—such as persistent high temperatures near the Arctic, destructive fires of unprecedented virulence, and deadly flooding even in nations with robust infrastructure—are already telling us quite a different story than what our economic models have been assuming: we are vastly unprepared for the times ahead. My informed assessment is that we are undoubtedly falling short of stepping up to the challenge: the uncertainty lies in how much (which papers like Barnett et al. can help assess), why, and what to do about it.

Endnotes

Author email address: Mar Reguant (mar.reguant@northwestern.edu). For acknowledgments, sources of research support, and disclosure of the author's material financial relationships, if any, please see https://www.nber.org/books-and-chapters/nber-macroeconomics-annual-2021-volume-36/comment-climate-change-uncertainty-spillover-macroeconomy-reguant.

1. See, for example, figure 7 in Barnett et al. It shows that the threshold after which climate damages are relevant is only achieved after more than 50 years. Under many realizations, significant climate damages only occur after more than 80 years.

2. The parameter γ_3 is set to zero in the benign scenario, 0.016 in the medium case, and 0.09 in the extreme case. The scenarios mimic the three cases presented in an earlier version of Barnett et al.

3. For example, the International Energy Agency recently recommended stopping new fossil fuel developments (IEA 2020), a policy that seems entirely outside the feasible set.

4. Each period is a decade; 2020 should be interpreted as emissions in the 2020s, 2030 as emissions in the 2030s, etc.

References

Barnett, M., W. Brock, and L. P. Hansen. 2020. "Pricing Uncertainty Induced by Climate Change." *Review of Financial Studies* 33 (3): 1024–66.
Burke, M., S. M. Hsiang, and E. Miguel. 2015. "Global Non-linear Effect of Temperature on Economic Production." *Nature* 527 (7577): 235–39.
Cai, Y., K. L. Judd, T. M. Lenton, T. S. Lontzek, and D. Narita. 2015. "Environmental Tipping Points Significantly Affect the Cost-Benefit Assessment of Climate Policies." *Proceedings of the National Academy of Sciences of the United States of America* 112 (15): 4606–11.
IEA (International Energy Agency). 2020. *Net Zero by 2050*. Paris: IEA.

Joos, F., R. Roth, J. S. Fuglestvedt, G. P. Peters, I. G. Enting, W. Von Bloh, V. Brovkin, et al. 2013. "Carbon Dioxide and Climate Impulse Response Functions for the Computation of Greenhouse Gas Metrics: A Multi-model Analysis." *Atmospheric Chemistry and Physics* 13 (5): 2793–825.

Lemoine, D., and C. P. Traeger. 2016. "Ambiguous Tipping Points." *Journal of Economic Behavior and Organization* 132:5–18.

Peng, W., G. Iyer, V. Bosetti, V. Chaturvedi, J. Edmonds, A. A. Fawcett, S. Hallegatte, et al. 2021. "Climate Policy Models Need to Get Real about People—Here's How." *Nature* 594 (7862): 174–76.

Comment

Per Krusell, Stockholm University, Sweden, *and NBER,* United States of America

The authors develop a climate-economy framework whose main purpose is to illustrate the importance of taking "the unknown" seriously in this area. More precisely, the paper considers risk, model ambiguity, and model misspecification. The focus is on the decision problem of a planner whose preferences embody uncertainty aversion. That is, a market outcome is not considered. The key contribution of the paper is to propose a framework—that is, methods useful for addressing this kind of issue—and then to apply it to three examples. None of the examples can be viewed as full-fledged, quantitative settings, so it is difficult to draw concrete policy conclusions from them. At the same time, they illustrate possible magnitudes that could arise. Overall it is an impressive paper. My comments will be organized into three sections: I will discuss the broad motivation for focusing on uncertainty, I will comment on the specific modeling approach, and I will make concluding remarks.

I. Uncertainty?

The authors emphasize the (perhaps striking) lack of knowledge about the carbon dynamics, the temperature dynamics, and the economic effects of climate change. But is the climate-economy area really so full of uncertainties? Do we not know already that the burning of fossil fuel significantly affects the global climate in a negative direction? On this point, I am in full agreement with the authors: there is far from a scientific consensus on the quantitative importance of emissions for atmospheric carbon

© 2022 National Bureau of Economic Research. All rights reserved. Published by The University of Chicago Press for the National Bureau of Economic Research. https://doi .org/10.1086/718670

concentration, for the climate, and for human welfare. To be clear, the authors do not dispute the logic behind the argument that human activity affects the climate: this logic, which is present in all the Intergovernmental Panel on Climate Change reports and which is well-known far beyond the research sphere, is really a consensus when it comes to the main channels and their qualitative features. The disagreements—between climate researchers, to the extent there is disagreement—are instead about the relative importance of different mechanisms and about the overall magnitude of the effects. It is, for example, not wholly implausible that the effects of burning even rather large amounts of fossil fuel are negligible. Here, the argument would be that there are feedback effects working in the direction of cooling, such as increased reflection of sunlight from aerosols and clouds, whose prevalence can be increased as a result of a higher atmospheric carbon concentration.[1] Of course, there are also well-known feedback effects working to increase warming. So the point here, rather, is that the net effect contains much uncertainty, as reflected in the figure in the paper showing how climate sensitivity varies greatly across the 144 models considered. What is of course key is that there is a sizable right tail in these experiments: severe warming is possible too.

Turning to the damages to humans, my own summary is that there is even greater uncertainty in this domain than for the natural-science variables. The literature on damage measurements, though growing rapidly at the moment, is nascent and is typically based on short enough time series that it is difficult to draw reliable inferences, especially about the effects of significant warming over the longer run. The longer run is key here because climate change is mostly about how future generations are affected by warming; most models predict a slow warming process. One line of defense against "radical" climate policy, such as carbon taxes at the level proposed in the Stern Review and by many others, is that even large drops in gross domestic product will be more than canceled by economic growth (assuming that growth continues at its historic rates). Another line of defense is that adaptation—say, in the form of slow migration away from areas hit hard by warming—ought to be feasible. Of course, there are many reasonable counterarguments as well.

Finally, a separate, powerful argument in favor of immediate, radical action may be that of tipping points. More precisely, the idea would be that beyond a certain temperature level, or atmospheric carbon concentration, we enter into different dynamics that, moreover, are irreversible—at least for hundreds if not thousands of years. My own perception, when entering into this research area, was that my skills in solving for and understanding nonlinear dynamics in macroeconomic models would be key precisely because of tipping points. It did not take long to realize, however, that there was no consensus in this area either, making it difficult to formulate quantitative models of climate change embodying global tipping points. First, there is agreement on a long list of different kinds of local tipping points (or tipping points specific to limited phenomena) and each of these can perhaps be argued to be well understood. However, what the implied global system would look like need not involve severe nonlinearities but could perhaps equally well be described as smooth and linear. Second, to be sure, there are some global tipping points, such as the melting of the ice caps and the release of methane from the tundra, but the speed of these changes may not be so high or, in the case of methane, so long-lasting.[2] Then again, we really do not know, and recent measurements of the thickness of ice caps are alarming, so it may be that the global system is more nonlinear than previously thought.

In conclusion, the best way to summarize is that there is, again, large uncertainty. We just do not know, and the range of possible outcomes is uncomfortably large. At the very least, with this understanding it is easy to counter the climate skeptics: they are simply hoping that, when the uncertainty has been revealed, we are in the left tail of warming and climate change, and the mere reliance on hope does not seem responsible. A more sophisticated argument would be that radical climate action is very costly for our economies, indeed so costly that it is not worth it. However, then explicit cost-benefit analyses are needed, and the point of the present paper is precisely to move the debate in this direction.

II. The Approach

The authors present two related climate-economy models. In the first one, underlying the first two examples, emissions have direct utility benefits; in the second, emissions are useful in production.[3] On the cost side in both models, consumption is "damaged," along the lines of how damages are described in the literature, but allowing for (random) nonlinearities. Both models are global—no regional heterogeneity is considered—and, in terms of the economics, quite stripped down. A feature they have in common is that fossil fuel is not modeled as a resource in finite supply, nor is it costly to produce. Thus, market economies not subject to regulation of taxation would generate emissions without bound in every period.[4] The setting may still be appropriate for studying illustrative planning problems but is probably less suited for analyses of how to achieve good outcomes in market economies. Relatedly, in a market economy one would need to be specific about whether or not different agents/generations have the same kind of preferences, knowledge, and concern for model misspecification as the planner here.

On a pure methodological level, the model is set up in continuous time and the authors argue that this formulation facilitates some of the analysis. I have a slight concern here, as I worry that most economists, including those otherwise well versed in dynamic macroeconomic theory, are not sufficiently skilled on a technical level to fully grasp all the subtleties. This is certainly true for myself. The topic is a very important one and I worry that too much of the potential audience is lost by carrying out the analysis at this level of technicality. Perhaps it helps that a large part of the paper is devoted to discussing how to model and evaluate uncertainty and misspecification, but it could also be a hurdle. Could perhaps a simple static model with an ex ante/ex post distinction have been used, at least as an introduction?

On a more substantive level, is it necessary to also consider recurrent shocks and risk? As I argue above, I am fully convinced that uncertainty is key in the area, but I wonder whether risk could be dispensed with, thereby simplifying matters significantly. I do not think that fluctuations per se, and smoothing/worrying about them, are the main issue in this area. In my view, rather, it is the significant uncertainty about outcomes that ought to drive modeling. In Hassler, Krusell, and Olovsson (2018), we examine this issue informally. We define two kinds of major errors regarding permanently selecting the wrong climate policy. One type of policy error would result if we follow the advice of the climate skeptics (essentially setting the carbon tax to zero) and it turns out they are wrong: that both climate change and the damages from it are at the extremes of the intervals indicated by researchers. The other major policy error is that we are wrong in the opposite direction: we drastically reduce carbon use when it turns out ex post not to have been needed. Our contention implicit in that work is that we should mostly worry about the extremes—and also not about the fluctuations per se—and that simple calculations of this sort can also be helpful. We find, in particular, that the second type of error—that of being overzealous about fighting climate change—is far smaller than the first.[5] Relative to our analysis (aside from differing in various details), the current paper allows for aspects of slow learning, which could certainly be important, and it formalizes preferences allowing us to choose one policy.

The paper is also related to the discussion about the size of the optimal carbon tax. Obtaining a large value for this tax appears to have been an aim for some researchers, and a number of candidates have been developed. The list includes: (i) a low discount rate, (ii) strong convexity in the mapping between global temperature and damages, (iii) fat tails in climate/damage outcomes and utility curvature, (iv) long-run growth effects, and (v) distributional aspects (lack of interregional transfers and a stronger concern for the developing world than expressed by available measures of foreign aid). The present research could be seen as providing another candidate, which is ambiguity aversion, as formalized in the paper. I would like to have seen more discussion of how we can obtain guidance in selecting numerical values for the relevant preference parameters, because these are key; the paper, as I understand it, mostly gives us illustrations. There is also a parallel here to the discussion of discount rates, where the following issue arises. If one selects a very low discount rate—one that is much lower than rates typically used in, say, the cost-benefit analyses of potential long-term infrastructure investments—then it would be important to square this value with the much higher market interest rates. In the case of ambiguity, is the degree of such aversion mainly to be present among climate-policy planners, or should it be present in other realms of government policy as well? Do we expect private agents to embody it too? If so, one should guide calibration/estimation of these important parameters accordingly.

III. Concluding Remarks

The paper outlines a thorough and ambitious agenda toward formalizing and analyzing uncertainty in the climate-economy context. It is laudable and I very much hope it will have major impact. I have not commented on the specific findings in the paper, in part because they are reasonable given the assumptions but most importantly because they are illustrative examples and thus not yet full-fledged analyses of policy. Aside from the comments and recommendations I have made, let me add that I think the authors' contributions could be boosted significantly by considering richer economic settings. One of the main ways in which economists can contribute in this area is to offer our specialized expertise in, precisely, economics: how markets work or do not work, and how people can be expected to respond to various forms of policy. The present paper does not leverage our knowledge and key insights as economists as much as it could. Rather, it focuses on how to conceptualize uncertainty and formalize preferences with aversion to the unknown, and I worry that actual policy makers do not perceive a need for such insights. Thus I would highly recommend a combination of the approach in this paper with a more full-fledged description and analysis of market economies and available policy instruments.

Endnotes

Author email address: Krusell (per.krusell@iies.su.se). For acknowledgments, sources of research support, and disclosure of the author's material financial relationships, if any, please see https://www.nber.org/books-and-chapters/nber-macroeconomics-annual-2021-volume-36/comment-climate-change-uncertainty-spillover-macroeconomy-krusell.

1. Indeed, some climate models predict a higher global temperature increase due to historic emissions than that observed today, and one hypothesis is that those models overpredict warming because they do not incorporate aerosol formation.

2. Methane is a very potent greenhouse gas but does not stay very long in the atmosphere, unlike carbon dioxide, which depreciates extremely slowly.

3. Though not described this way exactly, the setup is similar to assuming a production function that is Leontief in capital and emissions.

4. This would not need to occur in the second model the authors present, because the benefits of emissions are zero here beyond a certain point.

5. In recent work, we study the roots of these findings in more detail (Hassler, Krusell, and Olovsson 2021).

References

Hassler, John, Per Krusell, and Conny Olovsson. 2018. "The Consequences of Uncertainty: Climate Sensitivity and Economic Sensitivity to the Climate." *Annual Review of Economics* 10:189–205.

———. 2021. "Suboptimal Climate Policy." Mimeo, Stockholm University.

Discussion

Daron Acemoglu opened the discussion by recognizing the importance of the topic. Then, in agreement with the discussants, he argued for a number of potentially fruitful extensions of the model. First, he expressed the desirability of widening the scope of the analysis to include issues such as irreversibility and tipping points. He added that it would be useful to jointly analyze emissions and mitigation actions, which are themselves uncertain or subject to uncertain learning. In the presence of uncertainty, it might be optimal to be conservative in emissions but more experimental in mitigation policies such as investment in renewable energy and carbon sequestration. This is because the latter act as insurance mechanisms. Mar Reguant expressed concern that in the current model, dire scenarios can be avoided by losing only 20% of utility, and this seems infeasible. Lars Hansen agreed that he and his collaborators look forward to pushing the analysis in the ways mentioned and in other directions, while preserving tractability. The point of this paper is to argue for taking a broader approach to uncertainty than is typical in this and other literatures and to show that this can be quantitatively important. In regard to tipping points in particular, Hansen added that the introduction of a probabilistic structure on tipping points opens up new research challenges by pushing beyond pure risk models to a more nuanced approach that recognizes the limited knowledge of the timing and magnitude of such events.

The discussion then centered around the issue of discounting.

James Stock pointed out that implementing a stochastic approach to discounting under uncertainty is a complex procedure that requires information on outcomes of covariances and consumption paths, which might

NBER Macroeconomics Annual, volume 36, 2022.
© 2022 National Bureau of Economic Research. All rights reserved. Published by The University of Chicago Press for the National Bureau of Economic Research. https://doi .org/10.1086/718671

be hard to obtain. He inquired whether there exists a simplified approach that could inform real-world discussion of social cost of carbon calculation. Hansen responded that stochastic discounting in cost-benefit analysis should reflect the type of uncertainty that agents, including policy makers, are exposed to, and, therefore, it cannot be easily reduced to a single rate. Following up on the discussion, Robert Hall argued that issues of discounting can be understood by thinking about the assignment of Arrow-Debreu prices to the space of climate outcomes crossed with time. Such a space clarifies how risk aversion across climate outcomes cannot be separately identified from discounting. Hansen agreed with Hall's argument while noting that this point continues to apply when embracing broader notions of uncertainty as is explored in this paper. He also noted that the model posed in the paper cannot speak to market prices because it features a social planner's solution. Nevertheless, he concurred that there are important connections between discounting and uncertainty that cannot be easily decoupled, adding that entities that affect social valuation will carry over to market valuation.

The authors concluded the discussion by addressing some of the concerns raised by the discussants. First, Hansen conceded that the Cobb-Douglas function is not an ideal specification and that it might distort some calculations. Second, he addressed the issue of learning in the model. He argued that to some extent, dynamic learning is important in the model, positioning the paper in between the two extremes of a static setup and full Bayesian learning. He argued that introducing Bayesian learning over different climate change models is not feasible. However, in contrast to a static setup with no learning, the current model allows for the learning process to begin at a slow pace and to speed up as the economy becomes severely damaged. Third, he noted that the direct calibration of ambiguity aversion parameters from decision theory is challenging because such parameters are not easily transportable across economic environments. Instead, what is more revealing are the implied worst-case distributions computed as part of the solution to the dynamic decision problem. Finally, Michael Barnett emphasized that the discussion about enriching the elements of the economy reinforces the importance of studying uncertainty in connection to climate change.

5

Converging to Convergence

Michael Kremer, *University of Chicago and NBER,* United States of America
Jack Willis, *Columbia University and NBER,* United States of America
Yang You, *The University of Hong Kong,* Hong Kong SAR, China

I. Introduction

Studies of convergence in the 1990s found no tendency for poor countries to catch up with rich ones. If anything, there was divergence: rich countries growing faster than poor. National accounts data showed weak divergence across a large set of countries since the 1960s (Barro 1991), whereas historical data, for a smaller set of countries, showed stronger divergence starting as early as the sixteenth century, with the ratio of per-capita incomes between the richest and the poorest countries increasing by a factor of five from 1870 to 1990 (Pritchett 1997). The lack of convergence was a major challenge to models where growth is based on accumulation of capital subject to decreasing returns or where copying technology is easier than developing new technologies. It led to two responses: first, a rejection of the neoclassical growth models and the development of poverty trap models and AK endogenous growth models, some of which predict divergence (Romer 1986); second, an emphasis on underlying determinants of steady-state income, such as human capital, policies, and institutions, leading to growth regressions and tests of convergence conditional on them (Barro and Sala-i-Martin 1992; Durlauf, Johnson, and Temple 2005).

To update the stylized facts of convergence, we revisit these empirical exercises with 25 years of additional data. We consider global trends in income and growth, as well as factors that might determine them—which we term *the correlates of growth*—such as human capital, policies,

NBER Macroeconomics Annual, volume 36, 2022.
© 2022 National Bureau of Economic Research. All rights reserved. Published by The University of Chicago Press for the National Bureau of Economic Research. https://doi .org/10.1086/718672

institutions, and culture. We find substantial changes since the late 1980s in growth, in its correlates, and in the cross-country relationship between them. Although we do not provide a full analysis of the reasons, or causal determinants, we think this is still useful, as any understanding of development should match the cross-country patterns.

We begin with absolute convergence—poor countries growing faster than rich, unconditionally—and document convergence in income per capita in the last 2 decades. To study the trend in convergence, we regress 10-year growth in income per capita on income per capita and consider the evolution of the relationship since 1960. Doing so shows a steady trend toward convergence since the late 1980s, leading to absolute convergence since 2000, precisely when empirical tests of convergence fell out of fashion. In terms of magnitude, from 1985 to 1995 there was divergence in income per capita at a rate of 0.5% annually, whereas from 2005 to 2015 there was convergence at a rate of 0.7%.[1] Although lower than the 2% "iron law of [conditional] convergence" (Barro 2012), this still represents a substantial change. Looking further back to 1960, when the widespread collection of national income data began, the trend in convergence was initially flat, with neither convergence nor divergence, followed by a decade of a trend toward divergence in the late 1970s and early 1980s.

Breaking down the trend toward absolute convergence since 1990, by subsets of countries, provides a fuller picture of the change. There has been both faster catch-up growth and a slowdown of the frontier. The richest quartile of countries had the fastest growth in the 1980s but the slowest growth since, being flat in the 1990s and then declining since 2000. In contrast, the three other quartiles all experienced substantially accelerating growth through the 1990s and early 2000s, inconsistent with certain poverty trap explanations for the change in convergence, in which countries catch up once above a certain income threshold. Fewer lower-income countries have had growth disasters since the mid-1990s—but removing them has little effect on the recent trend toward convergence; instead, it removes the divergence in the late 1970s and early 1980s. The trend is also not driven by any one specific region, and convergence becomes stronger upon removing sub-Saharan Africa or the bottom quartile of the income distribution from the data set.

Is convergence in the last 20 years just a blip, or does it represent a turning point in world history? It certainly could be a blip, as others have argued (Johnson and Papageorgiou 2020), for example due to high commodity prices. Yet the trend has lasted for 25 years and is robust to removing resource-rich countries, so we entertain the idea that it represents a turning point and consider its potential causes.

Within the framework of conditional convergence, we classify possible causes into two broad groups. First, those that lead to faster convergence conditional on growth correlates, which could include faster spread of technologies due to globalization, as well as greater capital and labor mobility. Second, our main focus, convergence in the growth correlates themselves—human capital, policies, institutions, culture—may close the gap between unconditional and conditional convergence. Although recent literature on economic growth and institutions emphasizes the stability and persistence of such correlates, using their historical determinants to identify their causal effects on economic outcomes (Acemoglu, Johnson, and Robinson 2001; Nunn 2008; Dell 2010; Michalopoulos and Papaioannou 2013), the finding that certain determinants of growth are highly persistent is not inconsistent with others changing, potentially rapidly, and being subject to global influences on policies and culture, for example.

To study whether growth correlates have changed, we classify them into four groups: (a) enhanced Solow fundamentals (investment rate, population growth rate, and human capital)—variables that are fundamental determinants of steady-state income in the enhanced Solow model (Mankiw, Romer, and Weil 1992); (b) short-run correlates—variables considered by the 1990s growth literature that may change in a relatively short time scale, typically policies; (c) long-run correlates—those that change slowly if at all, and for which we will not have time variation, typically historical determinants of institutions and geography; and (d) culture. Far from being static, even among highly persistent correlates we find that many have undergone large changes and themselves converged substantially across countries, toward those of rich countries.

For the Solow fundamentals and short-run correlates, we examine 35 variables in six categories: Solow fundamentals, labor force, political institutions, governance quality, fiscal policy, and financial institutions. To tie our hands over which variables we include, and hence reduce the risk of specification search, we started from a list of variables commonly used in growth regressions, from the *Handbook of Economic Growth* chapter entitled "Growth Econometrics" (Durlauf et al. 2005). We then constrained ourselves to those variables that were available for at least 50 countries by 1996, and we chose to focus on the period 1985–2015 as a compromise between the number of countries and the number of time periods. Among the 20 variables that are comparable across time, we find significant β-convergence (a negative slope of growth regressed on level) in 17. Only credit to the private sector diverged. Moreover, of the 18 variables that were correlated with income in 1985, 15 "improved" on average, meaning they converged toward those associated with higher income. For a subset of correlates, we are also able to look further back, and we find similar, albeit slower, trends in 1960–85.

Using different rounds of the World Values Survey (WVS), we also find evidence of convergence in culture. While culture does show persistence, eight out of the 10 cultural variables we consider have been converging since 1990. For example, views on inequality, political participation, the importance of family, traditions, and work ethic have all been converging. While limited, the results of the exercise are consistent with papers in sociology and psychology studying cultural convergence (Inglehart and Baker 2000; Santos, Varnum, and Grossmann 2017). In contrast, convergence was unlikely or impossible for long-run correlates, and we do not have time variation to test for it.

Are these two changes since the late 1980s related: the trend toward convergence in income and the convergence of many of the correlates of growth? We are naturally unable to do a full causal analysis, and causality can run both ways. On the one hand, an extensive empirical literature argues that such correlates are important for economic development (Glaeser et al. 2004; Acemoglu, Johnson, and Robinson 2005), and the convergence literature itself turned toward convergence conditional on correlates (determinants of the steady state). On the other hand, modernization theory suggests that causation may run the other way, with converging incomes causing policies, institutions, and culture to converge. While recent literature uses instrumental variables to provide evidence on both directions of causation (Acemoglu et al. 2001, 2008, 2019; Dell 2010; Michalopoulos and Papaioannou 2013), these studies build on earlier analysis that focused on stylized facts from empirical cross-country relationships (Barro 1996; Sala-i-Martin 1997; Durlauf et al. 2005; Rodrik 2012), facts that any theory of growth should fit and which we revisit and update.[2]

To link the trends in growth and its correlates, we develop a simple empirical framework, revisiting two central cross-country relationships and documenting how they have changed since the 1980s. First, regressing correlates on income; a cross-sectional representation of the modernization hypothesis. Second, regressing growth on correlates, controlling for income; the basic specification for both growth regressions and tests of conditional convergence. By the omitted variable bias formula, the gap between absolute convergence and conditional convergence is then given by the product of the slopes of these two relationships (correlate-income slopes and growth-correlate slopes), allowing us to break down the trend in absolute convergence into trends in these slopes, together with any trend in conditional convergence. In the main exercise, we do so comparing 1985 to the present, as that is when we have the best data and can run a balanced panel exercise. In supplementary analysis, we also present trends since 1960, which is important as we want to understand why there was a change in income convergence in the late 1980s.

While the cross-sectional relationships between income and the correlates have changed in levels, their slopes have mostly remained stable, despite large changes in both income and the short-run correlates. Among 32 Solow and short-run correlates, regressing the cross-sectional correlate-GDP slope of 2015 on that of 1985 gives coefficients of 0.90 and 0.89, respectively, and R^2 of 0.90 and 0.70. Moreover, although there is substantial prediction error by individual correlate, on average Solow and short-run correlates themselves have changed as much as would have been predicted by the changes in income, given the baseline cross-country relationship between the two.

In contrast, growth-regression coefficients have shrunk substantially across the period and show relatively little autocorrelation. The coefficients of the Solow fundamentals have remained the most stable, with a slope of 0.86 and an R^2 of 0.95 when regressing coefficients in 2005 on those in 1985. The coefficients of short-run correlates have shrunk the most, such that there is almost no correlation in coefficients between the periods (slope 0.18, R^2 0.06). For example, in 1985, a 1 standard deviation higher Freedom House political rights score predicted 0.6% higher annual gross national product (GDP) growth for the subsequent decade, yet the predictive power is negligible in the decade 2005–15. Long-run correlates and culture fall somewhere between the two, with coefficients that are somewhat stable across the periods, although on average they also shrank.

As a result of the flattening of the growth-correlate relationships, absolute convergence converged toward conditional convergence, by the omitted variable bias formula. This helps to explain the trend toward absolute convergence but has conditional convergence itself also become faster? While conditional convergence regressions typically condition on multiple correlates, our baseline specification conditions on one variable at a time, because of the difficulty in forming a balanced panel with multiple correlates and to tie our hands in terms of specification search. In our multivariate analysis, although not our main focus, we find no obvious trend in conditional convergence itself, which held throughout the period.

These results suggest an interpretation that is consistent with neoclassical growth models. Conditional convergence has held throughout the period. Absolute convergence did not hold initially, but as human capital, policies, and institutions have improved in poorer countries, the difference in institutions across countries has shrunk, and their explanatory power with respect to growth and convergence has declined. As a result, the world has converged to absolute convergence because absolute convergence has converged to conditional convergence.

However, this narrative leaves a key question unanswered: Why did the growth-regression coefficients shrink? One interpretation, consistent with a Fukiyama end of history view, is that policies and institutions used to matter, but now that they have converged, they matter less—their effects are nonlinear. For example, perhaps terrible institutions are bad for growth, but so long as institutions are not disastrous, they matter much less, and there is convergence. However, our results could also be viewed as demonstrating the limits of our collective understanding: many of the policies that were significant in growth regressions in the 1990s no longer significantly predict growth today, and basic patterns of divergence that held for centuries have not held for the past 20 years. Consistent with this, perhaps earlier growth-regression specifications suffered from an overfitting problem and are now failing an out-of-sample test using subsequent data? Relatedly, it is natural to think that there is a very large number of factors that determines steady-state income—some observable, many unobservable. The correlation between the observable and unobservable determinants may have shrunk. While these alternatives would also explain the shrinking of the gap between absolute and conditional convergence, they cannot explain the trend toward absolute convergence, although that could result from faster conditional convergence. The multitude of possible interpretations acts as a reminder of the difficulty of projecting the current trends we document forward, and the dangers of extrapolating from trends over the past quarter century, especially considering rising authoritarian populism, climate change, and pandemic threats, a theme we return to in the conclusion.

This paper describes trends in major macroeconomic variables and the relationships between them, some of which have changed substantially in the last 20 years. The goal is descriptive, not causal. The first literature we contribute to is that regarding convergence, which flowered in the 1990s. Despite absolute convergence being a central prediction of foundational growth models, multiple papers found no evidence for absolute convergence in incomes across countries (Barro 1991; Pritchett 1997) but evidence of convergence within countries and across countries conditional on similar institutions (Barro and Sala-i-Martin 1992). While we identify off cross-country variation, Caselli, Esquivel, and Lefort (1996) and Acemoglu and Molina (2022) argue that countries should have fixed effects in convergence regressions, corresponding to their individual steady-state incomes. The tradeoffs are discussed at length in Durlauf et al. (2005), and we discuss our specification choice in Section II. In short, we think that the country fixed effects absorb exactly the variation relevant for studying convergence. Consistent with this, if we allow country fixed effects to vary by decade, then they themselves have converged since the 1990s, so that our results do still appear in that framework but are just absorbed into the "nuisance" parameters. More recently there have been several important additions to the classic convergence findings. Rodrik (2012) looks specifically at manufacturing and shows that within manufacturing, there has been absolute convergence. In a paper closely related to ours, Grier and Grier (2007) also consider convergence both in income and in policies and institutions from 1961 to 1999. They contrast convergence in policies and institutions with divergence in incomes, arguing that this difference is hard to reconcile with neoclassical growth models. We agree with their conclusion for the period 1960–90 but benefit from 20 years of additional data, and we argue that convergence changed around 1990 and is since consistent with models of neoclassical growth and inconsistent with a class of endogenous growth theory models that predict divergence, such as AK models (Romer 1986) or some poverty trap models.

This is not the only paper to revisit the question of convergence with updated data. Roy, Kessler, and Subramanian (2016), in particular, make the point that there has been absolute convergence in the last 20 years, and in concurrent work to ours, Patel, Sandefur, and Subramanian (2021) emphasize how this is in contrast to the previous stylized facts about convergence. Johnson and Papageorgiou (2020), in contrast, also use the latest data and conclude that there is still no absolute convergence. The difference results in part from Johnson and Papageorgiou (2020) considering convergence from a fixed base date (1960), while we consider the trend in convergence over a moving time interval, and in part because we are willing to speculate that the trend in the last 25 years represents a fundamental change. Indeed, although we find a sustained trend toward convergence, we only find actual convergence for a relatively short period, whereas historically divergence has been the norm for several hundred years (Pritchett 1997).

The paper also adds to the literature on the effects of culture and institutions. Recent papers use historical variation to identify the effect of institutions and culture on income, using either instruments (Acemoglu et al. 2001; Algan and Cahuc 2010) or spatial discontinuities (Dell 2010), and generally find that both play a central role. That empirical strategy requires focusing on long-run, persistent components of steady-state determinants, which can easily slide into a pessimistic view: the things that matter for growth can only change very slowly. However, although some, such as legal systems and trust, have deep historical roots and may change very slowly (Michalopoulos and Papaioannou 2013), many change rapidly, and there is no contradiction in culture both having a long-run effect and being subject to recent change. For example, gender roles have deep and important historical determinants (Alesina, Giuliano, and Nunn 2013), but they have also changed substantially in the last 50 years, differentially across countries. While historical determinants continue to persist, we should also remain open to asking how recent changes in policies and institutions have affected growth, especially when considering policy changes.

Our growth-regressions exercise also provides an out-of-sample test of sorts for the predictive power of policies and institutions: with a limited sample size and many potential covariates, the growth-regressions literature is vulnerable to overfitting; events since the publication of earlier papers provide a (limited) out-of-sample data set (Hastie, Tibshirani, and Friedman 2009).

Finally, in studying changes to, and convergence in, policies, institutions, and culture, the paper adds to expansive literatures in political science, sociology, and psychology whereby the diffusion and convergence of numerous policies, institutions and cultural traits have been documented and studied (Dobbin, Simmons, and Garrett 2007).[3] Some of the changes in correlates have been gradual, possibly consistent with modernization theory (Inglehart and Baker 2000; Acemoglu et al. 2008), and indeed we do find that on average changes in correlates are consistent with predictions from income growth, based upon the cross-country relationship. However, many recent changes in policies and institutions are dramatic, such as global trends in the adoption of VATs, or marriage equality, or the Me Too movement, which may be better thought of as technology adoption through information diffusion. This technology diffusion may be passive or may, for example, result from the work of international organizations, which provide norms and information on perceived best practices (Clemens and Kremer 2016) and sometimes directly incentivize the adoption of different policies through conditionality. For example, the Washington Consensus encouraged lower tariffs, lower inflation, and privatization of state-owned firms, all of which have been broadly adopted since. The end of the cold war ushered in a period of growth in democracy. In a closely related paper, Easterly (2019) argues that such Washington Consensus reforms may have been better for growth than previously believed, as growth has been higher recently in countries that adopted them. Finally, convergence and diffusion of culture are central topics in sociology and psychology. Two recent examples studying them, using the WVSs (among other data sources) as we do, are Inglehart and Baker (2000) and Santos et al. (2017).

The paper proceeds as follows. In Section II, we present the results on absolute convergence in income per capita and document a trend toward convergence since the 1990s. In Section III, we consider global trends in the correlates of growth—policies, institutions, human capital, and culture—and document considerable convergence across multiple dimensions. In Section IV, we relate the trend toward convergence in income to the convergence in the correlates of growth, first considering the cross-country relationships between income and correlates (modernization theory), which have remained stable, then turning to the cross-country relationships between correlates and growth (growth regressions), which have flattened, and finally turning to the gap between unconditional and conditional convergence, which has shrunk. Section V concludes.

II. Convergence in Income

Neoclassical growth models predict convergence toward steady-state income: poor countries should catch up with rich countries, at least among countries with similar underlying determinants of steady-state income. Empirical tests in the 1990s of absolute convergence—convergence across countries without conditioning on determinants of steady-state income—found little evidence for it: if anything, rich countries were growing faster than poor (Barro 1991). We begin by revisiting these tests of absolute convergence, with 25 additional years of data. We use the same data sources and focus mainly on β-convergence, defined below.[4]

A. Empirical Setup: Measuring Convergence

The convergence literature in the 1990s used three different data sets. First, standard cross-country sources such as the World Development Indicators (WDIs) and the Penn World Tables (PWT), which covered a sizeble span of countries from the 1960s onward. Second, the Maddison data set, which collected many sources of data to derive income per capita going back much further in time, for a smaller set of countries, which showed that divergence had been the norm for several hundred years (Pritchett 1997). Third, within-country panel data sets, to look at convergence within countries. For example, Barro and Sala-i-Martin (1992) examined convergence within the United States.

Our goal is to document what has happened to global cross-country convergence since the heyday of the literature in the 1990s. As such, we use the standard cross-country data sources, which cover 1960 to the present. In the main specification, we use the GDP per capita, adjusted for Purchasing Power Parity (PPP), from the Penn World Tables v10.0.[5] It is an unbalanced panel, as for many countries GDP per capita data only becomes available partway through the period. Nevertheless, we use the unbalanced panel for our main specification so as not to drop many of the poorer countries that become available later in the period (we also show robustness to using balanced panels, which make little difference to our results). We also drop very small countries and those that are extremely reliant on natural resource rents, as is common in studies of convergence. Specifically, we drop countries whose maximum population during the period was <200,000 and those for whom natural resources accounted for at least 75% of GDP (as reported in the WDIs) at some time during the period.[6]

We examine both β-convergence and σ-convergence. β-convergence is when poor countries grow faster on average than rich, whereas σ-convergence is when the cross-sectional variance of (log) income per capita is falling over time. The relationship between the two notions of convergence is well documented (Barro and Sala-i-Martin 1992; Young, Higgins, and Levy 2008). We focus on β-convergence for most of the analysis, with equivalent results for σ-convergence reported in the appendix.

Formally, the β-convergence coefficient from time t to time $t + \Delta t$ is the coefficient β in the following country-level regression:

$$\log(\text{GDPpc}_{i,t+\Delta t}) - \log(\text{GDPpc}_{i,t}) = \alpha + \beta\log(\text{GDPpc}_{i,t}) + \epsilon_{i,t}$$

where $\log(\text{GDPpc}_{i,t})$ is log GDP per capita of country i at time t. To show how β-convergence has changed over time, we plot β_t versus t, where β_t comes for the following country-year level regression, clustered at the country level (μ_t is a year fixed effect on growth):

$$\log(\text{GDPpc}_{i,t+\Delta t}) - \log(\text{GDPpc}_{i,t}) = \beta_t \log(\text{GDPpc}_{i,t}) + \mu_t + \epsilon_{i,t}. \quad (1)$$

Much of the existing empirical convergence literature plots how β varies when holding the starting point t fixed (often at 1960) and varying the end point, $t + \Delta t$. Since we are interested in how the process of convergence may itself have changed over time, we instead hold Δt fixed and vary t. In the main specification, we use 10-year growth averages, that is, $\Delta t = 10$.[7]

B.   Results: Converging to Convergence

Figure 1 shows the scatter plot and regression of equation (1) for each decade since 1960. Convergence corresponds to a negative slope, and the shift to convergence since 2000 can clearly be seen in the raw data. Figure A2 presents summary boxplots of these basic scatter plots, plotting the average growth by income quintile for each decade.

Figures 2A and 2B show the β- and σ-convergence coefficients from these regressions over the whole period of 1960–2007. The first striking result is that there has been absolute convergence since the late 1990s, precisely when the best-known empirical tests of convergence were published. The point estimate for β-convergence becomes negative in the early 1990s, becoming significant in the late 1990s and staying significant since. Table 1 shows a point estimate of –0.65 in the 2000s, and –0.76 in the 10 years after 2007, the most recent period we can consider. σ-convergence, represented by a negative slope in panel B of figure 2, started slightly later, with the standard deviation in GDP per capita falling since the early 2000s. The difference in timing is consistent with β-convergence being a function of subsequent 10-year average growth.

The second result is that there has been a trend toward β-convergence—converging to convergence—since 1990. The coefficient started at around

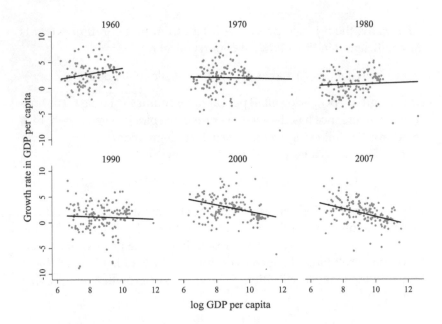

Fig. 1. Income convergence by decade. This figure plots, by decade, the raw scatter plots for the decade's β-convergence regression, as well as the regression line itself. $100 \left(\log(\text{GDPpc})_{i,t+10} - \log(\text{GDPpc})_{i,t}/10\right) = \alpha_t + \beta_t \log(\text{GDPpc})_{i,t} + \epsilon_{i,t}$. The income measure is income per capita, adjusted for PPP, from the Penn World Tables v10.0. The sample is all countries for which data are available, excluding those with a population less than 200,000 or for whom natural resources account for >75% of their GDP. Data availability means that the number of countries is growing over time. For 2007, the period considered is 2007–17. A color version of this figure is available online.

0.5 in 1990 and has trended down toward −1 today. Looking further back to 1960, initially there is no clear trend, and then there is a trend toward divergence in the 1980s.[8] Table 1, column 2, reports the results of our basic absolute convergence regression, equation (1), with the addition of a linear year variable interacted with $\log(\text{GDP}_{i,t})$. The interaction terms, representing the "convergence toward convergence," is negative and significant, with a point estimate of −0.025. The trend toward convergence is also apparent in the σ-convergence figure, where it is represented by a gradual decrease in slope, that is, concavity of the plot.

This trend toward convergence is consistent with models of growth in which capital is subject to diminishing marginal returns, or where catch-up growth is easier than growth at the frontier. It is inconsistent with models of growth that predict long-run divergence, such as AK models, or some poverty trap models.

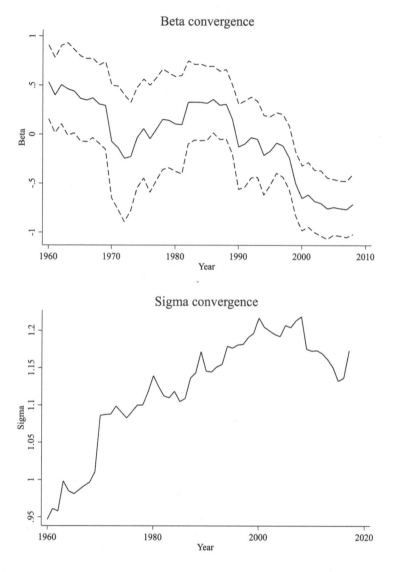

Fig. 2. Trend in income convergence, 1960–2007. These figures show the trend in convergence from 1960 to 2007. The top panel plots the β-convergence coefficient, for growth in the subsequent decade, over time. It is the coefficient from equation (1)—regressing, across countries, the average growth in GDP per capita in the next decade (in %) on the log of GDP per capita, with year fixed effects, and with standard errors clustered by country. Income per capita is adjusted for PPP and comes from the Penn World Tables v10.0. The sample is growing over time and excludes countries with a population less than 200,000 or for whom natural resources account for >75% of their GDP, as in figure 1 (neither exclusion has a meaningful effect on the trend). The bottom panel plots the evolution over time of the cross-country standard deviation in GDP per capita. σ-convergence corresponds to a negative slope. Equivalent panels using balanced panels are in figure A5.

Table 1
Converging to Convergence. Absolute Convergence 1960–2017

	Average Annual Growth in Next Decade		
	(1)	(2)	(3)
log(GDPpc)	−.270**	.449**	
	[.118]	[.224]	
log(GDPpc) × (1960)		−.025***	
		[.006]	
log(GDPpc) × 1960s			.532***
			[.191]
log(GDPpc) × 1970s			−.075
			[.293]
log(GDPpc) × 1980s			.106
			[.246]
log(GDPpc) × 1990s			−.127
			[.221]
log(GDPpc) × 2000s			−.651***
			[.168]
log(GDPpc) × 2007s			−.764***
			[.146]
Year FE	Y	Y	Y
Observations	863	863	863

Note: This table reports absolute convergence regressions, equation (1). The independent variable is the average annualized GDP per capita growth (%) for the subsequent decade, in PPP (from the Penn World Tables v10.0), and the sample contains the data for the first year of each decade since 1960, with 2007 replacing 2010. We exclude countries with population <200,000, and for which natural resources account for >75% of GDP. Specification (1) pools the data since 1960. Specification (2) includes a time trend of absolute convergence β. Specification (3) estimates the absolute convergence β by decade. Year fixed effects (FE) are included in all three specifications. Standard errors, clustered at the country level, are reported in the parentheses.
*$p < .05$.
**$p < .01$.
***$p < .001$.

C.   Econometric Considerations and Robustness to Alternative Specifications

There is an extensive literature on the tradeoffs of different econometric specifications to test for convergence, summarized in Durlauf et al. (2005). We follow the most standard approach, testing for β convergence using OLS with fixed effects for year, clustered at the country level. This approach is not without limitations, which we discuss below, but it is transparent and captures the cross-country variation that is our main focus.

We begin by replying to the three main critiques of the specification noted in the comment of Acemoglu and Molina (2022): unobserved country fixed effects, cross-country heterogeneity in convergence rates, and using annual growth rather than 10-year growth. We then discuss several additional considerations and robustness questions, such as whether measurement error may drive toward convergence through mean reversion, whether results are driven by panel imbalance, in particular the larger number of poor countries entering the panel over time, and whether results depend on the macroeconomic data set used.

Specification, Country Fixed Effects, and Heterogeneity

Our regression specification assumes homogeneous rates of convergence across countries and does not account for potential differences in steady-state income, as discussed in Acemoglu and Molina (2022). We agree with the empirical finding of the authors and Caselli et al. (1996): the coefficients on current income change substantially when incorporating heterogeneity and country fixed effects, with strong convergence toward countries' individual steady-state income levels throughout, at a rate of at least 10%. However, we disagree that their specification is more economically meaningful for the question of convergence (or, in particular, that the coefficient on income in these specifications can be interpreted as causal). It is a different exercise, and one that is not without its own econometric issues (Durlauf et al. 2005).

We are interested in what has been happening across countries, over time; by definition, country fixed effects absorb cross-country differences and treat them as nuisance parameters. We agree that there are likely to be cross-country differences in steady-state income, but we wish to know how these differences have evolved. A priori, we do not know whether convergence to a fixed steady state, or evolution of country-level "steady-state" income itself, is likely to be a more important determinant of growth, so we do not want to assume away the latter. Investigating the evolution of the potential determinants of the country-level steady states is precisely our exercise below, when we turn to conditional convergence, and to whether the potential determinants of steady-state income have converged. We view doing so with variation that we can explain—changes in correlates—as providing additional insights, but we can also do so with a fixed effects approach, which can be interpreted as another form of conditional convergence. To do so, however, we need to allow for the possibility that country "fixed effects" vary over time. Specifically, we modify the framework of Acemoglu and Molina (2022) to allow country fixed effects to vary by decade:

$$\log(\text{GDP}_{i,t+\Delta t}) - \log(\text{GDP}_{i,t}) = \beta_d \log(\text{GDP}_{i,t}) + \mu_t + \gamma_{i,d} + \epsilon_{i,t}, \qquad (2)$$

$\gamma_{i,d}$ being a country-decade fixed effect.

Table A1 reports the β_d estimated with average decade growth in panel A and annual growth in panel B, confirming the results of Acemoglu and Molina (2022). The coefficient stays strongly negative since 1960. The magnitude is quite stable and does not exhibit any declining pattern over time. We also find that using annual growth gives stronger convergence, and we speculate below that annual GDP measurement errors might bias upward a short-term reversal pattern.

In this paragraph in an earlier version of this paper, in analysis undertaken to respond to Acemoglu and Molina's discussion at the National Bureau of Economic Research (NBER) Annual Conference on Macroeconomics, we incorrectly claimed that the fixed effects in this model show little stability over time. Our error was pointed out in Acemoglu and Molina (2022), their subsequent discussion paper. We thank the authors for this correction and have updated this paragraph accordingly (and removed the appendix figure that it referred to). As shown in Acemoglu and Molina (2022), the country fixed effects in this model are stable over time and have a high F-test statistic. This persistence of the fixed effects is primarily from the persistence of country income levels; country growth rates show little autocorrelation from decade to decade.

In this specification, country-decade fixed effects have converged across countries since 1990, suggesting that much of the action for studying the global income distribution may be being absorbed by these fixed effects. Figure A3 plots standard deviations of fixed effects over time with a rolling time window of 10 years. We see a fall in the standard deviation of the country fixed effects since 1990, the period in which we see a trend toward unconditional convergence in our preferred specification. This encourages us to study whether unconditional convergence has converged toward conditional convergence, the question we turn to below.

Moreover, the country fixed effects approach has its own econometric limitations, discussed further in Durlauf et al. (2005). The convergence coefficient in the country fixed effects model, β_d in equation (2), is identified from time-series variation for all years in decade d, whereas the convergence coefficient in our main specification, β_t in equation (1), is identified from cross-sectional variation in year t. Bernard and Durlauf (1996) show that the two specifications may give very different answers and argue that the time-series β_d is a good estimate of convergence only if the sample distribution is a good approximation of the true underlying growth process; if historical growth is not stable, then the time-series model can be substantially biased. Our analysis uses a large set of countries, most of which experienced substantial changes in growth correlates during the period, potentially perturbing them far away from their steady states.

Averaging Period

Many of the original convergence studies used a fixed baseline year, considering how convergence in income per capita changed when varying the endline year. We argue that to consider trends in convergence itself, rather than use a fixed baseline year, it is better to consider convergence over a fixed interval of time and how it changes when varying the baseline year. This raises a natural question of what the fixed interval of time should be and whether that interval matters. In the main results, we used a 10-year interval, considering 10 years a good trade-off between allowing us to see medium-frequency trends, without overloading the trend with annual noise. Acemoglu and Molina (2022) suggest we should use annual data. We think that annual data gets at high-frequency phenomena (e.g., weather streaks, business cycles), whereas 10-year data gets at lower-frequency phenomena, such as long-run growth. Annual data is likely to introduce substantial noise. If this noise is measurement error in GDP, then growth regressions will be biased toward convergence and this bias will be larger over shorter periods, via mean reversion. Figure A4 shows how the convergence coefficient varies when using 1-, 2-, 5-, and 10-year averages. Ten-year averages show the clearest trend toward convergence. Once we get to 1-year averages, the year-to-year variation dominates, and the trend that is apparent in 5- and 10-year averages is much less apparent.

Balanced Panel

Since the number of countries in the data set is growing over time, our results could reflect the inclusion of the new countries over time, rather than global trends. To investigate this, we show, by decade, what convergence looks like from that decade until present day, among the balanced panel of countries whose data is available from the start of that decade. So, for example, for the 1970s, we plot the 10-year average convergence coefficient, from 1970 to present, for the set of countries that have been in the data set since 1970.

Figure A5 displays the results of these investigations that hold the set of countries fixed over time. It shows that the change in convergence has little to do with the expansion of the set of countries over the time period—results are remarkably robust to different balanced panels, showing that the original results do indeed reflect a trend toward convergence since 1990.

While the trend toward convergence began around the time of the dissolution of the Soviet Union, the repercussions of which may have been an important driver of the change in convergence, the robustness of the trend to countries that existed before 1990 shows that the change was not mechanical from the addition of the former Soviet countries.

Measure of Income

Figure A6 shows that our finding of a trend toward convergence is not specific to looking at income per capita (as opposed to per worker), nor to using income per capita in PPP-adjusted terms from the Penn World Tables v10.0. Namely, we find a broadly similar pattern using income per worker instead of income per capita, using different measures of income from the PWT, and using the WDIs data with income measured in constant 2010 US dollars. Indeed, in the latter, the trend is more apparent and seems to start from 1960, again with a decade of regression in the 1980s.

D.   Which Countries Have Driven the Change?

To provide more details on the trend to absolute convergence, and to take a first step toward understanding its causes, we consider which countries have driven the change. We do so mainly by showing how the trend in convergence changes when removing different groups of countries.

Faster Catch-up Growth and a Slowdown of the Frontier

Two very different and popular narratives could each lead to the observed trend to convergence: stagnation of the frontier (a drop in the growth rate of richer countries), or faster catch-up growth (a rise in the growth rate of poorer countries).

Figure 3 shows average 10-year growth rate by income quartile, where income quartile is recalculated each year. The richest quartile of countries had the highest growth rate of all quartiles in the 1980s and then switched position entirely to have the lowest growth rate since 2000. The shift was driven both by a slowdown of growth at the frontier—the richest quartile of countries experienced flat growth in the 1990s and then a growth slowdown since 2000—and by a faster catch-up growth—the other three quartiles experienced a substantial acceleration in growth in the 1990s. Removing one quartile at a time from our standard test for convergence, figure A7, it does appear that in the last decade the trend toward convergence is driven by the richest quartile versus the other quartiles, and that

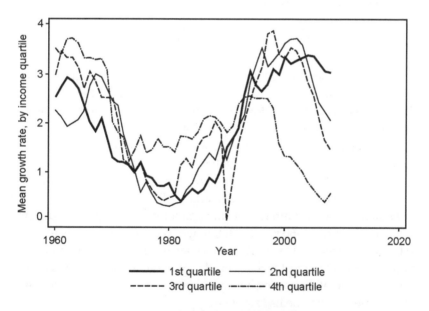

Fig. 3. Trend in income growth by income quartile, 1960–2007. The plots show the average annual growth in GDP per capita, PPP, for the subsequent decade, averaged by income per capita quartile. Income per capita quartile is classified based on GDP per capita in that year, with the first quartile being the lowest income and the fourth quartile the highest. A color version of this figure is available online.

the poorest quartile has, if anything, been a drag on the trend toward convergence within the other quartiles.

Fewer Growth Disasters and More Growth Miracles

Figure A8 presents the trend in coefficients from equation (1) when excluding countries that experienced disasters or growth miracles. The trend toward convergence remains robust, whether we drop episodes of especially low or episodes of especially high growth. Interestingly, the reversion in the 1980s disappears when excluding countries that had a negative 10-year growth rate.

Which Regions Are Driving the Change?

Figure A9 presents the trend in coefficients from equation (1) when excluding countries from different regions. Again the trend remains robust, although the trend toward convergence in the last 20 years becomes stronger upon excluding sub-Saharan Africa.

E. Club Convergence

Convergence among OECD countries (or rich countries), a group of relatively homogeneous countries (Barro and Sala-i-Martin 1992), has been documented as evidence for club convergence—convergence among groups of countries that have similar institutions and culture. We revisit this result and show that convergence among the rich countries has slowed and shifted toward the general global convergence pattern.

Figure A10 plots the convergence coefficients in the country subsample with income above the Xth percentile.[9] Three decades from 1965 to 1995 yield a similar pattern—strong convergence among high-income countries (above the 60 percentile), whereas overall there was little absolute convergence. This pattern has changed in the period from 1995 to 2005, and in the most recent decade convergence holds across a sample containing all countries, whereas convergence among the top 40% of countries by income has stopped.

These results, together with the above finding that growth has increased across the bottom three quartiles, are inconsistent with certain poverty trap explanations for the trend toward absolute income convergence. Namely, we see no evidence of there being an income threshold above which there is convergence, with more countries crossing the threshold over time.

III. Convergence in Correlates of Income and Growth

We next consider global trends in factors that might be determinants of growth—policies, institutions, human capital, and culture—using the same empirical approach as above. While much recent literature emphasizes the persistence of institutions over time (Acemoglu et al. 2001; Dell 2010; Michalopoulos and Papaioannou 2013), we find substantial change and convergence. Overall, 17 out of the 32 Solow fundamentals and short-run correlates for which we have temporal variation exhibit β-convergence from 1985 to 2015, and the correlates have generally converged in the direction of those of more advanced economies, toward what we term development-favored institutions. Moreover, culture has also convergence, with eight out of 10 measures of culture we consider displaying β-convergence in the WVS data.

A. Policies, Institutions, Measures of Human Capital, and Cultural Traits Considered

We divide such potential correlates of income and growth into four groups: (a) enhanced Solow fundamentals (investment rate, population growth rate, and human capital)—variables that are fundamental determinants of steady-state income in the enhanced Solow model (Mankiw et al. 1992); (b) short-run correlates—other policy and institution variables considered by the 1990s growth literature that may vary at relatively high frequency; (c) long-run correlates—institutions and their historical determinants that do not change or only change slowly, which have been the focus of the recent institutions literature, and geographic correlates of growth; and (d) culture.

To tie our hands, we started from a list of variables commonly used in growth regressions, from the *Handbook of Economic Growth* chapter titled "Growth Econometrics" (Durlauf et al. 2005), constraining ourselves to those variables that covered at least 40 countries from 1996. We then added to this list numerous cultural variables and historical determinants of institutions that have played a central role in the empirical growth literature since Durlauf et al. (2005). While we obviously cannot consider convergence for historical or geographic variables—they are, however, included in the empirical exercises in the next section—we are able to study convergence of multiple cultural variables, albeit with a smaller country sample than for the policy and institutional variables.

Table 2 summarizes the data sources and sample period of the resulting correlates. There are five enhanced Solow fundamentals and 27 short-run correlates divided into four broad categories: political institutions, governance, fiscal policy, and financial institutions. Not all the short-term correlates are comparable over time; for example, the World Governance Indicators and Heritage Freedom Scores are standardized each year. We obviously cannot study convergence or average changes for such variables, but we include them in the table as we do use them for our analysis of the gap between unconditional and conditional convergence, in Section IV of the paper. For certain figures in the paper, we pick one representative variable from each category, displayed in bold in the table: Polity 2 score, the Worldwide Governance Indicators (WGI) rule of law, government spending (% GDP), credit provided by the financial sector (% GDP). Equivalent figures with the other variables can be found in the appendix.

To help interpret the direction of change of correlates, table 3, column 2 shows which correlates were "development-favored" in 1985 (or the earliest available year), defined by their correlation with log GDP in 1985. Correlates are defined as high (or low) development-favored if the coefficient from regressing the correlate on log GDP is positive (or negative), with statistical significance at a 10% level. A high-income country tends to have a higher Polity 2 score, higher rule of law score, higher government spending (as a % of GDP), more financial credit, and higher education attainment. Five correlates cannot be signed: taxes on goods and services, tax burden score, military expenditure, inflation, and central bank independence (CBI).

We first supplement Solow fundamentals with two measures about the labor force: gender inequality in education (male minus female in educational attainment) and labor force participation rate. High-income countries enjoy more gender equality in education and lower labor force participation.

Then, we use five variables to measure political institutions: the Polity 2 score from the Center of Systematic Peace (1960–2018), the Freedom House political rights score (1973–2018), the Freedom House civil liberty score (1973–2015), the Press Freedom score (1979–2018),[10] and the political stability score (1996–2018) from WGI.

Governance variables—distinct from political institutions—measure whether the public system functions well. We use four variables (1996–2018) from the WGI Project: government effectiveness, regulatory quality, the rule of law, and control of corruption; and five variables (1995–2019) from the Index of Economic Freedom by the Heritage Foundation: Overall economic freedom, government integrity, business freedom, investment freedom, and property rights. The sample size of countries in the Economic Freedom database rises from 97 in 1995 to 145 in 2005, and then 159 in 2015. Variables under the governance and political institutions categories are all positively correlated with economic development.

The fiscal policy category mainly captures the following three dimensions: taxation, tariffs, and government interventions/expenditures. Taxation measurements include taxes on income and capital gains (percentage of total tax revenue), taxes on goods and services (percentage of total tax revenue), and a tax burden score. Equal-weighted and value-weighted tariffs are measures of the policy-induced barriers to trade. A state with strong government interventions and expenditures tends to have a lower private investment (% total investment), more government spending (% spending), and higher military expenditure. In general, high-income countries are more likely to adopt free trade and low government intervention, but there is not a clear pattern in our data on taxation.

The financial institutions category includes six variables: a CBI index constructed by Garriga (2016); inflation, credit to the private sector (% GDP), and credit provided by the financial sector (% GDP), all from the WDIs; and financial freedom and investment freedom scores from the Index of Economic Freedom. Higher financial development is positively associated with economic development, whereas CBI and inflation are ambiguous according to our approach. The high inflation of 1990 was not constrained to developing countries but was a global issue. CBI adoption rose over time and inflation was brought under control (Rogoff 1985; Alesina 1988; Grilli, Masciandaro, and Tabellini 1991; Alesina and Summers 1993; Alesina and Gatti 1995; Fischer 1995).

The following sections examine average changes in correlates from 1985 to 2015 as well as their rate of convergence, β_{Inst}, estimated from the following equation:[11]

$$\Delta_{1985 \rightarrow 2015} Inst_i = \beta_{Inst} Inst_{i,1985} + \alpha_{\text{Inst}} + \epsilon_i.$$

The country sample is time-varying (mostly increasing) as data sets add new countries into the sample. In the appendix, we also plot the

Table 2
List of Solow Fundamentals, Growth Correlates, and Cultural Variables

Category	Variable	Data Source	Data Period
Enhanced Solow fundamentals	**Gross Capital Formation (% GDP)**	WDI	1960–2017
	Population Growth Rate	WDI	1960–2017
	Barro-Lee Years of Education Age 25–29	Barro-Lee Data	1950–2010
Labor force	Education Gap (Male-Female)	Barro-Lee Data	1950–2010
	Labor Force Participation Rate	WDI	1960–2017
Political Institutions	**Polity 2 Score**	Polity IV Project	1960–2018
	Freedom House Political Rights	Freedom House	1973–2018
	Freedom House Civil Liberty	Freedom House	1973–2018
	Media Freedom Score	Freedom House	1979–2018
	WGI Political Stability	WGI	1996–2018
Governance Quality	**WGI Rule of Law**	WGI	1996–2018
	WGI Government Effectiveness	WGI	1996–2018
	WGI Regulatory Quality	WGI	1996–2018
	WGI Control of Corruption	WGI	1996–2018
	Overall Economic Freedom Index	Heritage Freedom	1995–2019
	Government Integrity	Heritage Freedom	1995–2019
	Business Freedom	Heritage Freedom	1995–2019
	Property Rights	Heritage Freedom	1995–2019

Category	Variable	Source	Years
Fiscal Policies	Taxes on Income & Cap. Gains (% of Revenue)	WDI	1972–2017
	Taxes on Goods and Services (% of Revenue)	WDI	1972–2017
	Equal-weighted Tariff	WDI	1988–2017
	Value-weighted Tariff	WDI	1988–2017
	Tax Burden Score	Heritage Freedom	1995–2019
	Private Investment (% Total Investment)	IMF	1960–2015
	Government Spending (% GDP)	WDI	1960–2017
	Military Expenditure (% GDP)	WDI	1960–2017
Financial Institutions	Inflation	WDI	1960–2017
	Central Bank Independence (Weighted)	Garriga (2019)	1970–2012
	Credit to Private Sector	WDI	1960–2017
	Credit by Financial Sector	WDI	1960–2017
	Financial Freedom	Heritage Freedom	1995–2019
	Investment Freedom	Heritage Freedom	1995–2019
Culture	Power Distance	Hofstede VSM	–
	Individualism	Hofstede VSM	–
	Masculinity	Hofstede VSM	–
	Uncertainty Avoidance	Hofstede VSM	–
	Indulgence vs Restraint	Hofstede VSM	–
	Long-term Orientation	Hofstede VSM	–
Long-Run Variables	Population in 1900	Maddison Project	–
	Legal Origin (UK)	LaPorta et al. (2008)	–
	Legal Origin (France)	LaPorta et al. (2008)	–
	Legal Origin (Germany)	LaPorta et al. (2008)	–
	Legal Origin (Scandinavia)	LaPorta et al. (2008)	–
	Legal Origin (Socialist)	LaPorta et al. (2008)	–
	Log Settler Mortality Rate	Acemoglu et al. (2001)	–
	Mean Temperature	Acemoglu et al. (2001)	–
	100 km of the Coastline	Acemoglu et al. (2001)	–

Table 2
Continued

Category	Variable	Data Source	Data Period
	Ethno-linguistic Fractionalization	Acemoglu et al. (2001)	—
	Landlocked	Acemoglu et al. (2001)	—
	Absolute Latitude	Acemoglu et al. (2001)	—
	Tropical Climate	Sachs and Warner (1997a)	—

Note: This table summarizes all enhanced Solow fundamentals, growth correlates, and cultural variables considered in the analysis, which we divide into four broad groups: enhanced Solow fundamentals, short-run correlates (comprising political institutions, governance, fiscal policy, financial institutions), long-run correlates, and culture. Columns 3 and 4 report the data source and data period for each variable. The variables in bold are the representative correlates reported in figures A14 and 4. Some of the correlates are not directly comparable across time; for example, the WGI indicators are standardized each year. In subsequent analysis, we only consider such variables for conditional-versus-absolute convergence, where such standardization does not matter.

standard deviations of the correlate metrics as the σ-convergence for correlates (figs. A11–A13).

Before presenting results for individual correlates, we test the convergence of all of our short-run correlates jointly in table A2, which presents the joint significance of each category using seemingly unrelated regressions. All variables are available since 1996. Thus we report results for 1996–2006 in panel A and 2006–16 in panel B. For both decades, we confidently hypothesize that convergence in correlates does not exist.

B. Enhanced Solow Fundamentals

Human Capital

Human capital is a robust predictor of income growth, as emphasized in the seminal literature from Lucas (1988), Barro (1991), Mankiw et al. (1992), Sala-i-Martin (1997), and Barro and Lee (1994).[12] Education augments labor productivity (Lucas 1988), facilitates technological progress (Romer 1990), and can help promote structural transformation into industry (Squicciarini and Voigtländer 2015).[13]

We measure time-varying human capital with the Barro-Lee average schooling years of population—ages 20–60. Figure A14, panel C reports the β-convergence. The convergence in human capital starts in 1975. Beginning in 1975, poor countries start to gain faster growth in educational attainment and gradually catch up with rich countries. In addition, education levels in some well-educated populations have stagnated, and the data imply that 13 average years of education appears to be a soft cap for many countries.[14] We also observe a meaningful shrinking in education attainment inequality across gender. The education gender gap reduced by 8.1% per decade on average.

Investment

Investment is development-favored, according to our definition, and we observe a moderate growth from 22.07% in 1985 to 24.18% in 2015, which translates to 0.23 standard deviations in 1985. Figure A14, panel B indicates that convergence in investment has been stable (around −6) since 1985. Figure 4, panel B exhibits strong mean reversion, with 1% higher investment in 1985 corresponding to a negative growth of 2.98% per decade. With most countries slowly decreasing their investment, certain

Table 3

Change and Convergence in Enhanced Solow Fundamentals and Growth Correlates from 1985* to 2015*

	Dev-Favored	Mean in 1985*	Mean in 2015*	Change (in σ_{1985}) Estimate	Change (in σ_{1985}) p-value	Convergence β
Gross Capital Formation (% of GDP)	High	22.07	24.18	.23	.06	−2.98***
Population Growth (Annual %)	Low	1.99	1.42	−.43	0	−1.53***
Barro-Lee Education Age 20–60	High	6.19	8.80	.86	0	−.16
Average of Solow Fundamentals						−1.56
Education Gap (Male-Female)	Low	.97	.33	−.66	0	−.81***
Labor Force Participation Rate	Low	62.48	62.61	.01	.79	−.66***
Polity 2 Score	High	−.87	4.69	.73	0	−2.03***
Freedom House Political Rights	High	5.86	6.53	.30	0	−1.39***
Freedom House Civil Liberty	High	5.72	6.56	.41	0	−1.36***
Media Freedom Score	High	52.63	49.93	−.12	.02	−.88***
WGI Political Stability	High	−	−	−	−	−
WGI Government Effective	High	−	−	−	−	−
WGI Regulatory Quality	High	−	−	−	−	−
WGI Rule of Law	High	−	−	−	−	−
WGI Control of Corruption	High	−	−	−	−	−
Overall Economic Freedom Index	High	−	−	−	−	−
Government Integrity	High	−	−	−	−	−
Property Rights	High	−	−	−	−	−
Business Freedom	High	−	−	−	−	−
Equal-weighted Tariff	Low	9.46	4.36	−.47	0	−3.46***
Value-weighted Tariff	Low	8.11	3.09	−.70	0	−3.38***
Taxes on Income and Capital Gain	High	25.54	28.79	.20	.06	−1.61***
Government Spending (% GDP)	High	15.90	15.96	.01	.90	−1.61***
Taxes on Goods and Services	N/A	28.47	31.38	.21	.17	−2.51***
Tax Burden Score	N/A	−	−	−	−	−
Private Investment	High	.63	.63	0	.99	−1.60***
Military Expenditure (% GDP)	N/A	3.38	1.89	−.47	0	−2.10***
Inflation	Low	16.19	2.25	−.54	0	−3.07***

Table 3
Continued

	Dev-Favored	Mean in 1985*	Mean in 2015*	Change (in σ_{1985}) Estimate	Change (in σ_{1985}) p-value	Convergence β
Central Bank						
Independence	N/A	.38	.60	1.77	0	−2.56***
Credit to Private Sector	High	31.46	55.60	.95	0	.89**
Credit by Financial						
Sector	High	49.42	69.15	.47	0	−.98
Financial Freedom	High	–	–	–	–	–
Investment Freedom	High	–	–	–	–	–
Average of Short-Run						
Correlates						−1.66

Note: This table presents the average correlate in 1985 (or the earliest available year, denoted 1985*) and 2015 (or the latest available year, denoted 2015*) and convergence rate over the 3 decades. Column 2 reports the development-favored correlates determined by their correlation with GDP per capita in 1985. "N/A" refers to the potential correlates that are not significantly correlated with income in our base year 1985, that is, where δ_{1985} is insignificant. Columns 3 and 4 report the raw mean of correlates in 1985* and 2015*, respectively. Columns 5 and 6 report the change in the correlates between 1985* and 2015*, normalized by the standard deviation in 1985* and corresponding t-statistics. Column 7 is the correlate convergence β, obtained by regressing the decade-average correlate change from 1985* to 2015* on the correlate in 1985*. Missing entries correspond to correlates that are not directly comparable across time, for example, if they are standardized each year. Results for culture are in table A6.
*$p < .05$.
**$p < .01$.
***$p < .001$.

developing countries like Mozambique, Ethiopia, and Angola have increased investment.

Population Growth

Developed economies feature lower population growth. Population growth slows down from 1.99% in 1985 to 1.42% in 2015, translating to −0.43 standard deviations in 1985. Figure A14, panel A reports the beta convergence that fluctuates between −4 and −2 before 2000, after which we witness a sharp decline toward −6. After 2000, population growth has fallen for poor countries, whereas it has stagnated for most of the rich countries. Figure 4, panel A reports that most countries in our sample witnessed a decrease in population growth from 1985 to 2010.

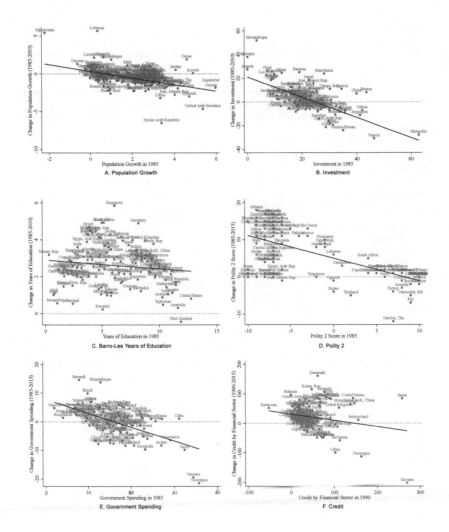

Fig. 4. Convergence in growth correlates: level in 1985 versus change 1985–2015. This figure plots β-convergence for growth six representative correlates (potential determinants of steady-state income) from 1985 (or the earliest available year) to 2015 against the baseline correlate level in 1985. We include six of the correlates, which are comparable over time, for illustration: population growth rate (%), investment rate (% of GDP), Barro-Lee average years of education among 20-to-60-year-olds, Polity 2 score, government spending (% of GDP), and credit by the financial sector. The sample for each figure is the complete set of countries for which the relevant data are available in 1985 and 2015. A color version of this figure is available online.

C. Short-Run Correlates

Labor Force

Education attainment became more gender-balanced from 1985 to 2015. Male education was 0.97 years more than women in 1985, and the number reduces to only a 0.33-year advantage. Not surprisingly, countries with larger gender differences experienced more gap reduction. The labor force participation rates remain stable around 62.5% in the recent 3 decades, but β-convergence also holds—1% higher labor participation rate correlates with a 0.66 % reduction in 1985–2015.

Political Institutions

Political institutions exhibit pervasive β-convergence and σ-convergence, with particularly strong convergence in the 1990s. We use the Polity 2 score from the Polity IV project as our primary democracy measure, which ranges from −10 to 10; −10 represents dictatorship and 10 represents perfect democracy. Figure A15 shows that the average Polity 2 score hits its low point in 1978, at below −2, then the score gradually climbs back to zero in 1990. Then, the average democracy score jumps up to 2 after the dissolution of the Soviet Union and persistently improves to above 4 in the next 25 years.

Figure A11 shows the plot of coefficients for β-convergence in political institutions. Polity 2 score, political rights, and civil liberty yield similar results, including in the rate of convergence. The long-run average of coefficients is around −0.2. The deep institutional reforms in the 1990s lead the coefficients to drop below −0.3 in that decade and then gradually move back the historical average of −0.2. The institutional convergence is statistically significant in any single year's cross-sectional regression. β-convergence in media freedom and political stability also holds since 1995, and the convergence pattern is very stable in the recent 2 decades.

Panel B of Figure A11 reports the standard derivation of the four political institutions.[15] The σ-convergence of democracy starts in 1990. The standard deviation of Polity 2 score fluctuates around 7.5 before 1990, sharply declines to 6.5 in 2000, and persistently decreases to 6 in 2015. The four other variables show a similar pattern: the standard deviation after 2000 is lower than that prior to 1990.

The broad adoption of democracy is a central aspect of the convergence of political institutions. Figure 4 plots the change in the democracy score from 1990 to 2010 against the democracy score in the baseline year 1990. The spread of democracy is a global phenomenon, not just constrained to Soviet Union countries. Many countries with a Polity 2 score below 5 radically shift their political institutions toward democracy.

Meanwhile, movements away from democracy are also relatively common. Table A3 summarizes the proportion of countries with increases and downgrades in democracy scores. Even after 1980, in each decade roughly 10% of countries experienced falls in their democracy scores. If we focus, admittedly somewhat arbitrarily, on countries with a Polity 2 score reduction of at least 3 in a decade, then most democracy degeneration events happen in countries with positive democracy scores—6 out of 8 in the 1980s, 5 out of 5 in the 1990s, 7 out of 7 in the 2000s, and 4 out of 5 in 2010–15.

Developing countries are much more likely to experience political reforms, both toward democracy and against democracy, whereas rich countries successfully maintain their democratic politics. Table A4 shows logit regressions of increases or decreases in Polity 2 score on income level for the 6 decades. Panel A reveals that low-income countries are only more likely to gain democracy in the 1960s and 1990s but not much in other periods. However, in panel B, low-income countries are also more exposed to democracy setbacks, except in the 1990s.

Fiscal Policy

Despite a lack of consensus on optimal fiscal policy, global average government spending stayed close to 16% of GDP throughout 1985–2015. Moreover, there was sizeble and statistically significant beta convergence in government spending. Figure 4, panel E shows that 1% higher government spending in 1996 predicts 1.61% reduction in the next 2 decades, where a high t-stat of 9.6 and the R^2 are as high as 41%.

This pattern is not unique to government spending but is common to all fiscal policy variables. The convergence β ranges from −3.46 (equal-weighted tariff) to −1.60 (private investment), significant at the 1% level.

A large empirical literature argues that lower policy-induced barriers to trade are associated with faster economic growth (Frankel and Romer 1999). We document a significant trade liberalization from 1990 to 2010—equal-weighted tariffs drop from 9.46% to 4.36%, and value-weighted tariffs drop from 8.11% to 3.09%—more than a 50% cut on average. The β-convergence coefficient fluctuates around −6 but gradually moves to −4 in recent decades. The magnitude is notably large compared with other correlates, in both equal-weighted and value-weighted tariff data. Figure A12, panel B3 shows that the variance of tariffs sharply reduces in 1995 and that trade liberalization expands internationally. The standard deviation of tariffs stays below 5 after 2010.

Financial Institutions

We see mixed evidence regarding financial credit convergence: there is modest convergence, although there is also substantial credit growth in a few large highly leveraged developed economies.[16] Credit is development favored, according to our definition, and we do observe substantial credit expansion from 49.4% of GDP in 1990 to 69.15% of GDP in 2010, which translates into 0.47 standard deviations in 1990. One percent higher credit in 1990 corresponds to a −0.98% decrease per decade. However, the convergence pattern is less persistent over time—figure A14, panel F shows the convergence is particularly concentrated in the 1980s and 1990s.

Figure 4, panel F implies that convergence happens in both directions. Underleveraged economies, such as Denmark, Australia, and South Korea, expanded their financial sector. At the same time, many countries deleveraged: out of 123 countries in our sample, 40 reduced the amount of credit. Highly leveraged economies were more likely to contract credit, potentially to manage the risk of recessions. In total, 12 countries held credit-to-GDP ratio above 100% in 1990; they reduced credit by 23% on average after 2 decades.[17] At the other extreme, 17 countries with credit below 15% of GDP in 1990 expanded their credit by 21% through 2010.

Financial stability also increased significantly. For example, episodes of high inflation became much less frequent. Figure A13, panels A1 and B1 report the convergence pattern for inflation. We do not find robust convergence until 1980, when episodes of very high inflation were still widespread. The β-convergence coefficients have stayed significantly negative since 1980. σ-convergence has happened since 1990: the standard deviation runs from the peak above 30 to the trough below 5 in 2010. Modern monetary policy reduced the occurrence of hyperinflation and contributed to the convergence in inflation. Figure A16 plots the proportion of countries that experience (a) inflation above 200%, (b) inflation above 100%, (c) inflation above 50%, and (d) inflation above 15% in a specific year. All the four lines start to decline starting in 1995. From 1972 to 1995, about 35% of countries had annual inflation above 15% and 10% countries experienced inflation more than 100%. After 2000, almost no country had inflation above 50% whereas less than 10% countries had inflation above 15%.

D. Culture

We adopt two data sources to measure culture. The WVS allow us to study the evolution of culture. To best match the time horizon considered for other correlates, we pick countries surveyed in wave 3 (1995–1998) and wave 6 (2010–14), leaving us with 33 countries in our sample to test cultural convergence. To expand the country sample, we turn to the Hofstede dimensions of national culture, which are available for 69 countries. Section IV studies the culture-growth relationships using the Hofstede data.

Each cultural variable constructed from the WVS aggregates responses from age groups 20 to 40, using population weights.[18] For each country, we compare perceptions held by those aged 20–40 in wave 6, to those aged 20–40 in wave 3. We compute the annualized cultural change between waves 3 and 6 and adjust for the survey year difference in a given wave. We then regress the annualized cultural change on the wave 3 level to obtain the cultural convergence β.

We report our results in table A6, which shows that β-convergence holds for eight out of 10 cultural variables. In political views, the willingness to participate in boycotts converges by 6.4% annually, interest in politics by 2.7%, opinions on the importance of politics by 1.8%, and the recognition of authority by 1.8%. In views on work-life balance, the importance of family and work converge by 4.4% and 3.3%, respectively. Also, the younger generation reaches more agreements on social issues than the older generation. Between the waves, perceptions on the importance of tradition and of reducing inequality also converged by 7.1% and 2.7% per year, finding them less and more important on average, respectively. Finally, on two deep cultural variables, the level of trust and the importance of religion, we find no convergence.

IV. Linking Converging Income with Convergence of Its Correlates

Are these two changes since the late 1980s related—the trend toward convergence in income and the convergence of many of the correlates of income and growth? We are naturally unable to do a full causal analysis, and causality can run both ways. On the one hand, an extensive empirical literature argues that such correlates are important for economic development (Glaeser et al. 2004; Acemoglu et al. 2005), and the convergence literature itself turned toward convergence conditional on correlates (determinants of the steady state). On the other hand, modernization theory suggests that causation may run the other way, with converging incomes causing policies, institutions, and culture to converge. Recent literature uses instrumental variables to provide evidence on both directions of causation, using historical determinants of institutions to establish their effect on long-run growth (Acemoglu et al. 2001, 2019; Dell 2010; Michalopoulos and Papaioannou 2013), and using instruments for income to test modernization theory (Acemoglu et al. 2008). These studies build on earlier analysis that focused on stylized facts that any theory of growth should fit, either from growth regressions (Barro 1996; Sala-i-Martin 1997; Durlauf et al. 2005; Rodrik 2012) or from the observation that rich countries often share a common set of policies and institutions: on average, they are more democratic, less corrupt; they have robust financial systems, more effective governance, better social order, and the like. It is these earlier analyses—of empirical cross-country relationships—that we return to in this section, updating their findings with 20 years more data.

We revisit the cross-sectional relationships between correlates and income levels and growth rates, detailing how the relationships have changed since 1985 and linking these changes to the emergence of absolute convergence in the past 2 decades. First, we consider the relationship between income levels and correlates, a simple cross-country representation of modernization theory. Then, we turn to the relationship between income growth and correlates, controlling for income levels—the classic growth regressions. Finally, we turn to conditional convergence—the prediction of neoclassical growth models. A simple decomposition, combining the two cross-country relationships via the omitted variable bias formula, of the gap between unconditional and conditional convergence provides a partial answer to the question of whether the trend to absolute convergence occurred because absolute convergence has converged to conditional convergence, or because conditional convergence itself has become faster?

A. Simple Empirical Framework

For our simple empirical investigation of the link between income, correlates, and growth, we consider two basic cross-country regressions.

First, the cross-country relationship between income and correlates, a simple test of modernization theory:

$$I_{i,t} = \nu_t + \delta_t \log(\text{GDPpc}_{i,t}) + \epsilon_{i,t}, \tag{3}$$

where δ_t is the slope of the relationship, and ν_t is a year-t fixed effect.

Second, the relationship between correlates and growth, controlling for income—the classic growth regression and the standard formulation of conditional convergence:

$$\Delta_t \log(\text{GDPpc}_{i,t}) = \alpha_t + \beta_t^* \log(\text{GDPpc}_{i,t}) + \lambda_t I_{i,t} + \epsilon_{i,t}, \tag{4}$$

where $I_{i,t}$ can be an individual correlate or a set of correlates; λ_t is the growth-regression coefficient(s) of the correlate(s), when controlling for baseline income; and β_t^* is the conditional convergence coefficient, controlling for the correlate(s).

In this framework, when conditioning on a single correlate, the omitted variable bias formula allows us to decompose the difference between absolute convergence (β) and conditional convergence (β^*) as the product of the income-correlate slope, δ_t, and the growth-regression coefficient, λ_t:

$$\beta_t - \beta_t^* = \delta_t \times \lambda_t. \tag{5}$$

In turn, we can decompose any change in absolute convergence ($\beta_{t_2} - \beta_{t_1}$) into changes in four components: the underlying process of conditional convergence ($\beta_{t_2}^* - \beta_{t_1}^*$), the income-institution relationship ($\lambda_{t_1}(\delta_{t_2} - \delta_{t_1})$), the income-growth relationship ($\delta_{t_1}(\lambda_{t_2} - \lambda_{t_1})$), and the interaction term.

Data availability varies substantially across different correlates, making it difficult to construct a balanced panel with many correlates. This has two implications for our analysis. First, we largely focus on univariate versions of the growth regression, that is, equation (4) including one correlate at a time. This misses the effect of changes in the relationships across correlates, so we also run several multivariate analyses trading off the number of correlates with the size of the panel. Second, in the main analysis we focus on the time period 1985–2015, because that is the period over which the majority of our correlate variables are available for a large number of countries. We also present trends in results since 1960, for those correlates for which we have the data to do so.

B. Correlate-Income Relationship and Modernization Theory

Prosperity is correlated with the rule of law, democracy, fiscal capacity, and education, among others. We have shown above that income has started to convergence and that correlates have converged substantially. Are these changes related? Did countries simply shift along the lines in the cross-country relationship between income and correlates, in line with the predictions of modernization theory, or did the lines themselves change?

Figure A17 investigates this, plotting whether changes in correlates are as would be expected from changes in income, given the baseline cross-country relationship between the two. Overall, we see that actual changes are on average in line with those predicted from income growth: the fitted line is approximately on the 45-degree line. This can be viewed as modernization theory passing a (weak) out-of-sample test for the correlates specified in the 1990s, using new data. It also suggests that overall, levels of correlates conditional on income have remained constant.

However, for individual correlates, the actual changes are generally quite far from those predicted by baseline relationships, pushing back on the explanatory power of a simple modernization theory explanation. Education and financial development have improved by much more than predicted by income growth. Education has increased, and the gender gap in education became significantly smaller. Many "best practices" of financial institutions have been broadly pursued as well: well-managed inflation, CBI, credit expansion as a crucial part of the economic stimulus package, and lower tariffs to embrace globalization. Political institutions improved almost as much as predicted. Meanwhile, from 1985 to 2015, measures of governance stagnated or even declined: property rights protection, investment freedom, business freedom, and political stability experienced a sizable decline.

We have shown correlates have changed as predicted by their cross-country relationship with income, on average, but what has happened to these cross-country relationships themselves? Figure 5, which normalizes correlates by their standard deviation in 1985 shows the slopes of these correlate-income regressions, the δ_t in equation (3), changed remarkably little. The slopes in 1985 are sufficient to explain the 69% of variation in slopes 3 decades later. The explanatory power (R^2) rises to 87.5% if three outliers (financial credit, credit to private sector, and tertiary education) are excluded. The other 30 correlates scatter precisely along the 45-degree line. The results are also reported in table 4.

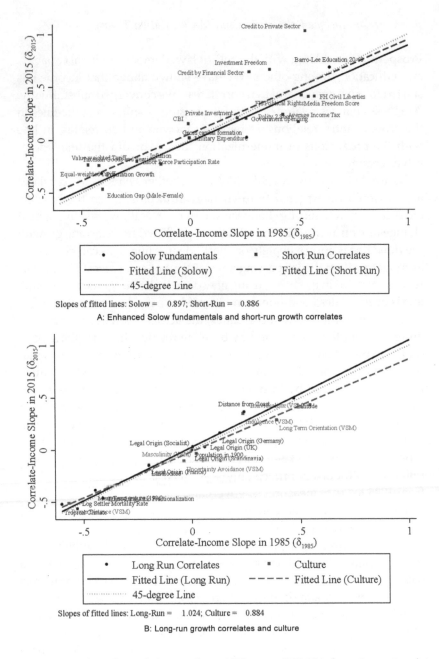

Fig. 5. Correlate of growth-income slopes, 1985 versus 2005. This figure is a scatter plot of the coefficients from regressing correlates on (log) income per capita, plotting the coefficient in 1985 versus 2015. The correlates are normalized by their standard deviation in

While the 1985-versus-2015 comparison is our main specification, in figure A18 we also report the trends in the correlate-income slopes since 1960, averaged within each group of correlates. To make the average meaningful, we first renormalize the correlates such that their correlate-income slope is positive in 1985 (i.e., we multiply the correlate by −1, throughout, if the slope is negative in 1985). The signs of the correlate-income relationships are highly stable, so this normalization does not bias our results for the average slope in 1985 relative to other years. Also, as many correlates are not available before 1985, and the set of countries for which correlates are available is growing, we repeat the exercise for several different balanced panels. In particular, for each decade, we trace one plot holding constant the set of correlates and the set of countries for which they were available at the start of the decade. The exercise shows the robustness of the correlate-income slopes over time for each of the four correlate types.

C. Growth-Correlate Relationship and Growth Regressions

Recent empirical growth papers use historical variation to identify the effect of institutions and culture on income, using either instruments (Acemoglu et al. 2001; Algan and Cahuc 2010) or spatial discontinuities (Dell 2010), and generally find that both play a central role. Such an approach can only identify the effect of persistent institutions and cultural traits, and although some, such as legal systems and trust, have deep historical roots and appear to change very slowly (Michalopoulos and Papaioannou 2013), many change rapidly as we have shown above, and there is no contradiction in institutions both having a long-run effect and being subject to recent change. While historical determinants continue to persist, we should also remain open to asking how recent changes in policies and institutions have affected growth, especially when considering policy changes.

Here we return to the basic growth-regression specification, cognizant of its limitations as a causal framework. For this question—the

---

1985. Namely, the y-axis is δ_{2015}, and the x-axis δ_{1985}, from equation (3), which is the following regression: $Inst_{i,t}/SD(Inst_{1985}) = \delta_t \log (GDPpc)_{i,t} + v_t + \epsilon_{t,i}$. δ_{2015} and δ_{1985} are estimated using a balanced panel, balanced separately for each correlate. The solid lines are the fitted lines of the scatter plot; the numbers beneath the plots refer to their slopes. The dashed lines are the 45-degree line, as a benchmark. Panel A presents results for Solow fundamentals and short-run correlates; panel B presents results for long-run correlates and culture. We exclude those correlates that are normalized each period and hence are not comparable over time. A color version of this figure is available online.

Table 4
Correlate-Income and Growth-Correlate Relationships

	δ_{1985}	δ_{2005}	λ_{1985}	λ_{2005}	$\delta\lambda_{1985}$	$\delta\lambda_{2005}$	N
Gross Capital Formation							
(% of GDP)	.276**	.109[+]	.253	.382[+]	.070	.042	115
Population Growth (Annual %)	−.384**	−.192**	−.636**	−.656**	.244*	.126	136
Barro-Lee Education Age 20–60	.656**	.639**	.963*	.700*	.632*	.447*	118
Average of Solow Fundamentals					.32	.20	
Education Gap (Male-Female)	−.412**	−.501**	−.550*	−.257	.227*	.129	118
Labor Force Participation Rate	−.268**	−.257**	−.424	.367*	.114	−.094	160
Polity 2 Score	.494**	.197**	.891**	.340	.440**	.067	124
Freedom House Political Rights	.540**	.353**	1.107**	.189	.598**	.067	132
Freedom House Civil Liberty	.568**	.351**	.959**	.173	.544**	.061	132
Media Freedom Score	.517**	.468**	.117	.004	.061	.002	152
WGI Political Stability	–	–	–	–	.069	.069	159
WGI Government Effective	–	–	–	–	−.115	.262	158
WGI Regulatory Quality	–	–	–	–	−.270	.044	159
WGI Rule of Law	–	–	–	–	−.175	.075	159
WGI Control of Corruption	–	–	–	–	−.173	−.032	159
Overall Economic Freedom Index	–	–	–	–	−.267[+]	−.150	97
Government Integrity	–	–	–	–	−.113	−.042	97
Property Rights	–	–	–	–	−.106	−.125	97
Business Freedom	–	–	–	–	−.012	−.120	97
Equal-weighted Tariff	−.758**	−.271**	.298	−.265	−.226	.072	45
Value-weighted Tariff	−.696**	−.256**	.026	−.799	−.018	.205	45
Taxes on Income & Capital Gain	.416**	.280*	−.113	.082	−.047	.023	48
Government Spending (% GDP)	.262**	.237**	−.192	−.245	−.050	−.058	111
Taxes on Goods and Services	−.182	−.155	−.579[+]	.185	.106	−.029	49
Tax Burden Score	–	–	–	–	.017	.004	97
Private Investment	.234**	.195**	.026	.121	.006	.024	133
Military Expenditure (% GDP)	.034	.044	.089	−.565	.003	−.025	110
Inflation	−.156[+]	−.043[+]	−.081	−1.117*	.013	.048[+]	124
Central Bank Independence	−.022	.339**	−.606*	.023	.013	.008	100
Credit to Private Sector	.549**	.963**	.761*	.170	.418**	.164	104
Credit by Financial Sector	.267**	.574**	.371	.132	.099	.076	104
Financial Freedom	–	–	–	–	−.059	−.069	97
Investment Freedom	–	–	–	–	.133	.005	97
Average of Short-Run Correlates					.04	.03	
Population in 1900	−.230[+]	−.145	.472	.472*	−.109	−.068	58
Legal Origin (UK)	.059	.039	.533*	.056	.031	.002	136
Legal Origin (France)	−.213**	−.191**	−.600**	−.308[+]	.128[+]	.059	136
Legal Origin (Germany)	.127*	.137*	.187	.480*	.024	.066*	136
Legal Origin (Scandinavia)	.283**	.234**	−.076	−.065	−.022	−.015	136
Legal Origin (Socialist)	−.132	−.089	.007	.345*	−.001	−.031	136
Log Settler Mortality Rate	−.610**	−.569**	−.774*	−.426	.473*	.243	84
Mean Temperature (1986)	−.583**	−.476**	.024	.381	−.014	−.181[+]	60
Distance from Coast	.239[+]	.329**	.806*	.130	.192	.043	61
Ethno-linguistic Fractionalization	−.413**	−.441**	−.555*	.029	.229[+]	−.013	124
Landlocked	−.200**	−.142*	.301	.183	−.060	−.026	129
Latitude	.494**	.481**	.618*	.059	.305*	.029	129
Tropical Climate	−.601**	−.518**	−.083	.752**	.050	−.390*	89

Table 4
Continued

	δ_{1985}	δ_{2005}	λ_{1985}	λ_{2005}	$\delta\lambda_{1985}$	$\delta\lambda_{2005}$	N
Average of Long-Run Correlates					.09	−.02	
Power Distance	−.588**	−.513**	−.017	.679**	.010	−.348**	60
Individualism	.573**	.459**	−.574⁺	−.626**	−.329⁺	−.287*	60
Masculinity	.023	−.006	−.247	−.092	−.006	.001	60
Uncertainty Avoidance	−.040	−.105	−.492⁺	−.114	.020	.012	60
Indulgence	.242*	.292**	.783**	.458*	.190⁺	.134*	69
Long-term Orientation	.412**	.297**	−.092	−.268	−.038	−.080	70
Average of Culture Determinants					−.03	−.09	

Note: This table reports the coefficients of the cross-sectional regressions of correlates on income and of (10-year average) growth on correlates, in 1985*–2005*. In particular, the coefficients δ and λ are estimated from the following regressions: $\Delta \log(\text{GDPpc}_{i,t}) = \beta_t \log(\text{GDPpc}_{i,t}) + \lambda_t I_{i,t}/SD(I_{1985}) + \alpha_t + \epsilon_{i,t}. I_{i,t}/SD(I_{1985}) = \delta_t \log(\text{GDPpc}_{i,t}) + \nu_t + \epsilon_{i,t}$. Columns 2 and 3 report the cross-section relationship δ estimated estimated in 1985* and 2005*. Columns 4 and 5 report regressions of income growth in the next decade on correlates, controlling for income at the start of the decade, in 1985*–95 and 2005*–15. Columns 6 and 7 report the difference between absolute converge and conditional convergence constructed using the standard omitted variable bias formula by constructing the product $\lambda\delta$. Column 8 reports the number of observations in the specifications, respectively. The sample only includes countries with nonmissing correlate variables in 1985. Missing entries correspond to correlates that are standardized each year: the standardization makes comparisons over time of λ and δ difficult to interpret but cancel out for the product $\lambda\delta$.
⁺$p < .10$.
*$p < .05$.
**$p < .01$.

effect of correlates on growth—we are more sympathetic to the view of Acemoglu and Molina (2022) and agree that including country fixed effects may make sense, although our results in Section II point to shortcomings of that framework too. Our exercise, without country fixed effects, has the advantage of providing an out-of-sample test of sorts for the predictive power of policies and institutions identified as important in the 1990s literature. With a limited sample size and many potential covariates, the growth-regressions literature is vulnerable to overfitting; events after the publication of papers provide an out-of-sample data set. In 20 years, we could run a similar exercise to test the correlates and identification strategies proposed more recently.

Growth-regression coefficients, the λ_t in equation (4), fell somewhat in magnitude over time for human capital and other Solow fundamentals (the investment rate and the population growth rate), but they were correlated. Education, for example, strongly predicts higher economic growth at a roughly similar magnitude in decades 1985–95 and 2005–15. A 1-standard deviation increase in educational attainment predicts 0.96% annualized GDP growth in 1985–95, and the number falls to 0.70% in 2005–15. Countries in which females and males have more equal access to education resources have grown faster: a 1-standard deviation reduction in the gender gap (in schooling years) predicts 0.55% higher GDP growth in 1985–95 and 0.26% in 2005–15.

In contrast, coefficients on short-run correlates beyond the enhanced Solow fundamentals (those correlates that can change over relatively short horizons) fell more substantially from 1985 to 2005, with essentially zero correlation between the two periods. Table 4, columns 4 and 5 report λ_{1985} and λ_{2005}.[19] Figure 6 plots λ_{2005} reestimated with the same country sample[20] 2 decades later (2005–15). The slope of the correlate-growth relationships has shrunk toward zero and the slope of fitted line in figure 6 is only 0.206.

Long-run correlates (those that can only change slowly, if at all) and culture fall in between Solow fundamentals and short-run correlates in the persistence of their correlation with growth. Figure 6, panel B shows that the slope of the long-run correlate-growth relationship has shrunk toward zero with 0.408 as the slope of the fitted line. However, the correlate-growth relationship is more stable for culture with 0.739 as the slope of the fitted line.

As we did for correlate-income slopes, whereas the 1985-versus-2005 comparison is our main specification, in figure A19 we also report the trends in the growth-correlate slopes since 1960, averaged within each group of correlates. We apply the same normalization as for correlate-income slopes, namely we first renormalize the correlates such that their correlate-income slope is positive in 1985 (i.e., we multiply the correlate by −1, throughout, if the slope is negative in 1985). Again, as many correlates are not available before 1985, and the set of countries for which correlates is available is growing, we repeat the exercise for multiple balanced panels, one from the start of each decade. The figures support the results above, showing that the flattening of growth-regression coefficients from 1985 to 2005 reflects a gradual trend over that period. It also appears that growth-regression coefficients peaked around the 1980s, but we do not place too much weight on that result, as data availability is sparse prior to then, especially for short-run correlates.

Why did growth-regression coefficients shrink as correlates converged? We provide two hypotheses, for future work. First, many correlates, both observable and unobservable, are likely correlated with each other, so that the regression coefficient on any one will reflect not just its underlying causal impact but also its correlation with others. The rapid convergence in correlates may have been associated with a reduction in the correlation between them, and hence a reduction in this omitted variable bias. Second, correlates may have nonlinear effects: perhaps policies and institutions used to matter when there were large differences across countries, but now that they have converged, any remaining differences matter less.

D. Shrinking Gap between Conditional and Unconditional Convergence

One response to the failure of unconditional convergence was to move to the idea of conditional convergence—convergence conditional upon possible determinants of steady-state income, such as policies and institutions (Barro and Sala-i-Martin 1992)—which has been widely supported in the data (Durlauf et al. 2005). This suggests a natural question: does the shift toward unconditional convergence represent a shrinking of the gap between conditional and unconditional convergence, for example, due to rapid convergence of correlates, or did conditional convergence itself became faster? Globalization could have resulted in either. For example, international institutions have promoted convergence across many policies, and higher capital mobility has increased capital inflows into some lower-income countries, potentially reducing the effect of conditioning on such correlates, whereas at the same time the spread of technology and of production processes through increased trade may have made convergence conditional on correlates faster.

Univariate

While conditional convergence regressions often condition on multiple correlates, our baseline specification conditions on one variable at a time, because of the difficulty in forming a balanced panel with multiple correlates, and to tie our hands in terms of specification search. When conditioning on a single correlate, according to the omitted variable bias formula, the gap between unconditional and conditional convergence can be written as the product of the correlate-income slope δ and the growth-correlate slope λ.

Figure 7 and table 4 report the changes in this gap from 1985 to 2005. Correlate-by-correlate, qualitatively the trend in the effect of conditioning

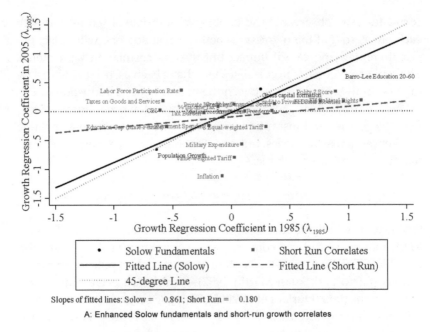

Slopes of fitted lines: Solow = 0.861; Short Run = 0.180

A: Enhanced Solow fundamentals and short-run growth correlates

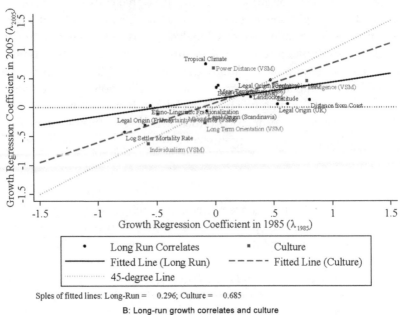

Sples of fitted lines: Long-Run = 0.296; Culture = 0.685

B: Long-run growth correlates and culture

Fig. 6. Growth-correlate of growth slopes, 1985 versus 2005. This figure is a scatter plot of the growth-regression coefficients for different correlates, in 1985 versus 2005, that is, the coefficients from regressions of average growth in (log) income per capita in the next

is similar to that of the growth-regression coefficients: Solow fundamentals have the most stable effect, long-run correlates and culture are intermediate, and short-run institutions have the least stable effect. However, what is harder to see from this figure but can be seen clearly in figure A20, is that the effect on conditioning has on average shrunk to around zero for short-run and long-run correlates since 1980, whereas for Solow fundamentals and culture it has remained more steady. The same figure also shows that the effect of conditioning on correlates increased substantially between 1960 and 1980, although for a much smaller set of countries and correlates.

Multivariate

Many of the classic conditional convergence regressions control for a large set of policies and institutions. In attempting to run such multivariate regressions, there is a harsh trade-off in constructing the country-year sample, between the number of observations and the number of available correlates, which is why we consider the univariate results our main results in this section. However, to attempt to run a multivariate version, we (somewhat arbitrarily) selected a sample of 72 countries and include the following institutional variables: Polity 2 score, Freedom House political rights, Freedom House civil liberty, private investment ratio, government spending, inflation, credit provided to the private sector, credit by the financial sector, Barro-Lee educational attainment, and gender gap in schooling years.

Figure 8 plots both the conditional and unconditional convergence coefficients, from 1985 to 2007. We see that although the unconditional convergence coefficient has trended down, there has been no clear trend in the conditional convergence coefficient, and the gap between the two has closed substantially. Thus, in terms of what has driven the change in unconditional convergence, unconditional convergence has become

---

decade, on correlates, controlling for baseline (log) income per capita. Namely, the y-axis is λ_{2005}, and the x-axis λ_{1985}, from equation (4), which is the following regression: $100\{[\log(\text{GDPpc})_{i,t+10} - \log(\text{GDPpc})_{i,t}]/10\} = \beta_t \log(\text{GDPpc})_{i,t} + \lambda_t[I_{i,t}/SD(I_{1985})] + \alpha_t + \epsilon_{i,t}$. λ_{1985} and λ_{2005} are estimated using a balanced panel, balanced separately for each correlate. The solid lines are the fitted lines of the scatter plot; the numbers beneath the plots refer to their slopes. The dashed lines are the 45-degree line, as a benchmark. Panel A presents results for Solow fundamentals and short-run correlates; panel B presents results for long-run correlates and culture. We exclude those correlates that are normalized each period and hence are not comparable over time. A color version of this figure is available online.

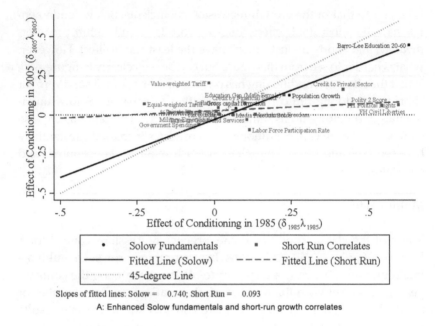

Slopes of fitted lines: Solow = 0.740; Short Run = 0.093

A: Enhanced Solow fundamentals and short-run growth correlates

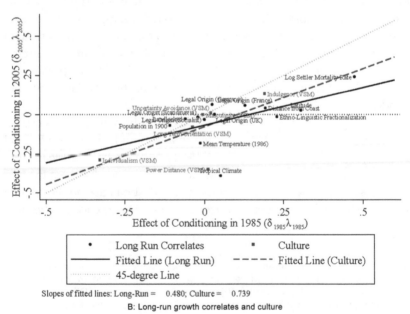

Slopes of fitted lines: Long-Run = 0.480; Culture = 0.739

B: Long-run growth correlates and culture

Fig. 7. Gap between unconditional and conditional convergence (univariate), 1985 versus 2005. This figure plots the gap between unconditional and (univariate) conditional convergence, in 1985 versus 2005, across different correlates. In particular, it plots

closer to conditional convergence. We do not find clear trends in conditional convergence itself, although that is not our focus.

Table 5 reports the coefficients for growth in 3 decades from 1985 to 2015. From 1985 to 1995, correlates explain substantial variation in economic growth and convert absolute divergence to conditional convergence. The 10 correlates jointly take down the coefficient from 0.42 ($t = 1.67$) to −0.816 ($t = −1.79$). In 2005–15, the unconditional economic growth rate is −0.79% ($t = −5.16$). Correlates still effectively cut the convergence rate to −1.14% ($t = −4.63$), however, no sign indicates conditional convergence is faster than 2 decades ago.

These results suggest an interpretation that is consistent with neoclassical growth models. Conditional convergence has held throughout the period. Absolute convergence did not hold initially, but, as policies, institutions, and human capital have improved in poorer countries, the difference in institutions across countries has shrunk, and their explanatory power with respect to growth and convergence has declined. As a result, the world has converged to absolute convergence because absolute convergence has converged to conditional convergence.

V. Conclusion

We document a trend toward absolute convergence since the late-1980s, resulting in absolute convergence since 2000. This trend is consistent with neoclassical growth models and with models in which catch-up growth is easier than growth at the frontier, and inconsistent with the set of endogenous growth models, which predict divergence. While incomes have diverged across countries for centuries (Pritchett 1997), the rapid trend to convergence over the last 20 years suggests something important has changed. Breaking down convergence by income quartiles shows both a growth slowdown at the frontier and a broad increase in the rate of catch-up growth away from the frontier, the breadth of which does not support an explanation in which countries catch up only above a certain income threshold, with more countries recently crossing

---

$\delta_{1985}\lambda_{1985}$ and $\delta_{2005}\lambda_{2005}$, which link together unconditional and conditional convergence through the omitted variable bias formula, equation (5): $\beta_t = \beta_t^* + \delta_t\lambda_t$. Coefficients are estimated using a balanced panel, balanced separately for each correlate. The solid lines are the fitted lines of the scatter plot; the numbers beneath the plots refer to their slopes. The dashed lines are the 45-degree line, as a benchmark. Panel A presents results for Solow fundamentals and short-run correlates; panel B presents results for long-run correlates and culture. A color version of this figure is available online.

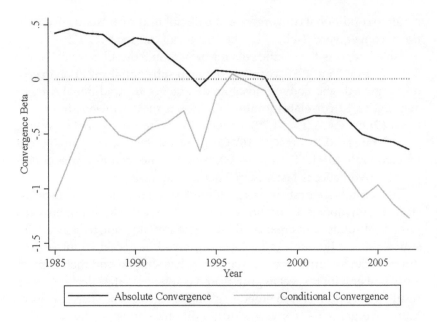

Fig. 8. Absolute convergence converging to conditional convergence (multivariate). The black line represents the absolute convergence β-coefficient, and the gray line represents the conditional convergence β^*-coefficient, using one particular set of correlates to condition on. Choosing the set of correlates is a trade-off between sample size and number of correlates, which leaves a lot of choice to the researcher—one of the reasons we view the univariate results as our main specification. The particular choice here gives a sample of 72 countries, using the following set of correlates: Polity 2 score, Freedom House political rights, Freedom House civil liberty, private investment ratio, government spending, inflation, credit provided to private sector, credit by financial sector, Barro-Lee education attainment, and education gender gap. Minor imputations apply: missing values in institutions are imputed with the latest available data point. The dotted line is the benchmark of no convergence. A color version of this figure is available online.

the threshold, as might be suggested by certain poverty trap models. What could have driven this change: faster catch-up conditional on correlates, for example due to the globalization of production, improved communication, faster technology flows, greater access to (international) finance, and migration; or the convergence of correlates themselves, which could also have followed not only from globalization but also from the end of the Cold War, trends in democratization, the reduction in conflict, and the adoption of the Washington Consensus, among other reasons?

Most correlates of growth and income—policies, institutions, and culture—have converged during the same period, toward those of rich countries. Some of these changes have been gradual, such as changes

Table 5
Absolute and Conditional Convergence in 1985 and 2005

	Annual Growth in GDPpc (1985–1995)				Annual Growth in GDPpc (2005–2015)			
	(1)	(2)	(3)	(4)	(5)	(6)	(7)	(8)
Log GDP PC	.420$^+$	−.447	−.435	−.816	−.794**	−1.215**	−.791**	−1.139**
	(.252)	(.661)	(.457)	(.619)	(.154)	(.205)	(.233)	(.246)
Investment		.298		−.0469		.384		.416
		(.377)		(.478)		(.319)		(.300)
Population growth		−1.034		−1.024		−.392**		−.415**
		(.626)		(.661)		(.129)		(.148)
Barro-Lee Education 20–60		.428		.492		.463$^+$		.535*
		(.525)		(.619)		(.270)		(.267)
Polity 2 Score			−.558	−.916			.693$^+$	.0514
			(.704)	(.728)			(.378)	(.400)
FH Political Rights			1.304	1.567$^+$			−.193	.378
			(.989)	(.931)			(.464)	(.428)
Private Investment			−.184	−.267			.223	.143
			(.332)	(.329)			(.394)	(.344)
Government Spending			−.0168	.0773			−.551*	−.764**
			(.386)	(.415)			(.275)	(.256)
Inflation			−.0994	−.0284			−1.438$^+$	−1.273$^+$
			(.235)	(.243)			(.772)	(.722)
FH Civil Liberties			.0958	−.481			−.0784	−.333
			(.647)	(.749)			(.782)	(.724)
Credit to Private Sector			.915$^+$	.875			.483	.494$^+$
			(.467)	(.531)			(.313)	(.291)
Credit by Financial Sector			−.394	−.546			−.733$^+$	−.798*
			(.507)	(.573)			(.376)	(.368)
Constant	−2.172	5.546	1.213	6.644	9.387**	11.42**	10.90**	12.31**
	(2.230)	(5.458)	(3.313)	(4.687)	(1.471)	(1.732)	(2.277)	(2.306)
Observations	73	73	73	73	113	113	113	113
R^2	.0283	.155	.152	.228	.214	.333	.306	.417

Note: This table reports absolute and conditional convergence regressions, for 1985*–95 and 2005*–15, for the fullest list of Solow and short-run correlates that allow a reasonable sample size of 72 in 1985. The covariates include investment, population growth, Barro-Lee education attainment, Polity 2 score, Freedom House political rights, Freedom House civil liberty, private investment ratio, government spending, inflation, credit provided to private sector, credit by financial sector, and education gender gap. Columns 1–4 report regressions for 1985–95, and columns 5–8 for 2005–15. Column 1 is the absolute convergence regression. Column 2 conditions on the enhanced Solow fundamentals—the fundamental determinants of steady-state income in the Solow model. Column 3 conditions on other policies and institutions and column 4 conditions on both. Robust standard errors are reported in parentheses.
$^+p < .10.$
$^*p < .05.$
$^{**}p < .01.$

in government spending and in fertility, consistent with modernization theory (Inglehart and Baker 2000), and on average the size of the changes has been as predicted by income growth, under the cross-country correlate-income relationship. However, other changes have happened remarkably quickly, such as the adoption of VATs, or marriage equality, or the spread of democracy after the fall of the Soviet Union, and these more rapid changes may be better explained with theories of contagion or technology adoption (Dobbin et al. 2007). While some aspects of convergence happened independently of external forces, international institutions played a role in other aspects of convergence; for example, the International Monetary Fund (IMF) and the World Bank encouraged the adoption of the Washington Consensus (Easterly 2019), and the World Health Organization provides technical guidance and best practice for health policy.

As correlates and growth have changed, so have the relationships between them: the coefficients of growth regressions. All types of correlates considered—Solow fundamentals, other short-run correlates, long-run correlate, and culture—have seen their growth coefficients shrink. Most robust are the Solow fundamentals, for which a regression of the coefficients in 2005 on those of 1985 has a coefficient of 0.86. Long-run correlates and culture were somewhat stable, whereas short-run correlates' coefficients in 2005 bore little relation to their coefficients in 1985.

As a result of this shrinking in growth-regression coefficients, the gap between unconditional and conditional convergence has also shrunk substantially. Absolute convergence has converged toward conditional convergence, a central prediction of neoclassical growth theory that has held throughout the period. In the parlance of club convergence, policies and institutions have (partially) converged, so that now more countries are "in the convergence club."

What drove these changes since the late 1980s? Why was there not also a trend toward convergence in the preceding 2 decades, when correlates were already converging? And why have growth-regression coefficients shrunk since? While faster catch-up conditional on correlates may be part of the explanation for the trend in convergence (although not our focus, we do not find evidence of it), and the shrinkage in growth-regression coefficients may in part be explained by earlier overfitting, we have focused on the convergence of correlates themselves, the potential determinants of steady-state income.

Our preferred narrative in terms of parsimony, which is admittedly speculative, is as follows. Steady-state incomes are determined by a very large number of factors, from the quality of transport infrastructure, to the quality of education systems, to the quality of bankruptcy law. Many of these determinants are correlated with each other, and although some are observable to us, many are not. As such, the regression coefficient on any observable determinant will not just reflect its underlying causal impact but also patterns of correlation with unobservable determinants. Since the fall of the Soviet Union in 1991 and the adoption of the Washington Consensus, there has been rapid convergence in observable policies and institutions (perhaps endogenously as policy makers reacted to the 1990s growth literature), explaining the shrinking gap between absolute and conditional convergence. If they have simultaneously become less correlated with the unobservable determinants, it would also explain the shrinking growth-regression coefficients, although then it would also likely predict slower conditional convergence, counterfactually. However, unobserved factors might also be converging, pushing toward faster convergence conditional on observables: just as international institutions like the World Bank and IMF are promoting convergence in economic policy, a host of other international bodies are promoting convergence on policies from civil aviation, to smoking (the World Health Organization), to standardized testing in schools (the Program for International Student Assessment), and the globalization of education and media exposure of elites is likely leading to convergence across many factors. An alternative narrative is that correlates have nonlinear effects: policies and institutions used to matter, but now that they have converged, any remaining differences matter less. While we found little evidence for such nonlinearities in our exploratory work, we were underpowered, and the hypothesis merits further investigation.

Do these results give cause for optimism or pessimism regarding whether changes in policies and institutions can lead to catch-up growth? Of course, our results are not causal, so care should be taken here, and further work is needed to assess the causal consequences of the convergence in correlates documented here. Even without taking a causal stance, the results push back on an interpretation of the persistence literature, as indicating that steady-state income is determined only by deep, persistent determinants, which are hard to change. We have shown evidence of convergence in culture, suggesting that even persistent determinants may change relatively rapidly. If we do entertain that our growth regressions at least partially reflect a causal relationship, then our results suggest that malleable policies and institutions did matter for growth in the 1990s, and that when they subsequently (partially) converged, there was a shift to income convergence. Yet malleable policies now seem to have less explanatory power, whereas long-run correlates (and especially Solow fundamentals) have continued to be correlated with growth.

While we cannot predict whether absolute convergence will continue, we can discuss reasons to believe that it may or may not. On the one hand, there are at least two reasons for pessimism. First, both Acemoglu and Molina (2022) and Pande and Enevoldsen (2022) understandably point to recent deteriorations in democracy. This is of concern in its own right, but if democracy is the key correlate, from which others follows, this may undermine the convergence of other correlates. Second, as discussed in Pande and Enevoldsen (2022), the economic costs of climate change are growing and faced disproportionately by developing countries. These costs—both the direct costs and, perhaps more importantly, the indirect costs of induced conflict and emigration—will be a force against convergence going forward. While these are reasons for pessimism, there are also substantial reasons for optimism. Conditional convergence is a robust phenomenon across many settings, and so if the convergence of correlates continues, absolute convergence is a reasonable hypothesis. In the 1960s, there were the growing pains from postcolonial independence, and in the 1980s there was the breakup of the Soviet Union, both periods in which transitional forces may have eclipsed trends toward convergence. In the more stable, postcolonial world order since the 1980s, we observe rapid convergence of correlates, a shrinking of the gap between unconditional convergence and conditional convergence, and ultimately, unconditional convergence.

Appendix

Figures and Tables

A.1. Convergence in Income

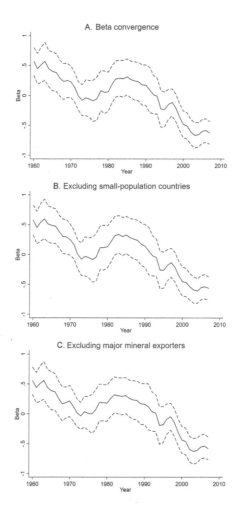

Fig. A1. Robustness of β-convergence to excluding small countries and major mineral exporters. These graphs show the robustness of the β-convergence plot to natural changes in the set of countries: (*A*) is the original, main specification; (*B*) excludes countries whose maximum population during the period was <200,000; and (*C*) excludes countries whose natural resources accounted for at least 75% of GDP (as reported in the World Development Indicators) at some time during the period. Dashed lines represent the 90% confidence intervals.

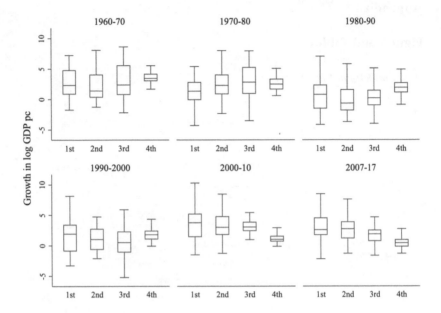

Fig. A2. Boxplot of growth versus country quartile, split by decade. These are boxplots of the country's average growth in GDP per capita for a decade. Each facet shows 1 decade. Within a facet, the plot shows how decade-average growth varied by quartile of baseline GDP per capita. The top of the box is the 75th percentile of average growth in that quartile, the center is the median (the 50th percentile), and the bottom is the 25th percentile. The whiskers represent the corresponding maximum and minimum. The last decade starts in 2007 because our data run to 2017. A color version of this figure is available online.

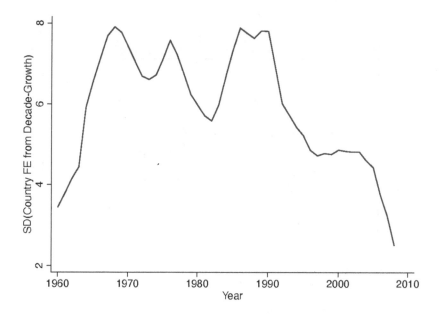

Fig. A3. σ-convergence of country fixed effects. The figure plots the standard deviations of (decade) country-fixed effects in the convergence regression, by year (eq. [2] but with a rolling 10-year window). A color version of this figure is available online.

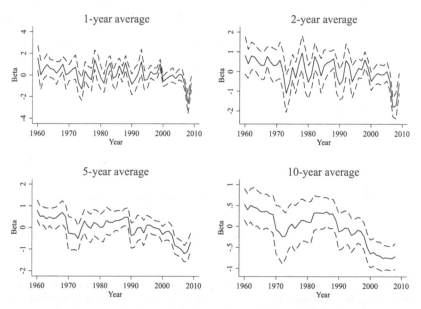

Fig. A4. Robustness of β-convergence to averaging period. This figure shows robustness to the averaging period used for β-convergence. In particular, the plots show the β-convergence coefficients using subsequent 1-, 2-, 5-, and 10-year average growth rates.

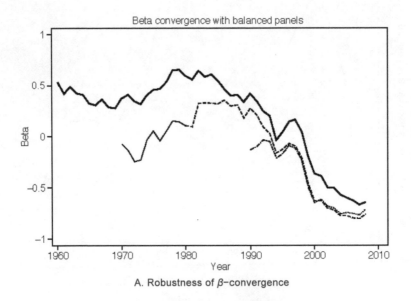

A. Robustness of β-convergence

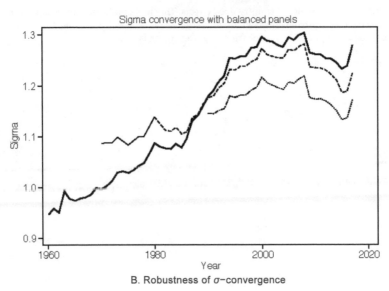

B. Robustness of σ-convergence

Fig. A5. Robustness of convergence to balanced panel. This figure shows robustness of the convergence coefficients to using balanced panels. Since countries are joining our data set over time, we plot five different curves, one starting at the beginning of each decade. A given decades curve shows the evolution of the convergence coefficients going forward from the start of that decade, based upon the constant set of countries that were in the data set at the start of that decade. A color version of this figure is available online.

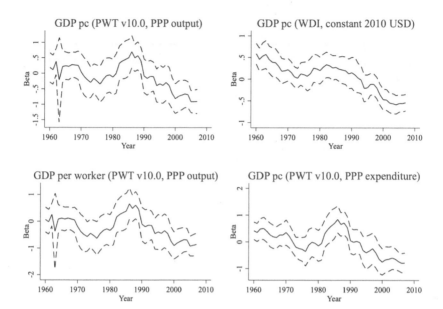

Fig. A6. Robustness of β-convergence to measure of output. This figure shows robustness to the outcome used for β-convergence. Our baseline specification uses GDP pc in constant PPP output, from the PWT v10.0.

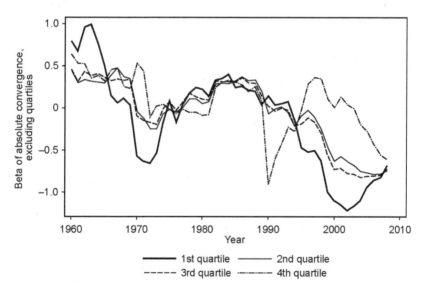

Fig. A7. Catch-up of the poor or slowdown of the rich? β-convergence when excluding countries from different quartiles of per-capita income. This figure reports the sensitivity of the absolute convergence coefficient β to excluding different quartiles of wealth from the sample. The legend refers to which wealth quartile is being dropped, where the first is the poorest. A color version of this figure is available online.

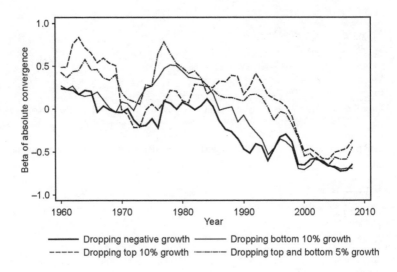

Fig. A8. Disasters, growth miracles, and stagnation. β-convergence when excluding outlying growth rates. This figure reports the sensitivity of the absolute convergence coefficient β to excluding countries based on their subsequent 10-year growth (which is conditioning on an outcome variable, but we report here for diagnostic purposes). The legend refers to which countries are being dropped. A color version of this figure is available online.

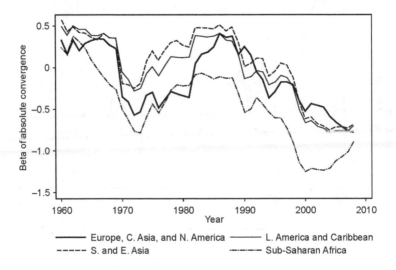

Fig. A9. Which regions are converging? β-convergence when excluding regions. This figure reports the sensitivity of the absolute convergence coefficient β to excluding different regions. The legend refers to which region is being dropped. A color version of this figure is available online.

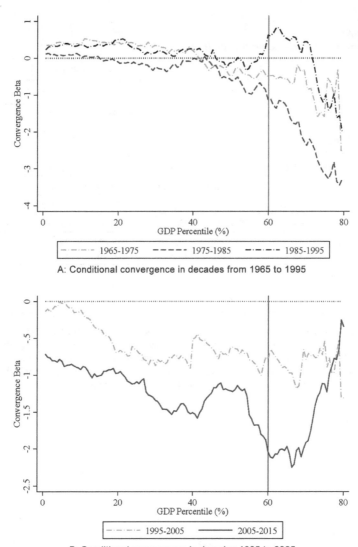

Fig. A10. Club convergence by income. This figure plots β convergence conditional on the rank of GDP per capita (>X%), from absolute convergence β ($X = 0$) to β conditional in top 20% income percentile ($X = 80$). Panel A reports the convergence β conditional on income for the 3 decades in the preconvergence era: 1965–75, 1975–85, and 1985–95. Panel B reports the β for the 2 decades in the postconvergence era: 1995–2005 and 2005–15. The vertical lines imply the cutoff for the country subsample in the top 40% income percentile. The dotted lines are the benchmark of no convergence. A color version of this figure is available online.

Table A1
Convergence β with Country Fixed Effects

	Panel A: Average Growth in Next Decade ($\Delta t = 10$)				
	1960–1969	1970–1979	1980–1989	1990–1999	2000–2007
log(GDPpc)	−7.794***	−7.990***	−8.552***	−10.38***	−9.186***
	(.896)	(.820)	(.685)	(.625)	(.849)
Year FE and					
Country FE	Y	Y	Y	Y	Y
Observations	1,107	1,370	1,371	1,600	1,440

	Panel B: Growth in the Next Year ($\Delta t = 1$)					
	(1)	(2)	(3)	(4)	(5)	(6)
	1960–1969	1970–1979	1980–1989	1990–1999	2000–2009	2010–2017
log(GDPpc)	−21.56***	−15.30***	−15.76***	−19.99***	−12.86***	−11.52*
	(3.561)	(3.419)	(3.366)	(3.698)	(3.481)	(4.570)
Year FE and						
Country FE	Y	Y	Y	Y	Y	Y
Observations	1,107	1,370	1,371	1,600	1,600	1,120

Note: This table reports the β-convergence estimation with both country and year fixed effects (FE) included. $\log(GDP_{i,t+\Delta t}) - \log(GDP_{i,t}) = \beta \log(GDP_{i,t}) + \mu_t + \gamma_i + \epsilon_{i,t}$. The data sample is 1960–2017. Each column reports the β coefficient estimated for each decade. Panel A reports average growth in the next decade ($\Delta t = 10$), and panel B report growth in the next year ($\Delta t = 1$). Standard deviations are clustered at the country level.
*$p < .05$.
**$p < .01$.
***$p < .001$.

A.2. Convergence in Correlates of Growth

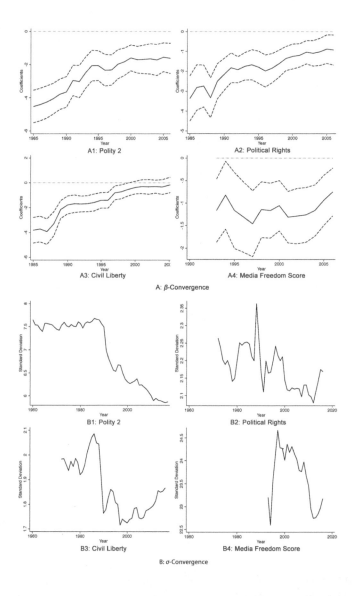

Fig. A11. Convergence in political institutions. Political institution measures include Polity 2 score from Center of Systematic Peace (1960–2015), Freedom House political rights score (1973–2015), Freedom House civil liberty score (1973–2015), Press Freedom score (1995–2015), and WGI political stability. The top panels (*A1–A4*) report results of β-convergence. The bottom panels (*B1–B4*) report results of σ-convergence. Dashed lines represent the 90% confidence intervals. A color version of this figure is available online.

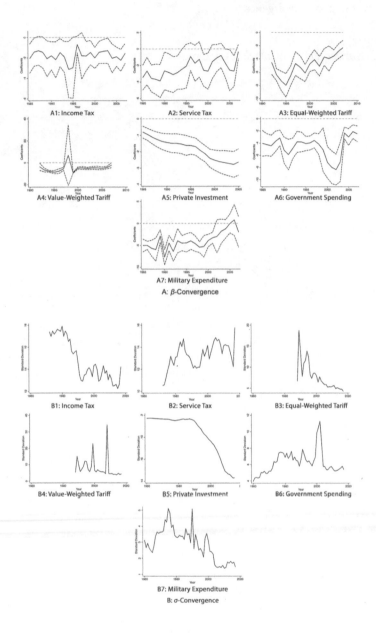

Fig. A12. Convergence in fiscal policies. Fiscal policy measures include tax on income and capital gain (% tax revenue), tax on goods and service (% tax revenue), tax burden score, equal-weighted tariff rate, value-weighted tariff rate, private investment (% total investment), government spending (% GDP), and military expenditure (% GDP). The top panels (*A1–A7*) report results of β-convergence. The bottom panels (*B1–B7*) report results of σ-convergence. Dashed lines represent the 90% confidence intervals. A color version of this figure is available online.

398

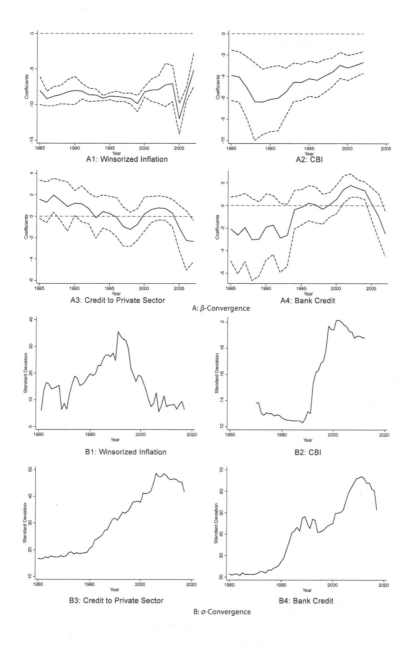

Fig. A13. Convergence in financial institutions. Financial institution measures include winsorized inflation, CBI, credit to private sector, credit by financial sector (bank credit), and financial freedom score. The annual inflation data are winsorized by 100% to reduce the impact of outliers. The top panels (*A1–A4*) report results of β-convergence. The bottom panels (*B1–B4*) report results of σ-convergence. Dashed lines represent the 90% confidence intervals. A color version of this figure is available online.

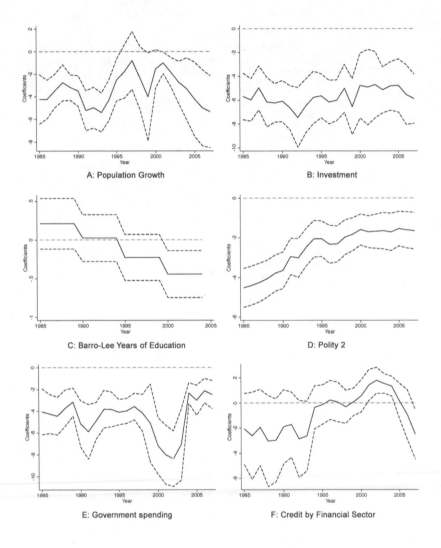

Fig. A14. Convergence in correlates of growth. This figure plots the correlate convergence β_t as a function of year t estimated from regressing the correlate change in the next decade (from year t to $t + 10$) on the current correlate (in year t): $100 \ [(Inst_{i,t+10} - Inst_{i,t})/10] = \beta_t Inst_{t,i} + \mu_t + \epsilon_{t,i}$. Five institutions are included: Polity 2 score, rule of law (WGI), government spending (% GDP), credit provided by the financial sector, and Barro-Lee education attainment of age cohorts from 20 to 60. The dashed horizontal lines are benchmark $\beta_t = 0$. A color version of this figure is available online.

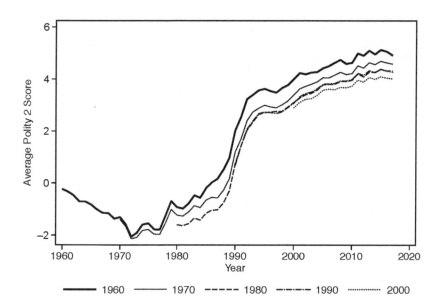

Fig. A15. Polity 2 score with fixed country samples. Average Polity 2 score with the country samples available in 1960, 1970, 1980, 1990, and 2000. A color version of this figure is available online.

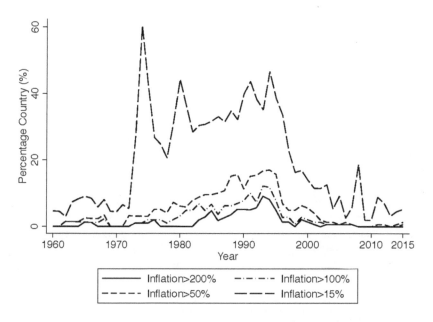

Fig. A16. Hyperinflation over time. This figure plots four series of the percentage of countries experience inflation above 200%, 100%, 50%, and 15%.

Table A2
Short-run Correlate Convergence: Joint Tests

	Chi-squared	p-value	Number of Institutions
	Panel A: 1996–2006		
Labor force	4.600	.100	2
Political institutions	139.749	0	4
Fiscal policies	512.293	0	7
Financial institutions	216.534	0	4
	Panel B: 2006–2016		
Labor force	21.405	0	2
Political institutions	65.906	0	4
Fiscal policies	239.728	0	7
Financial institutions	284.074	0	4

Note: This table reports the joint significance test for 2 decades, 1996–2006 and 2006–16. The null hypothesis is that there is no correlate convergence in all Solow fundamentals and short-run correlates (all βs are zeros). 1996 is the first year, and we have a full data for all institutional variables. Barro-Lee education and private investment are extended to 2016 with the latest value available in our data (2010 and 2014, respectively).

Table A3
Polity 2 Score Change by Decade

Decade	Increase in Polity 2 (%)	Decrease in Polity 2 (%)	Unchanged Polity 2 (%)	Observations
1960–70	19.4	30.1	50.5	103
1970–80	23.8	25.4	50.8	122
1980–90	37.3	9.7	53.0	134
1990–2000	52.9	10.1	37.0	134
2000–10	31.6	13.3	55.1	158
2010–15	19.3	6.8	73.9	161

Note: This table reports the portion of countries with an increase, decrease, and unchanged Polity 2 score for each decade: 1960–70, 1970–80, 1980–90, 1990–2000, 2000–10, and 2010–15.

Table A4
Democratization and Income by Decade

	1960–1970	1970–1980	1980–1990	1990–2000	2000–2010	2010–2015
	(1)	(2)	(3)	(4)	(5)	(6)
	Panel A: Dummy {Increase in Polity 2 Score}					
log(GDP)	−.403**	.0575	.0707	−.468***	−.137	−.0173
	(−2.36)	(.44)	(.63)	(−3.99)	(−1.46)	(−.18)
Observations	91	114	137	169	193	203
	Panel B: Dummy {Decrease in Polity 2 Score}					
log(GDP)	−.328*	−.690***	−.438*	−.0895	−.292*	−.280
	(−1.68)	(−3.32)	(−1.81)	(−.47)	(−1.79)	(−1.22)
Observations	68	96	114	127	154	158

Note: This table reports the logit regressions of dummies of Polity 2 score increase or decrease on log(GDP). The dependent variable in panel A is the indicator dummy of the increase in Polity 2 score, and the sample excludes the countries with perfect democracy (where the score increase is not possible). The dependent variable in panel B is the indicator dummy of the decrease in Polity 2 score, and the sample excludes the countries with perfect dictatorship (where the score decrease is not possible). t-statistics are in parentheses.
*$p < .05$.
**$p < .01$.
***$p < .001$.

Table A5
Culture Variables from the WVS

Variable	WVS Question ID	Question Content
Trust	A165	Generally speaking, would you say that most people can be trusted or that you need to be very careful in dealing with people?
Perception on inequality	E035	Incomes should be made more equal/ we need larger income differences as incentives for individual effort
Politics—Respect for Authority	E018	Greater respect for authority (Good/ Don't mind/Bad)
Interest in Politics	E023	How interested would you say you are in politics?
Political actions	E026	Whether you might do the political action or would never under any circumstances do it? Joining in boycotts
Importance of politics	A004	How important it is in your life? Politics
Importance of Family	A001	How important it is in your life? Family

Table A5
Continued

Variable	WVS Question ID	Question Content
Importance of Work	A005	How important it is in your life? Work
Religion	A006	How important it is in your life? Religion
Tradition	B016/A198	Tradition is important to this person/which one is more important? Tradition or economic growth.

Note: The list of WVS questions used to study the dynamics of culture.

Table A6
Convergence in Culture using the WVSs

Cultural Variable	Convergence β	Sample Size
Trust	−.00645	
	(.008)	33
Perception on Inequality	−.0265*	
	(.0123)+	32
Politics—Respect for Authority	−.0177*	
	(.0083)+	32
Interest in Politics	−.0269*	
	(.0104)+	31
Political Actions (Boycott)	−.0214**	
	(.0051)*	33
Importance of Politics	−.0184*	
	(.0078)+	33
Importance of Family	−.0435**	
	(.0085)*	33
Importance of Work	−.0329**	
	(.0111)*	33
Religion	.00376	33
	(.0048)	
Tradition	−.0708**	
	(.0131)*	33

Note: This table reports β-convergence regressions for country-level changes in cultural traits in the WVSs. Country-level traits are calculated as the population-weighted average of the traits reported in the WVS. The sample is countries that are surveyed both in wave 3 (1995–98) and wave 6 (2010–14) of the WVS. To adjust for the different survey frequency, we take the annualized change. Robust standard errors are reported in parentheses.
+$p < .10$.
*$p < .05$.
**$p < .01$.

A.3. Linking Converging Income with Convergence of Its Correlates

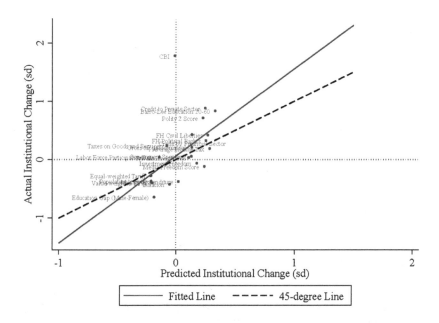

Fig. A17.   Actual and predicted change in correlates of growth from 1985 to 2015. This figure plots the actual average correlate change from 1985 to 2015 versus the predicted average correlate change due to GDP growth, predicted using the GDP-correlate relationship in 1985, which is estimated by the following regression: $Inst_{i,1985}/SD(Inst_{1985}) = \delta_{1985} \log(GDPpc)_{i,1985} + \nu_{1985} + \epsilon_{i,1985}$. The predicted correlate change (on X-axis) is defined as $\delta_{1985} mean_i(\log (GDPpc)_{i,2015} - \log(GDPpc)_{i,1985})$. The actual correlate change (on Y-axis) is defined as $mean_i(Inst_{i,2015} - Inst_{i,1985}/SD(Inst_{1985}))$. The solid line is the fitted line of all correlates. The dashed line is the 45-degree degree line as a benchmark. A color version of this figure is available online.

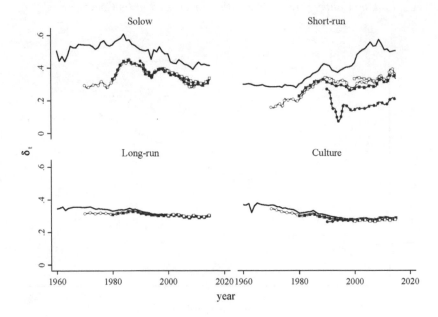

Fig. A18. Trends in relationship between income and correlates of growth (δ). These figures plot δ_t—the slope of the relationship between income and correlates of growth—averaged across the different correlates. Each line represents a balanced panel, so that, for example, the line starting in 1960 is estimated from those country-correlate pairs for which data were available in 1960. A color version of this figure is available online.

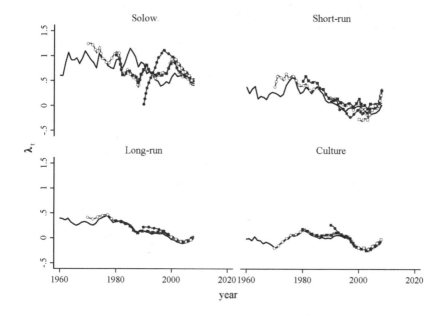

Fig. A19. Trends in relationship between growth and correlates of growth (λ). These figures plot λ_t—the growth-regression coefficient, controlling for baseline income—averaged across the different correlates. Each line represents a balanced panel, so that, for example, the line starting in 1960 is estimated from those country-correlate pairs for which data were available in 1960. A color version of this figure is available online.

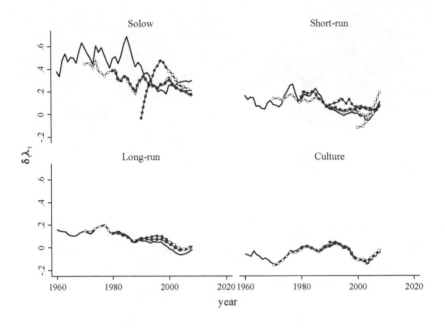

Fig. A20. Trend in difference between unconditional and conditional convergence, univariate ($\delta\lambda$). These figures plot $\delta_t\lambda_t$—the difference between unconditional and conditional convergence—averaged across the different correlates. Each line is estimated from balanced panels of correlate-country pairs, so that, for example, the line starting in 1960 is the average of those country-correlate coefficients for which data were available starting in 1960, and each country-correlate coefficient is estimated for the set of countries for which income data and that specific correlate were available in 1960. A color version of this figure is available online.

Endnotes

Authors' email addresses: Michael Kremer (kremerassistant@uchicago.edu), Jack Willis (jack.willis@columbia.edu), Yang You (yangyou@hku.hk). William Goffredo Felice Labasi-Sammartino, Stephen Nyarko, and especially Malavika Mani provided excellent research assistance. We thank the two discussants, Daron Acemoglu and Rohini Pande, as well as Robert Barro, Brad DeLong, Steven Durlauf, Suresh Naidu, Tommaso Porzio, and seminar audiences at the Portuguese Economics Association, NEUDC, HKUST, the IMF, and Berkeley. For acknowledgments, sources of research support, and disclosure of the authors' material financial relationships, if any, please see https://www.nber.org/books-and-chapters/nber-macroeconomics-annual-2021-volume-36/converging-convergence.

1. Our base specification uses income per capita adjusted for PPP, from the Penn World Tables v10.0, but a similar trend is found using income per capita from the WDIs, measured in constant 2010 USD, and also when using income per worker.

2. Obviously we need to wait another 20 years to perform similar out-of-sample tests of the recent literature. Maseland (2021), in a related paper, studies long-run trends in the relationships between long-run correlates and income, using the trends to distinguish different models of growth.

3. The social science literature on the diffusion of policies has proposed four theories for policy diffusion: social construction, coercion, competition, or learning. See Dobbin et al. (2007) for a review.

4. Parallel results for σ-convergence are in figure 1, panel B and figure A5, panel B with a fixed country sample.

5. Specifically, for growth rates we use the variable "rdgpna," real GDP at constant 2017 national prices (2017 USD), and for growth levels we use "rdgpo," output-side real GDP at chained PPPs (2017 USD), as recommended by the PWT user guide.

6. Figure A1 shows the β-convergence after excluding small population countries and major mineral exporters.

7. The dependent variable is the annualized growth—the geometric average growth rate in the next decade.

8. In subsequent robustness exercises, not using PPP adjustments, the trend looks more like a steady trend toward convergence since 1960, except for a major reversal in the 1980s.

9. $X = 0$ corresponds to absolute convergence. X stops by 80, corresponding to the top 20% high-income countries. The sample size would be too small to obtain stable β if X rises above 80.

10. The Press Freedom score ranges from 0 to 100. A high score represents less press freedom in the original data. We transform the data as 100 minus the original data so that high score translates into more press freedom.

11. If data were not available in 1985, we use the earliest available year for the analysis. For example, the rule of law score from WGI starts in 1996. Table 3, col. 4 reports the 1996 average and the baseline year for the correlate convergence β_{Inst} in col. 7 is 1996 as well.

12. Although human capital is not something that can be directly manipulated by policy, many policies can significantly influence educational attainment, such as budgetary decisions, school-building campaigns, curriculum, and minimum school-leaving age.

13. See Krueger and Lindahl (2001) for extensive reviews on micro- and macro-empirical evidence on schooling and growth.

14. In 2010, only nine countries—Switzerland, Denmark, United Kingdom, Iceland, Japan, South Korea, Poland, Singapore, and the United States—have a population with more than 13 years of education. South Korea and Singapore are the only two nations that are above 14 years.

15. WGI political stability scores are rescaled year by year. Thus, β and σ convergences are not well redefined.

16. There is almost surely divergence if we weight countries by their credit market size. Credit growth is highly concentrated in countries with low interest rates and in reserve currencies, e.g., US dollars, Euro, and Japanese yen.

17. Three developed economies—the United States, the United Kingdom, and Japan—are notable exceptions: highly leveraged economies that continue to expand bank credit. Japanese credit was more than 200% of GDP in 1990, and the interest rate dropped below 1% in 1996. The United States and the United Kingdom were both highly leveraged, more than 100% relative to GDP, and continued to increase by approximately another 100%. Similarly, both countries lowered interest rates to near zero after the 2008 financial crisis and the 2020 COVID-19–induced recession. The unprecedented low interest rates further fueled outstanding credit.

18. Table A5 provides the survey question list for each cultural variable.

19. Our time horizon shrinks to 1985–2005 to accommodate the growth regression. Table 4, cols. 2 and 3 report δ_{1985} and δ_{2005}, instead of δ_{2015} discussed in Subsection IV.2.

20. The country sample is selected with valid GDP and correlates data in the starting year. The sample size typically decreases slightly from 1985 to 2005 because some countries vanish in the 2 decades.

References

Acemoglu, D., S. Johnson, and J. A. Robinson. 2001. "The Colonial Origins of Comparative Development: An Empirical Investigation." *American Economic Review* 91 (5): 1369–401.
———. 2005. "Institutions as a Fundamental Cause of Long-run Growth." In *Handbook of Economic Growth*, vol. 1A, ed., P. Aghion and S. N. Durlauf, 385–472. Amsterdam: Elsevier.
Acemoglu, D., S. Johnson, J. A. Robinson, and P. Yared. 2008. "Income and Democracy." *American Economic Review* 98 (3): 808–42.
Acemoglu, D., and C. Molina. 2022. "Comment on 'Converging to Convergence.'" *NBER Macroeconomics Annual* 36 (1): 423–440.
Acemoglu, D., S. Naidu, P. Restrepo, and J. A. Robinson. 2019. "Democracy Does Cause Growth." *Journal of Political Economy* 127 (1): 47–100.
Alesina, A. 1988. "Macroeconomics and Politics." *NBER Macroeconomics Annual* 3:13–52.
Alesina, A., and R. Gatti. 1995. "Independent Central Banks: Low Inflation at No Cost?" *American Economic Review* 85 (2): 196–200.
Alesina, A., P. Giuliano, and N. Nunn. 2013. "On the Origins of Gender Roles: Women and the Plough." *Quarterly Journal of Economics* 128 (2): 469–530.
Alesina, A., and L. H. Summers. 1993. "Central Bank Independence and Macroeconomic Performance: Some Comparative Evidence." *Journal of Money, Credit and Banking* 25 (2): 151–62.
Algan, Y., and P. Cahuc. 2010. "Inherited Trust and Growth." *American Economic Review* 100 (5): 2060–92.
Barro, R. J. 1991. "Economic Growth in a Cross Section of Countries." *Quarterly Journal of Economics* 106 (2): 407–43.
———. 1996. "Democracy and Growth." *Journal of Economic Growth* 1 (1): 1–27.
———. 2012. "Convergence and Modernization Revisited." Technical report no. 18295, NBER, Cambridge, MA.
Barro, R. J., and J.-W. Lee. 1994. "Sources of Economic Growth." *Carnegie-Rochester Conference Series on Public Policy* 40:1–46.
Barro, R. J., and X. Sala-i-Martin. 1992. "Convergence." *Journal of Political Economy* 100 (2): 223–51.
Bernard, A. B., and S. N. Durlauf. 1996. "Interpreting Tests of the Convergence Hypothesis." *Journal of Econometrics* 71 (1–2): 161–73.
Caselli, F., G. Esquivel, and F. Lefort. 1996. "Reopening the Convergence Debate: A New Look at Cross-country Growth Empirics." *Journal of Economic Growth* 1 (3): 363–89.
Clemens, M. A., and M. Kremer. 2016. "The New Role for the World Bank." *Journal of Economic Perspectives* 30 (1): 53–76.
Dell, M. 2010. "The Persistent Effects of Peru's Mining Mita." *Econometrica* 78 (6): 1863–903.
Dobbin, F., B. Simmons, and G. Garrett. 2007. "The Global Diffusion of Public Policies: Social Construction, Coercion, Competition, or Learning?" *Annual Review of Sociology* 33 (1): 449–72.
Durlauf, S. N., P. A. Johnson, and J. R. W. Temple. 2005. "Growth Econometrics." In *Handbook of Economic Growth*, vol. 1A, ed. P. Aghion and S. H. Durlauf, 555–677. Amsterdam: Elsevier.
Easterly, W. 2019. "In Search of Reforms for Growth: New Stylized Facts on Policy and Growth Outcomes." Working Paper no. 26318, NBER, Cambridge, MA.

Fischer, S. 1995. "Central-bank Independence Revisited." *American Economic Review* 85 (2): 201–206.

Frankel, J. A., and D. H. Romer. 1999. "Does Trade Cause Growth?" *American Economic Review* 89 (3): 379–99.

Garriga, A. C. 2016. "Central Bank Independence in the World: A New Data Set." *International Interactions* 42 (5): 849–68.

Glaeser, E. L., R. La Porta, F. Lopez-de-Silanes, and A. Shleifer. 2004. "Do Institutions Cause Growth?" *Journal of Economic Growth* 9 (3): 271–303.

Grier, K., and R. Grier. 2007. "Only Income Diverges: A Neoclassical Anomaly." *Journal of Development Economics* 84 (1): 25–45.

Grilli, V., D. Masciandaro, and G. Tabellini. 1991. "Political and Monetary Institutions and Public Financial Policies in the Industrial Countries." *Economic Policy* 6 (13): 341–92.

Hastie, T., R. Tibshirani, and J. Friedman. 2009. *The Elements of Statistical Learning: Data Mining, Inference, and Prediction.* New York: Springer Science & Business Media.

Inglehart, R., and W. E. Baker. 2000. "Modernization, Cultural Change, and the Persistence of Traditional Values." *American Sociological Review* 65 (1): 19–51.

Johnson, P., and C. Papageorgiou. 2020. "What Remains of Cross-country Convergence?" *Journal of Economic Literature* 58 (1): 129–75.

Krueger, A. B., and M. Lindahl. 2001. "Education for Growth: Why and for Whom?" *Journal of Economic Literature* 39 (4): 1101–36.

Lucas, R. E., Jr. 1988. "On the Mechanics of Economic Development." *Journal of Monetary Economics* 22 (1): 3–42.

Mankiw, N. G., D. Romer, and D. N. Weil. 1992. "A Contribution to the Empirics of Economic Growth." *Quarterly Journal of Economics* 107 (2): 407–37.

Maseland, R. 2021. "Contingent Determinants." *Journal of Development Economics* 151:102654.

Michalopoulos, S., and E. Papaioannou. 2013. "Pre-colonial Ethnic Institutions and Contemporary African Development." *Econometrica* 81 (1): 113–52.

Nunn, N. 2008. "The Long Term Effects of Africa's Slave Trades." *Quarterly Journal of Economics* 123 (1): 139–76.

Pande, R., and N. Enevoldsen. 2022. "Comment on 'Converging to Convergence.'" *NBER Macroeconomics Annual* 36 (1): 411–422.

Patel, D., J. Sandefur, and A. Subramanian. 2021. "The New Era of Unconditional Convergence." Working paper no. 566, Center for Global Development, Washington, DC.

Pritchett, L. 1997. "Divergence, Big Time." *Journal of Economic Perspectives* 11 (3): 3–17.

Rodrik, D. 2012. "Unconditional Convergence in Manufacturing." *Quarterly Journal of Economics* 128 (1): 165–204.

Rogoff, K. 1985. "The Optimal Degree of Commitment to an Intermediate Monetary Target." *Quarterly Journal of Economics* 100 (4): 1169–89.

Romer, P. M. 1986. "Increasing Returns and Long-run Growth." *Journal of Political Economy* 94 (5): 1002–37.

———. 1990. "Endogenous Technological Change." *Journal of Political Economy* 98 (5, Part 2): S71–S102.

Roy, S., M. Kessler, and A. Subramanian. 2016. "Glimpsing the End of Economic History? Unconditional Convergence and the Missing Middle Income Trap." Working Paper no. 438, Center for Global Development, Washington, DC.

Sala-i-Martin, X. X. 1997. "I Just Ran Two Million Regressions." *American Economic Review* 87 (2): 178–83.

Santos, H. C., M. E. W. Varnum, and I. Grossmann. 2017. "Global Increases in Individualism." *Psychological Science* 28 (9): 1228–39.

Squicciarini, M. P., and N. Voigtländer. 2015. "Human Capital and Industrialization: Evidence from the Age of Enlightenment." *Quarterly Journal of Economics* 130 (4): 1825–83.

Young, A. T., M. J. Higgins, and D. Levy. 2008. "Sigma Convergence versus Beta Convergence: Evidence from U.S. County-level Data." *Journal of Money, Credit and Banking* 40 (5): 1083–93.

Comment

Rohini Pande, *Yale University and NBER,* United States of America
Nils Enevoldsen

I. Paper Summary

Neoclassical growth theory posits that countries with access to identical technologies should converge to a common income level. However, an important literature, exemplified by Barro and Sala-i-Martin (1992), tested this prediction using cross-country data from 1960 to 1990 and instead found conditional convergence. That is, poor countries converged in growth to rich countries only after conditioning on policies, institutions, and other country-specific factors such as human capital.

"Converging to Convergence" extends the underlying data series up to 2015, reestimates cross-country growth regressions, and documents a striking change. Since the mid-1980s, there has been a trend toward unconditional convergence culminating in absolute convergence since 2000 (roughly 1% per annum). The paper examines convergence in correlates of growth, and finds that enhanced Solow fundamentals (s, n, h), short-run correlates (political and financial institutions, fiscal policy), and culture all show β-convergence. This evidence, the authors suggest, is supportive of "institutional homogenization" contributing to absolute convergence: short-run growth coefficients diminished because convergence of "development-favored" policies outpaced that of income. Importantly, the same is not true of Solow fundamentals.

The paper is based on an impressive collation of data sets and careful standardization of conditioning variables. Using the original empirical specification developed in Barro and Sala-i-Martin (1992), it documents

© 2022 National Bureau of Economic Research. All rights reserved. Published by The University of Chicago Press for the National Bureau of Economic Research. https://doi .org/10.1086/718673

changing trends and evaluates proximate determinants of the paper. The authors provide a battery of robustness checks and acknowledge the difficulty of identifying causal drivers of the absolute convergence findings. In line with Patel, Sandefur, and Subramanian (2021), they provide three pieces of descriptive evidence on the role of different income quartiles in driving absolute convergence. First, growth rates for richest countries slowed down post-2005, and convergence patterns are weaker if the top income quartile of countries is removed. Second, laggards remain: absolute convergence is stronger if sub-Saharan African countries or the bottom income quartile of countries are removed. Third, there is an "absence of middle-class trap": growth is particularly strong for the second quartile countries.

In their discussion of this paper, Acemoglu and Molina discuss the appropriateness of the original empirical specification if the aim is to evaluate economic relationships. Here, we provide a complementary discussion that examines the implications—both positive and normative—of absolute convergence for individual well-being. We take a development economics perspective and focus on poverty as the relevant welfare metric.

In Section II, we discuss how the time period associated with absolute convergence has also been a period marked by greater clustering of the world's poor within lower middle-income (second quartile) countries and rising within-country inequality. Drawing on recent research, Section III highlights how the changing nature of structural transformation—potentially driven by greater automation of manufacturing—has contributed to these patterns such that today a high share of labor fails to benefit from a more productive manufacturing sector. Thus, if disequalizing growth is to benefit the poor, then institutions that support domestic redistribution are critical. In Section IV, we argue that strong democratic institutions can enable this but there is growing evidence of democratic backsliding—a phenomenon often linked to growing economic inequality. Inequality, combined with weak institutions for redistribution, may limit progress on the poverty reduction front in the coming years, especially in the face of the COVID-19 pandemic. Moreover, a growing incidence of climate breakdowns suggests that the policies that may have helped absolute convergence are likely to be increasingly inadequate in ensuring that growth benefits the poor. Section V concludes.

II. The Changing Distribution of World Poverty

Development economists have long concerned themselves with poor households and with poor countries. For much of the discipline's history, the association was natural: poor countries were predominantly home to poor households, and poor households were predominantly found in poor countries. Thus, countries rising out of poverty should be more or less equivalent to households rising out of poverty.

There are, certainly, income distributions within countries as well. If certain policies narrow the income distribution, this provides another way to reduce household poverty in middle-income countries, even holding mean income fixed. Using household survey data for 118 countries from 1970 to 2010, Dollar and Kraay (2002) and Dollar, Kleineberg, and Kraay (2016) find that the poorest quintile of a country earns on average 7% of its income. Although this proportion varies somewhat between continents, it is invariant across levels of mean income, across decades, and across periods of economic growth and economic crisis. The same result holds when using national accounts income data. "The good news," they conclude, "is that institutions and policies that promote economic growth in general will on average raise incomes of the poor equiproportionally." So long as income shares remain constant, absolute poverty will naturally decline as countries grow.[1] In this view, finding absolute convergence is reassuring: as poor countries grow, so too do the incomes of the poor individuals within those countries. And poor individuals in poor countries make up the world's extreme poor, do they not?

The answer is, increasingly, no. The period since 1980 has seen a weakening correlation between country income and the share of the world's poor in that country. Though country convergence remains monotonically beneficial for poor individuals, its relative importance diminishes as within-country inequality has begun to dominate between-country inequality. In our discussion, we build on the changing profile of world poverty across countries to argue that absolute convergence in an increasingly unequal world is driving a wedge between country incomes and living standards of vulnerable groups, especially within lower middle-income (second quartile) countries.

A. Poor Are Increasingly Living outside Poor Countries

A common presumption is that poor people live in poor countries, many impoverished by colonialism. This was not always the case. Bourguignon and Morrisson (2002) find that in 1820, almost 90% of global inequality was due to within-country inequality rather than between-country inequality. This proportion fell in the subsequent century, and by 1950 within-country inequality accounted for only 40% of global inequality. That proportion remained stable for the next 4 decades. In *The Bottom*

Billion (2007), for instance, Collier argued that 58 countries—largely in sub-Saharan Africa—were home to the majority of the world's impoverished, and it is toward these countries that antipoverty efforts should be directed.

In response, Sumner (2010) coined the "New Bottom Billion," pointing out that by World Bank definitions, three-quarters of the world's poor live in middle-income countries. Indeed, in recent decades, the global income inequality decomposition trend is reversing. World Bank Group (2016) finds that between 1988 and 2013, the proportion of global inequality due to within-country inequality rose from 20% to 35%.[2]

Page and Pande (2018) identify the subset of middle-income countries that contain 1% or more of the world's poor—high-poverty middle-income countries (HiPMIs)—typically in the second quartile of gross domestic product (GDP) per capita. Just five HiPMIs are home to half of the world's poorest: India, Nigeria, Bangladesh, Indonesia, and Kenya (see fig. 1). Although the mean incomes of these countries are not among the lowest in the world, the trends of inequality within them have an outsized impact on the global convergence between rich and poor regions, communities, households, and individuals.

B. Poor Are Increasingly Clustered within Countries

Within HiPMIs themselves, poverty is, naturally, nonuniform. As though viewing a fractal through a loupe, the spatial clustering of poverty so visible on a global scale is replicated within middle-income countries. The distinction between a poor region of a HiPMI and a poor country is not demographic but political.

In populous middle-income countries like HiPMIs, some such regions are massive (see fig. 2). In fact, if the Indian state of Bihar were a sovereign state, it would be the world's most populous low-income country, with 127 million people and a GDP per capita of just $650. Or, were the northern region of Nigeria to break away, the low-income country it became would be second in population only to Ethiopia.

A large part of this spatial clustering of poverty reflects patterns of urbanization. As of the 2011 census, Bihar's urbanization rate of 11.3% was ahead of only Himachal Pradesh's, a much smaller state. Fully 80% of the world's extreme poor live in rural areas (Castañeda et al. 2016), whereas urban areas are engines of growth and labor productivity (Glaeser et al. 1992). The authors' ongoing surveys of economic migrants from two poor, rural Indian states find that the incomes of migrants who returned

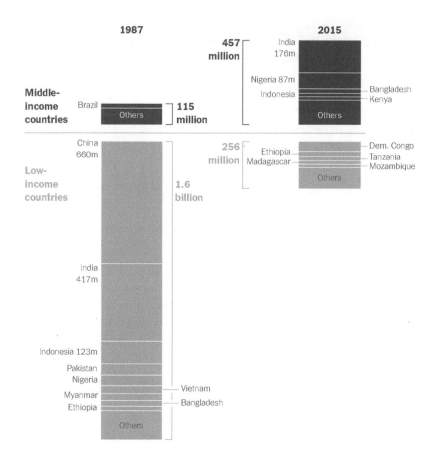

Fig. 1. Most poor live in middle-income countries (Pande, McIntyre, and Page 2019). Graph reprinted courtesy of *The New York Times*. A color version of this figure is available online.

to their villages during the COVID-19 lockdown fell by more than 80%, whereas the incomes of those who subsequently remigrated—mostly to urban areas—rebounded to 85% of their previous levels (Allard et al. 2021).

Because such a large proportion of the world's poor are clustered in so few middle-income countries, the trends of within-country inequality in these specific countries matter quite a lot for global poverty, arguably more than all between-country inequality combined. The trends here are mixed but are especially concerning in the South Asian HiPMIs of India and Bangladesh, and more or less neutral in other HiPMIs such as Nigeria and Indonesia (see fig. 3).

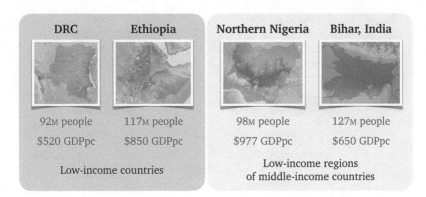

Fig. 2. Low-income regions of middle-income countries. DRC = Democratic Republic of the Congo. GDPpc = gross domestic product per capita. A color version of this figure is available online.

Indeed, the same convergence tests that are done between countries can also be done between subnational regions, and here there is suggestive evidence from India of within-country divergence in regional per capita income (Sachs, Bajpai, and Ramiah 2002; Ghosh 2008, 2012; Kalra

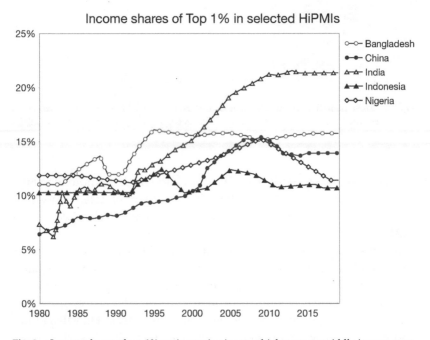

Fig. 3. Income shares of top 1% are increasing in some high-poverty middle-income countries. World Income Inequality Database. A color version of this figure is available online.

and Sodsriwiboon 2010) or limited club convergence (Baddeley, McNay, and Cassen 2006; Bandyopadhyay 2011; Ghosh, Ghoshray, and Malki 2013).

III. Structural Transformation and Disequalizing Growth

If poor countries converged with rich ones with respect to mean income, then of course residual poverty must reflect within-country inequality. The important question, then, is whether processes of economic growth that imply absolute convergence are increasing within-country inequality.

Historically, processes of economic development have been marked by a decline in the share of agriculture in both country income and labor employment. For today's rich countries, the process of structural transformation was accompanied by the manufacturing sector demonstrating a double advantage. It was both more productive than farming and absorbed a larger population share.

More recently, lower-income countries have continued to see relative increases in the income shares of manufacturing and, in some cases, services. Using data on (formal) manufacturing in 118 countries, Rodrik (2012) shows that up to 2005 manufacturing exhibited strong unconditional convergence in labor productivity. However, this was not accompanied by aggregate convergence due to the small share of manufacturing employment in low-income countries and the slow pace of industrialization. Figure 4 shows that HiPMIs continue to lag in manufacturing employment.

Service growth shows a similar pattern, India being the exemplar case here. Between 1950 and 2009, the share of agriculture in India's GDP fell from 55% to 17%, manufacturing rose but remained under 30%, and services increased to 57%. Fan, Peters, and Zilibotti (2021) show that the rise in services was driven by consumer, not producer, services and reflected limited employment gains. It was also urban-biased.

Thus, recent trends in manufacturing and services suggest these remain productive sectors that are gaining GDP share in the world's less well-off countries. However, they are less likely to provide high levels of well-paid employment. Diao et al. (2021) show that this is leading to a new form of dualism: In Ethiopia and Tanzania, the manufacturing sector is made up of larger firms that exhibit superior productivity performance but do not expand employment much, and small firms that absorb employment but lack productivity growth. Clearly, the declining

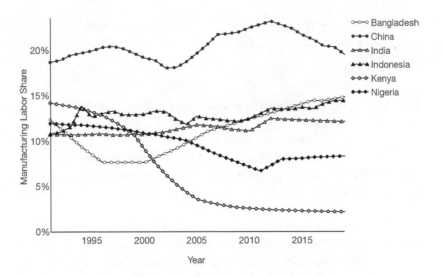

Fig. 4. High-poverty middle-income countries lag in manufacturing employment. International Labour Organization. A color version of this figure is available online.

labor share of income in many developing countries may further weaken link between GDP convergence and household well-being.

IV. The Present and the Future

Disequalizing growth can still benefit the poor if the state is willing and able to redistribute resources to those who need them. Pande (2020) shows that most of the world's poor now live in democratic states, but many of these states are relatively nonegalitarian. The twenty-first century has, concerningly, been marked by significant democratic backsliding, which Haggard and Kaufman (2021) define as "the processes through which elected rulers weaken checks on executive power, curtail political and civil liberties, and undermine the integrity of the electoral system." They identify more than 16 democracies that have seen such backsliding in recent years (see fig. 5).

Democratic backsliding and reduced redistribution are particularly costly for the poor and near-poor when economic growth falters—a possibility that has come to pass with COVID-19 in many HiPMIs. The year 2020 was the first in the twenty-first century in which world poverty rose. The newly poor are concentrated in "second quartile" countries: 61% in South Asia and 27% in sub-Saharan Africa (Lakner et al. 2021). At the $3.20/day threshold, 68% of the newly poor are in South Asia.

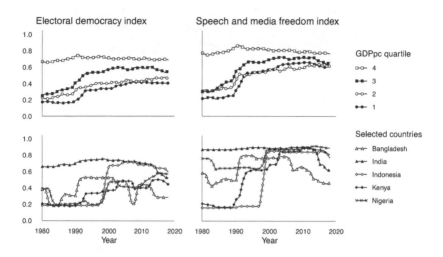

Fig. 5. Democratic backsliding. V-Dem Project. GDPpc = gross domestic product per capita. A color version of this figure is available online.

In the medium term, climate breakdowns will likely constrain fossil-fuel-based growth and this may particularly reduce growth in lower-income settings. For the average developing country, economic convergence is accompanied by a convergence toward the global average usage of most primary energy carriers, consumption of final energy in most sectors, and total carbon dioxide emissions. Current economic growth in lower-income countries is no less energy intensive than past growth in industrialized countries (van Benthem 2015).

In addition to potentially lower growth as countries transition away from fossil-fuel-based growth, HiPMIs are also significantly exposed to direct climate change adverse effects. The University of Notre Dame's ND-GAIN scores each country on its exposure to climate change (Chen et al. 2015). "Exposure" is a purely biophysical assessment, unrelated to a country's mitigation capacity. Factors include the proportion of land that will be submerged under the sea, how annual groundwater runoff and recharge will change, how cereal yields will change, and so forth. Of the top five most-exposed countries with populations of more than 1 million, thereby excluding most small island nations, three are HiPMIs (see fig. 6).

International climate change mitigation policies are a double-edged sword for poor countries and HiPMIs. If adopted, they will make fossil-fuel-based convergence more expensive. If not, climate change itself may reverse their growth via droughts, floods, storms, or rising sea level.

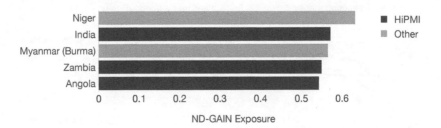

Fig. 6. Exposure to climate change. Notre Dame Global Adaptation Initiative. HiPMI = high-poverty middle-income country. A color version of this figure is available online.

It is essentially a growth-and-carbon accounting exercise to then conclude that there are only a handful of possible outcomes: economic convergence will stagnate, industrialized countries will experience dramatic degrowth, economic growth will decouple from energy use, energy use will decouple from carbon dioxide emissions, carbon sequestration technology will scale up massively, and/or humanity will engage in brinkmanship with climate catastrophe.

V. Conclusion

The paper convincingly documents a trend toward absolute convergence in GDP per capita and provides suggestive evidence that policy convergence played a role. From a development perspective, it is useful to link a narrative about country-level convergence to income distribution within countries: poor regions, communities, households, and individuals. Doing so highlights the need for institutions that will ensure greater domestic redistribution and, possibly, also a rethinking of domestic industrial policy. This, we argue, is critical if absolute convergence is to be the tide that lifts all boats. The need is amplified by the ongoing COVID-19 pandemic and the increasing likelihood of significant climate breakdowns.

Endnotes

    Author email address: Pande (rohini.pande@yale.edu). For acknowledgments, sources of research support, and disclosure of the authors' material financial relationships, if any, please see https://www.nber.org/books-and-chapters/nber-macroeconomics-annual -2021-volume-36/comment-converging-convergence-pande.
    1. Deaton (2005) notes that nonclassical measurement error in using either consumption surveys or national accounts to identify how economic gains are distributed within a country restricts our ability to conclude that this finding implies that growth is good for the poor. Consumption surveys undersample richer households and national accounts may assign incorrect consumption bundles to the poor.

2. The difference in estimates between when Bourguignon and Morrisson ends and World Bank, based on Lakner and Milanović, begins is in part due to different methodologies and measures—the former use Thiel index; the latter, mean log deviation—but we draw attention only to the direction and magnitude of the change, rather than the exact level.

References

Allard, Jenna, Nils Enevoldsen, Maulik Jagnani, Charity Troyer Moore, Yusuf Neggers, Rohini Pande, and Simone Schaner. 2021. "Over a Year after the First Covid-19 Lockdown, Migrants Remain Vulnerable." Blog post, Yale University Economic Growth Center, April.
Baddeley, Michelle, Kirsty McNay, and Robert Cassen. 2006. "Divergence in India: Income Differentials at the State Level, 1970–97." *Journal of Development Studies* 42 (6): 1000–22.
Bandyopadhyay, Sanghamitra. 2011. "Rich States, Poor States: Convergence and Polarisation in India." *Scottish Journal of Political Economy* 58 (3): 414–36.
Barro, Robert J., and Xavier Sala-i-Martin. 1992. "Convergence." *Journal of Political Economy* 100 (2): 223–51.
Bourguignon, François, and Christian Morrisson. 2002. "Inequality Among World Citizens: 1820–1992." *American Economic Review* 92 (4): 727–44.
Castañeda, Andrés, Dung Doan, David Newhouse, Minh Cong Nguyen, Hiroki Uematsu, and João Pedro Azevedo. 2016. "Who Are the Poor in the Developing World?" Policy Research Working Paper no. 7844, World Bank, Washington, DC.
Chen, Chen, Ian Noble, Jessica Hellmann, Joyce Coffee, Martin Murillo, and Nitesh Chawla. 2015. "University of Notre Dame Global Adaptation Index: Country Index Technical Report." Technical Report, University of Notre Dame.
Collier, Paul. 2007. *The Bottom Billion*. Oxford: Oxford University Press.
Deaton, Angus. 2005. "Measuring Poverty in a Growing World (or Measuring Growth in a Poor World)." *Review of Economics and Statistics* 87 (1): 1–19.
Diao, Xinshen, Mia Ellis, Margaret S. McMillan, and Dani Rodrik. 2021. "Africa's Manufacturing Puzzle: Evidence from Tanzanian and Ethiopian Firms." Working Paper no. 28344, NBER, Cambridge, MA.
Dollar, David, and Aart Kraay. 2002. "Growth Is Good for the Poor." *Journal of Economic Growth* 7:195–225.
Dollar, David, Tatjana Kleineberg, and Aart Kraay. 2016. "Growth Still Is Good for the Poor." *European Economic Review* 81:68–85.
Fan, Tianyu, Michael Peters, and Fabrizio Zilibotti. 2021. "Service-Led or Service-Biased Growth? Equilibrium Development Accounting across Indian Districts." Working Paper no. 28551, NBER, Cambridge, MA.
Ghosh, Madhusudan. 2008. "Economic Reforms, Growth and Regional Divergence in India." *Margin: The Journal of Applied Economic Research* 2 (3): 265–85.
———. 2012. "Regional Economic Growth and Inequality in India during the Pre- and Post-Reform Periods." *Oxford Development Studies* 40 (2): 190–212.
Ghosh, Madhusudan, Atanu Ghoshray, and Issam Malki. 2013. "Regional Divergence and Club Convergence in India." *Economic Modelling* 30 (C): 733–42.
Glaeser, Edward L., Hedi D. Kallal, José A. Scheinkman, and Andrei Shleifer. 1992. "Growth in Cities." *Journal of Political Economy* 100 (6): 1126–52.
Haggard, Stephan, and Robert Kaufman. 2021. *Backsliding: Democratic Regress in the Contemporary World*. Cambridge: Cambridge University Press.
Kalra, Sanjay, and Piyaporn Sodsriwiboon. 2010. "Growth Convergence and Spillovers among Indian States: What Matters? What Does Not?" Working Paper no. 10/96, International Monetary Fund, Washington, DC.

Lakner, Christoph, Nishant Yonzan, Daniel Gerszon Mahler, R. Andrés Castañeda Aguilar, and Haoyu Wu. 2021. "Updated Estimates of the Impact of COVID-19 on Global Poverty: Looking Back at 2020 and the Outlook for 2021." Blog post, World Bank, January.

Page, Lucy, and Rohini Pande. 2018. "Ending Global Poverty: Why Money Isn't Enough," *Journal of Economic Perspectives* 32 (4): 173–200.

Pande, Rohini. 2020. "Can Democracy Work for the Poor?" *Science* 369 (6508): 1188–92.

Pande, Rohini, Vestal McIntyre, and Lucy Page. 2019. "A New Home for Extreme Poverty: Middle-Income Countries." *New York Times*, January 28.

Patel, Dev, Justin Sandefur, and Arvind Subramanian. 2021. "The New Era of Unconditional Convergence." Working Paper no. 566, Center for Global Development, Washington, DC.

Rodrik, Dani. 2012. "Unconditional Convergence in Manufacturing." *Quarterly Journal of Economics* 128 (1): 165–204.

Sachs, Jeffrey, Nirupam Bajpai, and Ananthi Al Ramiah. 2002. "Understanding Regional Economic Growth in India." *Asian Economic Papers* 1:32–62.

Sumner, Andy. 2010. "Global Poverty and the New Bottom Billion: What if Three-Quarters of the World's Poor Live in Middle-Income Countries?" *IDS Working Papers* 2010 (349): 01–43.

van Benthem, Arthur A. 2015. "Energy Leapfrogging." *Journal of the Association of Environmental and Resource Economists* 2 (1): 93–132.

World Bank Group. 2016. *Poverty and Shared Prosperity 2016: Taking on Inequality.* Washington, DC: World Bank.

Comment

Daron Acemoglu, *Massachusetts Institute of Technology and NBER,* United States of America

Carlos Molina, *Massachusetts Institute of Technology,* United States of America

Abstract

The contribution by Kremer, Willis, and You revisit cross-country convergence patterns over the past 6 decades. They provide evidence that the lack of convergence that applied early in the sample has now been replaced by modest convergence. They also argue this relationship is driven by convergence in various determinants of economic growth across countries and a flattening of the relationship between these determinants and growth. Although the patterns documented by the authors are intriguing, our reanalysis finds that these results are driven by the lack of country fixed effects controlling for unobserved determinants of gross domestic product per capita across countries. We show theoretically and empirically that failure to include country fixed effects will create a bias in convergence coefficients toward zero and this bias can be time varying, even when the underlying country-level parameters are stable. These results are relevant not just for the current paper but also for the convergence literature more generally. Our reanalysis finds no evidence of major changes in patterns of convergence and, more importantly, no flattening of the relationship between institutional variables and economic growth. Focusing on democracy, we show that this variable's impact continues to be precisely estimated and if anything a little larger than at the beginning of the sample.

I. Introduction

Kremer, Willis, and You (2021) revisit how the global distribution of prosperity and growth have evolved over the past 6 decades and the role of various factors in shaping these distributions. Building on the conver-

© 2022 National Bureau of Economic Research. All rights reserved. Published by The University of Chicago Press for the National Bureau of Economic Research. https://doi .org/10.1086/718674

gence framework of Barro (1991) and Barro and Sala-i-Martin (1992), they investigate how a country's gross domestic product (GDP) per capita today depends on its GDP per capita in the past (unconditional convergence) and whether this relationship is different when conditioning on various determinants or "correlates" of growth (conditional convergence). Although the earlier literature concluded that there was unconditional divergence and conditional convergence, Kremer et al. report a trend toward unconditional convergence (meaning that growth in rich countries is no longer faster, and in fact may be slower, than in poor countries). They also find that this trend toward convergence has been accompanied by rapid convergence among the correlates of income—in particular human capital, policies, institutions, and culture. Finally, they report results suggesting that the relationship between growth and these correlates is now flatter, which they interpret as these factors becoming less important for economic growth, perhaps because remaining differences between institutions and policies are more minor or are confined to areas that matter less. Although the authors are careful in not pushing a very strong interpretation of this last finding, some may read these findings as suggesting that improving institutions and policies may have become less important in the modern era.

There is no doubt that these are first-order questions for economic growth and development, and the authors' voice and novel analysis are welcome additions to this debate. Their paper documents intriguing and thought-provoking facts. However, our assessment is that their findings suffer from some of the shortcomings that are inherent in the convergence framework. We take this opportunity to comment both on Kremer et al. and the broader convergence literature pioneered by Barro and Sala-i-Martin.

We argue that unconditional convergence regressions, especially in the form formulated by the authors, do not allow a straightforward causal interpretation. Lack of convergence may be because countries differ in their institutions and policies. It may be because of technological divergence due to other reasons. Or it may be because of statistical problems, in particular when the framework at hand does not properly account for permanent differences rooted in other factors. These shortcomings do not just make it difficult to interpret what estimates of unconditional convergence/divergence mean but also imply that changes in convergence patterns may be a statistical artifact of the same problems as well.

To elucidate these issues, we start with a framework that is more amenable to thinking and estimating causal effects—specifically, by allowing heterogeneity across countries, for example, as captured by country fixed effects. Using this framework, we first establish that convergence estimates do not have a straightforward economic interpretation. For example, even if every country had a negative convergence coefficient (indicating convergence), the authors' estimates could be strongly positive. This bias is not only first-order but also potentially time varying and can create the impression that convergence patterns are changing, when, in reality, it is the statistical properties responsible for the bias that are evolving over time.

We then reanalyze the same data as the authors and report several important findings.[1] First, in the data, there is indeed a major discord between estimated convergence coefficients (without fixed effects) and economically meaningful parameters summarizing how growth depends on current level of income. For example, we estimate that more than 88% of all countries show evidence of convergence, whereas the authors' regressions for the whole sample show no convergence. Second, the biases responsible for this discord are indeed time varying and account for the changes in convergence patterns the authors report. Third, this framework also enables us to estimate the effects of key institutional factors and policies on growth. Carrying out these estimates for one specific institutional characteristic—whether a country is a democracy—we find very different results from those reported by Kremer et al. Specifically, we confirm the results in Acemoglu et al. (2019), showing that democracy has a statistically robust and economically large positive effect on GDP per capita. Moreover, contrary to the findings of Kremer et al., there is no evidence of the relationship between democracy and growth flattening over time. This suggests there should be no presumption that institutional factors in general have become less important for explaining and spearheading economic growth.

The rest of the paper is organized as follows. In the next section, we start with a brief review of a minimalist framework that can shed light on the causal relationship between different factors and GDP per capita (or growth). We contrast this framework, which crucially includes country fixed effects to control for unobserved or unmodeled country-level determinants of GDP per capita, with the authors' model, which omits these fixed effects. In Section III, we theoretically and empirically explore the implications of our framework, establishing that the failure to include country fixed effects will lead to a (potentially time varying) downward bias in estimates of convergence. We document that this bias explains both the lack of convergence estimated in the earlier literature (and by the authors in the full sample) and the pattern toward greater convergence over time. In Section IV, we examine whether the relationship between economic growth and its potential determinants (and especially democracy) has become weaker over time, and we find no evidence that it has. In Section V, we respond to the adjustments that the authors have made following our conference comments, and in Section VI, we conclude. The appendix (appendix is available online) includes the proof of our theoretical result and some additional empirical findings.

II.   A Minimalist Framework

Consider the following relationship linking a country's economic growth to various characteristics, including its current level of GDP per capita

$$\Delta y_{ct} = \beta_c x_{ct} + \rho_c y_{ct-1} + \delta_t + \alpha_c + \varepsilon_{ct}, \tag{1}$$

where y_{ct} is the level of log GDP per capita of country c at time t and x_{ct} is some institutional/policy feature potentially affecting economic growth. In addition, α_c stands for country fixed effects, which capture various dimensions of country heterogeneity that influence economic growth. These may include other institutional features or various unobserved and/or unmodeled factors. Finally, ε_{ct} is an error term and δ_t denotes time effects. This relationship allows for heterogeneities, including in how institutional/policy features affect growth (β_c) and the extent of persistence (ρ_c), but is assumed to be linear for simplicity.

In what follows, we assume that equation (1) is the true model/data generating process (DGP), and also assume that x_{ct} is orthogonal to ε_{ct} (conditional on x_{ct} and α_c).

Equation (1) is similar to the conditional convergence framework of Barro (1991) and Barro and Sala-i-Martin (1992), because the relationship between Δy_{ct} and y_{ct-1} is conditional on x_{ct} and α_c. However, these articles do not typically include country fixed effects capturing unobserved permanent differences across countries, which will prove to be important.[2]

Now consider a typical unconditional convergence equation

$$\Delta y_{ct} = \rho y_{ct-1} + \delta_t + \varepsilon_{ct}. \tag{2}$$

This equation is a special case of equation (1), with three differences. First and most important, the α_c term is not present, implying that the model does not allow for (unobserved) heterogeneity across countries that could be correlated with initial GDP per capita. Second, there is no x_{ct}, which could capture some of the observed differences across countries. Third, this equation does not allow for any cross-country heterogeneity in the relationship between GDP per capita and its growth (captured by ρ_c in eq. [1]). Kremer et al. use this equation to estimate ρ and study unconditional convergence, though they look at the 10-year change, $\Delta_{10} y_{ct} = y_{ct+10} - y_{ct}$, on the left-hand side, rather than the annual change as in equation (2). We next show that the omission of appropriate country heterogeneity in equation (2) makes their estimates of ρ difficult to interpret.

III. Implications of Country Heterogeneity

Let us now suppose that the DGP is given by our equation (1). What happens when ρ is estimated from equation (2)? We answer this question first in theory, and then in the context of the authors' analysis of convergence.

A. Theory

To separate the implications of country heterogeneity from those of country covariates, which Kremer et al. later incorporate, we first set $\beta_c = 0$ for all c in equation (1). This ensures that the only difference between the underlying causal model, (1), and the authors' statistical model, (2), is the absence of country fixed effects.

Proposition 1. Suppose the DGP is equation (1) with $\beta_c = 0$ for all c. Let $\hat\rho$ be the ordinary least squares (OLS) estimator of ρ in equation (2). Then:

1. $plim\hat\rho = \sum_{c=1}^{C} \omega_c \rho_c$, where ω_c's can be negative or greater than one, and $\sum_{c=1}^{C} \omega_c$ is typically not equal to one.
2. Let $\theta_c = \omega_c - \frac{\theta_0 k}{C \rho_c}$, where $\theta_0 = 1 - \sum_{c=1}^{C} \theta_c$, $\theta_c \in [0,1]$ for all c, and $k \in \mathbb{R}$. Then:

$$plim\hat\rho = \sum_{c=1}^{C} \theta_c \rho_c + \theta_0 k.$$

3. Suppose that $-2 < \rho_c < 0$ for all c (which ensures that the process for each country is stationary), and let T_c be the effective number of observations for country c. Then, as $\min_c\{T_c\} \to \infty$, k, θ_c, ω_c and $\hat\rho$ all limit to zero (and the limit of θ_0 is one).

The proof of this proposition is provided in the appendix.

Proposition 1 contains several important lessons. First, part 1 of the proposition establishes that the estimate $\hat{\rho}$ does not correspond to a meaningful (local) average, or local average treatment effect (LATE), of the underlying parameters—the ρ_c's. Some of the ω_c's in the proposition can be negative, and they need not sum to one. Therefore, one could have cases where $\hat{\rho}$ may be estimated to be zero or positive, even when the underlying (true) ρ_c's are all negative. Part 2 expresses this same result in a different way. By writing the probability limit of $\hat{\rho}$ as the local average of the underlying ρ_c's plus a bias term, it shows that this estimator is inconsistent and biased.[3] We can also see that this bias is related to the covariance of α_c's with initial conditions (and of course, there is a natural reason for α_c to be highly correlated with initial conditions, especially when countries are close to their steady states). In addition, the bias in question is downward, pushing the coefficient estimate toward zero.[4] Third, part 3 shows that as sample size grows, $\hat{\rho}$ will tend to zero—regardless of the true values of the ρ_c's. This sharp result clarifies the intuition for the bias as well: asymptotically, all countries converge to their steady state, and without the α_c's, the only way the model can capture this is by imposing $\hat{\rho} = 0$. This bias, which becomes extreme asymptotically, is present for any time length. Finally, because the ω_c's or the θ_c's are functions of data moments, the estimate $\hat{\rho}$ (without country fixed effects) will change over time even when the underlying ρ_c's are stable.

We also note that the results in proposition 1 are relevant beyond Kremer et al.'s paper. These biases and challenges of interpreting the estimates of $\hat{\rho}$ apply to most of the work in the convergence literature.

What do the biases identified in proposition 1 imply for Kremer et al.'s empirical analysis? We answer this question in the next subsection.

B.   Empirical Implications

To illustrate the issue of the bias identified in proposition 1, we first estimate equation (1)—the true DGP under our hypothesis. The estimates of ρ_c's rely on time-series variation in a country's growth rate.[5] The average number of periods for a country in our sample is 46.

Figure 1 plots the empirical probability density (panel A) and the cumulative density (panel B) of the underlying ρ_c's. We also indicate the estimate $\hat{\rho}$ from equation using a dashed line. A significant bias toward zero in $\hat{\rho}$, as predicted by proposition 1, is visible from these results. For

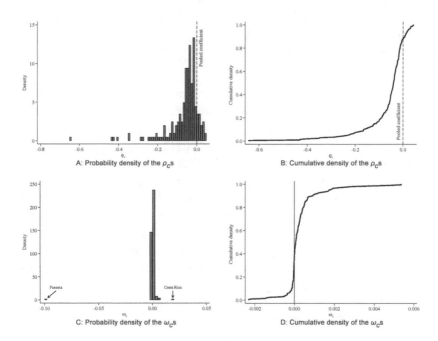

Fig. 1. Empirical distribution of the underlying ρ_c's and ω_c's. The figure presents estimates of the distribution of the country-specific coefficients of convergence (the ρ_c's) and the weights (the ω_c's, defined in proposition 1). The empirical probability density and the cumulative density are reported on the left- and right-hand panels, respectively. In panel A, the dashed line indicates the estimate $\hat{\rho}$ from equation (2) (when no country heterogeneity is allowed). A color version of this figure is available online.

example, our estimates of the ρ_c's are negative all the way up to the 88th percentile, but $\hat{\rho}$ is positive.[6]

Panels C and D of the figure explore the sources of this significant bias in $\hat{\rho}$ by plotting the distributions of the weights (ω_c) from proposition 1. Had $\hat{\rho}$ been a meaningful average of the underlying ρ_c's, we would expect all of these weights to be nonnegative. However, in practice, 37% of them are negative, their sum is also negative (= –0.024), and there are two massive outliers (Costa Rica and Panama).[7] This picture confirms that, under the presumption that equation (1) is the true model/DGP, estimates of $\hat{\rho}$ do not correspond to economically meaningful objects: even when the vast majority of countries are converging, $\hat{\rho}$ may create the impression that there is no convergence.

We now turn to part 2 of proposition 1 and explore where the bias of $\hat{\rho}$ comes in the sample studied by the authors. The next equation summarizes the results by presenting the empirical counterparts of the decomposition given in part 2 of proposition 1:

$$\underbrace{\hat{\rho}}_{0.00004} = \underbrace{\sum_{c=1}^{C}\theta_c\hat{\rho}_c}_{-0.00112} + \underbrace{\theta_0}_{0.93445}\underbrace{k}_{0.00120}.$$

The advantage of this equation is that it provides a decomposition of $\hat{\rho}$ into an average of the underlying parameters (the first term) and the bias (the second term). Recall in particular that $\theta_c \in [0, 1]$ and $\Sigma_{c=0}^{C}\theta_c = 1$. In our sample, we find that $\Sigma_{c=1}^{C}\theta_c\hat{\rho}_c = -0.00112$, suggesting that at least on average, most country-specific coefficients of convergence tend to be negative (in line with 88% of them being negative as we saw above). However, the coefficient of unconditional convergence $\hat{\rho}$ is positive (= 0.00004), because the second term is very large—comprising a huge weight $\theta_0 = 0.93445$ and a positive bias $k = 0.00120$.

We now turn to the question of what accounts for over-time changes in $\hat{\rho}$. In figure 2, we report the same decomposition from part 2 of proposition 1 but now separately by decade. Consistent with Kremer et al., we find that estimates of $\hat{\rho}$ from equation (2) are decreasing over time, as shown by the medium gray bars. Strikingly, however, this pattern

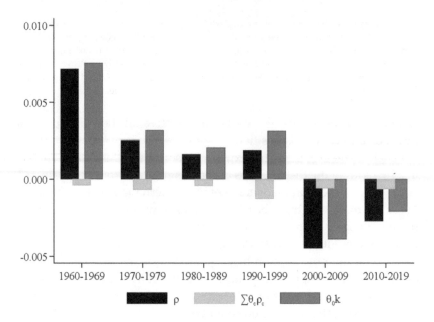

Fig. 2. Decomposition of $\hat{\rho}$ across decades. The estimate $\hat{\rho}$ from equation (2) (when no country heterogeneity is allowed) by decade shown by the black bars. This estimate is decomposed in two terms (see proposition 1): the underlying distribution of the ρ_c's shown by the light gray bars and the bias shown by the medium gray bars. A color version of this figure is available online.

is entirely driven by changes in the bias term (shown by the medium gray bar). The underlying distribution of the ρ_c's (shown by the light gray bars) has remained quite stable over time. Therefore, all of the dynamics in the authors' estimate of $\hat{\rho}$ seem to come from the bias term rather than from a faster rate of economic convergence.

We also explored the determinants of convergence patterns for the key covariates used by Kremer et al.[8] Table 1 reports the coefficient estimate $\hat{\rho}$ from equation (2) as well as key statistics about the distribution of estimates of the underlying ρ_c's estimated from equation (1). In all cases, estimates of $\hat{\rho}$ are significantly above the mean or the median of the distribution of the estimates of the ρ_c's (and except for Polity 2, they are also above the 75th percentile). These results again underscore that estimates that ignore country heterogeneity are going to be significantly biased toward zero.

IV. Estimating the Effects of Institutions and Policies

In the second part of their paper, Kremer et al. add the covariates mentioned in the previous section to the right-hand side of equation (2) and assume that they have the same impact across countries, although still

Table 1
Convergence Patterns for the Key Covariates

	Pooled Coefficient	Mean	Country-Level Coefficients		
			25th Quantile	50th Quantile	75th Quantile
	(1)	(2)	(3)	(4)	(5)
Log GDP per capita	0	−.063	−.074	−.040	−.017
Polity 2	−.029	−.107	−.165	−.087	0
Rule of law	−.008	−.346	−.487	−.295	−.169
Property rights	−.032	−.239	−.360	−.228	−.133
Government expenditure	−.055	−.215	−.313	−.168	−.069
Credit	.004	−.221	−.404	−.114	−.013
Years of schooling	−.020	−.506	−.653	−.440	−.321

Note: The table reports estimates of coefficient of unconditional convergence (ρ, see eq. [2]) in column 1. The remaining columns report moments (including the mean and the 25th, 50th, and 75th quantiles) of the distribution of the underlying country-specific estimates of convergence (ρ_c's, see eq. [1]). We show results for the key variables used by Kremer et al. (2020) including (source in parentheses): Polity 2 (Polity IV Project), Rule of law (Worldwide Governance Indicators), Property rights (Heritage Freedom), Government expenditure (World Development Indicators), and Years of schooling (Barro-Lee). GDP = gross domestic product.

not including country fixed effects. As they again consider 10-year changes on the left-hand side, their model is now

$$\Delta_{10} y_{ct} = \beta_t x_{ct} + \rho y_{ct} + \delta_t + \varepsilon_{ct}, \tag{3}$$

where $\Delta_{10} y_{ct} = y_{ct+10} - y_{ct}$.

Estimating this equation on the same sample, they conclude that conditional convergence patterns have been stable over the sample and the change in unconditional convergence implied by their estimates of $\hat{\rho}$ is due to the correlation between growth and institutions (or policies or other country characteristics) having become weaker over time. They also report that their estimates of β from this equation, $\hat{\beta}$, are getting smaller over time, which they interpret as the relationship between these factors and economic growth becoming weaker.

Although in the revision of their paper the authors recognize that these estimates are not causal and should be interpreted with caution, the same issues highlighted in the previous section are still relevant and, as we will see, are responsible for the majority of their results. In the rest of this section, we develop this point by focusing on one dimension of institutions that has been explored in detail in the literature and found to be robustly related to growth: democracy (see Acemoglu et al. 2019). Before doing this, however, in the next subsection we highlight that even ignoring these problems, the data do not unambiguously point out to a decline in β_t.

A. The Importance of Horizons

As noted above, Kremer et al. use the 10-year change on the left-hand side of equation (3) and then compare the estimates for 1985 and 2005. In panel A of figure 3, we reestimate their model, still with 10-year changes but separately by year. We focus on their main measure of democracy, Polity 2 score. Indeed, the coefficient estimates from this model are greater for 1985 and 2005, but the pattern we see is not one of decline but a cyclical one. This suggests that whatever is driving the authors' results may be more complex than a simple secular flattening.

Panel B of the same figure reestimates the authors' model but using annual changes on the left-hand side. Now, although the estimates do change over time, there is no evidence of a decline. We conjecture, instead, that the patterns shown in panel A are driven by the interaction of the changing bias terms, highlighted in the previous section, and the 10-year horizon on the left-hand side, which cumulates these changes.

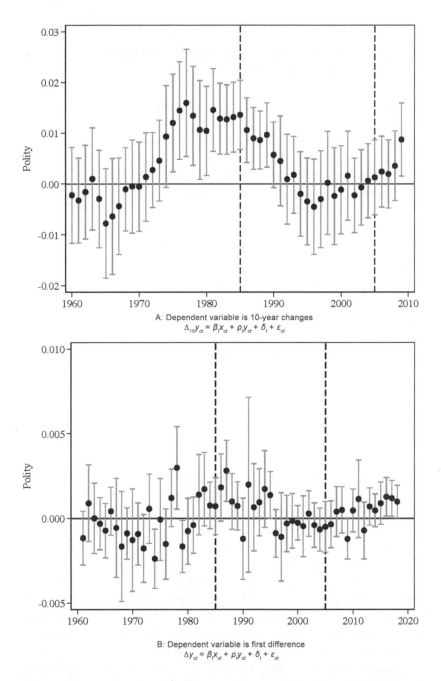

Fig. 3. Estimates of the relationship between the Polity 2 score and economic growth and 95% confidence intervals over time. We plot the coefficient β_t in the equation indicated in the panel labels. Panel A uses as dependent variable the 10-year change in log of gross domestic product (GDP) per capita, whereas panel B uses annual changes (first differences). Standard errors are clustered at the country level. A color version of this figure is available online.

We explore whether the effects of institutions are indeed diminishing over time more systematically in the next subsection.

B. Have the Causal Effects of Institutions Declined over Time?

We now study this question, focusing on the effects of democracy. We follow Acemoglu et al. (2019) in focusing on a dichotomous measure of democracy (to minimize measurement error) and extend (1) to include several lags of GDP per capita on the right-hand side, and, as in their paper, simplify the model by assuming constant effects of democracy and the lags; however, in line with the focus here, we allow the effect of democracy to be time varying. This gives

$$\ln y_{ct} = \beta_t D_{ct} + \sum_{j=1}^{p} \rho_j \ln y_{ct-j} + \alpha_c + \delta_t + \varepsilon_{ct}, \qquad (4)$$

where D_{ct} denotes the dichotomous measure of democracy (dictatorship vs democracy). All the other variables are as in equation (1), and crucially, as in that equation, we have country fixed effects, represented by the α_c's.

First, suppose that $\beta_t = \beta$. Then, under sequential exogeneity, the within-estimator of this equation recovers an interpretable estimate of an economically meaningful object, β.[9] We also report alternative estimators (including IV estimate using as instrument waves of democratization), which are consistent under related but slightly different assumptions.[10]

We first replicate the results of Acemoglu et al. (2019), estimating a time-invariant β in equation (4). The results are reported in panel A of table 2. All regressions include four lags of log GDP. As in Acemoglu et al. (2019), and common with all the other results we will report, the democracy variable is estimated to have a precise and significant positive impact on GDP per capita, with a coefficient of 0.787 (standard error = 0.226) in the OLS specification in column 1. This estimate implies that a permanent transition to democracy leads to an approximately 20% increase in GDP per capita after about 25 years.[11] As in the original results in Acemoglu et al. (2019), the other columns, including the IV procedure exploiting regional waves of democratization, show similar estimates.

Have these effects changed over time? To answer this question in the simplest possible way, we parameterize β_t in equation (4) as a linear function of time, which is equivalent to including an interaction between the democracy score and time, D_{ct}, as an additional regressor. Results from this exercise are reported in panel B. In all cases, this interaction has a positive coefficient, and shows no evidence of a decline over

Table 2
Estimates of the Effect of Democracy on (log) GDP per Capita

	Dependent Variable Is Log GDP per Capita			
	Estimator . . .			
	Within	Arellano-Bond	HHK	IV
	(1)	(2)	(3)	(4)
	A. Effect of Democracy on Log GDP			
Democracy	.787	.875	1.165	.966
	(.226)	(.374)	(.370)	(.562)
Observations	6,336	6,161	6,336	6,312
	B. Effect of Democracy on Log GDP and Its Change over Time			
Democracy	.678	.872	.886	1.346
	(.214)	(.374)	(.394)	(.616)
Democracy × Trend	.383	.270	.442	.716
	(.246)	(.362)	(.357)	(.368)
Observations	6,336	6,161	6,336	6,312

Note: This table presents estimates of the effect of democracy on log gross domestic product (GDP) per capita following Acemoglu et al. (2019). Democracy is measured as a dichotomous variable to minimize measurement error. Panel A replicates the results in Acemoglu et al. (2019), and panel B extends the regression by allowing an interaction between the measure of democracy and a linear function of time. Columns 1, 2, 3, and 4 present results from the within-estimator, Arellano and Bond's (1991) GMM estimator, the HHK (Hahn, Hausman, and Kuersteiner 2001) estimator, and an IV (exploiting regional waves of democratization), respectively. All regressions include four lags of log GDP per capita. Standard errors are clustered at the country level.

time. For example, with OLS in column 1 the coefficient estimate is 0.383 (standard error = 0.246), whereas with IV in column 4, it is 0.716 (standard error = 0.368), which is significant at 10%. We therefore conclude that, once one focuses on a model that allows for unobserved country heterogeneity which proves to be important in all of these specifications, there is no evidence of the causal effect of democracy having declined over time.[12]

C. Squaring the Circle

The model in equation (4) also gives us an opportunity to unify the two parts of our analysis so far—relating to changes in convergence patterns and changes in the effects of institutions. We now estimate this equation separately by decade and report the implied convergence estimates $\hat{\rho}$ (assumed to be the same across countries for this exercise). We focus

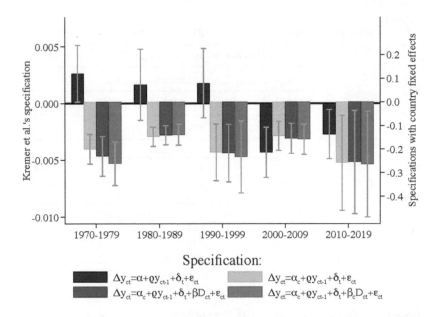

Fig. 4. Estimates of ρ across different specification and decades. Estimates of the coefficient of convergence (ρ) as well as 95% confidence intervals across four different specifications. The first is Kremer et al.'s specification of unconditional convergence, which does not include country fixed effects (shown by the black bars). The second is a specification that adds country fixed effects to this baseline (shown by the light gray bars). The third adds our dichotomous measure of democracy as a control, focusing on the OLS specification (shown by the darkest gray bars). Our final specification allows the effects of democracy to be varying across countries (medium gray bars). Standard errors are clustered at the country level. A color version of this figure is available online.

on four specifications, which are all reported in figure 4. The first is Kremer et al.'s specification of unconditional convergence, which does not include country fixed effects (shown by the black bars on the left axis). The second is a specification that adds country fixed effects to this baseline (shown by the light gray bars on the right axis). The third and fourth add our dichotomous measure of democracy as a control, with constant and heterogeneous effects across countries, respectively (shown by the darkest gray and medium gray bars on the right axis).

The black bars confirm the pattern emphasized by the authors: in the 1970s, 1980s, and 1990s, the estimate of $\hat{\rho}$ is positive and then declines to be negative in the 2000s and 2010s. However, the other bars show that this pattern is driven entirely by the absence of country fixed effects. As soon as these are included, the light gray bars are uniformly negative and do not show a clear trend either way. The same pattern is visible with the remaining bars. Another noteworthy feature, highlighting the downward bias in the convergence coefficient without fixed effects identified in proposition 1, is that the coefficient estimates shown by the black bars are about 1/50th of the others, hence the need for two vertical axes to be able to depict these estimates.[13]

We conclude once again that the time trends in the estimates of $\hat{\rho}$ in equation (2) do not appear to be related to a change in the causal relationship between economic growth and its country-level determinants.

V. Authors' Response to Our Comments

In response to our conference discussion, the published version of Kremer et al. includes various adjustments (in addition to the change of data set we noted above). We welcome several of these adjustments. They estimate an augmented version of their model in the appendix, which allows for fixed effects and confirms our results that there is no major change in convergence patterns in this case. However, the authors argue against including country fixed effects. They allow these fixed effects to vary across decades and then plot these decadal fixed effect estimates against each other. They state that there is little correlation between decadal fixed effects and conclude that this lack of correlation "call[s] into question the benefit of a model including fixed effects."

We reproduce this exercise in figure 5. Our results are very different from theirs. We find that the fixed effect estimates are highly persistent and the correlation between fixed effects in different decades is always above 95%. This is true regardless of whether we compare fixed effects for a decade starting with year t versus $t + 10$ or $t + 20$, and regardless of the exact specification of the dependent variable (panel A is for models with first differences of GDP per capita on the left-hand side, and panel B is for models with 10-year changes).[14] These patterns, combined with the very high F-statistics for the significance of the country fixed effects in all of our models, indicate that these fixed effects belong in the models and their omission is responsible for estimates that are difficult to interpret in terms of underlying economic effects.

VI. Conclusion

Kremer et al. is a timely paper revisiting the evolution of convergence cross-country patterns over the past 6 decades. The authors provide evidence that the lack of convergence that applied early in the sample has

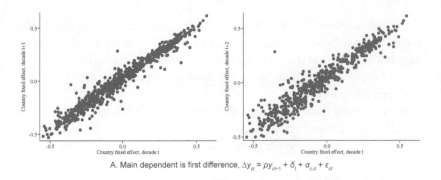

A. Main dependent is first difference, $\Delta y_{ct} = \rho y_{ct-1} + \delta_t + \alpha_{c,d} + \varepsilon_{ct}$

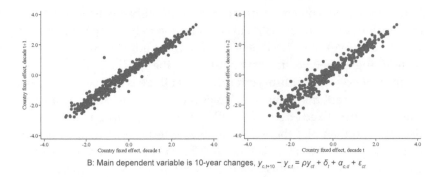

B: Main dependent variable is 10-year changes, $y_{c,t+10} - y_{c,t} = \rho y_{ct} + \delta_t + \alpha_{c,d} + \varepsilon_{ct}$

Fig. 5. Correlation of country fixed effects over decades. We estimate the regression specified in the panel label that allows the country fixed effects to vary across decades and then plot these decadal fixed effect estimates against each other. The graphs in panel *A* use as dependent variable the first difference (the 10-year change) in log of gross domestic product (GDP) per capita, whereas the graphs in panel *B* use 10-year changes. The panels show the correlation between the estimated country fixed effect for a decade starting at year *t* with a decade starting at year *t* + 10 for the panels to the left, and with a decade starting at year *t* + 20 for the panels to the right.

now been replaced by modest convergence. They also argue this relationship is driven by convergence in various determinants of economic growth across countries and a flattening of the relationship between these determinants and growth. Although the patterns documented by the authors are intriguing, our reanalysis finds that these results are driven by the lack of country fixed effects controlling for unobserved determinants of GDP per capita across countries. We establish theoretically that failure to include for such potential determinants will create a bias in convergence coefficients toward zero and, equally important, the resulting estimates may not have straightforward economic interpretations (e.g., they will not correspond to any type of local average of the effects at the country level). The root cause of this bias is simple: when there are permanent differences across countries and each country is close to its steady state, a model that does not include fixed effects can only fit the data by having a convergence coefficient very close to zero. This point is of more general relevance, because it applies not just to Kremer et al.'s study but also to the majority of the convergence literature.

Empirically, we show that estimated convergence coefficients (from models that do not include fixed effects) are indeed biased toward zero. Moreover, this bias is time varying, even though the underlying country-level parameters appear to be constant and stable.

The authors' finding that the relationship between economic growth and its country-level determinants (such as institutions) is flattening is notable. If true, it might suggest that improving institutions and policies may have become less important for explaining and spearheading growth. It might also have important policy implications. However, our reanalysis finds no evidence of a flattening in the relationship between institutional variables and economic growth. Focusing on democracy, we show that this variable's impact continues to be precisely estimated and, if anything, a little larger than the beginning of the sample.

Endnotes

Authors' email addresses: Daron Acemoglu (daron@mit.edu), Carlos Molina (camolina@mit.edu). We gratefully acknowledge financial support from the Bradley Foundation. For acknowledgments, sources of research support, and disclosure of the authors' material financial relationships, if any, please see https://www.nber.org/books-and-chapters/nber-macroeconomics-annual-2021-volume-36/comment-converging-convergence-acemoglu.

1. Namely, we follow Kremer et al.'s first draft, on which our comments were based, in using GDP per capita data from the World Development Indicators database. Their final draft switches to GDP numbers from the Penn World Tables. We use the former data set in the text and repeat all of the same exercises with the Penn World Tables in the appendix to verify that the choice of data set does not matter for any of the points we emphasize.

2. Other papers that have explored this type of linear model with country fixed effects include Knight, Loayza, and Villanueva (1993); Loayza (1994); Islam (1995); Caselli, Esquivel, and Lefort (1996); and Acemoglu et al. (2019).

3. Islam (1995) and Caselli et al. (1996) have also noted that estimates of growth regression will be biased when country heterogeneity is not properly controlled for. We are, however, unaware of any other characterization of this bias as in proposition 1.

4. If $Cov(\varepsilon_{ct}, y_{t-1}) = 0$, then:

$$plim\hat{\rho} = \frac{Cov(\alpha_c, y_{ct-1})}{Var(y_{ct-1})} + \sum_{c \in C} \gamma_c \rho_c$$

with $\gamma_c = \frac{\Sigma_{t \in T_c}(y_{ct-1} - \bar{y}_{t-1})^2}{\Sigma_{i \in C}\Sigma_{t \in T_i}(y_{it-1} - \bar{y}_{t-1})^2}$ and $\bar{y}_{t-1} = \frac{\Sigma_{c \in C}\Sigma_{t \in T_c} y_{c,t-1}}{\Sigma_{c \in C} T_c}$.

5. Like Kremer et al.'s original sample, our data come from the World Development Indicators database. As noted in endnote 1, the final version of their paper uses data from the Penn World Tables. The two data sets give very similar results. We keep the original data in our analysis in the text and report analogous results with the Penn World Tables in the appendix.

6. As in all of the other empirical models we report in this paper, the country fixed effects, the α_c's, are highly significant when we estimate these country-specific convergence parameters. In panel A, for example, the F-statistic for their joint significance is 276,182.

7. With the Penn World Tables data, Costa Rica and Panama are no longer outliers, but now Belarus is a massive outlier. The rest of the results are very similar. See fig. A-1.

8. These are (sources in parentheses): Polity 2 (Polity IV Project), Rule of law (Worldwide Governance Indicators), Property rights (Heritage Freedom), Government expenditure (World Development Indicators) and Years of schooling (Barro-Lee).

9. Sequential exogeneity requires that $\mathbb{E}[\varepsilon_{ct} \mid y_{ct-1}, \ldots, y_{ct_0}, D_{ct}, \ldots, D_{ct_0}, \alpha_c, \delta_t] = 0$ for all $y_{ct-1}, \ldots, y_{ct_0}, D_{ct}, \ldots, D_{ct_0}, \alpha_c,$ and δ_t and for all c and $t \geq t_0$.

10. See Acemoglu et al. (2019) for a discussion of these assumptions.

11. The F-statistic for the significance of country fixed effects in the specification is 1,417, again indicating that these fixed effects are highly significant.

12. All of the results reported so far are very similar using data from the Penn World Tables; see fig. A-1.

13. The only difference with the Penn World Tables comes in this analysis, where the analogues of the black bars in this figure show even less precision and are not uniformly positive before the 2000s. However, the other aspects of this figure and the overall conclusion from this alternative data set are identical. See fig. A-4.

14. These exercises should still be interpreted with caution. As is well known, estimates of fixed effects are inconsistent for finite T (Wooldridge 2010).

References

Acemoglu, D., S. Naidu, P. Restrepo, and J. A. Robinson. 2019. "Democracy Does Cause Growth." *Journal of Political Economy* 127 (1): 47–100.

Arellano, M., and S. Bond. 1991. "Some Tests of Specification for Panel Data: Monte Carlo Evidence and an Application to Employment Equations." *Review of Economic Studies* 58 (2): 277–97.

Barro, R. J. 1991. "Economic Growth in a Cross Section of Countries." *Quarterly Journal of Economics* 106 (2): 407–43.

Barro, R. J., and X. Sala-i-Martin. 1992. "Convergence." *Journal of Political Economy* 100 (2): 223–51.

Caselli, F., G. Esquivel, and F. Lefort. 1996. "Reopening the Convergence Debate: A New Look at Cross-Country Growth Empirics." *Journal of Economic Growth* 1 (3): 363–89.

Hahn, J., J. Hausman, and G. M. Kuersteiner. 2001. "Bias Corrected Instrumental Variables Estimation for Dynamic Panel Models with Fixed Effects." https://ssrn.com/abstract=276592.

Islam, N. 1995. "Growth Empirics: A Panel Data Approach." *Quarterly Journal of Economics* 110 (4): 1127–70.

Knight, M., N. Loayza, and D. Villanueva. 1993. "Testing the Neoclassical Theory of Economic Growth: A Panel Data Approach." *IMF Staff Papers* 40 (3): 512–41.

Kremer, M., J. Willis, and Y. You. 2021. "Converging to Convergence." *NBER Macroeconomics Annual 2021*. https://www.nber.org/books-and-chapters/nber-macroeconomics-annual-2021-volume-36/converging-convergence.

Loayza, N. 1994. "A Test of the International Convergence Hypothesis Using Panel Data." Policy Research Working Paper no. 1333, World Bank, Washington, DC.

Wooldridge, J. M. 2010. *Econometric Analysis of Cross Section and Panel Data*. Cambridge, MA: MIT Press.

Discussion

Michael Kremer opened the discussion by addressing some of the points raised by the discussants. First, he conceded that within-country inequality is very important and that there has been a large reduction in world poverty, as argued by Rohini Pande. He added that within-country inequality is easier to address through policy than cross-country inequality. For example, China and India have implemented policies to reduce inequality that have been very effective, he argued. Second, he agreed with the discussants that democracy is an important factor and thus erosion of democracy must not be overlooked. Third, he responded to the question of the future of convergence. Although after centuries of divergence we now see unconditional convergence, it is too early to tell if this is a fundamental change in history, he argued. He acknowledged that it is a plausible story that this change in trend was brought about by the end of colonialism and the rise of democracy.

Erik Hurst followed up on the future of convergence and asked whether Daron Acemoglu would agree that there has been a change in convergence patterns. Acemoglu responded that the descriptive regressions reported by the authors are correct, but the distribution of the underlying country-level parameters has not changed.

The discussion then centered around methods of estimation. Christopher Sims posited that the estimated country fixed effects are a bad estimator of the true underlying fixed effects. He encouraged the authors to use a random effects model instead of a fixed effects model. Following up on this remark, Acemoglu argued that country fixed effects are not

© 2022 National Bureau of Economic Research. All rights reserved. Published by The University of Chicago Press for the National Bureau of Economic Research. https://doi .org/10.1086/718675

consistently estimated, whereas convergence coefficients are estimated consistently with the Hausman-Kuersteiner estimator, if the model is correctly specified. Andrew Levin seconded the point raised by Sims, and he emphasized the challenges of estimation in panel models. He recognized that the paper studies an important topic and expressed hope for extensive future research. He highlighted that convergence is not a linear process and thus future research should address nonlinear dynamics and nonstationarity.

The authors concluded by addressing some additional points raised during the discussion. First, Jack Willis offered a comment on welfare considerations. He acknowledged that welfare considerations should include within-country inequality and population-weighted regressions. He added that when weighting regressions by country population, the authors obtain similar results. Second, he addressed comments on estimation and argued that the literature has not offered a definitive answer on the correct regression specification. He recognized that trends are different when including country fixed effects or when using 10-year growth rates instead of 1-year growth rates. Kremer further added that it is not even clear how to think about the question of convergence in a world with country fixed effects, which are part of the convergence puzzle themselves. In conclusion, Kremer emphasized that the scope of the paper is to offer a descriptive analysis and a set of facts that growth models need to match, leaving an interesting open agenda for future research.